The Prophetic Tradition
and Radical Rhetoric
in America

The Prophetic Tradition and Radical Rhetoric in America

James Darsey

NEW YORK UNIVERSITY PRESS

New York and London

NEW YORK UNIVERSITY PRESS
New York and London

Library of Congress Cataloging-in-Publication Data
Darsey, James Francis.
The prophetic tradition and radical rhetoric in America/James Darsey
p. cm.
Includes bibliographical references and index.
ISBN 0-8147-1876-0 (alk. paper)
1. Political oratory—Social aspects—United States.   2. Rhetoric–
Social aspects—United States.   3. Radicalism—United States.
4. Prophecy—Social aspects—United States.   5. United States—
Social conditions–1980–   6. Social problems—United States.
I. Title
PN4055.U53D37   1977
808.5'1'08835—dc21   97-4772
                              CIP

New York University Press books are printed on acid-free paper,
and their binding materials are chosen for strength and durability.

Manufactured in the United States of America

10 9 8 7 6 5 4 3 2 1

To Edwin Black

Contents

Preface   ix

1   Radical Rhetoric and American Community:
     Threnody for *Sophrosyne*   1

Part I

2   Old Testament Prophecy as Radical Ursprach   15
3   Prophecy as Sacred Truth: Self-Evidence and
     Righteousness in the American Revolution   35
4   Prophecy as *Krisis:* Wendell Phillips and the
     Sin of Slavery   61
5   The Prophet's Call and His Burden: The Passion of
     Eugene V. Debs   85

Part II

6   The Word in Darkness   111
7   A Vision of the Apocalypse: Joe McCarthy's Rhetoric of
     the Fantastic   128
8   Prophecy as Poetry: The Romantic Vision
     of Robert Welch   151
9   Secular Argument and the Language of Commodity:
     Gay Liberation and Merely Civil Rights   175
10   The Seraph and the Snake   199

     Notes   211
     Index   269

Preface

I did not begin this book with the idea of engaging the current crop of polemics on the disintegration of American society here at the turn of the millennium. Rather, this study has its origins in my own history, coming of age surrounded by the radical rhetorics of the 1960s, and my later professional dissatisfaction as a student of rhetoric with attempts to explain the behavior of the radicals. It was widely held then that the strident, often violent discourse of blacks, students, feminists, and other disaffected groups would not only hinder their various causes, but threatened to rend the very fabric of society.

Today's complaints bear a remarkable similarity to those voiced thirty years ago, with this important difference: there is no longer a strong sense of a source of the societal decay. It is now precisely the absence of radical discourse that signals the cultural root rot bemoaned by contemporary critics on the left and right. The disintegration they decry indicates something missing at the core, something held as fundamental by a sufficient number of us to be worth engaging over, worth exercising ourselves for. There were portents of our current rootlessness on the horizon ten years ago when this project began its present incarnation. Robert Bellah and his colleagues claimed the entire book review section of an issue of the *New Republic* with *Habits of the Heart*, an analysis of the degeneration of community and its associated moral discourse in America. Today, Bellah's lament is the cause *de jour*. Not only do the choirs on the political right continue to sing the old refrains, but quondam radicals who were once the objects of this approbation have joined in.

Yet, while the general diagnosis has been confirmed and amplified by sages more estimable than I, my specific reading and my prognosis have not been. My reading of the history of American rhetoric (and most of the current assessments are remarkably ahistorical) draws me to the conclusion that it is not an absence of what some writers term "civility," "civil discourse," "reasonable debate," what Matthew Arnold called "sweetness and light," that is the paramount symptom of our ills. Rather it is the absence of meaningful incivility, of radical engagement, of what Arnold called "fire and strength," that is by far more meaningful.

This "fire and strength," which Arnold saw as the tradition of the Old Testament prophets, derives from the vitality of sacred principle, and its whole shape reflects the logic of sacred principle, that is, immutable law, beyond the reach of humankind and uncompromisable. Such principles entail mystery and transcendence, qualities that are in short supply in our world. Given this analysis, I am in agreement with those who, in various ways, call for a renaissance of a religious idea as the umbilicus of a national community. I am not in agreement that such a religion can or should be either "civil" or that it will be at all like attending service at St. Stephen's Episcopal. In fact, I will confess, before anyone has the opportunity to expose me as a fraud, that I have no idea how such principles are created except through the most calculated and strategic of Platonic or Machiavellian means, and I am not at all certain that now moribund ideas that have sustained us in the past can be revived. (A friend once suggested Wagner as the aesthetic foundation for my new religion, but I demurred that something rather too close to that had already been tried with disastrous results.) Despite the fact that my reading of American history through some of its significant public discourses has a certain periodic quality, the alternation of engagement and disengagement, the argument is finally progressive, not cyclical. I believe that our epistemology has undergone, and will continue to undergo, irremediable change, and that those changes have mitigated against the viability of prophetic claims on our credibility.

If I have another manuscript containing the answers to the difficulties we currently face in finding or creating a discursive community, it may take me another ten years to realize that. In the meantime, I will only say that my analysis does not dispose me to think that this is something we can settle once and for all, but that the fate of democracy, if not to fertilize its roots every fifteen years with the blood of revolution as Jefferson believed, is at least to engage periodically in serious acts of redefinition based on radical principles. The goal cannot and should not be a state of restfulness. Quite the contrary, the goal must be endlessly competing zealotries. In vigorous opposition, we (re)invent those principles that define us as a people.

Some may be surprised to have such radical conclusions drawn in a work populated with so many deeply conservative sources—not only Arnold, but Leo Strauss, Richard Weaver, Daniel Bell, Peter Berger, to name only a few—but this surprise is only a further symptom of our fundamental misunderstanding of radicalism. Conservatives may certainly engage "root" issues in a society in important ways and may, given their conservatism, engage them at a deeper historical level than ersatz liberals. I would also note a fair number of sources here from the radical left, chief among whom, in terms of an influence that runs throughout, is Kenneth Burke.

A decision that troubles me and for which I could discover no easy solution is my use of the generic masculine pronoun when referring to prophets and generally when referring to American radicals. Too many factors entered into this decision to detail them here, but it was not thoughtless, for better or worse. It was, in the end, a balancing of stylistic clarity and accuracy in representing my subject. Both Old Testament prophecy and the received notion of American virtue that provides the essential motive for the radicals examined here are products of a patriarchal theology that explicitly holds virtuous action in opposition to "effeminacy." In choosing not to evaluate this aspect of the tradition, I do not mean to condone it, but only to acknowledge that I had another job to do. I hope, at least, that in not camouflaging the sexism in this tradition, I have made it available for others who may choose to evaluate it on these grounds.

Part of chapter 5 was published in the *Quarterly Journal of Speech* in 1988 and part of chapter 7 in *Communication Monographs* in 1995. I am grateful to the Speech Communication Association for permission to use that material. Chapter 9 was originally intended to be a mild revision of an essay published in R. Jeffrey Ringer, ed., *Queer Words, Queer Images: Communication and the Construction of Homosexuality* (New York University Press, 1994). The gay liberation movement, however, would not hold still, and I felt compelled to address trends, nascent in the earlier study, now fully articulated. Though the final product is more like an extension or a sequel, parts of the essay in Ringer's volume are still recognizable here in chapters 6 and 9. My appreciation to New York University Press for permission to use that material.

I have also assumed many personal debts over the course of this project. I have tried to acknowledge some of them along the way. I am not the least bit less indebted for having done so. I hope that those who have contributed their insights, suggestions, criticisms, and support will recognize here my continuing appreciation. There are some, however, who, for various reasons, must be recognized in this final product. They include Murray Edelman, Michael Leff, Stephen Lucas, and Donald K. Smith. David Zarefsky, Daniel Boyarin, and an anonymous reviewer gave the manuscript very helpful reviews, their suggestions improving and clarifying my thinking and writing. The Department of Communication at Northern Illinois University provided me a course reduction in the Spring of 1996 to assist me with the timely completion of the final revisions. My appreciation, too, to the staff at New York University Press: a more professional yet humane treatment I cannot imagine. Jennifer Hammer, my editor, exhibited a remarkable balance of sympathy, strictness, and indulgence that enabled this book to be published in something like the appointed time.

Roderick Hart has been my most stalwart and unflagging professional cheerleader. His wise and warmhearted counsel has, on more than one occasion, saved me from my own worst instincts. Ann Speltz graciously helped me through the copyediting process. As the project went into the home stretch, Valdan Pennington often put forward a brave face and provided courage when it was elsewhere not to be found.

This book is dedicated to Edwin Black whose mark is apparent in its best moments. The luminosity of his criticism sets a standard that we are all better for having before us, even if we can only be frustrated in aspiring to it.

1

Radical Rhetoric
and American Community
Threnody for Sophrosyne

People always think well of speeches adapted to, and reflecting, their
own character: and we can now see how to compose our speeches so
as to adapt both them and ourselves to our audiences.

—Aristotle, *Rhetorica*

Now nothing in oratory, Catulus, is more important than to win for
the orator the favour of his hearer, and to have the latter so affected as
to be swayed by something resembling a mental impulse or emotion,
rather than by judgment or deliberation.   —Cicero, *De Oratore*

The orator indeed is obliged to adapt himself to his audience if he
wishes to have any effect on it and we can easily understand that the
discourse which is most efficacious on an incompetent audience is not
necessarily that which would win the assent of a philosopher.
—Chaim Perelman and L. Olbrechts-Tyteca, *The New Rhetoric*

On May 2, 1996, Billy and Ruth Graham were awarded the
Congressional Gold Medal. In remarks entitled "The Hope for America,"
the Reverend Graham looked backward to George Washington, the first
recipient of the Congressional Gold Medal, and forward to the "Third
Millennium." Though a message of hope, Graham's short speech was full
of the darkness of the moment:

> racial and ethnic tensions that threaten to rip apart our cities and neighbor-
> hoods; crime and violence of epidemic proportions in most of our cities;
> children taking weapons to school; broken families; poverty; drugs; teenage
> pregnancy; corruption; the list is almost endless. Would the first recipients of

this award even recognize the society they sacrificed to establish? I fear not. We have confused liberty with license—and we are paying the awful price. We are a society poised on the brink of self destruction.[1]

Dire as the warning is and prominent as the platform from which it was given, what is most notable about Graham's jeremiad is its lack of notability, receiving not even so much as a remark in the *New York Times.* The complaints suffer the contempt of familiarity; the phrasing, in the current climate, is pedestrian; and perhaps, coming from this source, it is all simply too predictable. The news here lies in the fact that such an ominous portent, delivered by a man who has occupied a significant place on the public stage for as long as any American now living, should be so commonplace.

Such pronouncements have long been the steady fare of the so-called religious right, enjoying greater and lesser degrees of credibility as the fortunes of the country—and the fortunes of individual Americans with it—have waxed and waned. Today, however, these *topoi* have become rhetorical staples of the left as well, the lamentation over, in Todd Gitlin's phrase, *The Twilight of Common Dreams.*[2] Treatments range from the esoteric and rarefied—Gertrude Himmelfarb's *On Looking into the Abyss,*[3] which makes contemporary literary theory its bête noire—to the decidedly practical—*Miss Manners Rescues Civilization from Sexual Harassment, Frivolous Lawsuits, Dissing and Other Lapses in Civility.*[4] The common issue in these various productions is the perceived erosion of any ethical basis for "civil society," or "civic virtue," the "common good," the usurpation of the life of the citizen by privatized, selfish interests. As Gitlin describes it,

> In the land of the free market, civil society, the fine mesh of self-organized groups and initiatives is embattled. The public square, formally open, is usurped by private concessions. Meanwhile, among the general population, it becomes harder to see citizens motivated by obligations beyond their immediate circles. Institutions of public discourse—the press, political parties, vital trade unions, serious books—have become the concern of minorities.[5]

"Little by little," Gitlin warns, "our cultural infrastructure seems to be coming apart along with the bridges and roads."[6]

If there is a trace of reason left in the universe, someone, somewhere must be smiling, even amidst the overwhelming dolor, to hear Professor Gitlin sounding so like the Reverend Billy Graham. Thirty years ago, Gitlin and his associates on the New Left would have been, as they were for many, the object of Graham's criticism, the engine of the cultural doom. In a 1968 review of Abbie Hoffman's book *Revolution for the Hell of It,* Jack Newfield contrasted the traditional liberal values of "reason, democracy, tolerance, and truth," to Hoffman's "distortion, violence, chaos, and mindless action."[7] Justice Abe Fortas expressed the view that what was at stake was no less than the formal processes which make society possible.[8] In his first inaugural address, Richard Nixon, who had run on a law and order campaign, characterized the "difficult years" of the 1960s as ones in which America had "suffered from a fever of words; from inflated rhetoric that promises more than it can deliver; from angry rhetoric that fans discontents into hatreds; from bombastic rhetoric that postures instead of persuading," and he urged us to "stop shouting" and to "speak quietly enough so that our words can be heard as well as our voices."[9]

In these assessments, admonitions, and pleas from both the Sixties and the Nineties, radical speech, unmannerly rhetoric, is a symptom, a harbinger of a more extensive disorder. It strikes, explicitly in Fortas's caveat, at something essential to our social organization. The failure of communication, recognized by both critics and defenders of the radical stance, is taken as signaling a failure of community. The phrase "civil society" itself, expressing our preference for the mannerly, the courteous, the amenable, the proper, is contrasted to the decay of process we sense around us. There is a widely held belief that the ties that bind us are eroding. We are alarmed by what we see as the rise of force over reasoned discourse as "the chief means whereby social borders, hierarchies, institutional formations, and habituated patterns of behavior are both maintained and modified."[10] Robert Bellah and his colleagues have framed the problem as one where the language of individualism has run amuck, mutated, and become anarchic, obliterating the moral language of duty and commitment that makes the *polis* possible,[11] and Lee C. Bollinger questions the benefits of a free speech principle so broad that it allows "extremist speech" to strike "more and more deeply at the personal and social values we cherish and hold fundamental to the society."[12] The production of eulogies for civil discourse in America has become a minor industry.[13]

The parallels notwithstanding, there are important and potentially informative differences between Franklyn Haiman's "Farewell to Rational Discourse" (1968)[14] and Mary Ann Glendon's diagnosis that our political discourse has been "impoverished" by a faulty and undisciplined conception of rights.[15] Haiman and other observers of the Sixties mourned a society apparently being torn apart at the seams, an act of violent division, perhaps an excess of definition.[16] Glendon and her colleagues, on the other hand, address a diffusion of responsibility, a loss of definition. Billy Graham's talk of ripping, and weapons, and breakage, and destruction, for all its incipient violence, is peculiarly unfocused. There is no clear defendant in his indictment. He merely points to an "almost endless" list of symptoms. The story lacks a compelling villain. Even the recent bombings in the United States confirm this reading in their lack of attachment to a cause, their seeming senselessness and lack of meaning.

The real lesson is the lesson of license conceived as licentiousness— things fall apart—it is the unraveling of Gitlin's "fine mesh," each thread establishing its independent claims. This theme weaves it way through Jean Bethke Elshtain's analysis in which she refers to "corrosive forms of isola- tion, boredom, and despair; the weakening, in other words, of that world known as democratic civil society, a world of groups and associations and ties that bind," the "disintegration" of "social webs," the "thinning out" of the "skein of obligation," and "the unraveling of democratic civil society."[17] Fraying is not violent rending.

The persistent confusion lies in the common disregard by both forms of destruction of the social fabric for "civility." Elshtain reveals something of the root of this confusion in her celebration of the rhetorical legacy of ancient Athens. Rhetoric is the discourse of the public being, of the citizen, and Elshtain observes that the achievement of the common good depended, not only on the deliberative outcomes in the assembly, but also on the "day-to-day relations of Athenians with each other,[18] related to what Thomas Cole refers to as "the rhetoric of tact and etiquette.[19] Robert Hariman articulates the relationship of rhetoric and manners through the classical notion of "decorum," which he defines as consisting in "(a) the rules of conduct guiding the alignment of signs and situations, or texts and acts, or behavior and place; (b) embodied in practices of communication and display according to a symbolic system; and (c) providing social cohe- sion and distributing power."[20] From the time of Aristotle forward, the tradition of public discourse in the West has been one of civility, diplomacy, compromise, and negotiation. In the United States, the connection be- tween rhetoric as a mode of persuasion and rhetoric as civil behavior is most evident in those public speaking texts published circa 1900, which often represented themselves as guides to both public speaking and eti- quette. In 1902, the author of *The American Star Speaker and Model Elocution- ist* wrote,

It is a duty imposed at birth to make the best use of every talent of which we are possessed; it is equally a duty to make ourselves as agreeable in our intercourse with our fellow creatures as our opportunities may permit. Politeness, coupled with an attractiveness of manner, is the passport which admits us to the favorable attention of our fellow men.[21]

The etymological propinquity of "manners" and "manipulation" suggests something of the relationship between the preferred nature of rhetorical discourse and its goals.

Public discourse in this tradition assumes the existence of a community of mores, common operating assumptions, shared values, even as it seeks to rebuild, reinforce, and redirect that community. Indeed, the orator has often been seen as a central figure in cultural life and the state of oratory a significant measure of cultural health. James Boyd White only puts into contemporary language a Ciceronian conception of the role of oratory in society when he defines rhetoric as: "the study of the ways in which character and community—and motive, value, reason, social structure, everything, in short, that makes a culture—are defined and made real in performances of language."[22]

In such a conception, the rhetor becomes "representative" of his or her public, a usage reflected in our most common appellation for public officials. And just as the rhetor becomes representative of his or her public, the rules of rhetoric become synecdochal for the rules of society. "Fair speech," whether presented in *The American Star Speaker and Model Elocutionist* or elsewhere, reflects, in Kenneth Burke's formulation, "the individual person striving to form himself in accordance with the communicative norms that match the cooperative ways of his society."[23] The failure of this process, or worse, the rejection of it, is taken as a signal of the disintegration of society itself, the abandonment of the accepted rules of speech a portent of incipient chaos and the abandonment of the rule of order generally.[24]

Yet, Rosa Parks's refusal to surrender her seat on a bus in Montgomery, Alabama, is not the same as the belligerent occupation of a seat for two by a disaffected youth on a Chicago el at rush hour, and a critique of incivility that fails to recognize this distinction misses an essential difference between the threats to comity of the 1960s and those of the 1980s and 1990s. Further, I will argue, it misses the lessons that the American radical tradition holds for our current disquietude.

The recovery of a radical tradition in American public discourse, a tradition characterized by a steadfast refusal to adapt itself to the perspectives of its audience, a rhetoric *in extremis,* indicates something more complex than the breakdown of order; it indicates an alternative order, a rationality not accounted for in the Graeco-Roman model. A recrudescent rhetorical form entails a stable response to a recurrent historical situation, intimating the kind of discernible relationship among elements in a rhetorical situation constitutive of a genre.[25] Criticism of rhetorical genres, in turn, presupposes a logic underlying the shape of discourse. Such criticism is predicated on an accountability of discourse to the salient forces that have shaped it. A radical genre is not without rules, but its rules, of necessity, are shaped in large part by its significant opposition to the status quo. What we really mean when we complain about the lack of respect for process in radicalism is the lack of respect for *our preferred* process, a process that reinforces the situation that the radical seeks to change.

The notion of a rhetorical tradition includes and extends the idea of genre to encompass those forms that have been consciously fostered within a culture.[26] Consideration of the traditional aspects of genre encourages questions of development and evolution, and since they, in turn, suggest a point of origin, consideration of a rhetorical tradition proffers the possibility that the genre may be located in a nascent, primitive historical form, a form in which features and outlines were still firmly connected to the cultural features that engendered them. To speak of genres as subjects of evolution brings us close to the relationship between the generic and the genetic,[27] and makes perfectly reasonable the proposition that rhetorical traditions should retain vestigial elements that, unless understood in historical context, obscure the functions of the genre.

Such is the kind of explanation I have undertaken here as a perspective on some of that discourse in American history that has been characterized as "radical," "extremist," or "revolutionary," because of its failure to adopt its audience's frame of reference. Because its essential form appears to be both recurrent and stable, it cannot be reduced to the vagaries of the particular situation or of individual maladjustment. Before we can disqualify such rhetoric, we must first seek its sources in our culture.

The thesis I shall argue here is that the primitive source for much of the rhetoric of reform in America has been the prophetic books of the Old Testament. It seems an obvious connection given the prominence of the Bible in American culture, and there have been some studies that have traced influences of the Bible in our national life[28] and on our public discourse in particular.[29] Many of these studies might be considered studies of allusion, appraisals of the use of the content of a key cultural document.

Sacvan Bercovitch's influential work on the American jeremiad as a genre is an exception.[30] Even Bercovitch's work, however, is concerned, as its title indicates, with an American rhetorical creation, not with the form of prophetic speech as it appears in the books of the Old Testament.[31] Consequently, he refers to his jeremiads as "political sermons," the genre of priests and preachers, not prophets.[32] Old Testament prophecy operates in a different mode and is based on different epistemological assumptions than our public rhetorics derived from the Graeco-Roman tradition.

Assessing the reform efforts of another time and another place, Matthew Arnold once characterized the methods as conforming either to the ideal of "sweetness and light" or to that of "fire and strength." "Sweetness and light" is the ideal of our received rhetorical theory; its source, said Arnold, is Hellenic. "Fire and strength," on the other hand, is Hebraic in origin. Though in many ways antithetical to one another, both stand in opposition to anarchy, that state in which everyone is absorbed in "doing as one likes."[33] As Arnold expressed it: "The uppermost idea with Hellenism is to see things as they really are; the uppermost idea with Hebraism is conduct and obedience."[34] In this respect, Arnold's analysis is more precise than many of those in the present, which tend to regard both "fire and strength" and anarchy as destructive forms of incivility.

Rhetorical critics have been prevented from seeing as clearly as Arnold did the possibility of the continuing influence of the Bible on social action for two reasons. First, we have received no systematic theory of rhetoric from the ancient Hebrews. The prophets of the Old Testament left us with a considerable body of discourse, but they were not theorists and were not prone to spend time examining or articulating the assumptions on which their discourse was built. The failure of the prophets to provide a theory is a gap in our understanding of them and of ourselves that has only begun to be rectified in our own time.[35] Furthermore, the theory that we are likely to find implied in the rhetoric of Old Testament prophets will be foreign and alien when compared to our accustomed theories. As Michael Fox has stated, "In Israel we have a well-documented major rhetorical movement entirely independent of the classical tradition from which Western rhetoric and rhetorical criticism descend."[36] And Arnold's characterization of the Hebraic ideal as "fire and strength" suggests that it is not only foreign but also uncomfortable. Consideration of the prophetic aspects of discourse, then, has presented itself as an undertaking both unfamiliar and difficult.

Yet the "fire and strength" of the prophets is as much a part of our cultural inheritance as is the "sweetness and light" of the Greeks, and it is sheer folly to think that we can have an adequate explanation of radicalism in our culture so long as we ignore a discursive tradition marked by obvious similarities to those discourses we today term "radical," the influence of which is often attested to by the radicals themselves in their allusions and quotations.

A second reason, I would suggest, that we have avoided explanations that have their roots in anything like prophecy is our embarrassment at the prospect of considering seriously claims of divine possession or consecration. In our everyday usage, we acknowledge the possibility of something like a religious commitment at the base of radical social movements: we talk of revolutionary "faith" and "zeal"; we refer to radical leaders as "prophets"; and we analyze radical rhetoric according to its "God terms" and "devil terms."[37] At the same time, while we admit of the existence of some blatantly "messianic" or "millennial" or "revitalization" movements that have unmistakably religious roots, we are also victims of our own enlightenment and generally prefer explanations of a more secular order. This in spite of the fact, as George Bernard Shaw, humbling himself before the self-conception of Saint Joan, once reminded us, that "the nineteenth century, and still more the twentieth, can knock the fifteenth into a cocked hat in point of susceptibility to marvels and saints and prophets and magicians and monsters and fairy tales of all kinds." "The proportion of marvel to immediately credible statement in the latest edition of the *Encyclopaedia Britannica*," he went on to say, "is enormously greater than in the Bible."[38] Approaching the study of a discourse, the ultimate premises of which cannot be verified by conventional means, demands that we suspend, at least for a moment, our modern tendency toward rationalized incredulity and humble ourselves before what we understand only incompletely.

Here is the element that completes the triad initiated with the discussion of "community" and "communication" above. That third element is "communion." A community must find its rules in some common authority. The authority by which we seek to circumscribe radical rhetorics, to bring them from the realm of "fire and strength" into the realm of "sweetness and light," to make them agreeable,[39] the authority reflected in the criticisms of the protests of the 1960s by Haiman, Newfield, Fortas, and Nixon, is the secular authority of reason. Similarly, the authority invoked by Gitlin, Himmelfarb, Glendon, Elshtain against the anarchy of the 1980s and 1990s draws on the process orientation of the liberal democratic tradition. Reason is demystified—that is, it can be completely articulated; reasons can be given—and it describes process rather than content. There is ostensibly no leap of faith in reason. In politics, the rule of reason is expressed in the rationalist metaphor of the social contract. Robert Bellah has argued that in complex societies, "the legal order in some significant measure becomes a substitute for the religious order."[40] Such an arrangement allows "matters of ultimate religious and moral truth" to be declared "essentially private."[41] Money becomes the source of our public bonds. As Burke notes,

> Money endangers religion in that money can serve as universal symbol, the unitary ground of all action. And it endangers religion not in the dramatic, agonistic way of a "tempter," but in its quiet, rational way as a *substitute* that performs its mediatory role more "efficiently," more "parsimoniously," with less "waste motion" as regards the religious or ritualistic conception of "works."[42]

The consequence of such rationalization is that moral criticism is discredited, or at least deemed inappropriate in the public sphere. Social reform efforts are evaluated in terms of resource or rational exchange models, as, for example, reflected in William A. Gamson's description of influence: "Carrying out influence involves making commitments which place a future call on one's resources. The transactional cost of influence is the cost of fulfilling obligations contracted."[43] The language of economics makes incomprehensible all claims based on ideals. Consider the marked disparity between the number of Americans generally favorable to the notion of equal pay for equal work and those favorable to the larger goals of the feminist movement.

There is no communion in money; it is the great metonymy for private property. Radicalism, in contrast, is defined by its concern with the political roots of a society, its fundamental laws, its foundational principles, its most sacred covenants. It is common for radicals to claim to be the true keepers of the faith; they oppose their society using its own most noble expressions and aspirations.[44] A rootless society, a society where the power of once compelling ideas has atrophied, has no basis for authorizing radical activity. When General Motors' Mr. Goodwrench declares "Your car is your freedom," the solution to oppression is to buy and maintain an automobile (furthering insulation and rootlessness).

As I will argue in the following chapters, ours is a society that no longer recognizes radical activity for what it is. The failure of community is signaled, not by the rudeness and stridency of protest, but by the loss of a common faith in fundamental ideals and the loss of the long historical conversation in which these ideals were molded, preserved, and defended.

That the content of this conversation is derived largely from the liberal tradition of John Stuart Mill and John Locke has been well documented, but the prophetic form that unites much of that discourse in its more extreme manifestations has not been.

In the six case studies that follow, I have sought to examine the fundamental assumptions of prophetic discourse and to seek an understanding of the ways in which those assumptions have manifested themselves in the rhetoric of radical American reformers. In this endeavor, I have no claim to being a scholar of the Bible, nor need I make such a claim for my purpose here. Although I have borrowed heavily from biblical scholarship in my efforts to isolate those features that are salient to the prophetic message, I am less interested in scholarly debates over the fine points of biblical criticism than I am in the prophetic tradition as it has been received and generally understood and imitated by Americans.

The following chapter, the introduction to part I of this study, attempts to adumbrate a theory of prophetic discourse based on its origin in the divine word, the prophetic *logos;* its psychosocial situation, the prophetic *pathos;* and the prophet's personal mode of validation, the prophetic *ethos.* This chapter represents an initial assay of the shape and function of each aspect of prophetic discourse with reference to the Old Testament prophets themselves. What is sought is an articulation of the direct relationship between prophetic rhetoric and the cultural assumptions that engendered it. In this set of relationships is the most basic understanding of the discourse.

Chapters 3, 4, and 5 explore the appropriation of prophetic forms by American reformers. Each of these chapters is a case study in one of the text-context relationships of prophetic discourse, though it is assumed that each of these relationships could be found in any of the discourses: the self-evident truths of the American Revolution are a particularly suggestive study in the relationship of the prophetic *logos* to absolute truth; Wendell Phillips's condemnation of slavery, with its caustic energy, provides insights into the sources of the prophetic *pathos;* and the martyrdom of Eugene Debs is a model of the prophetic *ethos.*

In addition to permitting the drawing of analogs between American reformers and Old Testament prophets, the chronological ordering of the chapters allows us to see something of how a prophetic tradition developed in America. If the Old Testament prophets did not inspire each generation of reformers anew or *in vacuo,* how did their tradition become assimilated into an American tradition of radical reform? How and to what degree does each successive generation of radicals influence the rhetorical resources that are available to the next and the expectations of future audiences?

Part II of this study turns to the problem of public reform discourse in an age bereft of absolute principles. Beginning with chapter 6, having defined the most basic characteristics of the prophetic tradition or voice, I am interested in exploring the difference between its essential and nonessential attributes. In order to possess critical utility, a generic construction must be definitive; that is, it must not only be able to define the qualities of what is included, but it must be able to make meaningful exclusions; it must be able to distinguish the genuine article from the impostor. The postmodern era is widely regarded as a time of the negative. Todd Gitlin characterizes it as "a prolonged cultural moment that is oddly weightless, shadowed by incomplete revolts, haunted by absences . . . in general, by the erosion of that false and devastating universality embodied in the rule of the pyramidal trinity of Father, Science, and State."[45] Gitlin and Graham may be worlds apart in their evaluations of what has been lost, but there is a high degree of consensus that it is gone, and that we have found nothing yet to replace it. Radical discourse understood in terms of biblical prophecy has no potency in such a world. The shift parallels that in the Old Testament from a community that could be called into being by a prophetic reassertion of the covenant and the apparently forsaken and rootless aggregation to whom the message of the apocalypse was directed. Part II of this study looks at three possible avenues for a reform discourse with the power to command the assent of a significant public in a world deprived of principles.

The rhetoric of Joe McCarthy has often been referred to as radical, but that position has never been held without opposition, even in McCarthy's own day. His rhetoric, though audacious, never clearly defined its position in the manner of genuine radicalism. McCarthy's entertainment of a chaotic world in which judgment was suspended partakes of the literary genre of fantasy and has parallels with the devolution of Old Testament prophecy into apocalyptic. Robert Welch, like McCarthy, was widely hailed as a radical. His tactics were often compared to the tactics of those on the extreme left, yet we sense that there is a profound difference between a Robert Welch and, for example, a Eugene Debs. The similarities are undeniable, but one suspects superficial. Perhaps more interesting still is Welch's relationship to McCarthy since the two were publicly associated, but again, there is the strong suspicion that Welch was no more a McCarthy than he was a Debs. Welch provides evidence that he self-consciously aped the form of prophecy as he found it in nineteenth-century poetry, and in Welch's rhetoric we are able to look at the surface divorced from its animating source, a kind of autopsy.

Finally, having formed some relatively clear idea of the tradition's shape and its parameters, the last case seeks to highlight its features through contrast and to make some preliminary assessment of the rhetorical worth of the prophetic voice by comparing the possibilities it contains to the possibilities available in the traditional consensus view of rhetoric. What happens when a reform movement in a postreligious world capitulates and embraces the thoroughly secular, rationalized discourse of its time? Gay liberation, again a reform movement often held to be radical, is the subject of the last study, chosen because, although its programs have been characterized as radical, it has been decisively excluded from the argumentative premises of the prophetic voice, having no claim on the most prominent historical sources of authority: religion, science, and the law. In fact, I argue, gay liberation has attempted to make its argument by pushing the pluralistic, adaptive assumptions of traditional rhetoric to their limit. The comparison of the Hebraic and the Hellenic ideals in situations of contest should further our understanding of the function and place of prophetic discourse. It should also say something about the state of community in America.

Part I

2

Old Testament Prophecy as Radical Ursprach

In my powerlessness, it seemed that I was becoming identified with the very powers that had drained me of power. I knew, in other words, what hero, saint, Marxist, criminal, artist, and madman must know: identity with fate.

—Robert Penn Warren, *A Place to Come To*

A tornado of confusion swept whirling from wall to wall, and the madness of the moment seized irresistibly upon Presley. He forgot himself; he no longer was master of his emotions or his impulses. All at once he found himself upon the stage, facing the audience, flaming with excitement, his imagination on fire, his arms uplifted in fierce, wild gestures, words leaping to his mind in a torrent that could not be withheld.

—Frank Norris, *The Octopus*

In his treatise on rhetoric, Aristotle identified three modes of persuasion "furnished by the spoken word: . . . The first kind depends on the personal character of the speaker; the second on putting the audience into a certain frame of mind; the third on the proof, or apparent proof, provided by the words of the speech itself."[1] Though terms have changed, been altered, modernized, and extended, these three modes of proof, in one guise or another, still define much of the research agenda in communication studies and rhetoric. Certainly any rudimentary theory of rhetoric needs to incorporate them.

Though the study of the theory of rhetoric in the West has been largely restricted to a line of inheritance that runs from Plato and Aristotle through Cicero, Quintilian, Saint Augustine, into the Middle Ages, the neo-Classical rhetorics of the Renaissance, to the modern period, including George Campbell, Hugh Blair, and Richard Whately, to contemporary times and figures such as Kenneth Burke and Chaim Perelman, there is evidence of a body of rhetorical practice that has its roots in a very different tradition. Particularly in the United States, with its early self-conception as the New Israel, the "shining city on the hill," the rhetoric of the Christian Bible has had an enormous presence in our public discourse. James Turner Johnson, in his introduction to a collection of essays devoted to examining this presence, notes, "A cross-flow has existed between religion and American culture from the early colonial settlements onward to the present, and through much of American history that flow has involved reference to symbols, rhetoric, moral guidance, and an understanding of history derived from the Bible." [2]

Rhetorics of radical reform, in particular, exhibit similarities with the discursive tradition of the Old Testament prophets. Both have in common a sense of mission, a desire to bring the practice of the people into accord with a sacred principle, and an uncompromising, often excoriating stance toward a reluctant audience. Though there was no theory of rhetoric among the ancient Jews, prophetic practice offers a tradition highly articulated with its philosophical foundations, and these connections, especially as they have been filtered through Christianity and the King James Bible and received as part of the American tradition, provide important insights into the rhetorical practices of those who agitate on behalf of great causes.

The Prophetic Logos

Prophetic speech is incomprehensible except as the speech of a divine messenger; the prophet, properly understood, speaks for another.[3] The prophets of the Old Testament were spokesmen for Yahweh. They were called to deliver a message that was not their own, often against their will.[4] Ezekiel "went in bitterness, in the heat of my spirit; but the hand of the Lord was strong upon me."[5] Ezekiel was compelled to speak; he prophesied over his own resistance. Jeremiah spoke of the futility of refusing to "speak any more in His name . . . There is in my heart as it were a burning fire, Shut up in my bones, and I am weary with holding it in, And I cannot."[6] The words of Amos reveal the same compulsion: "The Lord Yahweh hath spoken; who can but prophesy?"[7] Contrary to the assumptions of traditional Graeco-Roman rhetorical theory, prophecy shatters the unity of rhetoric. *Inventio* and *actio* are not products of the same agent. Prophecy is in a significant respect a performance from script. As Margaret Zulick notes, "YHWH is shown to be the true agent of the prophetic word and the prophet is reduced to the status of agency, an unwilling instrument of the word."[8] The prophet cannot be held personally culpable for his message. Indeed he is only culpable to the extent that he asserts his will and throws off the yoke of God. The prophet acts responsibly only when he subordinates his will to the divine will and bears witness to God's word. As Zulick characterizes this transaction, "the whole responsibility of the agent for the act is passed over to YHWH, exonerating the prophet by entirely identifying his speech with that of YHWH.[9] So long as the prophet serves as God's trumpet, his activity is not only justified but mandated.

The role of the Old Testament prophet is often indicated by the use of the "messenger formula," "Thus saith the Lord."[10] The messenger formula makes clear the nature of the prophetic *logos* as the word of God, and the identification of God and the word quite literally suggests the character, the *ethos,* of the message. The formula preferred in Ezekiel is quite explicit: "And the word of the Lord came unto me saying . . ." This rendering of Ezekiel personifies the word and reveals the suasory power of the word to lie in who it is: "And the word was God." In Heschel's formulation,

> The certainty of being inspired by God, of speaking in His name, of having been sent by Him to the people, is the basic and central fact of the prophet's consciousness. Other people regard *experience* as the source of certainty; what singles out the prophet in the world of man is that to him *the source of experience* is the source of his certainty. To his mind, the validity and distinction of his message lie in the origin, not only in the moment of his experience.[11]

The word brought by the prophets was a reassertion of Yahweh's covenant with His people and a reminder of Yahweh's presence in the world, a reminder of God's will, not a revelation or the presentation of a startlingly new claim. The prophets addressed a community already defined by knowledge of the covenant.[12] The covenant was central to the shared history of the ancient Jews, and it was in history that its terms were realized. Prophetic instauration of the covenant served to reaffirm the hand of God behind events in the world. In the essentially theological view of history held by the ancient Hebrews,[13] history was, in Abraham Heschel's phrase, "the vessel for God's action."[14] The God of the Old Testament made Himself manifest in the affairs of the world as the perpetual author of events, the ceaseless creator; military victories and defeats, well-being and plagues, bountiful harvests and natural disasters, all were meaningful in terms of the covenant as evidence of Yahweh's mercies toward and judgments against His people.[15] This history was the common legacy of the peoples of Israel and Judah.

But the common legacy seems at odds with the historical reputation of the prophets. If the message of the prophets was the message of the covenant, if the prophets of the Old Testament were not endowed with an exclusive revelation, how were they set apart from their people? What made the prophet a voice crying from the wilderness? Why was the prophetic office exclusive? Although the terms of the covenant and the events of history were the common legacy of Israel and Judah, the prophets addressed a people whose vision had been clouded by the material benefits of a settled and agrarian lifestyle, a people "which have eyes to see, and see not; they have ears to hear, and hear not: for they are a rebellious house."[16] Unlike the prophets, who were responsible to God's will and responsive to His call, the people were at ease. As Amos described them: "That lie upon beds of ivory, and stretch themselves upon their couches, and eat the lambs out of the flock, and the calves out of the midst of the stall; That chant to the sound of the viol and invent to themselves instruments of musick, like David; That drink wine in bowls and anoint themselves with the chief ointments: but they are not grieved for the affliction of Joseph."[17] It was the prophet's task to reassert the terms of the covenant to a people who had fallen away, to restore a sense of duty and virtue amidst the decay of venality. Abraham Heschel finds the demands of God's covenant with His people "reflected in every word" of the prophet.[18]

The terms of the compact Yahweh had made with His people were accessible to all, but, said Isaiah, "the vision of all this has become to you like the words of a book that is sealed. When men give it to one who can read saying, 'Read this,' he says, 'I cannot, for it is sealed.' And when they give the book to one who cannot read, saying, 'Read this,' he says, 'I cannot read.' "[19] The peoples of Israel and Judah, then, were not condemned for their ignorance, but for their willful blindness to the message of Yahweh: "For three transgressions of Judah, and for four, I will not revoke punishment," proclaimed Amos, "because they have rejected the law of the Lord, and have not kept his statutes, but their lies have led them astray, after which their fathers walked."[20]

The defective vision of the people is often expressed in the metaphors of drunkenness and slumber, thus intimating the moral failings behind it: "These also reel with wine and stagger with strong drink; the priest and the prophet reel with strong drink, they are confused with wine, they

stagger with strong drink; they err in vision, they stumble in giving judgment."[21] The prophets were called by God as a corrective to this failure of
perception, this intoxication with the world. The prophets were, in part,
seers; for the most part, they were uninfected by and renounced worldly
comfort, and they commanded the people to use their senses, long fallen
into desuetude: "Hear this, O foolish and senseless people, who have eyes,
but see not, who have ears, but hear not."[22]

Heavy use of metaphors of vision in Old Testament prophecy suggests a
rhetoric of showing.[23] In the *Posterior Analytics,* Aristotle treats those truths
which are susceptible, not to persuasion or argument, but to "demonstration" as the most common English translation holds—demonstration
which comes from the Latin *monstare,* to show. The kind of truth Aristotle
was concerned with in the *Posterior Analytics* was *apodictic* (also *apodeictic*)
truth from the Greek *apodeiknyai,* to demonstrate, from *apo + deikynai,* to
show. For Old Testament prophets, apodictic law in the form of God's
revealed covenant with His people, is a topic for rhetoric or proclamation,
not an epistemological status belonging to some other discipline as in
Aristotle's conception,[24] and Heschel describes the activity of Old Testament prophets in terms that reflect the nature of their activity as a kind of
demonstration: "In speaking, the prophet reveals God. This is the marvel
of a prophet's work: in his words, *the invisible God becomes audible.* He does
not prove or argue."[25] It is impossible to adduce evidence for God's law, for
it contains its own evidence; it is self-evident, clear upon viewing.[26]

Chaim Perelman has noted the tautological character of self- evidence
"conceived both as a force to which every normal mind must yield and as
a sign of the truth of that which imposes itself because it is self-evident."[27]
Although Perelman would dismiss such reasoning as fallacious, he reveals its
coercive power as a substitute for argument. The logical refutation is
technical cavil against the social force of what Richard Weaver has called
"uncontested terms." Uncontested terms are such precisely because the
audience is unable or unwilling to question them.[28] For the ancient peoples
of Judah and Israel, the existence of a God active in history was just such a
matter of faith. Thus we can understand what Sheldon Blank means when
he says of Jeremiah as an example of the Old Testament prophet's understanding of his authority that the strongest argument for his authenticity is
not an argument at all, but the simple affirmation that God had sent him.[29]
To a people who hold what W. D. Hudson has termed a "constitutive
belief" in an irreducible God, such an affirmation is not only sufficient, but
the only proof consistent with that belief. Any other proof implies some-

thing more compelling than the revelation of God.[30] As Blank writes, "So Jeremiah rests his case with the prima-facie evidence of the message itself as the final test of its authenticity and his own veracity."[31]

The rhetoric of self-evidence is both profoundly conservative, even reactionary, and profoundly radical. It is conservative in that it has no power of invention; it can only reveal that which was already there, the sempiternal; it is always the rhetoric of the messenger. It is radical in its engagement of society at its root.

The values expressed in prophecy lay at the heart of ancient Hebrew society; they were the values of the covenant that defined the peoples of Israel and Judah. Prophetic discourse is thus highly enthymematic; it emphasizes the presence of a public tradition. A common belief in the viability of the covenant is the silent but acknowledged premise behind every judgment, a "common sense," at least of basic principles. Walter Brueggemann describes the prophet as one who must "move back into the deepest memories of his community and activate those very symbols that have always been the basis for contradicting the regnant consciousness."[32] But in the act of judgment, in opposing his understanding of the covenant against the more comfortable understanding of his people, in presenting his understanding as God's understanding, the prophet not only forebodes punishment, but threatens the basis of self-definition. Against Israel's complacency in her chosen status, the prophets decried her as a harlot. Judah's unearned sanctimoniousness is a scourge. It is precisely because the prophet engages his society over its most central and fundamental values that he is radical.[33]

The most accessible evidence of the prophet's radicalism is his opposition to the regnant power structure. As illustrated in the covenanting of David as King of Israel, even rulers were subject to the overarching covenant with Yahweh.[34] The prophets measured the performance of kings against the incontrovertible moral standards of that higher covenant and found the substitution of power for righteousness.[35] Isaiah condemned the princes of Judah as "rebellious, and companions of thieves: every one loveth gifts, and followeth after rewards: they judge not the fatherless, neither doth the cause of the widow come unto them. . . . Therefore saith the Lord . . . I will turn my hand upon thee, and purely purge away thy dross, and take away all thy tin: And I will restore thy judges as at the first, and thy counsellors as at the beginning: afterward thou shalt be called, The city of righteousness, the faithful city."[36] All power paled beside the supreme power of God, and no power was legitimate that was not in accordance with His will.[37] It is the central place of the covenant in prophetic discourse that gives that discourse its distinctly judicial or legal character.[38]

Despite its radicalism and the magnitude of its judgment, there is an element in prophecy that aspires to the mundane. The severity of the prophet's judgment must not be confused with hysteria. Vawter in fact describes the prophetic word as "usually calm" and "matter-of-fact" in tone,[39] and Westermann finds the highly formal legal antecedents to the major literary prophets in the early prophecy of first and second Kings.[40] The rationality of prophecy consists in its perfect consistency with the terms of the covenant as reflected in the *rîb* pattern of predicate (accusation) and consequent (punishment).[41] There is a logic to prophetic rhetoric, which, once the underlying premises are conceded, is inexorable.

What prophecy is not is reasonable. Egon Bittner, in the article on radicalism for the *International Encyclopedia of the Social Sciences,* makes an important distinction between reasonableness and rationality that suggests the rhetorical consequences of absolute *logos:* "Although radicalism is characteristically rational or at least rationalized," writes Bittner, "it is clearly and implacably inconsistent with reasonableness. In principle, pure radical thought and action is devoid of practical wisdom, of sensitivity to the occasion, of opportunistic economizing, of the capacity to learn from experience, of flexibility and looseness of interest. In sum, it lacks that bargaining side of intelligence that characterizes the conduct and thinking of 'reasonable' persons."[42]

What Bittner does not show but prophecy reveals are the reasons for the unreason. First, given a truth that is absolute, it makes no sense to talk of "practical wisdom," "sensitivity to the occasion," "opportunistic economizing," "the capacity to learn from experience," "flexibility and looseness of interest," or "bargaining."[43] As a manifestation of God's will, the word is absolute and immutable; it is beyond the reach and power of humankind; it is sacred in the critical sense of being separate, untouchable, pure,[44] and it exercises its claim on its auditors because it is; it cannot be compromised. Emile Durkheim expressed this distinctive circular power of the sacred "as expressly obligatory, and this obligation is the proof that these ways of acting and thinking are not the work of the individual but come from a moral power above him, that which the mystic calls God or which can be more scientifically conceived."[45] Secondly, as a messenger, the speaker cannot alter the message without violating his sacred trust. Indeed, the fact of the sacred trust itself places the speaker outside the frame of reference of his audience; the speaker's role is that of the extremist.[46] Thus prophetic rhetoric violates one of the traditional functions of rhetoric by emphasizing separation over identification.[47]

It may begin to seem that prophecy is not rhetorical at all since it lacks the pragmatic orientation that is a hallmark of rhetoric, and prophecy, with its emphasis on the *apodictic,* does threaten whatever Ramistic divisions we might want to create between rhetoric and philosophy in particular. But prophecy shares with rhetoric a situational nature and a raison d'être in ends.[48] The prophetic end, however, is qualitative, not quantitative; anything short of God's absolute will as expressed in His word is a profanation. "Compromise," Heschel reminds us, "is an attitude the prophet abhors. . . . Others may be satisfied with improvement, the prophets insist upon redemption."[49] The holy remnant, as illustrated in the stories of Noah or Sodom and Gomorrah, is more valuable to God than any contaminated consensus. The prophet achieves identification only when the holy remnant has joined him in the purity of the wilderness; the people must come to God; He cannot come to them.

The preeminent discourse of separation in American history, the discourse that first defined us as an American people, is that of the American Revolution. The apparent contradictions and complexity of the rhetoric that accompanied the creation of a new nation from thirteen British colonies continue to absorb our attentions two centuries after the fact. Certainly the frequent biblical allusions in the rhetoric of the Revolution confirm our historical understanding of the importance of the Bible as a prominent model of discourse in the lives of the colonists,[50] but that understanding may reflect no more than a crude *imitatio,* the superficial adoption of literary conceits. The more fundamental parallel lies in the inflexible posture of righteousness. With other models of discourse in the colonial repertoire— the tradition of parliamentary debates, the speeches of Cicero—is the special place of biblical rhetoric, Old Testament rhetoric in particular, in the speeches and broadsides of American Whigs symptomatic of something more than mere literary affinity? Does it perhaps indicate something about the Whig conception of themselves and their message as rooted in the *logos* of Old Testament prophecy? Certainly the discourse surrounding an event that Robert Bellah has boldly termed the provenance of "the American civil religion" deserves analysis from such a perspective, and in chapter 3 I will do so.[51]

The Pathos of Prophecy

To be a prophet it is not enough to speak on behalf of an absolute truth. While this may satisfy the etymological requirement, the historical requirement entails a time of crisis, from the Greek *krisis,* "decision," or "judgment."[52] As R. B. Y. Scott suggests,

> The call appears to have come to each prophet in a time of intellectual and emotional tension. "The year that King Uzziah died" marked the end of an epoch. The social strains following Jeroboam's wars and a series of natural calamities appear in the pages of Amos as affecting all but the very wealthy. Hosea spoke out of a welter of vice and confusion, bordering on anarchy. Micah cried out that the cities were draining the lifeblood from the country-side, and a foreign invasion must shortly come to complete the destruction. Jeremiah and Zephaniah began to prophesy when the world empire of the Assyrians was tottering under the onslaught of barbarian hordes, which were soon to appear on the northern horizon of Palestine. Nahum shouted that Nineveh was about to fall with a world-shaking crash.[53]

Common to these critical times is a sense of overwhelming threat, a sense that, in its intensity, achieves psychotic proportions, a threat to the self-definition of a people.

Jürgen Habermas finds crisis "when members of a society experience structural alterations as critical for continued existence and feel their social identity threatened. . . . Disturbances of system integration endanger continued existence only to the extent that *social integration* is at stake, that is, when the consensual foundations of normative structures are so much impaired that the society becomes anomic. Crisis states assume the form of a disintegration of social institutions."[54] Stressing "disintegration" and "anomie," Habermas presents a time of chaos, a time literally without law. The impact of anomic states is suggested by Peter Berger who finds in them a failure by society to perform its most important function, the imposition of order on the world. Consequently, the individual "loses his orientation in experience" and, in extreme cases, "his sense of reality and identity."[55] Amplifying Berger's conception, John Smith defines crises as "times when the purpose of life as such comes into question and when we have the sense that life is being judged, not in its details, but as a whole . . . the crisis times fill us with a sense of the finitude and frailty of man, of our creatureliness, of our dependence upon resources beyond our own, and of our need to find a supremely worshipful reality to whom we can devote ourselves without reserve."[56]

Against crisis, against chaos, the prophet posits sacred judgment, replicating the original ordering of creation by God. Claus Westermann, in his widely cited work on the forms of prophetic speech, asks the question, "What is the specifically prophetic speech form?" and answers, "If we look back now to earlier work, we can see that some agreement had been reached on one point. The announcement of judgment to their own nation, along with the reason given in the accusation, was recognized by all as the most essential, the most important, or the most frequent prophetic speech form."[57] Westermann concedes that the advent of the writing prophets and their judgments against the nation rather than the judgments against individuals characteristic of the preliterary prophets caused some changes in the form of the prophetic judgment-speech. The form became freer, more complex, and more reflective of the individual prophet's style and circumstance. Among the changes he notes in the transition from the preliterary prophets to the literary prophets are (1) an emphasis on one part (accusation or announcement) of the judgment over the other, sometimes the complete elimination of one of the parts from the speech itself (although it is usually implied) and (2) the elimination of the messenger formula or the relocation of it to the beginning of the speech. Neither of these changes, however, altered the fundamental nature of the prophet's speech: "that which is essential is not the external balance of emphasis nor the adherence to a pattern, but the correspondence of the judgment of God and the guilt of the people which is required by the proceedings."[58] Westermann maintains that the prophetic judgment-speech preserved the essential characteristics that relate it to the historical development of the genre and unite the writings of the literary prophets under one "basic-form."[59] What remains constant in all the speeches is the essential judgment-speech, "the announcement of Yahweh's judgment to the people for a transgression."[60]

The idea of a basic form of prophetic speech helps clarify the nature of the prophet and his discourse. The prophet is an accuser and judge;[61] he is called into being when the law has been violated, a critical time. The prophet announces both the charges and the verdict of God or nature against the transgressors of the law: "Woe to those who devise wickedness," proclaimed the prophet Micah,

> and work evil upon their beds! When the morning dawns, they perform it, because it is in the power of their hand. They covet fields, and seize them; and houses, and take them away; they oppress a man and his house, a man

and his inheritance. Therefore thus says the LORD: Behold, against this family I am devising evil, from which you cannot remove your necks; and you shall not walk haughtily, for it will be an evil time.[62]

When the worldly success of those who do evil confuses belief in the good, the prophet reestablishes the power of Yahweh's law and restores clarity to the world.

In the proclamation of Micah there is evidenced, not only the form of the judgment-speech, but also something of its character, a glimpse of the omnivorous pathos behind it. In a word often used in English translations of the Old Testament, it reeks of vengeance, of the anger of betrayal. Abraham Heschel in particular reminds us of "the centrality of pathos" in prophetic discourse, and finds God's wrath to be a manifestation of that pathos. As opposed to the gods of the Greeks, Heschel reveals the Hebrew God to be a compassionate god whose concern for His creation is boundless; His covenant with His chosen people is a great gift of love. Through the terms of the covenant, according to the conditions revealed therein, Yahweh binds His own conduct.

The conditions of the covenant provide the reasons or the rationality for the prophetic *logos* conceived as justice. Now it can be seen how they also form the basis for the prophetic *pathos*.[63] Justice, as prescribed by the covenant, is a painful and unsparing ideal. As Yahweh is bound against capricious action, He is as much bound to punish His people when they have rejected the covenant as He is to reward them with His blessings when they have been faithful. Heschel discloses in God's wrath, not the intemperate passion so feared by the Greeks and their intellectual heirs, but the anger of a loving God upon being made to punish His people.[64] Bruce Vawter captures the essence of the deity detailed by Heschel when he describes "this God of pathos, this God who cares, who weeps over his own inexorable justice."[65]

Judgment is a consequence of the fall of humankind, the failure to maintain the terms of the covenant, a failure to participate in the divine *pathos* or will. So understood, it discloses the basis of the alienation of the sacred. The sacred is always separate, always beyond the reach of mortals, but in judgment it is also antagonistic, God in opposition to humankind, thesis versus antithesis. In this antagonism lies the agony of *krisis,* the sense of disintegration, of despair, that characterizes critical times.

The relief of agony requires a new synthesis. To be restored to grace, the people must experience a revival of *pathos,* a resurrection from their spiritual death, for as Northrop Frye notes, the real enemies of "the myth of concern" "are not those who oppose but those who are indifferent," those who are unable to feel abhorrence at the world as it is.[66] God's anger is the motive for this revival. For Heschel, the anger of God is "the end of indifference."[67] Yahweh's pathos stands against the a-pathos or apathy of humankind, humankind as it has become inured to the demands of justice and righteousness, to the needs of the powerless.[68] The prophet, by his calling, becomes the vessel of Yahweh's pathos, a symbol of divine compassion, and a vehicle for the reconciliation of humanity to God.

Reflecting its sacred cause, the synthesis is extreme; it must be genuinely transcendent; it is not a compromise of the two opposing elements, but in the Old Testament metaphor, a purification. As Leo Strauss reminds us, "In every attempt at harmonization, in every synthesis however impressive, one of the two opposed elements is sacrificed, more or less subtly but in any event surely, to the other."[69] For the people of Israel and Judah to be restored to God's grace, they must rise above themselves, restore the sanctity of the root principles of their society, stand outside their current moral torpor. This is the example provided by the prophet. The opposition between the first person singular and the second person plural in prophetic discourse is both a measure of the prophet's estrangement from his people and of the distance of the people from God. The prophet does not speak as a member of the group he is addressing; he does not speak in the inclusive "we." As a messenger, the prophet speaks in the voice of the divine "I," and the message of judgment is against "you" the people.

Assuming the voice of the divine "I," the prophet presents the *ethos* of God in a radical confrontation with His people. In the revelation of the compassionate nature of that *ethos* and its agony in critical times lies the great *pathos* in prophetic discourse.[70] Such expression, far from fraudulent rhetorical practice, is the only honest representation of the nature of God's judgment. "Emotion enters prose not only as disguises for slipping into the reader's confidence," writes Richard Ohmann, "but as sheer expression of self. Complete honesty demands that the writer [or speaker] not only state his ideas accurately, but also take an emotional stance."[71] Only in revealing God's wrath does the prophet fully reveal God's will.

In prophetic discourse, then, we find the horrible anguish of Yahweh's alienation from His people and an overwhelming desire for reunion. Reconciliation, though, cannot be achieved through adjustment of the message, but only through purification of the audience. In the fire metaphor of the prophets, we confront the violent and destructive side of purification. "O house of David, thus saith the LORD; Execute judgment in the morning, and deliver *him that is* spoiled out of the hand of the oppressor, lest my fury go out like fire, and burn that none can quench *it,* because of the evil of your doings."[72] "But who may abide the day of his coming?" asks the prophet Malachi, "and who shall stand when he appeareth? For he is like a refiner's fire, and like the fullers' soap. . . . And he shall sit *as* a refiner and purifier of silver: and he shall purify the sons of Levi, and purge them as gold and silver, that they may offer unto the LORD an offering in righteousness. Then shall the offering of Judah and Jerusalem be pleasant unto the LORD as in the days of old, and as in former years."[73] The prophet demands that the people give up their worldly comforts and follow him into the purity of the wilderness. Regeneration is a necessary propaedeutic to reunion in prophetic discourse; Jeremiah shatters the vessel in order that it may be remolded.[74]

In remolding or reformation lies the essential optimism of the prophetic judgment. For all the terror of God's wrath, purification promises a resolution of crisis. The spiritual wilderness is harsh and exacting, but it is also invigorating; it provides an opportunity for the reassertion of the self as against the atrophy induced by profane comforts, and its vastness and incipient power rekindles a worshipful attitude toward that which is larger than the self. Furthermore, the moral status of the wilderness is unambiguous; it is not polluted or corrupted; it is virgin and innocent, thus the quality of one's participation is assured; the burdens of the wilderness do not include that most grievous of burdens, doubt.

Certainly one of the most passionate and divisive rhetorics in American history is the rhetoric of the radical abolitionists. The debates over strategies and tactics that so divided the abolition movement itself continue in the scholarship of historians and students of rhetoric today. As a prominent spokesman for the abolitionist cause and as one of its more articulate theoreticians, Wendell Phillips provides an excellent subject for an examination of radical judgment from the perspective of prophecy in chapter 4.

The Prophetic Ethos

At the center of prophetic rhetoric is the prophetic *ethos.* "Statements of belief or concern are existential," Frye reminds us, "and therefore one very obvious context for them, apart from doctrinal synthesis is the life of the person who makes or inspires them, and who is usually a leader or a culture-hero of some kind."[75] As the messenger of God's judgment, the prophet presents himself not as hero, but as God's servant. The role is one of submission to God's call, as suggested by the etymology of the word *nabi,* a Hebrew word closely associated with prophecy in the Bible. Abraham Heschel believes *nabi* to be associated with the Akkadian verb for "to call": "*Nabi,* then, would mean, literally, one who is called (by God), one who has a vocation (from God), as well as one who is subject to the influence of a demon or a false god, and who retains the condition imposed upon him by that call or influence."[76]

Heschel's definition is important because it highlights the element of subjugation in the call. The role of the prophet is not a role one seeks; it is a role with which one is burdened. In the words of Jeremiah, perhaps the most reluctant prophet,

> O Lord, thou hast deceived me, and I was deceived: thou art stronger than I, and hast prevailed: I am in derision daily, every one mocketh me. For since I spake, I cried out, I cried violence and spoil; because the word of the Lord was made a reproach unto me, and a derision, daily. Then I said, I will not make mention of him, nor speak anymore in his name. But *his word* was in mine heart as a burning fire shut up in my bones, and I was weary with forbearing, and I could not *stay.*[77]

The first verse of this passage becomes even more poignant in Heschel's translation: "O Lord, Thou hast seduced me, And I am seduced; Thou hast raped me And I am overcome."[78] The will of the prophet is overpowered and completely subjugated to the will of God. As R. B. Y. Scott describes the experience,

> The consciousness of the prophet that he had within him a word expressing the divine *will* shows itself in the sense of compulsion under which he labored. His mission was not of his own choosing. . . . Human prudence would keep silent, but the divine word must find utterance. Isaiah felt himself sent out with a hopeless and impossible task, and the stories of Elijah and of Jonah illustrate how some prophets would fain have escaped from the relentless will which drove them on. From the beginning Jeremiah protested in vain against the charge that was laid upon him; in an excess of agony he cursed the day he had been born to labor and sorrow and shame.[79]

The surrender of the prophet's will to Yahweh is most dramatically presented in the birth accounts related by the prophets. Jeremiah, for example, was born to prophesy: "Before I formed thee in the belly I knew thee; and before thou camest forth out of the womb I sanctified thee, *and* I ordained thee a prophet unto the nations."[80] Isaiah also speaks of being formed in the womb to be a prophet.[81] It is not always clear whether the prophets are speaking literally of their birth or metaphorically of a "second birth"—their conversion or calling. All the prophets had such an experience, which served to impose a new teleology on their lives, and it seems natural to express this event in terms of rebirth. Jonah's expulsion from the belly of the whale, for example, has traditionally been viewed as a metaphorical expression of a second birth to a life of prophecy.

William James wrote of the process of being twice-born as an element involved in the unification of the self:

> Now in all of us, however constituted, but to a degree the greater in proportion as we are intense and sensitive and subject to diversified temptation, and to the greatest possible degree if we are decidedly psychopathic, does the normal evolution of character chiefly consist in the straightening out and unifying of the inner self. The higher and the lower feelings, the useful and the erring impulses, begin by being a comparative chaos within us—they must end by forming a stable system of functions in right subordination.[82]

"To be converted," continued James, "to be regenerated, to receive grace, to experience religion, to gain an assurance, are so many phrases which denote the process, gradual or sudden, by which a self hitherto divided, and consciously wrong inferior and unhappy, becomes unified and consciously right superior and happy, in consequence of its firmer hold upon religious realities."[83] Applied to the prophet, rebirth is a mechanism for overcoming the anxiety of chaos by the complete subordination of the self to the divine will; the prophet exchanges self for certitude, the absolute negation of chaos.[84] It is from this position that the prophet makes his criticism of his society; the prophet stands as a synecdochal realization of God's will.

James stresses the personal and the egoistic side of rebirth, but it would be wrong to undervalue the magnitude of the prophetic sacrifice in the achievement of righteousness or to reduce conversion simply to psychopathological gratification. Salvation is not without its cost, and it is a shallow criticism to see in the experience of grace nothing but the mercenary motive. In order to be reborn, the prophet must first face what we most dread, death.[85] Death is suggested by the removal of the individual from the world in an act of consecration. Asceticism is an expression of this separation, an assertion of principle in opposition to worldly practice. The prophet is placed *in extremis* to the accepted routines of life.[86] Margaret Zulick finds "the full expression of the 'agon of Jeremiah' " in "the vindication of the word, against the people, at the expense of the (human) life of the prophet."[87] Gerhard von Rad expresses this sacrificial aspect of the calling as a "gulf which separates the prophets from their past" so deep that "none of their previous social relationships are carried over into the new way of life."[88] The profound discontinuity between the old life and the new noted by von Rad, the end of old social relationships, represents a kind of death.

The weight of the burden is attested to many times by the prophets, perhaps nowhere more stridently than in Jeremiah's curse of his (re)birth which is symbolized as an unwelcome expulsion from a death-like existence and from the possibility of death:

> Cursed *be* the day wherein I was born; let not the day wherein my mother bare me be blessed. Cursed *be* the man who brought tidings to my father, saying, A man child is born unto thee; making him very glad. And let that man be as the cities which the Lord overthrew, and repented not; and let him hear the cry in the morning, and the shouting at noontide; Because he slew me not from the womb; or that my mother might have been my grave, and her womb *to be* always great *with me*. Wherefore I came forth out of the womb to see labour and sorrow, that my days should be consumed with shame?[89]

Nietzsche, though his criticism of the ascetic ideal is harsh in the extreme (according to James, a symptom of Nietzsche's own sickly soul), testifies to the genuineness of the mortification. "Nor will the reader doubt," he writes, "that the *joy* felt by the self-denying, self-sacrificing, selfless person was from the very start a *cruel* joy."[90] Nietzsche is undoubtedly correct in identifying a masochistic impulse operating here, part of the paradox of prophecy—the pleasure in suffering and denial, the exercise of the will through self-sacrifice, freedom through subordination. What he refuses to recognize is the assertion of strength in suffering. Again, the Aristotelian idea of virtue, especially as realized by the Epicureans, virtue as the will to do right, is illuminating.

For the community confronted by the prophet, the problem is one of authenticating the prophet's call.[91] If the call is genuine, there can be no disputation of the message. As Burke Long writes: "For the storyteller, who accepts Jeremiah's authority, rejection of the prophet is tantamount to rejection of God, and to bringing about God's calamity (26:19). From the same partisan standpoint, Jeremiah 29:32 terms opposition to Jeremiah as 'rebellion against the Lord.' "[92] As is the case with the prophet's charge against the recalcitrant, the community's only option for disputing the prophet is *ad personam;* the tendency of radical confrontations to degenerate into name-calling sessions is understandable in this context. Presenting his *ethos* as nugatory, consumed in the divine *ethos,* the prophet succeeds in making his *ethos,* the authenticity of his call, the paramount question. James Crenshaw terms this "the Achilles-heel of ancient prophecy," "namely the absence of any validation for a prophetic word. . . . The prophet was particularly vulnerable since he claimed to speak what another had communicated to him, yet when challenged as to the source of his word, he could only affirm that God had indeed summoned him, sent the vision, spoken the word."[93]

Against claims that their ecstatic certitude and extreme passion are manifestations of God's will, prophets have historically encountered cries of "fanatic" and "madman"; for their posture as witnesses—those who know, *witan*—prophets have characteristically been martyred, a word which comes from a Latin transliteration of a Greek word for witness. As the Inquisitor in George Bernard Shaw's *Saint Joan* solemnly declares, "For two hundred years the Holy Office has striven with these diabolical madnesses; and it knows that they begin always by vain and ignorant persons setting up their own judgment against the Church, and taking it upon themselves to be the interpreters of God's will."[94] Convening the tribunal that will hear Joan's case, the Inquisitor continues, "God forbid that I should tell you to harden your hearts; for her punishment if we condemn her will be so cruel that we should forfeit our own hope of divine mercy were there one grain of malice against her in our hearts. But if you hate cruelty—and if any man here does not hate it I command him on his soul's salvation to quit this holy court—I say, if you hate cruelty, remember that nothing is so cruel in its consequences as the toleration of heresy."[95] Joan, of course, is first burned for her "diabolical madness" but later canonized. The history of prophecy is a history of martyrdom.[96] On the event of her canonization, Shaw's Joan returns to visit her judges, and it is Cauchon who phrases the human dilemma in the face of the prophet when he pleads, "The heretic is always better dead. And mortal eyes cannot distinguish the saint from the heretic. Spare them."[97]

The problem of the prophetic *ethos* lies in the nature of charisma. Max Weber defined the prophet as "a purely individual bearer of charisma, who by virtue of his mission proclaims a religious doctrine or divine commandment."[98] It is the call that, for Weber, distinguishes the prophet from the priest: "The latter lays claim to authority by virtue of his service in a sacred tradition, while the prophet's claim is based on personal revelation and charisma."[99] Bruce Vawter amplifies and clarifies Weber's conception of the prophet's call: "The prophets of Israel, whose words we have in the books that bear their names, found their credentials not in any official position they may have enjoyed, but in their direct call by God himself. To adapt another terminology to them, their status was not hierarchical but charismatic."[100] Weber defined charisma as "a certain quality of an individual personality by virtue of which he is set apart from ordinary men and treated as endowed with supernatural, superhuman, or at least specifically exceptional powers or qualities. These are such as are not accessible to the ordinary person, but are regarded as of divine origin or as exemplary, and on the basis of them the individual is treated as a leader."[101]

Overholt and Vawter both point to an extraordinary and personal experience as the source of prophecy, and Weber's definition of charisma betrays an uncomfortable tension between the experience and its recognition. The means of validation, deriving as they do from a sacred source, are beyond the reach of the people; charisma is an irrational concept.[102] It is the prophet's burden to make the extraordinary, invisible, and personal understandable, visible, and public; the prophet's presentation must somehow validate his commission. Consistent with the character of servitude, the message of the prophet must bear continuing testimony to his helplessness and loss of self, particularly self as conceived as a rational calculating faculty; through effacement of the self, the prophet strives to present the uncolored word of Yahweh. The studied anonymity of the author of the servant songs of Deutero-Isaiah is an extreme example of this tendency.[103] Deutero-Isaiah does not speak in his own voice, but is given "the tongue of the learned, that I should know how to speak a word in season to *him that is* weary."[104] Failure of the person of the prophet is, almost by definition, necessary to his success as God's servant. Personal success is self-serving and vitiates the purity of divine motive.

Martyrdom is the ultimate sacrifice of self to duty or commitment. As an outward manifestation of the prophet's sacrifice, martyrdom is a means of making public and visible the private, personal submission to the call; reflecting the nature of charisma, it is the perfect irrational act. Kenneth Burke finds in martyrdom a kind of exhibitionism,[105] and the sufferings of the prophets were often intended as allegory: Jeremiah's yoke, Isaiah's nakedness, and Hosea's wife come immediately to mind. More important for a bewildered people, the willingness to suffer is the most compelling evidence of the abandonment of the self. The logic of commitment demands that the only appropriate posture in the face of persecution be resignation. So it is that F. G. Bailey detects "a pervasive connection between emotion, faith and suffering," as the several meanings of the word "passion" suggest.[106] The exemplary case in Western mythology is, of course, the passion of Christ, a passion firmly grounded in the prophetic tradition of the Old Testament.[107]

Although the discussion here is heavily freighted with pathological overtones, it also reveals, once we have accepted the possibility of the spiritual dimension, an internal logic: martyrdom is a perfectly reasonable presentation of the claims of sacred commission. James is the first to warn that charges of psychopathology are not an adequate assessment of the spiritual value of the prophet's mission. "Their value," James writes, "can only be ascertained by spiritual judgments directly passed upon them, judgments based on our own immediate feeling primarily; and secondarily on what we can ascertain of their experiential relations to our moral needs and to the rest of what we hold as true."[108] James later characterizes the psychopathic temperament as containing "the emotionality which is the *sine quâ non* of moral perception." He continues,

> We have the intensity and tendency to emphasis which are the essence of practical moral vigor; and we have the love of metaphysics and mysticism which carry one's interests beyond the surface of the sensible world. What, then, is more natural than that this temperament should introduce one to regions of religious truth, to corners of the universe, which your robust Philistine type of nervous system, forever offering its biceps to be felt, thumping its breast, and thanking Heaven that it hasn't a single morbid fibre in its composition, would be sure to hide forever from its self-satisfied possessors?[109]

Finally, James notes of saintliness that "the best fruits of religious experience are the best things that history has to show."[110]

Whatever the motives of the prophet, his value lies in his reception, the quality of the *ethos* presented to his auditors. Charisma, we are reminded, is only validated when recognized; it is a social phenomenon.[111] And if the recognition of charisma depends on recognition of the quality of the birth, the calling, only in the quality of the death, it stands to reason that sainthood is always *posthumous*. Consistent with the metaphors of birth and death, and illustrated vividly in the Gospels, the problem of the prophetic office is biographical, and there is a real sense, as von Rad points out, in which it can only be judged in its completion, in the end of the prophet. It was necessary for Joan to be burned before she could be canonized, and it was necessary for Christ to be crucified before he could be resurrected.[112] As James writes of Saint Paul, "From the biological point of view Saint Paul was a failure, because he was beheaded. Yet he was magnificently adapted to the larger environment of history; and so far as any saint's example is a leaven of righteousness in the world, and draws it in the direction of more prevalent habits of saintliness, he is a success, no matter what his bad fortune may be."[113]

Considered as biography, the prophetic *ethos* is a kind of legend. The prophetic life as presented by the prophet and his disciples becomes its own rhetoric, and it must be judged according to the example it presents, not according to its motive, which we can never know with assurance anyway, nor even according to its strict historical veracity, but according to its aspirations and to the sympathies it creates. Margaret Zulick states the case with respect to Jeremiah this way: "The very act of preserving the memory of such a life in a narrative, it seems, consumes the life we are telling. Henceforth, that life will be known, and changed, only by our retelling it. In no other way can it survive to cast its voice in social memory, and to shape in turn the narratives of those who respond."[114] In chapter 5, I turn to an examination of the prophetic *ethos* in the example of Eugene Debs, one of America's most conspicuous radical failures, yet a man who has inspired one of the most perdurable and generous legacies in American thought outside George Washington and Abraham Lincoln.[115]

3

Prophecy as Sacred Truth

*Self-Evidence and Righteousness in
the American Revolution*

I am the Lord, I have called you in righteousness, I have taken you by
the hand and kept you; I have given you as a covenant to the people, a
light to the nations; To open the eyes that are blind, to bring out the
prisoners from the dungeon, from the prison those who sit in darkness.   —Isaiah 42:6–7

And it shall come to pass afterward, that I will pour out my spirit on
all flesh; your sons and your daughters shall prophesy, your old men
shall dream dreams, and your young men shall see visions.

—Joel 2:28

In 1764, Stephen Hopkins in "An Essay on the Trade of the
Northern Colonies" abjured resistance to current laws limiting American
trade, averring to his countrymen that "their whole expectations of relief,
depend altogether on a proper application to the British legislature." With
this appeal, Hopkins reveals a colonist's faith in "a King who delights in
doing good to all his subjects; to a peerage, wise and accurate, guided by
the principles of honor and beneficence; and to a representative body
penetrating and prudent, who consider the good of the whole, and make
that the measure of their public resolves."[1] Hopkins expresses here two
important characteristics of pre-Revolutionary colonial thought: first,
American colonists, including the Whigs, had a strong attachment to their
identities as British subjects, and second, the colonists sought to preserve
that identity through reconciliation with the mother country.[2] The attitude
of propitiation assumed by Hopkins is evident over the course of Whig
protest, though faith in specific agencies of the British government flagged
and failed. Even as they took up arms against the mother country, the

members of the Second Continental Congress maintained a pose of unimpeachable temperance: "We for ten years incessantly and ineffectually besieged the Throne as supplicants; we reasoned, we remonstrated with parliament, in the most mild and decent language. But Administration, sensible that we should regard these oppressive measures as freemen ought to do, sent over fleets and armies to enforce them. . . . Fruitless were all the entreaties, arguments."[3]

Although Bernard Bailyn, like the Whigs themselves, finds Whig pamphlets "essentially decorous and reasonable,"[4] noting of them in their "business like sanity" that "the pamphlets aim to persuade,"[5] his view of American Revolutionary rhetoric has been characterized as sympathetic to the Whigs; his interpretation of the ideas and mind-set of the Revolutionaries "shields the patriots from accusations that they reacted paranoiacally or demagogically to England's challenge and it makes understandable the American's bitter resistance to the introduction of a mild program of imperial taxation and administrative adjustment."[6] Gordon Wood directly counters Bailyn's scenario of sweet reason with Bailyn's own evidence:

> As Bailyn and the propaganda studies have amply shown, there is simply too much fanatical and millennial thinking even by the best minds that must be explained before we can characterize the American's ideas as peculiarly rational and legalistic and thus view the Revolution as merely a conservative defense of constitutional liberties. To isolate refined and nicely-reasoned arguments from the writings of John Adams and Jefferson is not only to disregard the more inflamed expressions of the rest of the Whigs but also to overlook the enthusiastic extravagance—the paranoiac obsession with a diabolical Crown conspiracy and the dream of a restored Saxon era—in the thinking of Adams and Jefferson themselves.[7]

The evidence suggests that the Whig rhetoric experienced by audiences of the time was the rhetoric characterized by Wood rather than that characterized by Bailyn. "A Gentleman at Halifax" found expressions of Whig sentiment sufficiently fissiparous to plead for a more "reasonable" discourse: "If we have anything to ask, we should remember that diffidence and modesty will always obtain more from generous minds than forwardness and impertinence."[8] The "Gentleman" had already noted that petitions then being sent to Britain protesting the Stamp Act "were of a very different temper" than their "extremely modest" antecedents like Mr. Partridge's petition against the Sugar Act. Thomas Bolton colorfully characterized much of the prevailing attitude toward the Whigs and their rhetoric in demurring that he could not "boast the ignorance of HANCOCK, the insolence of ADAMS, the absurdity of ROWE, the arrogance of LEE, the vicious life and untimely death of MOLLENEAUX, the turgid bombast of Warren, the treasons of QUINCY, the hypocrisy of COOPER, nor the principles of YOUNG."[9]

Virtually no advocate on behalf of the colonies escaped censure. John Dickinson, that most reasonable of Whigs, was challenged to defend his first two "Letters from a Farmer in Pennsylvania" against charges of attempting to foment "riots and tumult."[10] "Massachusettensis" saw the rhetoric of the Whigs as torrid and demagogic: "They [the Whig leaders] accordingly applied themselves to work upon the imagination, and to inflame the passions; for this work they possessed great talents; I will do justice to their ingenuity; they were intimately acquainted with the feelings of the human heart."[11] The fire imagery so often used to describe revolutionary causes, suggesting their intensity, is seen again in another "Massachusettensis" letter: "There is a latent spark however, in their [the common people's] breasts, capable of being kindled into a flame; to do this has always been the employment of the disaffected."[12] Joseph Galloway lamented the decline of a great and civilized country to a state "now governed by the barbarian rule of frantic folly, and lawless ambition."[13]

These are the complaints perennially raised as a conservative response to rhetorics of reform: it is not "reasonable." Joseph Galloway, for example, proposed a petition that he considered "reasonable and just" in contrast to those produced by the Whigs.[14] Most often the appeal was not couched in these terms, as "reasonable" tended still to mean the Cartesian method for arriving at truth. Samuel Johnson's *Dictionary* defined "reason" as "Right, justice," a usage evidenced in Thomas Paine's "the simple voice of nature and of reason will say 'tis right."[15] This imprecision in terms is symptomatic of a profound tension in the meaning of reason that divided emerging utilitarians from strict adherents of natural law on the question of the American Revolution.[16] Even in other terms, however, the sentiment is unmistakable; Whig discourse was widely regarded as immoderate.

According to Jay Fliegelman, the emotional character of public discourse in the eighteenth century simply reflected one current of ideas regarding human nature. Political authority, he argues, was increasingly identified with "an oratorical ability, not merely to persuade by rational argumentation, but to excite, animate, motivate, and impress. . . . An age preoccupied with efficacious persuasion and with uncovering hidden designs behind the masquerade of deceptive action and misleading speech," he continues, "translated a growing distrust of reason and rational persuasion into a wishful faith in an irresistible discourse of feelings."[17] Those who believed, then, that the truth was found in the unselfconscious and unrehearsed expression historically associated with the private sphere embraced this "natural display" of passion in the hope of creating a sympathetic response in the audience,[18] a position much in evidence in Peter Thacher's "Boston Massacre Oration":

> The tender feelings of the human heart are deeply affected with the fate of these and the other heroes who have bled and died, that their country may be free; but at the same time, sensations of indignant wrath are excited in the breasts of every friend to freedom: and to him for vengeance! he will feel himself animated with new vigor in the glorious cause nothing daunted by their untimely fate, he will rush into the midst of danger, that he may share their glory and avenge their death! every idea which can warm and animate him to glorious deeds, will rush at once upon his mind.[19]

Those, on the other hand, who believed that the truth lay in God's order of creation counseled that "the same virtue that gave the alarm, may sometimes, by causing too great a transport of zeal, defeat its own purpose; it being expedient for those who deliberate of public affairs, that their minds should be free from all violent passions."[20]

Fliegelman finds in the late eighteenth century, not a rhetoric of *pathos,* as his descriptions might seem to suggest, but a rhetoric of *ethos,* "an occasion for the public revelation of a private self. Such a private self would then be judged by private rather than public virtues: prudence, temperance, self-control, honesty, and, most problematically, sincerity."[21] On the basis of a dubious interpretation of classical rhetoric, Fliegelman nevertheless draws a valuable distinction: "Whereas *pathos* (emotion) is set in opposition to *ethos* (character) in classical rhetoric, here the former becomes the revelation of the latter."[22] Fliegelman's analysis is correct as far as it goes, and his description of the ideal of rhetorical "nakedness" in the late eighteenth century, a voice calculated to "blot out authorial innovation, to ventriloquize common sense and sensibility, and to 'harmonize' the wisdom of previous texts and voices,"[23] comports perfectly with the description of the prophetic *ethos* and its relationship to the prophetic *pathos* in the previous chapter. With regard to the rhetoric of the Revolution, what Fliegelman neglects is the role of exigence in the formation of rhetoric.[24] In other words, he neglects the Revolutionary cause, the *reasons* for the Revolution.

The Founding Fathers became prophetic figures because they argued on behalf of what they perceived to be a sacred cause and predicated their arguments, not on expediency, but on principle.[25] By locating principle in nature, beyond the reach of compromise and degradation, argument from natural law assured "the sovereignty of a principle" and the rendering of "a principled, unified, and internally consistent interpretation of the cosmos and the meaning of human life"; it reflected "the drive toward some sort of explicit intellectual generalization of the meaning of human action and experience" that Egon Bittner finds to be "a constitutive property of radicalism." Bittner writes, "By methodically correlating its interpretive principles with its maxims of conduct, radicalism provides ultimate, permanent, and 'objectively valid' grounds for moral choice."[26] In the case of the American Whigs, Stephen Lucas affirms that they "claimed moral, even divine, sanction for the most radical of their arguments and actions."[27]

Such a basis for argument makes both possible and necessary a rhetoric that conflates *ethos* and *pathos* as Fliegelman suggests, but also *logos*. Indeed the whole purpose of sacred discourse is truth; all else is merely vehicle. In speaking on behalf of what they saw as sacred principle, the Revolutionaries called upon rich, sometimes contradictory traditions, and in so doing, performed the epideictic function of (re)calling community into being out of slumber or lifelessness. It is this powerful act of necromancy that will be examined here.

Rights from Charter, Constitution, and Nature

That ideas of natural law, as revived in the seventeenth and eighteenth centuries, are basic to the structure of Whig argument prior to the Revolution is a position not beyond controversy. Over the years, there have been debates among those who maintain the importance of natural law to the American argument, those who emphasize constitutional issues, and various stripes of materialists, nationalists, and imperialists.[28] It is treacherous territory for the nonspecialist. Yet the rhetorical legacy reveals an intense preoccupation with "the laws of nature and of nature's God," with roots in the belief of the early Puritan settlers that America was the New Israel, God's new Chosen People,[29] and evident in much of America's foreign policy, even to the present time, in the form of "manifest destiny."[30] Unless there is posited a conspiracy pervasive enough to account for such a startling consistency from different sources over a number of years as that found in the public discussion leading up to the American Revolution, we must conclude, in Ernest Wrage's enduring formulation, that "a speech is an agency of its time, one whose surviving record provides a repository of themes and their elaborations from which we may gain insight into the life of an era as well as into the mind of a man. From the study of speeches given by many men, then, it is possible to observe the reflections of prevailing social ideas and attitudes."[31] What we find reflected in the rhetoric of the American Revolutionaries is a faith in the absolute rectitude of their position and in the God-ordered necessity of events that culminated in the appeal that Lucas has called "the apotheosis of American destiny."[32]

According to Merrill Jensen, the First Continental Congress was "deadlocked for weeks over a declaration of rights."

> The popular leaders insisted that it should be based on the 'law of nature.' The conservatives quite understandably opposed a foundation which had never been defined and which would allow every man to interpret its meaning for himself. They argued that American rights should be based on the colonial charters and the English constitution, which at least had the virtue of a certain amount of specific content. The outcome was a compromise. The declaration of rights finally adopted was based on the law of nature, the colonial charters, and the English constitution.[33]

Certainly these three themes are recurrent in the discourse of the decade prior to the convening of the Congress, and the separation Jensen makes seems a logical one, at least that between the laws of man and those laws that are *extra nos*. But it is important that the colonists did not separate these themes in their declaration of rights, nor were they separated in much of Revolutionary discourse. The framers of the "Declaration and Resolves" of the First Continental Congress exhibited a keen awareness of the distinction between issues of simple legality and issues of right, and the document leaves no doubt that the former were contingent on the latter. The language of rights is clearly predominate.[34]

Most often, arguments in the decade prior to the convening of the First Continental Congress conjoined several appeals in the same piece of discourse. In 1764, James Otis wrote, "Every British subject born on the continent of America, or in any other of the British dominions, is by the law of God and nature, by the common law, and by act of parliament (exclusive of all charters from the crown) entitled to all the natural, essential, inherent and inseparable rights of our fellow subjects in Great Britain."[35] The following year, another pamphleteer wrote, "Do we claim any [rights] but what are as clear as the noon day? Have we not by nature a right to liberty and property; as Englishmen by laws and charters, in terms as plain as words can express?"[36] A document, possibly by Samuel Adams, published in 1772 is a virtual echo of the statement quoted from Otis: "All persons born in the British American Colonies are by the laws of God and nature, and by the common law of England, *exclusive of all charters from the Crown,* well Entitled, and by Act of the British Parliament are declared to be entitled to all the natural essential, inherent & inseparable Rights Liberties and Privileges of Subjects born in Great Britain, or within the realm."[37]

Charters from the Crown might have been excluded in this and similar statements because, according to Charles McIlwain, they represented the weakest of the colonists' claims to rights, being a form of royal prerogative, although the colonists, as will be demonstrated, tried to make them much less arbitrary than they were.[38] But constitutional and legal theories aside, the clear rhetorical import of these arguments is to establish as the most basic rights of the colonists those rights they possessed as men and as subjects antecedent and supercedent to the specific rights granted them by charter. The repeated linkage of these appeals suggests something more complex than politics, and a review of the political philosophy that informed the period reveals more evidence of concatenation than of competition.[39]

American colonists held a notion of compact or covenant that was a product of the revolution in political theory begun by Thomas Hobbes. Throwing over the classical idea that human beings were political animals, creatures whose natural state was as members of the *polis,* seventeenth-century political theorists began to describe the individual, motivated by individual wants and needs, as the irremediable fact of natural law. Most agreed that humankind's natural state in this new view was not very appealing. Hobbes's famous dictum held life in the natural state, that state of war of everyman against everyman, to be "solitary, poor, nasty, brutish, and short."[40] Only by covenant, compact, or contract was there any hope of escape from this perdition.

At first glance, it would appear that covenants or contracts are simply agreements among humans, hence mutable, negotiable, not the basis for absolute and uncompromising appeals to principle. This conception, though, neglects the nature of those who made the contract. Although the seventeenth and eighteenth centuries were times of increasing secularization—including the displacement of mediaeval scholastic methodologies by the methods of observation and measurement, and the rise of history and science as disciplines independent of theology—most thinkers could not yet relinquish the notion that humanity was God's most special creation, and even those who denied God tended to conceive of humanity in terms of a nature that had become deified.[41] As God's creatures, it was widely assumed, human beings were possessed of certain inalienable rights, inalienable because they were part of a God-given nature, but the unrestrained exercise of which led to conflict. In order to assimilate these conflicting individual goals into a functioning society it was necessary that these rights be regulated, but they could not be abrogated. The covenant that created society ceded to society the power of governance, but the rights themselves remained with the people.[42] This is at the foundation of the idea of popular sovereignty. As Samuel West expressed it in an election day sermon in 1776,

> The law of nature is a perfect standard and measure of action for beings that persevere in a state of moral rectitude. But the case is far different with us, who are in a fallen and degenerate estate. . . . The strong propensities of our animal nature often overcome the sober dictates of reason and conscience, and betray us into actions injurious to the public, and destructive of the safety and happiness of society. . . . This makes it absolutely necessary, that societies should form themselves into politick bodies, that they may enact laws for the public safety, and appoint particular penalties for the violation of their laws, and invest a suitable number of persons with authority to put in execution and enforce the laws of the state. . . . This shews that the end and design of civil government, cannot be to deprive men of their liberty, or take away their freedom; but on the contrary the true design of civil government is to protect men in the enjoyment of liberty.[43]

The idea of popular sovereignty as found in seventeenth- and eighteenth-century thought granted a numinous quality to the nature of the covenant or the social contract. At the base of this contract were sacred rights, the rights of sovereign beings in their natural state, the violation of which annulled the contract itself. Behind the contract was an empyrean principle by which the validity of the contract could be judged. A society derived from the nature of humankind submits its supporting apparatus, its constitutions, its laws, to divine judgment; insofar as they are in keeping with their divine purpose, they may be appealed to unconditionally, and when not in keeping with this purpose, may be condemned absolutely.[44]

It is this hazy distillation of classical and modern political theory that is evident in the rhetoric of the Levellers in England and in turn in the rhetoric of the Whigs in America.[45] So it is that the author of "A State of the Rights of the Colonists" begins his account with the natural rights of colonists as men and notes,

> It is the greatest absurdity to suppose it in the power of one or any number of men at the entering into society, to renounce their essential natural rights, or the means of preserving those rights when the great end of civil government from the very nature of its institution is for the support, protection and defense of those very rights, the principal of which as is before observed, are life liberty and property. If men through fear, fraud or mistake, should *in terms* renounce & and give up any essential natural right, the eternal law of reason and the great end of society, would absolutely vacate such renunciation; the right to freedom being *the gift* of God Almighty it is not in the power of Man to alienate this gift, and voluntarily become a slave.[46]

At another point, the author writes, "When Men enter into Society, it is by voluntary consent; and they have a right to demand and insist upon the performance of such conditions, And previous limitations as form an equitable *original compact*."[47] The author of this pamphlet goes on to enumerate, in descending order, the rights of the colonists as Christians and as subjects. Near the conclusion of the discussion of rights, before turning to "A List of Infringements and Violations of Rights," the author ties his case to the colonial charters.[48]

The argument is consistent with the general tenor of the political philosophy reviewed here: the inalienability of rights; the requirement that government, to be legitimate, protect those rights; and the derivation of all government from a sacred compact. This is the philosophy echoed in the Declaration of Independence in the section beginning, "We hold these truths to be self-evident."[49] The "original compact" of which the author speaks assumes a sacred quality because of the rights involved; all other compacts are derivative. Even Tory Joseph Galloway, attempting to refute Whig arguments, referred to "the most solemn and sacred of all covenants; those upon which the existence of societies, and the welfare of millions depend,"[50] and Daniel Dulany, in his discussion of charter rights, made the connection quite succinctly: "By these charters, founded upon the unalienable rights of the subject, and upon the most sacred compact, the colonies claim a right of exemption from taxes *not imposed with their consent*."[51]

Extension of the logic of sacred compact reveals government itself to be sacred, and there is evidence that this was the prevailing conception in

England and in America on the eve of the Revolution.[52] Government, in seventeenth- and eighteenth-century England, was conceived, not primarily as a vehicle for legislating, but as a vehicle for judging the competing claims of members of the polity against the provisions of natural law. Parliament was less legislative than the supreme adjudicative agency of the land.[53] So it is that we have the British common law tradition, based as it is on an accretion of precedents which seem more the objective work of history than the manufacture of humankind. Edmund Burke, pleading the case of the colonies before Parliament, illustrated this devolution of sacred quality onto the law when he appealed to the precedent of a petition submitted to Parliament by the county of Chester. Describing Parliament's response to the petition, Burke said Parliament "made it the very preamble to their Act of address, and consecrated its principle to all ages in the sanctuary of legislation."[54] At another point in the same speech, Burke adopts an explicitly prophetic stance before the law: "Determining to fix articles of peace, I was resolved to use nothing else than the form of sound words, to let others abound in their own sense, and carefully to abstain from all expressions of my own. What the law has said, I say. In all things else I am silent. I have no organ but for her words. This, if it be not ingenious, I am sure is safe."[55] Here Burke treats the law as something holy, beyond the petty interests of men, the reflection of what is right. He is merely its mouthpiece. Thomas Paine, though an opponent of Burke by the time of the French Revolution, revealed a common conception of the sacral basis of the law when he wrote, "All the great laws of society are laws of nature."[56] And Whig pamphleteer James Otis made a compelling statement of this idea of government as sacred when he wrote, "The sum of my argument is, That civil government is of God."[57]

It may at first appear that a conception of government and the laws of government as sacred poses problems for the would-be revolutionary. How can revolution against the government be justified if the government is Right? This was the intention behind Calvin's ideas on natural law and government—to justify stable government by virtue of its divinity—but the fragility of the intention is illustrated by the revolutionary uses to which Calvin's doctrines were put by Congregationalists and later radical puritan sects.[58] The key to understanding this apparent paradox is to remember that government, especially in the two-contract theory held by most thinkers of the age, was simply the establishment of an adjudicative agency. The laws were the laws of nature; the specific pronouncements of government, insofar as they were correct and valid, were simply applications of those general laws.

As Locke wrote regarding legislative power, "The *Rules* that they make for other Mens Actions, must, as well as their own and other Mens Actions, be conformable to the Law of Nature, *i.e.* to the Will of God, of which that is a Declaration, and the *fundamental Law of Nature* being *the preservation of Mankind,* no Humane Sanction can be good or valid against it."[59] In the application of God's law, or what Locke was sometimes inclined to call "standing laws,"[60] it was possible for agencies of government to err.

In human error lies the revolutionary promise, a restoration of original law in its sanctity and glory. It is the possibility of error as measured against the Law of Nature, raised by Otis with regard to the Chancellor of the Exchequer and to Parliament "as infallibility belongs not to mortals, 'tis possible *they* may have been misinformed and deceived."[61] Otis's charge is a common one in Whig discourse,[62] although the presumption gradually faded to the point that actions of the British government unfavorable to America, initially viewed as mistakes, ultimately came to be represented as the products of invidious design born of corruption. This development did not change the form of the argument; it merely added the element of malign intent. Samuel West does not deal with motive. He says simply,

> If magistrates have no authority but what they derive from the people, if they are properly of human creation; if the whole end and design of the institution is to promote the general good, and to secure to men their just rights, it will follow, that when they act contrary to the end and design of their creation, they cease being magistrates, and the people, which gave them their authority, have the right to take it from them again. This is a very plain dictate of common sense, which, universally obtains in all similar cases.[63]

The colonists were extremely jealous of what they viewed as their natural, God-given freedoms, and they were ever mindful of the distinction between the power of government and its rights and quick to denounce perceived infringements in the harshest terms. According to Bailyn, "everywhere in this late seventeenth-century world of ideas there was fear—fear that a free condition of life was a precarious thing, ever beset by power-hungry, corrupt enemies who would destroy it."[64] So Thomas Jefferson queried, "But can his majesty thus put down all law under his feet? Can he erect a power superior to that which erected himself? He has done it indeed by force; but let him remember that force cannot give right."[65] Jefferson here echoes not only Locke,[66] but also the Old Testament prophet Jeremiah reflecting the prophetic dread of uncontrolled power and tyranny: "Their course is evil, and their might is not right."[67]

When the rights trammeled by force are absolute, the transgression must be absolutely wrong. There is an interesting etymological affinity here, as the rights referred to are the freedoms of humankind in its natural state. The word "absolute" comes from the Latin for "to be disengaged" or "to be free." In the opposition maintained by Whig rhetoricians, there is no incremental freedom; one is either free or one is not: "For it must be confessed by all men that they who are taxed at pleasure by others, cannot possibly have any property, can have nothing to be called their own; they who have no property, can have no freedom, but are indeed reduced to the most abject slavery. . . . One who is bound to obey the will of another, is as really a slave, though he may have a good master, as if he had a bad one."[68] Or in the words of "Novanglus": "There are but two sorts of men in the world, freemen and slaves."[69]

As the God term that functioned opposite "slavery" in the colonists' vocabulary, "freedom" was the most exalted concept in Whig thought; it was the fundamental natural right, the unrestrained individual. As Edmund Burke noted in his speech on conciliation, "In this character of the Americans, a love of freedom is the predominating feature which markes and distinguishes the whole. . . . This fierce spirit of liberty is stronger in the English colonies probably than in any other people of the earth."[70] Freedom was also intimately connected to property as Hopkins, quoted above, suggests. According to Hobbes, every man in the natural state had an equal right to everything, and Locke held that one legitimately possessed something only by the addition of one's labor to it. The Lockean version of the famous triad in the Declaration of Independence was "life, liberty, and property." It is easy to see how, in this rhetorical and ideological climate, there could be no compromise. It was not a question of lowering taxes or eliminating duties on particular items; there was no middle ground between freedom and slavery.

Whig argument ultimately devolved on the distinction between freemen and slaves. The terms describe the earthly consequence of the abstract and complex theories of natural law. A free man was natural man, man in harmony with God's will, man with the power of his personal sovereignty. A slave was a degraded man, castrated, a eunuch, subject to the will of another. "Freedom" and "slavery" and their derivatives functioned in Whig rhetoric dialectically as "God term" and "devil term," radically dividing the world into good and evil, between them a great yawning void.[71] The division is radical because it was at the very root of the self-definition of the colonists as free men.

Shall they who by office and profession engage to assert the cause of public liberty, own themselves such dastards as to be afraid to speak, when their country is injured in her most sacred rights, yea, inslaved, lest they provoke her oppressors? "Tell it not in Gath!"—Liberty and property are necessarily connected together; He that deprives of the latter without our consent deprives of the former. What is a slave, but one who depends upon the will of another for the enjoyment of his life and property?[72]

Here a relatively mild tax is transformed into the shackles of abject slavery, the usurper of sacred rights, the ravager of virtue. Note the biblical injunction against the cabalists: "Tell it not in Gath!"[73] There can be no countenancing any infringement on the natural freedoms of the colonists, for any infringement, in principle, annuls that freedom absolutely, making slaves of all who capitulate. The conflict with England became not a dispute over pecuniary measures, but a battle over the autonomy and moral status of men.

Whigs, then, found not only legitimation but a coercive moral force in their rectitude. When fighting on the side of God against the devil, even the most extreme measures of defense are not only sanctioned but mandated in the appeal to natural law or God's law. Again turning to Locke: "In all States and Conditions the true remedy of *Force* without Authority, is to oppose *Force* to it. The use of *force* without Authority, always puts him that uses it into a *state of War*, as the Aggressor, and renders him liable to be treated accordingly."[74] Locke's admonition suggests the relentless quality of natural law: it operates of necessity; violation of it foments revolution just as inexorably as the planets revolve according to its dictates. Questions of personal culpability are no longer applicable. "Novanglus" discussed what he called "revolution principles," which he termed "principles of nature and eternal reason" and which he compared to the law of gravity.[75] So the Whigs were able to proclaim: "Let no man then suffer his rights to be torn from him; for fear of the consequences of defending them,—however dreadful they may be, the guilt of them does not lie at his door."[76]

In the Old Testament, Israel's fate was a direct consequence of her keeping her covenant with Yahweh. The covenant operated with mechanical predictability. It sometimes seemed sacred even to Yahweh as it pained Him to see His people suffer, but justice was served, cause and consequence.[77] The perspective is one widely adopted by the American colonists. Following the events at Lexington and Concord, Jacob Duché preached a sermon, "The American Vine," which is said to have greatly inspired John Adams. In this sermon, Duché made clear the causes and consequences of recent events:

Injured and oppressed as we are, unmeriting the harsh and rigorous treatment, which we have received from such an unexpected quarter, let us, however, look up to an higher cause for the awful infliction; and whilst we are faithfully persevering in the defence of our TEMPORAL RIGHTS, let us humble ourselves before God, lay our hands upon our hearts, and seriously and impartially enquire, what returns we have made to Heaven for its past favours, and whether its present chastisements have not been drawn down upon us by a gross neglect of our SPIRITUAL PRIVILEGES.[78]

The war, in Duché's interpretation, became a test of colonial virtue: "Testify to the world, by your example as well as by your counsels, that ye are equally the foes of VICE and of SLAVERY—Banish the Syren LUXURY, with all her train of fascinating pleasures, idle dissipation, and expensive amusements from our borders."[79] Like the prophets, the Whigs in effect had no choice in their actions; they bore God's judgment to the people; they were burdened with revolution; the covenant had been violated: "When in the course of human events it becomes necessary," begins the Declaration of Independence.[80]

Morton White has argued that the colonist's conception of natural rights entailed the duty to preserve those rights. In a chapter entitled "Rebellion to Tyrants is Obedience to God," White writes, "The notion that they had a *duty* to rebel is extremely important to stress, for it shows that they thought they were complying with the *commands* of natural law and of nature's God when they threw off absolute despotism."[81]

As early as the Stamp Act crisis, the colonists couched their protests in the language of compulsion: "[The members of this congress], having considered as maturely as time would permit, the circumstances of the said colonies, esteem it our indispensable duty to make the following declarations, of our humble opinion, respecting the most essential rights and liberties of the colonists, and of the grievances under which they labor, by reason of several late acts of parliament."[82] James Otis reflected the same point of view when he wrote, "And he that would palm the doctrine of unlimited passive obedience and non-resistance upon mankind, and thereby or by any other means serve the cause of the Pretender, is not only a fool and a knave, but a rebel against common sense, as well as the laws of God, of Nature, and his Country."[83] The Declaration of Independence reflects the reluctance of duty in characterizing the action of the colonies as a last resort after all pleas and patient sufferance had failed: "But when a long train of abuses and usurpations pursuing invariably the same object, evinces a design to reduce them under absolute despotism it is their right, it is their *duty* to throw off such government, & to provide new guards for their future security. Such has been the patient sufferance of these colonies, & such is now the *necessity* which *constrains* them to alter their former systems of government." Like Old Testament prophets, Whigs were not responsible for the consequences of defending their freedoms, only irresponsible if they failed to do so.

Closely connected to discussions of duty in late-eighteenth-century thought was the notion of virtue.[84] Much of the logic as well as the language of these discussions was borrowed from classical sources, notably Aristotle and Cicero. Virtue for Aristotle consisted in the pleasure derived from acting in accordance with the good. Although the end is pleasure, virtue is not passionate self-indulgence, but exists in that sphere where right reason and the pleasurable coincide.[85] It is the rational capacity that distinguishes human beings from lesser creatures, and the failure to exercise that capacity was counted a fall into "effeminacy." Aristotle held defects in government, particularly tyranny, to be symptomatic of such failures, the overwhelming of the rational by the appetitive, the life of ease which makes easy prey of the *polis*.[86] Consequently, it was possible to read the pain of slavery as a failure of virtue, for only those who had not the virtue of rational deliberation were by nature fitted to be slaves.[87] The virtue of the good man is necessarily connected in Aristotle's view to the virtue of the citizen of the perfect state,[88] and Aristotle connects the right to rebel with virtue, that is, the exercise of right reason.[89]

Borrowing classical ideas of virtue, the Whigs were able to present rebellion as an act of virtue, meaning not only that the act was praiseworthy, but that failure to act would constitute moral degeneracy. Robert Bellah goes so far as to argue that virtue "was the organizing center of that initial Revolution in the minds of men that I have identified with the civil religion, the very spirit of the Declaration of Independence."[90] Clearly finding his model in classical Rome, "Brutus" proclaimed,

> The prevailing principle of our government is, *virtue.* If we would be happy, we must be more attentive to it than we hitherto have been. By that only can liberty be preserved; and on the preservation of liberty depends our happiness. By *virtue,* I here mean a love for our country, which makes us pursue with alacrity, such measures as tend to its preservation; and cheerfully resist the temptations of ease and luxury, with which liberty is incompatible. For luxury and idleness bring on a general depravation of manners, which sets us loose from all the restraints of both private and public virtue, and diverts our thoughts from examining the behavior and politics of artful and

designing men, who meditate our ruin, and would sacrifice their country for their private emolument. From immorality and excesses we fall into necessity, and this leads us to a servile dependence upon power, and fits us for the chains prepared for us.[91]

Paine, in discussing the excessive taxation of people by governments declared, "Man ought to have pride, or shame enough to blush at being thus imposed upon, and when he feel [sic] his proper character, he will."[92] The Second Continental Congress, in their Declaration of the Causes and Necessity of Taking up Arms "counted the cost of this contest, and find nothing so dreadful as voluntary slavery.—Honor, justice, and humanity, forbid us tamely to surrender that freedom which we received from our gallant ancestors, and which our innocent posterity have a right to receive from us. We cannot endure the infamy and guilt of resigning succeeding generations to that wretchedness which inevitably awaits them, if we basely entail hereditary bondage upon them."[93] The vocabulary of "shame," "honor," "gallantry," "guilt," "baseness," and "degeneracy," all served to define the revolutionary role as an act of expiation. The logic of the colonists ultimately served to make their claims self-validating, for the degree of autonomy they enjoyed was both interpreted as a measure of their virtue and their rectitude and served to encourage "manly resistance" to all infringements on liberty.[94]

The colonists lived in a world where things held ontologically certain status; it was a world in which things empirically were, things including the great principles of right and wrong. Moreover, it was possible to know what really, in nature, was, and thus what should be. Eighteenth-century man, especially eighteenth-century Englishmen, believed that in their natural state they had inalienable rights to life, liberty, and property; the role of government was to enhance, not to infringe upon, these rights. To the extent that it did infringe, it was a usurper, a tyranny, unjust and unjustified. At that point the Whigs felt the duty which was inseparable from the right to restore justice, even if it meant setting themselves *in extremis* from their government. For the colonists, in all discussions of rights, were talking not only of rights as privilege or entitlement, but of rights as rectitude. The rhetorical options consistent with such a philosophy were limited. The question remains, how did the colonists achieve certainty in their knowledge; what was their epistemology?

Self-Evident Truth, Moral Sense, and Common Sense

Sir Isaiah Berlin has written that "The eighteenth century is perhaps the last period in the history of Western Europe when human omniscience was thought to be an attainable goal."[95] "Theists and atheists, believers in automatic progress and skeptical pessimists, hard-boiled French materialists and sentimental German poets and thinkers, seemed united in the conviction that all problems were soluble by the discovery of objective answers, which, once found—and why should they not be?—would be clear for all to see and valid eternally."[96] Sir Isaiah's observation is important because it points to what characterizes the thought of a century. From this perspective, debates over which authors were read by Thomas Jefferson or which passages from which eighteenth-century writer most closely parallel the words of the Declaration of Independence diminish into caviling puerility,[97] and when the focus is extended beyond Jefferson and the Declaration to the philosophy of the American Whigs in general, nothing less than the catholic perspective suggested by Sir Isaiah's statement can be expected to do more than obscure the problem.

Though the Whigs were not trained philosophers and sometimes made rather facile and superficial use of their philosophical sources, they were, by all evidence, more familiar with the philosophical works of their day than leaders in our day are with contemporary works. As Berlin's characterization suggests, what the Whigs learned from their sources was that they were justified in holding that there were things that they could know beyond a doubt, just as the layperson on the street today has a vague faith in the products of science justified by a lingering, second-hand idea of positivism. The content of absolute beliefs held by the Whigs has been given attention in the previous section. Equally important to our understanding of how they functioned rhetorically is knowledge of how these beliefs were conceived to be held.

The terms used by the colonists to justify their beliefs reflect the philosophical vocabulary of the British Empiricists and the Scottish Common Sense school. Whether the philosophers talked in terms of "self-evidence," "moral sense," or "common sense," they were talking of truths for which no reasons can be given, truths that are axiomatic. These are truths based on "feeling," in the eighteenth-century understanding of the term.[98] Note in the following from Joseph Warren's "Boston Massacre Oration" how terms for feeling provide evidence for "universal" epistemological claims, terms such as "excited," "sentiment," "jealousy," "adamantine," "secure":

The attempt of the British Parliament to raise a revenue from America, and our denial of their right to do it, have excited an almost universal inquiry into the right of mankind in general, and of British subjects in particular; the necessary result of which must be such a liberality of sentiment, and such a jealousy of those in power, as will, better than an adamantine wall, secure us against the future approaches of despotism.[99]

In the wake of the collapsing hegemony of the church, the seventeenth and eighteenth centuries were forced to revive something similar to the geometrical ideal of the ancient Greeks as a foundation of knowledge.[100] First mathematics and then physics became the models of reason, and both rested ultimately on some brute truth which, as Aristotle noted, had to be known prior to demonstration or no demonstration was possible. Descartes's famous starting point *"Cogito ergo sum"* is an illustration of a system of knowledge based on what William James termed the "one indefectibly certain truth, and the truth that pyrrhonistic scepticism itself leaves standing,—the truth that the present phenomenon of consciousness exists."[101] Although Locke's starting point was different enough from that of Descartes to distinguish the empiricist from the rationalist, Locke, too, found "simple ideas" which it is not in the power of the mind to deny or to destroy to be the foundation of all knowledge.[102] Applied to the detection of conspiracies of power, Locke's doctrine queried, "Are the People to be blamed, if they have the sence of rational Creatures, and can think of things no otherwise than as they find and feel them?"[103] Even the skeptical Hume relied on the data of the senses to form the "experience" upon which he based knowledge, data for which no reasons can be adduced, but which are believed according to their vivacity.[104] And Thomas Reid, Hume's chief philosophical opponent, also placed his faith not in philosophical reasons, but in belief as "a single act of the mind, which cannot be defined."[105] What each of these otherwise contentious philosophies has in common is a foundation for knowledge that reflects Sir Isaiah's characterization of the time, a foundation which, in Aristotle's conception, "we must necessarily believe" upon being exposed to it.

American colonists on both sides of the debate were influenced by this epistemology and optimistic about the sheer power of the truth to impress itself on the minds of men. Early in the conflict with Britain, a petition by New York to the House of Commons denounced an "odious Discrimination" which "no Sophistry can recommend to the Sober, impartial Decision of common sense."[106] Thomas Jefferson's "Summary View" is "penned in the language of truth," [107] and he further declared, "The greatest principles of right and wrong are legible to every reader." [108] "Massachusettensis," arguing the Tory position, wrote, "There are hundreds, if not thousands, in the province, that will feel the truth of what I have written, line by line as they read it." [109] And Massachusettensis's opponent, "Novanglus," was no less confident when he wrote, "Speak out the whole truth boldly," or when he later concluded his exposition of Bernard's plan to subjugate America by noting, "No other evidence is necessary; it was plain to such persons, what this junto was about." [110] James Otis felt that he had "proved" with mathematical certainty the rights of the British colonies based on axioms of natural law and right when he wrote his "Rights of the British Colonies." [111] Charles Inglis, in impartially stating "The True Interest of America," wrote, "Let every man only consult his feelings—I except my antagonist—and it will require no great force of rhetoric to convince him, that a removal of those evils, and a restoration of peace would be a singular advantage and blessing." [112] The Second Continental Congress held that "a reverence for our great Creator, principles of humanity, and the dictates of common sense, must convince all those who reflect upon the subject, that government was instituted to promote the welfare of mankind." [113] But surely the Revolution's most famous exemplar of the popular version of eighteenth-century epistemology is Thomas Paine's "Common Sense" where Paine offered "nothing more than simple facts, plain arguments, and common sense." [114] Among the many responses occasioned by Paine's pamphlet was one appropriately entitled "Plain Truth." [115]

Argument from common sense assumes concordance with the audience; the truths are self-evident. Natural law philosophy in the eighteenth century equated natural law with reason, and in their common qualification as reasonable persons, it was expected that all who but exercised this power could perceive the truth.[116] Locke regularly appealed to "reason" as the supreme adjudicator, as when he wrote, "Reason, the common Rule and Measure, God hath given to Mankind," [117] or when he asserted, "The *State of Nature* has a Law of Nature to govern it, which obliges every one: And Reason, which is that Law, teach all Mankind, who will but consult it." [118] Reasons, then, the product of consulting reason, were things in themselves. Although they were held to be the common property of human beings, their status was not predicated on assent. Acceptance of the verdicts of reason was the measure of the reasonable being. The reasonable person was not held up as the standard of reason. In this sense, as well as in the very direct sense suggested by Locke, reason was sacred; it was not of human creation.

To say that reasons were sacred is not to deny their power to compel belief. The liberal-Lockean view of humanity was essentially optimistic. The occasional failure of character or virtue notwithstanding, human beings would generally reflect their God-given nature and assent to those reasons revealed in natural law. As with the Old Testament prophets, eighteenth-century citizens had faith in the suasory power of sacred truth upon being revealed. Metaphors of vision in both discourses are indicative of this common faith.

Eighteenth-century tracts on moral and political topics dealt with the senses and their functioning in an effort to ground conclusions in the ineffable. Hobbes in *Leviathan* asserts, "There is no conception in a man's mind which has not at first, totally or by parts, been begotten upon the organs of sense."[119] The relation between the external world and the senses became the preeminent problem in eighteenth-century empiricism, Locke's doctrine of primary and secondary qualities being perhaps the most influential attempted resolution of the problem. Even Thomas Reid who, unlike his empiricist adversaries, believed in innate ideas, devoted his entire *Inquiry* to the functioning of the five senses (especially sight, which he termed "the noblest" of the senses) in an attempt to establish their veracity.[120]

This emphasis on sensory data, particularly vision, as ground for belief is not peculiar to the eighteenth century. In our own day we still find the notion that "seeing is believing" quite accessible: rental properties and used cars must be seen to be believed; our most elemental affirmation of fact is "I saw it with my own two eyes;" an eye witness is one who knows (from the Old English *witan,* "to know") by seeing; and "Don't you see?" is our final frustrated response to one who refuses to be convinced. R. Hazelton has explored the use of vision as a metaphor for belief and has noted that "of all the metaphors we habitually use, that of vision must be among the commonest. It permeates our speech and thought—especially our speech about thought. Although our scientific and philosophical mentors have always warned against confusing percept with concept, image with idea, it seems safe to predict that metaphors of sight for insight will continue to be operative and controlling."[121]

Although not peculiar to the eighteenth century, the emphasis on the senses, vision in particular, did have special philosophical significance to eighteenth-century thinkers as sources of certain knowledge.[122] The twentieth-century skeptic counters "Seeing is believing" with "Appearances are deceptive." Not so for an American colonist at the time of the Revolution.

Capturing the epistemology and the revolutionary fervor of the time, the inimitable Paine wrote, "But such is the irresistible nature of truth, that all it asks, and all it wants, is the liberty of appearing. The sun needs no inscription to distinguish him from darkness." [123] In similar terms, "Massachusettensis" expressed a certainty that thousands would feel the truth of what he had written and felt that even "those who obstinately *shut their eyes* against it now, haply the fever of the times may intermit, there may be some *lucid* interval, when their minds shall be open to the truth, before it is too late to serve them; otherwise it will be revealed to them in bitter moments, attended with keen remorse and unutterable anguish." [124]

Most revealing was the use of the metaphor to define the moral quality of opponents. "Do we claim any but what are as clear as the noon day?" queries a writer in *The Constitutional Courant*. Earlier in the pamphlet, the writer uses a variant of the same metaphor to describe the coercive nature of truth: "The arguments by which these points have been established beyond all dispute, I need not repeat; their evidence is such as must flash conviction into the minds of all but the vile minions of tyranny and arbitrary power. The tremendous conclusion, therefore, forces itself upon us, that the public faith of the nation, in which, till now, we thought we might securely confide, is violated." [125] The writer makes it quite clear that failure to see the truth is attributable to a defect of character, not to any want of the truth. Disagreement with the Whig program becomes prima facie evidence of corruption. There is no possibility of honest difference of opinion, only ulterior motives.

If all parties, both Whigs and Tories, felt the truth to be both real and inexorable, if the philosophy of omniscience was as prevalent as here claimed, where is the source of debate, why the need for advocates? In the first place, it appears that they did build their case on values and belief held by the audience rather than being in opposition to or outside the audience's frame of reference. In the second place, it now appears that if the Whig rhetors are to be considered prophets, so must Tory rhetors, for they seemed to hold the same basic truths and with the same conviction.

Granting a common epistemology, an agreement on method, we can yet conceive different conclusions. There is room for a significant distinction to be made between Whig leaders, their Tory counterparts, and the people at large, and that distinction lies in the radical's basic orientation to the status quo. Tories like Daniel Leonard did not deny natural law, but found in its dictates a "duty to remain subject to the authority of parliament." [126]

Acting the part of true prophets, Whigs decried Tories like Leonard in terms similar to those used by Old Testament prophets to imprecate the priests and false prophets of their own day. Those who could not see the truth were victims of prejudice, deluded by the ephemeral rewards of loyalty to the Crown as opposed to the true virtue of loyalty to God. Paine spoke of the "prejudices which men have from education and habit, in favour of any particular form or system of government" and dismissed such prejudices as "nothing," having yet to stand "the test of reason and reflection."[127] "It can only be by blinding the understanding of man, and making him believe that government is some wonderful mysterious thing, that excessive revenues are obtained," he continued. "Monarchy is well calculated to ensure this end. It is the popery of government; a thing kept up to amuse the ignorant, and quiet them into taxes."[128] Recall here William Goddard's contempt for those "who by *office* and *profession* engage to assert the cause of public liberty [who] own themselves such dastards as to be afraid to speak when their country is injured in her most sacred rights," and Otis's injunction against him "that would palm the doctrine of unlimited passive obedience and non-resistance upon mankind, and thereby or by any other means serve the cause of the Pretender." Such a person, said Otis, "is not only a fool and a knave, but a rebel against common sense, as well as the laws of God, of Nature, and his Country." The argument is almost entirely *ad personam;* it heightens the sense of division in the discourse, and it correctly reflects the assumption that the defect is not in the truth but in the integrity of those who refuse it.

If the Whig spokesmen are to be set apart from the Tories, they are also to be set apart from the people at large. The prophet assumes an office in answer to a call. The prophet sees what we in our moral torpor cannot or will not see and hears what we either cannot or will not hear. According to Abraham Heschel, "to a person endowed with prophetic sight, everyone else appears blind; to a person whose ear perceives God's voice, everyone else appears deaf. . . . The prophet's word is a scream in the night. While the world is at ease and asleep, the prophet feels the blast from heaven."[129] This may at first seem at odds with the notions of self-evidence and the compelling nature of truth in the Revolution, but the contradiction is not real. Morton White has discussed at length the nascent elitism in the seemingly democratic concepts of self-evidence and moral sense and concludes that the Revolutionaries "operated within a philosophical tradition [which held] that a learned man can see as self-evident a truth which an ignorant and rude man cannot see as self-evident." Therefore, "the power to see self-evidence was attributed to a restricted group and not to every person."[130] In this notion of elitism, we find a strong parallel to the office of the prophet.

Failure to see the truth was not a failure of the truth but an impairment of the perceiver, a failure of virtue. The colonists found many ways of expressing this failure on the part of their peers. John Dickinson sought to shake his countrymen from indulgent sleep: "Here then, my dear country men ROUSE yourselves and behold the ruin hanging over your heads."[131] James Chalmers appealed to all those "not drunk with fanaticism,"[132] an echo of the Old Testament imagery for impairment, and Thomas Paine asked nothing more of his reader "than that he will divest himself of prejudice and prepossession, and suffer his reason and his feelings to determine for themselves."[133] At another point Paine presented himself as trying to correct a lack of (in)sight by awakening his peers "from fatal and unmanly slumbers."[134] Paine consistently held prima facie natural law to be the basis for the Whig argument: "Here then is the origin and rise of government; namely, a mode rendered necessary by the inability of moral virtue to govern the world; here too is the design and end of government, viz., Freedom and security. And however our eyes may be dazzled with show, or our ears deceived by sound; however prejudice may warp our wills, or interest darken our understanding, the simple voice of nature and of reason will say, 'tis right."[135] As Morton White, borrowing from Kant, suggests in the case of the colonists, they were ultimately reduced to a position of "Do not argue, but believe."[136] It was a question not of persuasion but of making men see.

Whigs and Old Testament prophets had in common that they knew an absolute truth and, to paraphrase William James, that they knew that they knew; it was by all appearance self-evident. They further had in common that their knowledge was of the law, the law of nature and of nature's God. The message of these rhetors, then, is largely determined; in the words of Isaiah, "A voice says, 'Cry!' And I said, 'What shall I cry?' "[137] The radical, like the prophet, is dedicated, the proclaimer of a divine and sacred principle. The radical bears witness. Here is the root, if you will, of radical rhetoric and of prophecy as a particular form of it: a commitment to an absolute, sacred truth. Elizabeth Cady Stanton, a later radical for another cause, played prophet against the male priesthood of her day and clearly advocated the sovereignty of the truth in reform discourse when she wrote in her introduction to *The Woman's Bible,* "Reformers who are always compromising, have not yet grasped the idea that truth is the only safe ground to stand upon."[138] It is precisely this unwillingness to compromise that I have sought to highlight in both Old Testament prophecy and the rhetoric of the American Revolutionaries. It is this same unwillingness to compromise that is routinely equated with "unreason" by those it opposes. But there is another commonality, one suggested by the idea that prophetic speech is "sanctioned," that must be examined before we can understand how it is that this knowledge, accessible to all, set both Whigs and prophets in radical opposition to their respective societies, and that is the common situation that called both Whigs and prophets forth as spokesmen on behalf of the law—the transgression of the law.

The Judgment Proclaimed

Locke concludes *The Second Treatise of Government* by examining the question, "Who shall be Judge?" On the question of who should adjudicate "Controversie . . . betwixt a Prince and some of the People," Locke determines that the first judge should be the people themselves, and, that failing, "the Appeal then lies no where but to Heaven: . . . and in that State the *injured Party must judge* for himself, when he will think fit to make use of that Appeal, and put himself upon it."[139]

In the Declaration of Independence, the colonists expressed their judgment of Britain's attempts on their freedoms and made their appeal to heaven and the world for vindication of their war for separation. The major part of the Declaration is a litany of charges against King George III which begins, "The history of the present king of Great Britain is a history of repeated injuries & usurpations, all having in direct object the establishment of an absolute tyranny over these states. To prove this let facts be submitted to a candid world." This is followed by a verdict based on this accusation:

> Nor have We been wanting in attentions to our British brethren. We have warned them from time to time of attempts by their legislature to extend an unwarrantable jurisdiction over us. We have reminded them of the circumstances of our emigration & settlement here, we have appealed to their native justice and magnanimity and we have conjured them by the ties of our common kindred to disavow these usurpations which interrupt our connection and correspondence. They too have been deaf to the voice of justice & of consanguinity, we must therefore acquiesce in the necessity which denounces our separation and hold them as we hold the rest of mankind, Enemies in War, in Peace Friends.

There is no argument in the accusation, no attempt to demonstrate that the king had "refused his Assent to Laws the most wholesome & necessary to the public good," no evidence that "He has called together legislative bodies at places unusual, uncomfortable, and distant from the depository of their public Records, for the sole purpose of fatiguing them into compliance with his measures," no data to support the claim that "He has affected to render the Military independent of, & superior to the Civil power." The law had been transgressed, and the faith of the Whigs in the raw power of the truth in support of their accusation is evidenced in the phrase "let facts be submitted to a candid world." Carl Becker described the form as "the steady, laborious piling up of 'facts,' the monotonous enumeration, without comment, of one bad action after another. How could a candid world deny that the colonies were rightly absolved from allegiance to so malevolent a will!"[140] The verdict follows from the accusation "of necessity."

This form is not peculiar to the Declaration.[141] The author of "A State of the Rights of the Colonists" begins by stating the rights of colonists as men, as Christians, and as subjects; he then proceeds to "A List of Infringements & Violations of Rights."[142] Henry Laurens's "Extracts from the Proceedings of the Court of Vice-Admiralty" is simply a long recitation of individual cases in which violation of natural law is supposed to be apparent to the reader,[143] and "A Short Narrative of the Horrid Massacre in Boston," with its repeated calling of witnesses to the stand to deliver their depositions, is almost a simulated courtroom.[144]

Whig rhetoric has this form in common with the judgment- speech of the Old Testament prophets, in which the transgressions of the covenant were held before the people. The argument suggests that Whig rhetoricians conformed to this pattern in important respects: that they were constrained to speak the truth, regardless of its tendency to alienate; that their truth was immutable and absolute; that they did not doubt their knowledge of the truth; and that they exposed the crimes of England against her colonies to the searing light of this truth and boldly proclaimed God's judgment against the mother country. The reasons *of* Whig rhetoric are contained in the terms of the covenant, which is also the reason *for* Whig rhetoric. In their act of judgment against England, the Whigs completed an ideological journey into the purity of the wilderness that had its geographical beginnings almost two hundred years prior. Whig rhetoric served to clarify a relationship that had become increasingly ambiguous and confused; it defined the American people without the encumbrances of being part of the British empire. Out of a crisis of meaning, the Whigs brought new order and definition, boldly proclaiming self-evident truths, truths already part of the community's common heritage, the iteration of which called that community into being again even as they disjoined that community from other parts of that complex heritage and other parts of itself. The following chapter turns to times of crisis as the setting for prophetic discourse.

4

Prophecy as *Krisis*

Wendell Phillips and the Sin of Slavery

The Lord will enter into judgment with the ancients of his people,
and the princes thereof; for ye have eaten up the vineyard; the spoil of
the poor is in your houses. What mean ye, that beat my people to
pieces, and grind the faces of the poor? saith the Lord God of hosts.

—Isaiah 3:14–15

And your covenant with death shall be disannulled, and your
agreement with hell shall not stand; when the overflowing scourge
shall pass through, then ye shall be trodden down by it.

—Isaiah 28:18

Wendell Phillips's most recent biographer, James Stewart, holds
Phillips to have been "Civil War America's greatest and most radical orator."[1] This is no small praise, given the oratorical giants who occupied
America's podiums and pulpits during Phillips's day—men like Daniel
Webster, Edward Everett, Lyman Beecher, and Henry Clay—but Stewart
is far from alone in his assessment. Critical opinion from Phillips's day to
our own has almost universally afforded the "brahmin radical" a place
among America's premier speakers.[2] His single run for the governorship of
Massachusetts aside, Phillips eschewed the bureaucratic authority of political
office and made the independent moral authority of the speaker's rostrum
the basis of his power. In his last major address, the Harvard Phi Beta Kappa
address of 1881, Phillips described this prophetic stance, the voice speaking
truth outside the temple walls, "with . . . no object but truth—to tear a
question open and riddle it with light."[3]

Phillips's uncompromising passion ensured a controversial status, many
having argued that he provided perhaps more heat than light in the public
forum. The claim has been often made that Phillips was "the wrongheaded

radical of the Civil War crisis—an emotional person, lacking in responsibility, but quick to condemn those who had it, standing always for extremes that public opinion would not sustain, reckless, mischievous, and vindictive."[4] Irving Bartlett is using the phrase of one of Phillips's contemporaries when he characterizes Phillips's discourse as "the eloquence of abuse."[5] And E. L. Godkin, also contemporary with Phillips and one of the few who shared many of his radical views, nonetheless felt constrained, as editor of *The Nation* magazine, to criticize Phillips's excesses.[6]

Phillips's alienation from his audiences is clear—the excoriation, the clamant tone, the sneering condescension are all part of his repertoire. Though his lecture "The Lost Arts" was enormously popular—given more than two thousand times over a forty-five-year period, it earned Phillips an estimated $150,000[7]—his defense of John Brown's effort to foment a slave rebellion in Virginia, given at a time when the spectre of slave insurrections in the Caribbean loomed large in the minds of Americans, seems perversely calculated to offend and alienate. It is impossible to read the following segment of a speech Phillips gave on the events at Harper's Ferry without feeling the distance he placed between himself and his audience. There is no third person plural here; Phillips is not a member of the same group of which they are all members, that is, he is not a citizen. Phillips is *in extremis* as he denounces the U. S. Constitution as a "covenant with death and agreement with hell," a phrase often used by William Lloyd Garrison and echoing the prophet Isaiah:

> Thank God, I am not a citizen. You will remember, all of you, citizens of the United States, that there was not a Virginia gun fired at John Brown. Hundreds of well-armed Maryland and Virginia troops rushed to Harper's Ferry, and—went away! *You* shot him! Sixteen marines, to whom you pay eight dollars a month,—your own representatives. When the disturbed State could not stand on her own legs for trembling, you went there and strengthened the feeble knees, and held up the palsied hands. Sixteen men, with the vulture of the Union above them [sensation] your representatives! It was the covenant with death and agreement with hell, which you call the Union of thirty States, that took the old man by the throat with a pirate hand; and it will be the disgrace of our civilization if a gallows is ever erected in Virginia that bears his body.[8]

The Union and the Constitution on which it is based are sources of legitimacy for Phillips's audience; it is the benediction of his audience that allows the justification of slavery. Phillips decries the legitimacy of these arrangements as a falsehood. In profaning the Union and the Constitution, and in ridiculing the feeble response at Harper's Ferry made under their aegis, Phillips reveals the impotence of false idols. As for himself, Phillips keeps his distance above the sordidness of the affair. Only once does he suggest any kinship with his hearers when he mentions the possible "disgrace of our civilization."

S. N. Eisenstadt's comments on moral fervor illuminate the impulse exampled here. It is a radical impulse because it "is rooted in the attempt to come into contact with the very essence of being, to go to the very roots of existence, of cosmic, social, and cultural order, to what is seen as sacred and fundamental." At the same time, there is a strongly critical element in this quest, a "predisposition to sacrilege: to the denial of the validity of the sacred, and of what is accepted in any given society as sacred."[9] Phillips's reversal is made plausible in the convergence of the sacred and the sordid beyond the reach of man; both are untouchable. Such a reversal reveals the tenuousness of the existing order, the threat of chaos, thus providing the conditions for crisis.

The Crisis of Slavery

Dread of chaos was epidemic in early-nineteenth-century America. Expressed as a fear of intemperance, it bordered on the paranoiac.[10] According to Timothy Smith, "the concern for virtue that the revolutionary generation bequeathed to the new nation was no mere exercise in social control, but an effort to deal with the central problem of what we call 'free' societies: maximizing self-control."[11] The revival movement of the Second Great Awakening is symptomatic of the uncertainties that haunted the new nation. Perry Miller called it "the dominant theme in America from 1800 to 1860" and saw in it an attempt to achieve a national identity based on the reformation of common sins.[12] Nineteenth-century Americans fueled the revival movement by relentless application of their moral yardstick to contemporaries who were invariably found deficient. Living in the shadow of those who had demonstrated the courage and discipline to lead the country to independence in a great vindication of God's will, Americans of Phillips's generation felt small, their horizons limited to the easily attainable rather than the possible. Moral indolence and self-gratification, the failure of virtue and moral athleticism, these conspired to consign the people to slavery. Slavery represents the apotheosis of intemperance.

For early-nineteenth-century revivalists, "slavery" was a devil term, not merely as it applied to the institution of chattel slavery, but as any degradation of human autonomy that threatened to reduce human beings to the status of animals. As for the colonists of the late eighteenth century, "freedom" and "slavery" were radical ideas for the early nineteenth century because they were fundamental to self-definition. With regard to the Temperance movement, a product of the same climate and sharing many parallels with abolitionism, Joseph Gusfield has stated the case quite succinctly: "The concept of Temperance has rested on . . . a specific vision of man's character in which self-mastery, industry, and moral consistency are prized virtues. Impulsive action is at the opposite pole from virtue. The good man is able, through his character, to win the victory of Will over Impulse."[13] Slavery was both a product of the triumph of impulse over will in the enslaver and an institution that abrogated the exercise of will by those enslaved. David Brion Davis provides a useful clarification of the sinfulness of slavery when he notes that its inherent contradiction "lies not in its cruelty or economic exploitation, but in the underlying conception of a man as a conveyable possession with no more autonomy of will and consciousness than a domestic animal. This conception has always raised a host of problems and has never been held without compromise."[14] In a word, slavery was destructive of virtue.

Davis refers to those who were victims of institutionalized slavery, those human beings who were owned by other human beings, but the connection of intemperance and autonomy reveals the owners to be no less enslaved. As Donald Scott suggests of the abolitionist view, "slavery in its essence did not differ from the broader American life, but seemed to take to its logical end point that lust for gain and the willingness to sacrifice all to selfish ends that dominated American life."[15] Slavery stood opposed to the self-control associated with civilized men; it was directly associated with licentious behavior on the part of Southerners and indirectly with the decadence of Northerners who benefited from the labor of the bondsman.[16] For abolitionists, slavery represented the highest form of self-gratification and was symptomatic of the general decay in society necessitating the revival movement.[17]

Using the language of degraded virtue, abolitionists represented slavery as a materialistic corruption, the placing of self above duty, selfishness. Personal well-being provided a kind of intoxication, an anesthetic effect against the pain of slavery. "I appeal from the American people drunk with cotton," said Phillips.[18] The mob that killed Lovejoy was "a community, staggering like a drunken man, indifferent to their rights and confused in their feelings. Deaf to argument, haply they might be stunned into sobriety."[19] The mayor of Boston and the mob that nearly cost Garrison his life there in 1835 "were only blind to what they did not wish to see, and knew the right and wrong of the case well enough, only, like all half-educated people, they were but poorly able to comprehend the vast importance of the wrong they were doing."[20] "What is it that thus palsies our strength and blinds our foresight? We have become so familiar with slavery that we are no longer aware of its deadening influence on the body politic."[21]

Abolitionists cried out against indulgence, an indulgence that created a shield against the pain of a sinful world. As with the rhetoric of the American Revolution, the metaphors of drunkenness suggest the moral quality of those who look at questions of right and wrong through the ethical equivalent of an alcoholic cloud. The moral stupor that is insinuated suggests a state in which critical differences among principles are slurred and confused.

In the Constitution of the United States, radical abolitionists found the institutionalization of America's failed virtue in the face of slavery. Allying themselves with the Revolutionaries, abolitionists easily carried the banner of 1776 but stopped short of assuming the burden of 1787. Phillips was one of that band of Garrisonian radicals that held the absolute idealism of the Declaration of Independence in judgment over the Constitution. In 1844, he played a role in creating the document *The Constitution a Pro-Slavery Compact* published by the American Anti-Slavery Society. A compilation of reprints from the Madison papers on the constitutional debates, "these pages prove the melancholy fact that willingly, with deliberate purpose, our fathers bartered honesty for gain and became partners with tyrants that they might share in the profits of their tyranny."[22] In 1847, Phillips furthered the charges in a response to Lysander Spooner's essay "The Unconstitutionality of Slavery."[23] In the spring of 1860, Phillips's "Plea for the Dissolution of the Union" attracted considerable attention,[24] and after the secession of South Carolina from the Union, he hailed, " 'The Lord reigneth; the earth rejoice.' 'The covenant with death' is annulled; 'the agreement with hell' is broken to pieces. The chain which has held the slave system since 1787 is parted."[25]

For Garrisonians, the Constitution represented a great compromise with sin, a proslavery document, a travesty to the ideals of the Revolution as expressed in the Declaration of Independence. The Constitution was not a reflection of absolute right, but of expediency: "They [Americans] have no idea of absolute right," said Phillips. "They were born since 1787, and absolute right means the truth diluted by a strong decoction of the Constitution of '89. They breathe that atmosphere; they do not want to sail outside of it; they do not attempt to reason outside of it. Poisoned with printer's ink, or choked with cotton dust, they stare at absolute right as the dream of madmen." [26] As the Founding Fathers were enlisted against the leaders of the Revolution, providing fuel on both sides of the slavery debate, a fissure was revealed in the national foundation placing a terrible strain on consensus. Abolitionists effectively questioned the integrity of principles, the unimpugned status of which was necessary to sustain a justification of slavery.

In the view of radical abolitionists, the same accommodating, facilitative politics that had produced the Constitution was a chronic symptom of the failure of moral vision in America, and Phillips and his coreligionists reserved some of their bitterest invective for the process and its practitioners. "We do not *play* politics," declared Phillips, "Antislavery is no half jest with us; it is a terrible earnest, with life or death, worse than life or death, on the issue." [27] In a speech made in 1845, Phillips contrasted the politician with the reformer:

> "The politician must conceal half his principles, to carry forward the other half—must regard, not rigid principle and strict right, but only such a degree of right as will allow him at the same time to secure *numbers*. His object is immediate success. When he alters his war cry, he ever looks back over his shoulder to see how many follow." The reformer, on the other hand, worships truth; "his object is duty, not success. He can wait, no matter how many desert, how few remain; he can trust always that the whole of truth, however unpopular, can never harm the whole of virtue." [28]

Phillips at one point compares compromising politicians to Milton's "earth's giant sons, Now less than smallest dwarfs, in narrow room Throng numberless, like that pygmean race Beyond the Indian mount," while the "healthy party—the men who made no compromise in order to come under that arch" is compared to "The great seraphic lords and cherubim, In close recess and secret conclave." [29] Politicians thus became a symbol of moral failure as representatives of the will and leaders of the new Zion. Like Moses, they were particularly culpable.

The final symbol of the moral decay in America as the abolitionists viewed it was the dereliction of the church on the issue of slavery. The reluctant church was perhaps the institution most defamed by the abolitionists after slavery itself. Dissatisfaction with the institution of the church inspired "come-outers" to cast aside its corrupted authority and inspired Stephen S. Foster to make his reputation by interrupting church services to speak on behalf of the antislavery cause.[30] In antebellum America, the Bible was used as much by false priests to legitimate slavery as it was to condemn it,[31] and though Phillips never went so far as to accept what he felt were the heresies of Garrison and some of Garrison's followers, he did decisively set himself apart from the church and the attitude of the church with regard to slavery.[32]

According to Phillips,

> the abolitionists early saw, that, for a moral question like theirs, only two paths lay open: to work through the Church, that failing, to join battle with it. Some tried long, like Luther, to be Protestants, and yet not come out of Catholicism; but their eyes were soon opened. Since then we have been convinced that to come out from the Church, to hold her up as the bulwark of slavery, and to make her shortcomings the main burden of our appeals to the religious sentiment of the community was our first duty and best policy.[33]

He noted that the church's reaction to *Uncle Tom's Cabin* was "either silent or hostile, and in the columns of the theological papers the work is subjected to criticism, to reproach, and its author to severe rebuke."[34] "Save us from a Church not broad enough to cover woman and the slave, all the room being kept for the grogshop and the theatre—provided the one will keep sober enough to make the responses, and the other will lend its embroidered rags for this new baby house."[35] Phillips found the church's appeal to the separation of church and state as a reason for not becoming involved in the controversy disingenuous: "The office of the pulpit is to teach men their duty. Wherever men's thoughts influence their laws, it is the duty of the pulpit to preach politics."[36] The position of the church was all the more disingenuous because of its failure to maintain it consistently:

> Free men are kidnapped in our streets, to be plunged into that hell of slavery; and now and then one, as if by miracle, after long years, returns to make men aghast with his tale. The press says, "It is all right"; and the pulpit cries, "Amen." They print the Bible in every tongue in which man utters his prayers; and get the money to do so by agreeing never to give the book, in the language our mothers taught us, to any Negro, free or bond, south of Mason and Dixon's line. The press says, "It is all right"; and the pulpit cries, "Amen."[37]

Again and again, Phillips pointed to the dereliction of instruction, the failure of political and moral leaders to provide clear direction, to make significant distinctions between good and evil.

The mentality of compromise that Phillips excoriated in both politics and the church was intended by its proponents as the vehicle for continued unity. It was a beguiling notion in its passivity—"live and let live." It was not a strenuous doctrine. It reflected the realities of the world in all its imperfections. But compromise also has a sharply dyslogistic element: it does not always preserve the interests of opposing elements in mutual deference and respect, but sometimes surrenders one to the other. Compromise can be "a shameful or disreputable concession," particularly when it is the self that is compromised. Here the lack of strenuousness belies the benign face of compromise. In an age where the self is asserted only through the exercise of virtue, the life of ease involves the horrible anxiety of the loss of self, a condition of slavery. Compromise, in this less charitable view, is not a stalemate between the white king and the black king, but a reduction of all players to a homogeneous gray mass. In such a state, no significant distinctions can be made, there is no line of demarcation, no foundation for judgment, only amorphous formlessness, chaos.

The Call to Judgment

In such a situation, it is the prophet's office to cry, "Hear, you deaf; and look, you blind, that you may see!"[38] "To waken the nation to its real state, and chain it to the consideration of this one duty, is half the work," said Phillips.[39] According to Hofstadter:

> Phillips's career illustrates the principle that the agitator is likely to be a crisis thinker. . . . In periods of relative social peace the agitator labors under intellectual as well as practical restraints, for he thinks in terms of the *ultimate potentialities* of social conflicts rather than the immediate compromises by which they are softened. His moral judgments are made from the standpoint of absolute values, with which the mass of men cannot comfortably live. But when a social crisis or revolutionary period at last matures, the sharp distinctions that govern the mind of the agitator become at one with the realities.[40]

Referring to America as a modern-day Sodom,[41] a device often employed by the Old Testament prophets to suggest the urgency of the moment, Phillips attempted to create the necessary atmosphere of crisis. "While drunk with the temptations of the present hour," he proclaimed, "men are willing to bow to any Moloch."[42]

Murray Edelman has suggested that "crisis" is perhaps the most powerful political term available for encouraging unity and common sacrifice.[43] Phillips's purposes could not be better represented as he sought to create a new community through the renewal of virtue. The tradition of the jeremiad in America attests to a long practical understanding of the principle. Sacvan Bercovitch writes, "From the start the Puritan Jeremiahs had drawn their inspiration from insecurity; by the 1670s, crisis had become their source of strength. They fastened upon it, gloried in it, even invented it if necessary. They took courage from backsliding, converted threat into vindication, made affliction their seal of progress. Crisis became both form and substance of their appeals."[44] Bercovitch traces the use of the jeremiad through the nineteenth century and finds the idea of crisis to be a stable theme.[45]

The revival culture of antebellum America was predicated on crisis. In the personal terms of revivalism, abolitionism was, for many, the resolution of a carefully nurtured personal crisis of vocation. Donald M. Scott has argued that a large number of abolitionists had been dutifully prepared by their parents for the experience of rebirth and conversion, as a result of which God's plan for their lives would be revealed.[46] Bearing the marks of a strong Puritan heritage, the life dedicated to God's purpose was strenuous and exacting. According to Scott, "rebirth led not to disregard of the world but to implacable hostility to the world as it was sinfully constituted. As Christians born to righteousness they were as obliged to combat the sinful world as they were to rid themselves of all remnants of sin."[47]

Phillips was very much a product of this revival culture. Raised in a very pious, Calvinistic household, his mother's earliest gift to him was a Bible. In 1826, after hearing Lyman Beecher preach on the theme "You Belong to God," he reported a conversion experience,[48] though he did not discover the nature of his mission for another decade. When he did find his way into the abolitionist movement, he described the event in revelatory terms: "I had read Greek and Roman and English history; I had by heart the classic eulogies of brave old men and martyrs; I dreamed, in my folly, that I heard the same tone in my youth from the cuckoo lips of Edward Everett— these women taught me my mistake. . . . These women opened my eyes."[49] The women Phillips refers to are the women who had invited Garrison to speak to them on the day Phillips saw him dragged in a noose through the streets of Boston. By remaining steadfast and refusing to surrender their meeting, these women presented Phillips with a vision of courage and virtue. Phillips stresses the extraordinary nature of the experience by contrasting it with his formal education, and he refers to it as an "anointing."[50]

It is certainly not implausible to see in Phillips's radical career an attempt to provide meaning to his life in a world where the clerical and political options of his forefathers had been made increasingly irrelevant.[51] A modern cynic might be tempted to find in Phillips's abolitionist activities a synecdochal rejection of a repressive Calvinist upbringing, but Max Stackhouse reminds us that the slavery question, calling into question as it did the absolute doctrine of the natural right to property, also raised criticisms of "decadent Calvinist theories, which saw personal wealth as a sign of special divine favor."[52] Stackhouse quotes James Dombrowski to the effect that a "this- worldly" Calvinism, as opposed to the "otherworldliness" of Lutheranism and the "next-worldliness" of Catholicism, manifested itself in those places where Calvinism was most deeply entrenched.[53] This "Puritan evangelical" Calvinism emphasized participation in the world with a view to transforming it.[54] Just as Emerson, during this era, faced the crisis of relevancy and found a meaningful vocation as a "scholar," Phillips was able to find a divinely sanctioned vocation in abolitionism. According to Ronald Walters, "to be an abolitionist was to declare allegiance to the principles of brotherhood and equality of opportunity, to suffer for those ideals, and to band together with like-minded individuals."[55] Their agitation "often came at a crucial moment in their lives and helped them find direction, meaning, and companionship."[56]

Abolitionism is almost universally described by modern writers as a "moral crusade," "a sacred vocation," or a "religious movement,"[57] and Phillips, armed with confidence in his righteousness and his vision of absolute truth, reflected the religious nature of the cause in his discourse. He described abolitionism as "an insurrection to restore absolute right," described John Brown as "the brave, frank, and sublime truster in God's right and absolute justice," and denied concern with the temporal and ephemeral: "You see I am talking of that absolute essence of things which lives in the sight of the Eternal and the Infinite; not as men judge it in the rotten morals of the nineteenth century, among a herd of States that calls itself an empire, because it raises cotton and sells slaves."[58] Phillips truly prophesied or "spoke for another" when he said of John Brown, "God makes him the text, and all he asks of our comparatively cowardly lips is to preach the sermon, and say to the American people that, whether that old man succeeded in a worldly sense or not, he stood a representative of law, of government, of right, of justice, of religion, and they were a mob of murderers who gathered about him, and sought to wreak vengeance by taking his life."[59] The rhetorical attitude suggested here is succinctly characterized by Bartlett: "No matter how bitter, how merciless, how seemingly vindictive his assaults on individuals, Phillips always felt justified in what he was doing. He did not think of himself as an ordinary lecturer or orator, but as a kind of minister to the public, preaching the gospel of reform."[60]

The assertion of God's presence in history, however harsh, carries the reassurance of order, a single motive power, a single guiding passion behind an otherwise inexplicable universe. The exegesis of sacred history is a critical prophetic device for revealing at critical moments God's will. The prophetic woe finds in catastrophe an adumbration of God's judgment. Abolitionist discourse of the late eighteenth and early nineteenth centuries is rife with such revelations. David Brion Davis finds the theme to be central in the emergence of immediatism over gradualism in antislavery thought and provides a number of examples. Notable among them is Granville Sharp's interpretation of hurricanes in the West Indies as "supernatural agencies to blast the *enemies* of *law* and *righteousness*," and American Thomas Branagan's plea to "bring a speedy end to slavery and avert the divine judgment of an apocalyptic racial war."[61]

The language of Sharp and Branagan, with its synthesis of *logos* and *pathos* expressed as righteousness and the conviction of divine order behind it, was shared by Phillips and his fellow Garrisonians. In the "Address of the Executive Committee of the American Anti-Slavery Society to the Friends of Freedom and Emancipation in the U. States," signed by William Lloyd Garrison as President and Wendell Phillips and Maria Weston Chapman as Secretaries, it was declared,

> After the independence of this country had been achieved, the voice of God exhorted the people, saying, "Execute true judgment, and show mercy and compassion, every man to his brother: and oppress not the widow, nor the fatherless, the stranger, nor the poor; and let none of you imagine evil against his brother in your heart. But they refused to hearken, and pulled away the shoulder, and stopped their ears, that they should not hear; yea, they made their hearts as an adamant stone." "Shall I not visit for these things? saith the Lord. Shall not my soul be avenged on such a nation as this?"[62]

Borrowing language directly from the Old Testament, Garrison, Phillips, and Chapman left no doubt as to the ultimate realization of God's will: order would be restored through the elimination of sin. Perhaps not all would be saved, but the power of an omnipotent God would not be thwarted by the puny obstinance of avaricious men. There is a promise here that chaos will succumb to justice; the wicked will be punished and the good rewarded; the moral qualities of the world will be clarified.

Frightful as the prospect of natural disasters and wars might have been, the most compelling evidence of Jehovah's wrath against His people was the threat of the "slave power conspiracy." Conceived as a plot by the slaveholding states to establish political hegemony over the free states, the idea of the slave power conspiracy implicated the North for its passive complicity in slavery far more than it implicated the South for the sin of slaveholding. There was, after all, something virtuous in the Southerner's aggressive defense of slavery, however misguided. It was for this reason that Phillips had a grudging admiration for the unregenerate John C. Calhoun and nothing but contempt for the great compromiser Henry Clay. The end of Northern fecklessness would be its own slavery, the "slave power conspiracy" being conceived as God's vehicle for the enslavement of all those who had forsaken virtue and the covenant. In a letter to Phillips from William Lloyd Garrison, "Sunday Morning, April 21 [1861]," Garrison ventured to suggest some "portions of Scripture" that he felt might be useful for an address Phillips was to make that day at the Music Hall. From chapters 50 and 51 of Jeremiah, Garrison made the following application: "Israel and Judah typify the North; and a recognition of their guilt, also, is made, with discrimination and hope:—'For Israel hath not been forsaken, nor Judah of his God; *though their land was filled with sin against the Holy One of Israel*'—i.e., the sin of complicity."[63]

For those with an acute moral vision, the design of the slave power conspiracy was evident in many of the events preceding the Civil War. It is in the nature of conspiracies to attempt to escape notice, to disguise pattern as random activity. Actions presented to the public as the independent pursuit of economic interests—the Kansas-Nebraska Act, the Fugitive Slave Law, the Compromise of 1850—were viewed by abolitionists as components of a concerted moral assault.[64] The abolitionists were burdened with the task of revealing the true nature of events to the degenerate who saw them only through the promiscuous language of politics. In reference to the annexation of Texas, Phillips said,

> How vigilantly, how patiently, did we watch the Texas plot from its com-
> mencement! The politic South felt that its first move had been too bold, and
> thenceforward worked underground. For many a year, men laughed at us for
> entertaining any apprehensions. It was impossible to rouse the North to its
> Peril. David Lee Child was thought crazy, because he would not believe

there was no danger. His elaborate *Letters on Texan Annexation* are the ablest and most valuable contribution that has been made toward a history of the whole plot.[65]

The conspiracy theme, as evidenced in the rhetoric of the American Revolution, is a vehicle for signification. God, or some other absolute value standing in His place, is implied in the notion that there are ideals to which the conspiracy can be opposed. Conflict achieves cosmic dimensions; quotidian appearances prove to be an inadequate account of events; the contest has profound implications. Indeed, it is precisely under the shroud of pedestrianism that conspiracies seek to escape notice, to avoid a true assessment of their consequences. As isolated and random occurrences, events beg to be dismissed without cross-examination. Against the tendency to reduce events to insignificance, the prophetic voice demands a thoroughgoing exegesis of sacred history. In doing so, it reveals the patterns and provides a rationale for the putatively innocuous and serendipitous.

Treatment of the slave power conspiracy theme by Phillips and his fellow Garrisonians reveals an obsessive concern with enslavement as a result of moral sloth. Radical abolitionism was often less concerned with working toward freedom of chattel slaves than it was with the integrity of Northern free states. In a letter to Phillips, Garrison, quoting Jeremiah, wrote, "Flee out of the midst of Babylon, deliver every man his soul, be not cut off in her iniquity."[66] Phillips himself bespoke a certain selfish complacency when he argued, "If we never free a slave, at least we have freed ourselves in our efforts to emancipate our brother men."[67] It would be unfair to say that Phillips was not concerned with the plight of the chattel slave. He was concerned, as, for example, remarks made in 1846 attest: "We must speak strongly because the crisis demands plain talking. Remember this is no evil which lynx-eyed ingenuity has discovered. We are not going about with a lamp at mid-day, in order to ferret out some little local evil. Every sixth man is a slave. The national banner clings to the flagstaff, heavy with blood."[68] At the same time, it appears that his legal background, his interest in the issues of the American Revolution, and the nature of his conversion to the antislavery movement inclined Phillips to a great concern with the infringement of the slave power conspiracy on the rights of free Northerners.[69] In his first speech as an abolitionist, "The Right of Petition," Phillips protested against the antiabolitionist gag-rule in the Congress and lamented the death of a right "we had thought as firmly fixed in the soil of America as the Saxon race which brought it here. It was the breath of life during our colonial history, and is recognized on every page of our history since as the bulwark of civil liberty." He went on to link the defense of civil liberty and abolitionism: "Upon the friends of abolition, of free discussion, of equal rights, throughout the land, insult had been heaped on insult, and outrage added to outrage, till we thought that malice had done its worst. All the outworks that guard the citadel of liberty had been in turn overthrown. The dearest rights of freemen had been, one by one, torn from us."[70] Phillips's famous speech "In Defense of Lovejoy" was a defense of freedom of expression; its only concern with slavery was the fact that Lovejoy had been the owner of an abolitionist press.[71]

For self-professed revolutionaries who disdained expedience, it is more than mere coincidence that their proselytizing was restricted to the North; it is more than mere coincidence that primary among their tactics was withdrawal from contaminated institutions—the refusal to vote, the come-outerist movement in the churches; and it is more than mere coincidence that the motto of the American Anti-Slavery Society was "No Union with Slaveholders." Possibly the influence of New England Calvinism with its doctrine of predestination inhibited Garrisonian abolitionism from ever realizing a posture of conversion, but it seems apparent that radical abolitionism, for whatever reasons, is more adequately characterized as a movement of separation. Given the absolutist philosophy behind it, it seems inevitable that it should be so. Radical abolitionism found a certain power in the ambiguity between fitting its situation as corrective and fitting within what the situation permitted and would receive.[72]

In the 1844 "Address of the Executive Committee," Phillips, Garrison, and Maria Chapman declared that they wished to separate from slaveholders

> not in anger, not in malice, not for a selfish purpose, not to do them an injury, not to cease warning, exhorting, reproving them for their crimes, not to leave the perishing bondman to his fate—O no! But to clear our skirts of innocent blood—to give the oppressor no countenance—to signify our abhorrence of injustice and cruelty—to testify against an ungodly compact—to cease striking hands with thieves and consenting with adulterers.[73]

In this excerpt, the end of judgment is clear. Although concern is summarily expressed for the "perishing bondman," judgment entails separation, decision, definition. In wishing to keep their skirts clean, to avoid the touch of "thieves," the abolitionists express less concern for the welfare of the slave than for their own moral purity.

But it would be unfair to be overly cynical regarding the intentions of the Garrisonians. Consistent with Phillips's emphasis on the language of instruction, it cannot be doubted that the signers sincerely expected their action to serve as a model for emulation. By setting themselves apart in opposition to those who act contrary to God's will, the abolitionists sought to demonstrate the proper exercise of virtue and encourage the emulation of others, as well as to affirm their moral status.

Abolitionists saw the Civil War as the culmination of crisis. The people had for years absorbed themselves in captious debates, feigning ignorance of God's will, exhibiting a moral timorousness. Finally, there was no recourse but for God to execute His judgment and to restore order: "It is in vain now, with these scenes about us, in this crisis, to endeavor to create public opinion; too late now to educate twenty millions of people," lamented Phillips. "Our object now is to concentrate and to manifest, to make evident and to make intense, the matured purpose of the nation. We are to show the world, if it be indeed so, that democratic institutions are strong enough for such an hour as this. Very terrible as is the conspiracy, momentous as is the peril, Democracy welcomes the struggle."[74] The crisis for Phillips is instructive; properly attended to, it provides the resolution of chaos and indecision; it is a judgment from which must be discerned "the matured purpose of the nation." Awful as the war was, it at least had meaning. It resolved all doubt concerning the moral quality of slavery.

Judgment provides the resolution of the *agon* in the sacred drama. The antagonist is either absorbed or vanquished. Either way, the new display of unanimity is equally impressive. Justice is both ruthless and benevolent. The radical polarization of the world eliminates confusion. In a world where political and religious leaders fail to offer clear direction, where the compromise of purity is innocuously presented as a process that leaves the greater part of principle intact, prophetic rhetoric posits a clear dramatic opposition of protagonist and antagonist. It clarifies moral identities and structures desires for denouement.

In order to achieve certainty in the face of chaos, Phillips indulged in a reactionary move characteristic of the prophet. In the values of the American Revolution, Phillips found a redoubtable consensus and a model of virtue. Phillips canonized the Founding Fathers, and much of their philosophy was continuous with his religion. In college, he displayed an affinity for the works of Locke, among others, and was particularly interested in the history of the American Revolution.[75] His speeches contain references to John Milton and Algernon Sidney.[76] He echoes the revolutionary motto that "resistance to tyrants is obedience to God,"[77] and he often spoke of "natural law" and "inalienable rights."[78] Two of his biographers attest to the fact that the spirit of the Revolution was still very much in evidence in the Boston of Phillips's boyhood,[79] and James Stewart makes the influence of Whig republicanism on Phillips's career a central theme in his biography. The many tributes paid to Otis, Hancock, the Adamses, and Jefferson in his speeches bear out these estimations and leave no doubt as to the lasting imprint of this tradition on Phillips.

In his "Defense of Lovejoy," one of his first speeches on behalf of abolition, a speech that gained him instant notoriety if not fame, Phillips pointed to the portraits of the Founding Fathers hanging there in Boston's Fanieul Hall and proclaimed: "Sir, when I heard the gentleman lay down principles which place the murderers of Alton side by side with Otis and Hancock, with Quincy and Adams, I thought those pictured lips would have broken into voice to rebuke the recreant American, the slanderer of the dead."[80] In his speech "The Argument for Disunion," he reminded his listeners, "We stand today just as Hancock and Adams and Jefferson stood when stamp act and tea tax, Patrick Henry's eloquence and the massacre of March 5th, Otis's blood and Bunker Hill, had borne them to July, 1776."[81] Not only in God, but in the overpowering virtue of the leaders of Revolutionary America, Phillips found a guide to action and a ground for judgment.[82]

There were natural continuities between the philosophy of the American Revolution and the philosophy of Phillips's day, continuities that the language of evangelicalism should not be allowed to obscure.[83] Phillips referred to "a thread which bridges over that dark and troubled wave, and connects us by a living nerve with the freemen of the Revolution."[84] The writings of the Scottish Common Sense philosophers were prominent in American colleges and universities of the early nineteenth century, and there was, if anything, an even greater reliance on "intuition" as a source of infallible knowledge than in the Revolutionary period. The Second Great Awakening in America was a time of immense faith in the power of the heart to discern truth.[85] Phillips displayed this common faith when, for example, he affirmed his commitment that the "Higher Law" stood opposed to slavery. "So speaks the *heart*," he said.[86]

Addressing the heart, Phillips spoke the language of the passions. It is the prophet's task to create an emotional response to sin, a reaction to the *pathos* of God. Phillips exhibited a powerful consciousness of his rhetorical choices. Apparently making the heart metaphor literal, he declared, "There is something in the blood which, men tell us, brings out virtues and defects, even when they have lain dormant for a generation." Abolitionism was "blood whose warm currents of eloquent aid" had sprung to life after the dormancy of a generation "to rouse the world by the vigor and pathos of its appeals."[87]

Phillips demonstrated both vigor and *pathos:* "If we now repudiate and denounce some of our institutions, it is because we have faithfully tried them, and found them deaf to the claims of justice and humanity."[88] "Prove to me now that harsh rebuke, indignant denunciation, scathing sarcasm, and pitiless ridicule are wholly and always unjustifiable; else we dare not, in so desperate a case, throw away any weapon which ever broke up the crust of an ignorant prejudice, roused a slumbering conscience, shamed a proud sinner, or changed, in any way, the conduct of a human being."[89]

Abraham Heschel asks, "What is the torment that prompts the prophet to hurl bitter words at the people? Is it a feeling of alarm, the threat of disaster? What is the direct inner impact the prophet seeks to make upon his people? Does he aim to strike terror in the heart, to alarm?" And he answers, "The prophet's purpose is to move people to repent, to convert the inner man, to revive devotion, love, to reconcile Israel with God."[90] Phillips made clear the exhortative nature of his enterprise when he said,

> It seems to us that in such a land there must be, on this question of slavery, sluggards to be awakened, as well as doubters to be convinced. Many more, we verily believe, of the first than of the last. There are far more hearts to be quickened than confused intellects to be cleared up—more dumb dogs to be made to speak than doubting consciences to be enlightened. [Loud cheers] We have use, then, sometimes, for something beside argument.[91]

Writing of the Old Testament prophets, Heschel concurs: "Their primary aim is to move the soul, to engage the attention by bold and striking images, and therefore it is to the imagination and the passions that the prophets speak, rather than aiming at the cold approbation of the mind."[92]

Edwin Black, not coincidentally, finds William Lloyd Garrison to be an example of this mode of speaking, which Black terms "exhortative discourse" as opposed to "argumentative discourse." Exhortative discourse, according to Black, "is that in which the evocation of an emotional response in the audience induces belief in the situation to which the emotion is appropriate. In this genre, a strong emotional experience does not follow the acceptance of a belief, or even accompany it; it precedes it. Emotion can be said to produce the belief instead of the reverse."[93] Black's analysis of exhortative discourse tends to corroborate much of what I have claimed about Phillips and to illuminate the dynamics of Phillips's speaking. He notes that the power of exhortation to promote intense conviction makes it an "alien tongue"[94] and goes on to describe the judgment in the exhortative genre and its imminence.[95]

Phillips's transformation of the world, then, lies in the revival of emotional orientation. Radically dividing the world into good and evil and providing an example of the proper emotional response to each, he attempted to bring order out of chaos. In the dull, homogeneous, ambiguous world of compromise, exhortation served to restore simplicity and order through the introduction of highly charged and distinctive emotional states. In Phillips's own words, "God has given us no weapon but the truth, faithfully uttered, and addressed, with the old prophets' directness, to the conscience of the individual sinner."[96] In accordance with the epistemology of the time, Phillips provided an unfettered, uncomplicated proclamation of absolute truth in terms designed to demand an emotional conviction on the part of the audience; he aimed to make his listeners feel the truth.

It may first appear that such a passionate discourse is at odds with the ideal of temperance that the discourse was supposed to elicit and enforce. James Stewart, in an illuminating analysis of Phillips's rhetoric, finds this contradiction between the ideal of control and the passionate, evangelical vehicle for achieving it central to antebellum America. According to Stewart, "the major source of Phillips's rhetorical mastery" lay in his unerring balance of these elements: "As he harmonized and articulated these seemingly conflicting impulses by making order the prerequisite of freedom, he spoke to some of the deepest feelings of his age."[97]

Certainly, Phillips stood as an example of the paradox of freedom through submission—like the prophet, the radical abolitionist was only genuinely free when completely given over to the divine will—but we should be wary of perceiving irreconcilable oppositions where none exist. In their critical assessment of classical systems of thought, eighteenth-century philosophy and rhetoric understood the passions as integral to human nature and not necessarily alien to humanity's higher nature. As David Hume claimed, "Reason is, and ought only to be, the slave of the passions, and can never pretend to any other office than to serve and obey them." But Hume also argued, "It is impossible . . . that this passion can be opposed by or be contradictory to truth and reason; since this contradiction consists in the disagreement of ideas, considered as copies, with those objects which they represent."[98] George Campbell's *Philosophy of Rhetoric,* a text Phillips studied at Harvard, extended Hume's thinking on the relationship between feeling and persuasion by making "vivacity" the foundation of belief. Phillips's exhortative discourse is completely consistent with Campbell's Humean emphasis, and Phillips's teacher of rhetoric at Harvard, Edward T. Channing, appears to have reinforced such ideas.[99] It was Channing's belief "that it takes nothing from the merit of modern political orators to concede, that our most impassioned popular eloquence is marked throughout with the intention of leading considerate men to responsible action."[100] Passion, far from being irresponsible in the view of nineteenth-century rhetoric, sought to make people responsive to the good. It was a manifestation of God's judgment and a vehicle for awakening something fundamental to the self, for only through the proper exercise of the passions was one virtuous and thus truly human.[101] As Mynheer Peeperkorn counseled Hans Castorp in another anodyne environment,

> Feeling, you understand, is the masculine force that rouses life. Life slumbers. It needs to be roused, to be awakened to a drunken marriage with divine feeling. For feeling, young man, is godlike. Man is godlike, in that he feels. He is the feeling of God. God created him in order to feel through him. Man is nothing but the organ through which God consummates his marriage with roused and intoxicated life. If man fails in feeling, it is blasphemy; it is the surrender of His masculinity, a cosmic catastrophe, an irreconcilable horror.[102]

Perhaps flinching at the metaphors of intoxication, nineteenth-century Americans would have understood perfectly Peeperkorn's meaning.

The *ethos* presented through passion is ambiguous. It may represent the most indulgent form of personal expression reflected in such characterizations as "He just let go" or "She really let loose." Certainly, the appeal of such a licentious mode of speaking in an otherwise constrained and repressive society should not be underestimated, and it also makes understandable the acrimonious reactions to abolitionist rhetoric as a further sign of the fear of intemperance. At its extreme, passionate discourse may bring the speaker attention in the form of recriminations or retaliation, hence the connection between passionate expression and, for example, the passion of Christ. Hazel Catherine Wolf reflected this point of view when she argued that the abolitionists used their histrionic martyrdoms as a kind of exhibitionism, neurotic displays of self.[103] Wolf's suggestion that martyrdom was the primary motivation for the abolitionists has sustained serious criticism, but even most scholars sympathetic to the abolitionists have agreed that it is a significant idea in abolitionist thought.

Alternately, passion may be seen as an overpowering urge external to the person, in the case of the prophet, Yahweh's will. The prophet is reduced to the status of vehicle; the self is not expressed but surrendered. Passion accurately reflects this sublimation, for we associate passion with the loss of self—"I was out of my mind," "She forgot herself," "I was beside myself," "I don't know what came over me." The passionate state of mind is essentially sacrificial; the prophet is compelled to suffer the divine suffering. This is the view held by Aileen Kraditor who suggests that "the evidence shows *willingness* to suffer for the cause as a probably necessary price to be paid, rather than a *desire* to suffer."[104] The difference between Wolf and Kraditor is the difference between seeing in martyrdom a perverse form of self-celebration and seeing in it a form of ethical proof. From Kraditor's standpoint, martyrdom is the logical culmination of a commitment to unpopular truths. Wolf, on the other hand, would have us see not the ultimate sacrifice of self to principle, but the ultimate self-serving. By either interpretation there is a marked failure to accommodate the audience, but the prophetic motive is servitude.

Phillips clearly presented his exertions and suffering as an inescapable duty. From the examples already provided, the ubiquity of the language of duty in his discourse is evident. It was a burden of which he was always cognizant, as the frequent references attest.[105] The performance of a sacred duty in an atmosphere of adversity is the formula by which martyrs are created, and Phillips had a keen understanding of the appeal of martyrdom. In a speech commemorating the occasion of the Boston mob that nearly took the life of Garrison, he praised the women of the antislavery society who stood firm in their adherence to principle regardless of the threats of the mayor:

> They taught me that down in those hearts which loved a principle for itself, asked no man's leave to think or speak, true to their convictions, no matter at what hazard, flowed the real blood of '76, of 1640, of the hemlock-drinker of Athens, and of the martyr-saints of Jerusalem. I thank them for it! My eyes were sealed, so that, although I knew the Adamses and Otises of 1776, and the Mary Dyers and Ann Hutchinsons of older times, I could not recognize the Adamses and Otises, the Dyers and Hutchinsons, whom I met in the streets of '35.[106]

He also cast Elijah Lovejoy and John Brown as martyrs "who teach us how to live and how to die."[107]

Phillips demonstrates his appreciation of the didactic function of martyrdom in his repetitions of the verb "teach." Martyrdom was understood as a corrective to the failure of instruction by political and religious leaders whom Phillips so bitterly indicted. That he had learned his lessons from these noble martyrs is evidenced in his own willingness to join them: "We are perfectly willing—I am, for one—to be the dead lumber that shall make a path for thee men into the light and love of the people. We hope for nothing better. Use us freely, in any way, for the slave. When the temple is finished, the tools will not complain that they are thrown aside, let who will lead up the nation to 'put on the topstone with shoutings.' "[108] And it is clear that Phillips believed he had laid himself on God's altar when he describes the abuses he has suffered in his pursuit of the cause, and nowhere clearer than when he explicitly links himself to the Old Testament prophet Nathan:

> Sir, when a nation sets itself to do evil, and all its leading forces, wealth, party, and piety, join in the career, it is impossible but that those who offer a constant opposition should be hated and maligned, no matter how wise, cautious, and well planned their course may be. We are peculiar sufferers in this way. The community has come to hate its reproving Nathan so bitterly, that even those whom the relenting part of it is beginning to regard as standard- bearers of the antislavery host think it unwise to avow any connection or sympathy with him.[109]

In martyrdom lies the perfect realization of duty, the radical sacrifice of the self. In a discourse opposed to slavery, martyrdom is also the most complete freedom and the most profound exercise of virtue. Most important, in all this we find a model for emulation. The martyred prophet presents himself as a synecdochal realization of God's will.

Divine Judgment in a Postsacral World

The language of duty is a language of relationship. It is both an assertion of the motive of the prophet and a continuing testimony to the existence of divine forces that have commanded the prophet's servitude. In the latter aspect, the community to which the prophet speaks must have a belief in the possibility of the sacred, or the prophet's claim is dismissed as madness. Furthermore, this belief must be in direct proportion to the claims the prophet makes against it. In Phillips's case, in the criticisms of his intensity by both his contemporaries and later historians, there is the persistent suspicion of something excessive in the passion. Phillips himself understood this, as his acknowledgments of the charges of madness and fanaticism attest. For all its promise of resolution in judgment, Phillips's rhetoric produces a lingering agitation.

The world presented in Phillips's discourse is a simple world, a world of uncomplicated Manichaean dichotomies, a world of "us" and "them," the pure and the sordid. It is also an unreal world. Phillips speaks in terms of the ideal. His reliance on hyperbole and antithesis reflects the magnitude of worldly events and the relationship of competing forces as seen from a sacred perspective. His untempered, unqualified judgments are heroic leaps onto the cosmic plane. For all but a small band of radicals, however, the vision was not compelling. The Civil War was not fought to restore the kingdom of God, but for reasons that were patently political and economic.[110] Although the early nineteenth century was ostensibly a time of religious revival, the existence of the revivals themselves reveals an underlying doubt. The overwrought style of revivalism indicates a kind of spiritual desperation. It is possible that the increasingly fragile religious conceptions of the day could not support the stringent demands Phillips placed on their credence.

But to say of Phillips that the vision was ultimately not persuasive, like saying that the Second Great Awakening did not bring about the kingdom of God, fails to confront the phenomenon itself. Phillips did draw large crowds, and he did command, if not discipleship, at least a certain fascinated popularity.[111] If Phillips's claims were grandiose and extravagant, there is some sense in which the performance of them was not. What we need to discover is some link between the prophetic impulse and the literary and dramatic conventions of Phillips's time. The genre of melodrama is the obvious place to look.

Melodrama is a product of the notably secular French Revolution, whence it was exported to England and America.[112] Peter Brooks finds in melodrama "a degenerate form of the tragic—a form of the tragic, we might say, for a world in which there is no longer a tenable idea of the sacred."[113] It shares with prophetic judgment a basic impulse "to locate and to articulate the moral occult."[114] As a poetic form, the melodrama is reassuring; in the end justice is done. Melodrama testifies to the presence of meaning in the world; it addresses the void.[115] Brooks finds its genesis "in a world where the traditional imperatives of truth and ethics have been violently thrown into question, yet where the promulgation of truth and ethics, their instauration as a way of life, is of immediate, daily, political concern." [116] Far from being frivolous, the stark diametric oppositions in melodrama suggest its kinship to primitive mythologies. The integrity of the dramatic form in both depends on a resolution that attests to the continuing viability of justice. In the dramatic conflict lies the promise of a new order out of the midst of chaos. As Brooks has written, "If the world at the start of a melodrama seems charged with moral ambiguities . . . these ambiguities are not inherent to ethics. They are rather appearances to be penetrated, mysteries to be cleared up, so that the world may bathe in the stark moral lighting of manichaeism." [117]

Considered as melodrama, Phillips's discourse enjoys the advantage of immediate comprehensibility and total involvement of the audience, its passionate side, hissing and cheering the appropriate parties, as well as its rational and contemplative side. By engaging the feelings of the audience, melodrama forces them out of their torpor, forces them to confront the dramatic conflict and to align themselves. Melodrama provides the therapeutic function of catharsis, according to Brooks, less through the tragic mode whereby pity and fear are purged than through the "total articulation and vigorous acting out of the emotions." [118]

Brooks's notion of melodramatic catharsis might be abbreviated with the term "exhaustion." The early nineteenth century was saturated with the melodramatic imagination. Popular dramas included such titles as "Boston in Ashes, or Homeless Tonight" and "The Rat Catcher's Daughter." Temperance songs like "Father's a Drunkard and Mother is Dead" were unabashedly extravagant. Nor is *Uncle Tom's Cabin,* with beatific Little Eva, long-suffering Uncle Tom, and the heartless Simon Legree, a work generally noted for its subtle shadings. To the extent that Phillips spoke in the language of exaggeration bordering on hysteria, he was speaking in the language of his day, a moralistic din that must have reached a deafening level. Rather than arousing their audiences, nineteenth-century radicals may only have left them numb.

Beginning with the analog of prophecy and ending in melodrama may seem a rather precipitous descent. The two generic attributions may further seem to imply quite different valuations of Phillips's discourse. In the comparison of prophecy to melodrama, it may seem that the prophetic is cheapened and degraded, but melodrama is not so easily dismissed. Confronting the melodramatic in Balzac's *Illusions perdues,* Henry James found himself torn between seeing it as either "a magnificent lurid document or the baseless fabric of a vision." [119] Peter Brooks finds James's indecision "close to the center of the problem of melodrama." [120] James's opposition parallels our question on the nature of martyrdom, and it points to the problem of *ethos*. It is the problem of prophetic *ethos* that must next be attended to, leaving Phillips with the self-assessment of a melodramatic reformer hero created by one of Phillips's contemporaries, Nathaniel Hawthorne. Quitting his "cosey pair of bachelor-rooms—with a good fire burning in the grate, and a closet right at hand, where there was still a bottle or two in the champagne-basket and a residuum of claret in a box," Miles Coverdale left the pollution of the city to journey in a snowstorm to Blithedale where he and his compatriots were to form a community based on virtue and self-reliance that would set an example for the world. On this occasion, Hawthorne allows his protagonist to observe,

> The greatest obstacle to being heroic, is the doubt whether one may not be going to prove one's self a fool; the truest heroism is, to resist the doubt— and the profoundest wisdom, to know when it ought to be resisted, and when to be obeyed. Yet, after all, let us acknowledge it wiser, if not more sagacious, to follow out one's day-dream to its natural consummation, although, if the vision have been worth the having, it is certain never to be consummated otherwise than by a failure. And what of that! Its airiest fragments, impalpable as they may be will possess a value that lurks not in the most ponderous realities of any practicable scheme. They are not the rubbish of the mind. Whatever else I may repent of, therefore, let it be reckoned neither among my sins nor follies, that I once had faith and force enough to form generous hopes of the world's destiny—yes!—and to do what in me lay for their accomplishment.[121]

5

The Prophet's Call and His Burden

The Passion of Eugene V. Debs

And he said unto me, Son of man, I send thee to the children of Israel
to a rebellious nation that hath rebelled against me: they and their fathers have transgressed against me, *even* unto this very day. For *they are*
impudent children and stiffhearted. I do send thee unto them; and
thou shalt say unto them, Thus saith the Lord God. And they,
whether they will hear, or whether they will forbear (for they *are* a rebellious house,) yet shall know that there hath been a prophet among
them.   —Ezekiel 2:1–5

Then spake the priests and the prophets unto the princes and to all
the people, saying, This man *is* worthy to die; for he hath prophesied
against this city, as ye have heard with your ears. Then spake Jeremiah
unto all the princes and to all the people, saying, The Lord sent me to
prophesy against this house and against this city all the words that ye
have heard. Therefore now amend your ways and your doings, and
obey the voice of the Lord your God; and the Lord will repent him of
the evil that he hath pronounced against you. As for me, behold, I *am*
in your hand: do with me as seemeth good and meet unto you.
                                                      —Jeremiah 26:11–14

Ethos stands at the center of this study, as it should. The reception of any truths, the perception of the legitimacy of any crisis, depends
on a sense of the authenticity of the speaker's commitment. Kenneth Burke
would have recognized here a problem of motive, particularly that moment
at which motive intersects with authority.[1] Authorship must, in the case of
the prophet, rest with God. The unity of *ethos* and *logos* comes about in the
prophet's definition as servant to the message. I. A. Richards's idea that "to

be sincere is to act, feel and think in accordance with 'one's true nature' "[2] is illuminating in this context. The prophet's sincerity derives from the abolition of personal motive, from abnegation, so that "one's true nature" becomes synonymous with the divine message and one's *pathos* with the divine *pathos*.

Eugene Debs was, by most accounts, successful in presenting a compelling sincerity to his audiences. Historical appraisals of him are unanimous in their assessment of his significance. Sidney Lens claims that, in his time, "Debs was the most idolized labor leader America had produced."[3] Described by Charles Madison as "one of the best platform speakers of his time,"[4] Debs was, by most accounts, "a *speaker* in the great tradition of American public speaking."[5] Charles Lomas calls him "the most popular and effective orator" of the radical leaders of the day,[6] and Bert Cochran states flatly, "There is no question that he [Debs] was the most popular and effective socialist figure ever to appear in America."[7] One of the few figures formidable enough to warrant individual mention in a broad survey of America in the Gilded Age, Debs is described by Richard L. McCormick as "an indigenous American radical" and "a brilliant orator."[8] Though Ronald Lee and James Andrews are inclined to see in such assessments evidence of Debs's latter-day rehabilitation by liberal historians,[9] these encomia are based on and are completely consonant with those heard in Debs's own time. However he may have failed as a reformer and politician, the record does not indicate that Debs's *ethos* was ever in need of rehabilitation.

Eugene Debs and the Crisis of the New World

The crisis Debs addressed was the cataclysmic emergence of the modern world through the process we dispassionately label industrialism. In the fifty years following the Civil War, the United States was transformed from a preindustrial society of individual artisans, craftsmen, and yeoman farmers into the world's preeminent industrial power.[10] The change was pervasive; it left virtually no aspect of American life untouched, and its unrelenting newness was the source of "profound social and economic dislocations."[11]

Robert Wiebe has termed *fin de siècle* America "a society without a core"; it lacked the "national centers of authority and information" that might have given order to the changing world; there was no national community to replace the local communities that had been uprooted.[12] For

Herbert Gutman, this failure of coherence is best described as a failure of culture, the confrontation of obsolescent values with the conditions of the new society;[13] Richard Hofstadter called it the failure of "the agrarian myth." As an ideal, the agrarian myth, which was as much the property of urban dwellers as rural folk, celebrated the purity, virtue, and independence of the yeoman farmer, the American *par excellence*.[14] It was a moral compass that, as the population tended increasingly to concentrate itself in the cities and in industrial occupations, provided increasingly deviant readings. Edward Bellamy, in his enormously influential utopian novel *Looking Backward*, wrote of his time: "Pale and watery gleams, from skies thickly veiled by doubt and dread, alone lighted up the chaos of the earth."[15]

For most, the primary communal experience in late-nineteenth and early-twentieth-century America was a product of its industrial paternity, work. Those who gathered in the new and expanding urban centers were there on the promise of jobs. Great masses of people found a new common status in the label "worker" or "laborer." Industrial production required high degrees of uniformity in the behavior of workers: factories were run on scheduled shifts; workers were regulated by the time clock; the work itself was highly routinized; the once independent worker was, in Debs's military metaphor, "recruited into regiments, battalions and armies" with the work "subdivided and specialized."[16] New techniques of scientific management, based on a behavioristic psychology, were less concerned with the individual worker than with productive efficiency; workers were viewed as activity, that is, as machines.[17] "Why he's a factory hand—a *hand*, mind you, and he gets a dollar and a quarter a day when the factory is running. . . . Just a hand! A human factory hand!" exclaimed Debs in a characteristic metonymy borrowed from Dickens's *Hard Times*. "Think of a hand with a soul in it! . . . The working hand is what is needed for the capitalist's tool and so the human must be reduced to a hand. No head, no heart, no soul—simply a hand."[18] The requirements of industrial production posed a threat both to those who had grown up aspiring to realize the agrarian myth and celebrating the self-reliant individual and to the traditional work habits of European artisans.[19] In the American dialectic between freedom and responsibility, industrialism touted responsibility exclusively; autonomy was eclipsed by discipline.[20]

Debs and his fellow radicals set themselves against this inevitable march of progress. They were profoundly conservative in that they sought to restore the values that had characterized America's past. They were, at the same time, profoundly liberal in their exploitation of the individualistic and egalitarian side of America's traditions. They appealed, in Hofstadter's phrase, to an "ethos of responsibility"[21] against which they posited a venerable devil from the radical arsenal, the specter of slavery. As Debs bluntly phrased it,

> Since you have looked yourself over thoroughly, you realize by this time that, as a workingman, you have been supporting, through your craft unions and through your ballots, a social system that is the negation of your manhood.
>
> The capitalist for whom you work doesn't have to go out and look for you; you have to look for him and you belong to him just as completely as if he had a title to your body; as if you were his chattel slave.
>
> He doesn't own you under the law, but he does under the fact.[22]

Debs and the Trumpet of Judgment

Debs's portrait of the modern worker was one of weakness, servility, and dependence; the laborer under capitalism was a supplicant, not a man. Addressing his auditors in the second person plural, Debs was not merely making an analysis, he was passing judgment. One may imagine on the occasion of this speech in Chicago in 1905, Debs emphasizing his judgment with what the *Los Angeles Herald* termed his "ever-lifted indicting forefinger."[23] His prose is derisive in the extreme; he taunted the workers with their impotence: witness his references to ownership, chattel slavery, petitioning, considerations. In a 1920 campaign flyer, Debs declared, "Plain talk is assuredly needed, and I'm going to say what I think if I don't get a vote. . . . A few, a very few there are who think and act like men and women, but the overwhelming majority of us only imitate like monkeys and follow like sheep."[24]

The failure of manhood, virtue, was a favorite theme with Debs, one that he shared with other reformers of his day who were concerned with the decline of the individual.[25] In his "Declaration of Revolt," Debs wrote, "This appeal we now make in behalf of a working class reduced to slavery. Their rights have been violated, their organizations tied hand and foot, their press muzzled, their officials imprisoned, and their liberties all but destroyed. To submit to such outrages in a republic would be the basest cowardice and the rankest treason." Debs called for an assertion of virtue against self-abasement: "In the name of American manhood and womanhood, our self-respect, our fidelity to principle and our love of justice."[26] He always emphasized that the sufferings of the working class were a product of its own moral failings; he was comparatively uninterested in vilifying the capitalists. Though such excoriation may have been unpleasant for Debs's audiences to accept, it did contain the assurance that the power to change conditions was within their grasp.

At stake in Debs's judgment of the working class are two "charismatic terms"[27] that figured prominently in the rhetorics of the American Revolution and of Wendell Phillips: "freedom" and "slavery." In a new and unsettled set of social and economic relationships, Debs sought to restore moral clarity by defining new roles in terms of the old values; he attempted to replace indecision and confusion with the stark Manichaean oppositions of a perfectly ordered world. "Liberty is not a word of modern coinage," Debs told one of his audiences. "Liberty and slavery are primal words, like good and evil, right and wrong; they are opposites and coexistent."[28] Capitalists claimed that labor was a free agent with the capacity to drive its own bargains in the marketplace. Looking to the moral examples of the past, however, Debs found man under capitalism to be small and mean in comparison; he believed labor under capitalism renounced all independence and sold itself into slavery. "In capitalist society," claimed Debs, "the working man is not, in fact, a man at all; as a wage-worker, he is simply merchandise; he is bought in the open market the same as hair, hides, slat, or any other form of merchandise. The very terminology of the capitalist system proves that he is not a man in any sense of that term."[29]

Debs's antidote for slavery was self-assertion, a display of virtue. He never allowed the worker to escape responsibility for his or her condition; he consistently provided examples of those who had refused to capitulate to a degrading system. In an article on the Pullman strike, he wrote of the American Railway Union members, "They determined not to pollute their hands and dishonor their manhood by handling Pullman cars and contributing to the suffering and sorrow of their brethren and their wives and babies. And rather than do this they laid down their tools in a body, sacrificed their situations and submitted to persecution, exile and the blacklist; to idleness, poverty, crusts and rags, and I shall love and honor these moral heroes to my latest breath."[30] Debs made it clear that there were things that were more to be valued than material comfort; there were conditions under which it was better not to have a job. He was concerned with the state of men's souls, their honor, and he made it clear that this could only be compromised to the degree that the worker allowed it to be. As long as the worker preserved the ability to say no, he was not yet a slave.

Debs's language reveals its sources. It echoes Wendell Phillips and the

American Revolutionaries. By the late nineteenth century, there was a well-established and revered radical tradition in America. Whatever their status had been in their own day, history had made heroes of some of America's great protesters, and they formed an American canon, a basis for appeal to an American community. In celebrating their memories, Americans sought an identity and a set of common values. Eugene Debs was fully cognizant of this tradition and sought to identify with it as, for example, in his identification of labor's struggle with the ideals of the American Revolution.[31]

But it was not enough to ally with a successful doctrine—the capitalists, too, sought to identify themselves with the fulfillment of the American dream. Debs also drew a parallel between himself and the Revolutionaries in their role as rebels standing against the tide of public opinion. He had to discover what Nick Salvatore has called the "dual aspect in his culture's tradition: the American Revolution was not a static event, embossed in marble and praised each July. Its essential meaning demanded a prophetic call to each succeeding generation to renew and reinterpret that heritage."[32] Debs called for a renascence of Revolutionary virtue:

> Washington, Jefferson, Franklin, Paine and their compeers were the rebels of their day. When they began to chafe under the rule of a foreign king and to sow the seed of resistance among the colonists they were opposed by the people and denounced by the press. . . . But they had the moral courage to be true to their convictions, to stand erect and defy all the forces of reaction and detraction; and that is why their names shine in history and why the great respectable majority of their day sleep in forgotten graves.[33]

Debs praised the leaders of the Revolution, not for the system of government they left us or for the brilliance of their vision, but because they were men. They exemplified those values of courage, conviction, and self-assurance that Debs found lacking in the contemporary worker. "Washington, Jefferson, Franklin, Paine and their compeers" were Debs's measure of what his audiences should aspire to be.

From the martyrology of a young but vigorous civil religion, from the Bible, and from Marxism, Debs derived his self-evident truths. As with the American Revolutionaries and the radical abolitionists, there is an apparent paradox in holding as self- evident something that the majority of one's fellow citizens fail to see. But as Aileen Kraditor suggests, "When Debs and others proclaimed that the truth was so plain that a child could see it, they were not contradicting their claim to superior knowledge. They were expressing the absolute certainty and clear perception possessed by anyone who looked at society from the standpoint of Truth."[34] As Debs expressed it, "The rank and file of all unions, barring their ignorance, are all right. The working class as a whole is all right. Many of them are misguided, and stand in the light of their own interest."[35] The radical leader, like the prophet, resolves the ambivalence observed by Debs of the working class. The radical leader sees clearly the covenant and understands its consequences; it is not an obscure knowledge, but it is stringent in its demands.

There is a story that, some fifty years after receiving from a teacher a Bible with the inscription "Read and Obey," Debs retorted, "I never did either," but even a cursory reading of his speeches reveals the duplicity of his brave defiance.[36] His material abounds with biblical allusions and analogies, some developed to a degree indicating more than casual familiarity with his source. In a letter to Mr. Ed H. Evinger, dated August 29, 1895, for example, Debs spends eight paragraphs comparing his imprisonment for activities associated with the Pullman strike to Daniel's defiance of Darius.[37] Consistent with his emphasis on persons, the example of Christ played an important role in Debs's rhetoric, a theme to be examined at greater length in the following section.

Biblical communism, celebration of work, condemnations of usury, and other ideas cardinal to a Judeo-Christian culture also provided Debs with a hermeneutic frame for reading Marxist theories of materialist history and analyses of the class struggle. Indeed, there is a pronounced tendency in his discourse to make Marxist materialism continuous with the Christian ethic. The intentions of its creators notwithstanding, Marxism lends itself to such conceptions,[38] and Debs freely mixed the language of the Bible and the language of class conflict: "The hordes of hell are all against us, but the hosts of justice are on our side," he exclaimed. "We can win and must. Comrades, I am counting on you, each of you, as if our very lives were at stake—and they are."[39] Explaining how he became a socialist, Debs said, "I was to be baptized in socialism in the roar of conflict and I thank the gods for reserving to this fitful occasion the fiat, 'Let there be light!'—the light that streams in steady radiance upon the broad way to the socialist republic."[40]

Viewed as religion or as Marxist science, Debs's philosophy suggests those truths that, in the earlier examination of the rhetoric of the American Revolution, were termed *apodeictic*. Rhetorically, such truths are in the realm of demonstration or showing with all the attendant metaphors of wakefulness and sight. For Debs, failure to view society as he did was not a matter of disagreement, it was a failure of vision: "The interests of the millions of wage workers are identical, regardless of nationality, creed or sex, and if they will only open their eyes to this simple, self-evident fact, the greatest obstacle will have been overcome and the day of victory will draw near."[41] "It is our conviction that no workingman can clearly understand what Socialism means without becoming and remaining a Socialist," he declared. "It is simply impossible for him to be anything else and the only reason that all workingmen are not Socialists is that they do not know what it means."[42] "Can you not see it?" he queried on another occasion. "If not, I advise you to consult an oculist. There is certainly something the matter with your vision."[43] Referring to the fallacy of craft unions, Debs said, "The workingman, if his eyes are open, is bound to see that this kind of unionism is a curse and not a benefit to the working class."[44] "It is so simple that a child can see it. Why can't you?" Debs asked later in the same speech. "You can if you will think for yourselves and see for yourselves."[45]

Girded by the righteousness of absolute truth and the example of his radical forebears, Debs assumed an uncompromising, "unreasonable," rhetorical posture that scorned hedging and trimming as the weakness of the faithless and the misguided where a strict orthodoxy was what was needed: "There is but one thing you have to be concerned about, and that is that you keep foursquare with the principles of the international Socialist movement. It is only when you begin to compromise that trouble begins," he told his audience in the famous "Canton Speech." Then, in an allusion to Patrick Henry's "I know not what course others may take," he continued, "So far as I am concerned, it does not matter what others may say, or think, or do, as long as I am sure that I am right with myself and the cause."[46] On another occasion he echoed William Lloyd Garrison's "I will be as harsh as truth" as he assured his audience, "I shall be as candid as may be expected from a Socialist agitator."[47] Like Phillips before him, Debs rejected "the crooked and disreputable methods of ward-heeling and politicians"[48] in favor of "preserving inviolate the principles which quickened it [the Socialist Party] into life and now give it vitality and force," moving it forward "with dauntless determination to the goal of economic freedom."[49] In one of his most direct statements of his conception of his mission, Debs said,

> Time will tell and I can wait. I am not courting your flattery nor evading your blame. I am seeking no office; aspiring to no honors; have no personal ax to grind. But I have something to say to you and shall look straight into

your eyes while saying it. I shall speak the truth—as I see it—no more and no less, in kindness and without malice or resentment.

I should tell you what I think you ought to know though all of you turned against me and despised me.[50]

In these quotations is the fulfillment of Debs's criticism of the worker. He contrasts the servile attitude of the faithless to the temerity of radical heroes of the past and by speaking in the voice of Henry and Garrison, he seeks recognition of his own heroic stature. Debs presented himself as a model for the worker to emulate, a man of superior virtue claiming kinship to earlier radicals, committed to sacred principles, willing to suffer the consequences of his faith. It is an attitude of incalculable self-righteousness, one that cannot be supported without some claim to an extraordinary vision, a sacred calling. The stance taken by Debs, unless made to appear as the subordination of self to some higher cause, must be the most insufferable egotism.

The Construction of a Legend

The sketch of the prophetic *ethos* offered in chapter 3 argues that the office of the prophet must have its roots in an extraordinary (re)birth or conversion. With Debs, we find a highly developed conversion myth surrounding the Pullman strike and its aftermath. Debs's description of the Pullman strike contains the following extraordinary vision, comparable to the visions of the Old Testament prophets: "At this juncture there was delivered, from wholly unexpected quarters, a swift succession of blows that blinded me for an instant and then opened wide my eyes—and in the gleam of every bayonet and the flash of every rifle *the class struggle was revealed.*"[51] Following the Pullman strike, during a time of his removal from society, his sentence in Woodstock Jail, Debs claimed to have come to an understanding of socialism, an understanding that clarified his earlier vision and gave his subsequent crusade a consistency and direction it had heretofore lacked.[52] Of the experience at Woodstock Debs said,

It was here that socialism gradually laid hold of me in its own irresistible fashion . . . the writings of Kautsky were so clear and conclusive that I readily grasped not merely his argument, but also caught the spirit of his socialist utterance—and I thank him and all who helped me out of darkness into light. . . .

> It was at this time, when the first glimmerings of socialism were begin-
> ning to penetrate, that Victor L. Berger—and I have loved him ever since—
> came to Woodstock, as if a providential instrument, and delivered the first
> impassioned message of socialism I had ever heard—the very first to set the
> "wires humming in my system."[53]

The metaphors are highly visual, as are the accounts of calling related by
most of the Old Testament prophets. The vision is an extraordinary one,
and Debs insinuates that it overwhelmed him, the helpless receiver: it "laid
hold of me in its own irresistible fashion." The vision also involves an
infection of spirit and passion, creating a new person, and the transition
from darkness into light suggests the newness of life after the conversion. In
his account of Woodstock, Debs presents a classic account of consecration.

Charisma must be recognized to be validated. The supernatural quality
of the conversion, the rebirth, the vision, must be conceded before the
ethos can bear the weight of witness. The anointed figure must be able to
inspire discipleship or his ability to make claims on the sacred is severely
limited. There must be a community for whom the possibility of prophecy
exists. Among Debs's followers, the Woodstock conversion myth was
widely perpetuated. In *Eugene Victor Debs: A Tribute,* August Claessens
offered the following account:

> Debs came out of Woodstock a considerably changed man. Victor Berger
> visited Gene during his stay, talked with him, gave him books by Karl Marx,
> Karl Kautsky and others. Gene's eyes saw a new light. The whole economic
> struggle and political situation took on a new meaning for him. Gene
> emerged from Woodstock like a butterfly from its cocoon.[54]

Louis Kopelin, in a booklet published by the *Appeal to Reason* press, called
Woodstock Debs's "political awakening,"[55] and a later piece of hagiography
said of the Woodstock experience, "But the Debs who emerged from jail
was not the same man who had gone in. A new idea—that of socialism—
was beginning to take hold of him."[56] Upton Sinclair, including in his
novel *The Jungle* a cameo of a Debs speech, wrote of Debs that he "came
out of his cell a ruined man; but also he came out a Socialist."[57] Each of
these accounts stresses the ideas of death and rebirth, profound discontinuity
between life before and life after, the newness of the man, his transformation emerging "like a butterfly from its cocoon." In a special edition of the
National Rip-Saw, Kate Richards O'Hare quoted the same segment of
Debs's own account quoted above and added the following comment by
Debs's wife, Katherine Metzel Debs:

Victor Berger and Gene both say that Victor made a Socialist out of Gene, but really I am sure they are both mistaken. Berger didn't make a Socialist out of Gene; he just uncovered the Socialist that was already there. It was not books and pamphlets that made Gene a Socialist; God did that. Gene was just like me and millions of other people; he was a Socialist and didn't know it. Victor Berger just helped him to find himself, that was all.[58]

Although Katherine Debs is the only one to invoke explicitly considerations of divine intervention, it is clearly implied in the other accounts. An experience so radically discontinuous with the sensory experiences of everyday life always carries implications of the sacred. Debs's friend Stephen Marion Reynolds, in a biographical preface to a collection of Debs's writings and speeches, gave him a place with the "poets and orators, the true advocates that speak for the people, seem to see from some high mountain a vision in the lonely hours, when their eyes are unbound, the Deity passing by, leaving commands to be obeyed."[59]

Like so much else concerning Debs, the nature of his call to serve and to suffer is largely a mythological reconstruction. As part of his overall purpose, Nick Salvatore dissects the conversion myth and replaces it with a detailed picture of Debs's tortuous and often faltering path to his mission.[60] But the concern here is less with the historical Debs than with the rhetorically constructed one, and from this perspective it is clear that the conversion myth played an important role in the Debs *ethos*. Although Debs, like Amos, claimed not to be a prophet, the language of the following vision unmistakably has its roots in Old Testament prophecy:

Cheerless indeed would be the contemplation of such sanguinary scenes were the light of socialism not breaking upon mankind. The skies of the East are even now aglow with the dawn; its coming is heralded by the dispelling of shadows, of darkness and gloom. From the first tremulous scintillation that gilds the horizon to the sublime march to meridian splendor the light increases till in mighty flood it pours upon the world.

From out of the midnight of superstition, ignorance and slavery the disenthralling, emancipating sun is rising. I am not gifted with prophetic vision, and yet I see the shadows vanishing. I behold near and far prostrate men lifting their bowed forms from the dust. I see thrones in the grasp of decay; despots relaxing their hold upon scepters, and shackles falling, not only from the limbs, but from the souls of men.[61]

Debs understood clearly the claims he was making to supranormal vision. He denies the gift of charisma, *yet* he sees something more than is seen by the human eye. Through a linguistic association, he sought to assume the mantle of the prophetic *ethos* or the prophetic *pathos,* for in prophecy they seem to merge into one. Debs sought to represent himself as a participant in the divine, a bearer of *charism.* As Salvatore has noted,

> As he first explored new interpretations of familiar themes, Debs discovered that his culture's Protestant religious imagery was particularly suited to both his emerging new message and to his public personality. In the patriarchs of the Old Testament and in the angry Christ of the New, Debs found a prophetic model that legitimized his critique and demanded no apologies for frank, even harsh, pronouncements. In the process he touched for the first time his powerful charismatic appeal with audiences.[62]

Whatever the advantages and opportunities afforded by the charismatic appeal, it cannot be understood as an unalloyed gift. In order to be effective, *charism* must be perceived in its burdensome aspect. The rhetorical image Debs nurtured was one, not of pride, but of service. He presented himself as one who had been sacrificed to serve the needs of others. "He who has dared to voice the protest of the oppressed and downtrodden, has had to pay the penalty, all the way from Jesus Christ to Fred Warren. . . . I am in revolt against capitalism because I love my fellow men, and if I am opposing you it is for what I believe to be your good, and though you spat upon me with contempt I would still oppose you to the extent of my power."[63] Here Debs explicitly associates himself with those who were tortured and tormented in the service of their fellowman. The willingness to suffer the insult of being spat upon is the most extreme servility and recalls the example of Christ. The martyr theme is an important one in Debs's rhetoric. Ray Ginger claims that the idea was "featured in every Debs speech for twenty years."[64]

The ideas of suffering and sacrifice take several different forms in Debs's rhetoric. The most obvious are his accounts of his own privations on behalf of the cause. In an article entitled "Serving the Labor Movement," Debs responded to a decision by the Brotherhood of Locomotive Firemen and Enginemen not to invite him to address their convention:

> For twenty years I was a member of the organization represented by that convention. When I joined it I paid the admission fee of half the charter members, who had not the money of their own to pay. Five years later, when I was city clerk of Terre Haute and the brotherhood was bankrupt, deeply in debt and its magazine threatened with suspension, I was called upon to take

charge and I did so. I secured the entire debt with indorsed notes and spent most of my salary as city clerk in redeeming the organization from bankruptcy. The first two years all my spare hours, late in the night, every night in the week, I gave freely to my task and I paid out more for clerical assistance than the paltry salary amounted to.[65]

In 1902, in "How I Became a Socialist," he was similarly unabashed in recording his sacrifices at the altar of labor:

> For eighteen hours at a stretch I was glued to my desk reeling off the answers to my many correspondents. Day and night were one. Sleep was time wasted and often, when all oblivious of her presence in the still small hours my mother's hand turned off the light, I went to bed under protest.
>
> My grip was always packed; and I was darting in all directions. To tramp through a railroad yard in the rain, snow or sleet half the night, or till daybreak, to be ordered out of the roundhouse for being an "agitator," or put off a train, sometimes passenger, more often freight, while attempting to deadhead over the division, were all in the program, and served to whet the appetite to conquer.[66]

Debs's indulgent, sometimes mawkish prose served to inflate the extent of his sufferings to heroic proportions; it also served to confirm his manhood and to make him a model for those workers whose manhood had failed them. Debs presented himself as an embodiment of strength and courage in the face of adversity. More important, in his selflessness, he became everyman, the possibility inherent in everyman, a cynosure.

The inflation of his sacrifices allowed Debs a second vehicle for the expression of his passion—identification with a martyred canon. Debs's concern with past martyrs was second only to that of the Roman Catholic Church, and he summoned their specters large before his audiences. Jesus Christ, Joan of Arc, Elijah Lovejoy, and John Brown all gave their lives for a cause, and Debs brought them together as part of a continuous tradition.[67] The celebration of martyrs was important for an appeal so heavily based on *ethos;* they served as realizations of virtue, the historical vindication of those who had suffered for a cause. In "The Issue," Debs put it this way:

> Do you know, my friends, it is so easy to agree with the ignorant majority. It is so easy to make the people applaud an empty platitude. It takes some courage to face that beast called the Majority, and tell him the truth to his teeth! Some men do so and accept the consequences of their acts as becomes men, and they live in history—every one of them. I have said so often, and

I wish to repeat it on this occasion, that mankind have always crowned their oppressors, and they have as uniformly crucified their saviors, and this has been true all along the highway of the centuries.[68]

In many eulogies to contemporary labor martyrs, Debs attempted to link them to this sacred tradition, to claim for them that conduct that "becomes men," to make of them paragons of virtue.[69] More important for our purposes is the fact that, by implication, Debs also attempted to link himself to this tradition, thus his attentions to the suffering of others also served to draw attention to his own sacrifices. After praising "Old John Brown" for his "example of moral courage of single-hearted devotion to an ideal for all men and for all ages," Debs asked, "Who shall be the John Brown of Wage-Slavery?" It was no one if not Debs himself.[70]

Debs did not have to await history's verdict on his own life. In 1908, a story consuming nearly the entire first page of the second section of the *Terre Haute Tribune* began and ended with the observation that "a prophet is not without honor save in his own country."[71] Such encomia were common. "The man that comes crying a message in the wilderness and pointing to the inevitable farther heights to which humanity must ascend, meets misunderstanding, insult and rejection," wrote Stephen Reynolds, "but he is 'The Darling of Tomorrow,' when the heights are reached and the risen races run to mark the fields of battle with the pathetic monuments of regret and grief."[72] John Spargo compared Debs to Joan of Arc listening to "unseen voices, . . . seeing visions where other men saw only a black void. . . . He obeyed the voices," wrote Spargo. "He spoke in the Assembly of the Law-makers—spoke for Labor and against Labor's wrongs. He spoke for the Dumb, for the Doomed and Damned. He spoke their protest and their curse. He spoke for Childhood and for Motherhood—spoke for the Makers of Laws. And when he spoke they answered with the howl of the Beast."[73] After Debs's imprisonment in 1919, Ruth Le Prade wrote a particularly worshipful piece entitled simply "The Martyrdom." In her essay, Le Prade calls forth some of Debs's favorite revered saints: "Jeanne d'Arc," Christ, Socrates, and John Brown. Of Debs's entry into prison, she wrote, "Such is the spirit God gives to his chosen ones, fearlessly they stand and speak the Truth; they tremble not at the scourge, the gaol, the cross; and when the hour comes, they walk unto the doom man has prepared for them, with a *smile!*"[74] Of course the idolatry did not end with Debs's death. A 1935 publication of the Socialist Party concerning Debs's resistance to the First World War carried an advertisement for a twenty-minute "nonflammable" film with the title *Eugene V. Debs—Labor's Martyr*.[75]

Debs's third vehicle for proclaiming his martyrdom lay in the rhetoric of acting out, a *characteristic* of prophetic discourse. It is widely noted that Debs was a kindly and generous man, and stories of him giving away watches, overcoats, money, not to mention his time and concern, are legion.[76] His most dramatic sacrifices were his two prison sentences, the first after the failure of the so-called "Pullman strike" in 1895 and the second, in 1919–21, for his dissent against U. S. involvement in the First World War. In describing the significance of Debs's jail term after the Pullman strike, Salvatore provides some insight into the function of the Debs myth in general. When Debs emerged from Woodstock Jail, the veneration he enjoyed was not the veneration of a successful strike leader; the strike had been an unqualified failure, and Debs's American Railway Union was in ruin. What Debs had become, according to Salvatore, was "a national symbol": "Due to his recent activities, Debs served to focus and, after a fashion, to direct the anger many Americans felt. In turn, he also drew a strength from this role that largely accounts for his appeal over the coming three decades."[77]

It is probably inevitable, given the strong themes of martyrdom in his rhetoric and his public acts of sacrifice that Debs should have been compared to Christ—the passion of Christ, as noted earlier, being the quintessential passion myth in Western thought. Salvatore finds the first overt comparison in a statement by J. A. Wayland, a close friend of Debs and the publisher of the *Appeal to Reason,* after Debs's release from Woodstock Jail. But as Salvatore notes, although it was the first such comparison, "it certainly would not be the last; . . . for Debs, as for many of his followers, only a thin line remained between the man and the symbol."[78] It was the author of *Elmer Gantry* who wrote to Upton Sinclair that Debs was the "Christ spirit,"[79] while on another occasion Lewis merely proclaimed Debs a saint.[80] A 1921 letter to Debs from Harriet Curry, daughter of Debs's purported lover Mabel Curry, begins "Dearest Gene—Mother says I am to call you this instead of the "Mister" [.] At first it seemed disrespectful or something, until I reflected that I wouldn't think of saying 'Mr. Jesus,' were I to meet him!"[81] That same year Kate Richards O'Hare, under the heading "Gesthemane," wrote, "For forty years Gene Debs served the working class of the United States as Jesus of Nazareth served the working class of Judea. Priest, architect and builder he renewed the faith in men that

had been crushed by poverty and social injustice."[82] "Like Christ," wrote
Louis Kopelin, " 'the common people heard him gladly.' "[83] Walter Hurt
was able to write without a trace of irony: "Of Debs it may advisedly be
said that no other man in history so approximates the attributes of Jesus of
Nazareth. In his all-understanding, all-forgiving, all-suffering nature Debs
closely resembles the reputed character of the divine Proletaraire of Pales-
tine."[84] As a final example, there is the widely reported incident from a
Debs speech at Carnegie Hall in 1908, where a woman suddenly leapt up
and proclaimed, "There he is, there he is! Gene Debs, not the missing link
but the living link between God and man. . . . Here is the God consciousness come down to earth."[85]

The comparison between Debs and Christ was nourished by Debs's
rhetoric and his deeds for the rest of his career. It therefore provides a
context from which to view his trial and conviction for violation of the
Espionage Act. The comparisons are almost painfully patent, and one
suspects, calculatedly so. Debs had no witnesses in his defense, did not
contest the prosecution's account of the speech in question, only their
definition of it, denied his ability to retract what he had said, and resigned
himself to the possibility that he might "be consigned, perhaps to the end
of my life, in a felon's cell." In his "Address to the Jury," he reflected on his
fate:

> When great changes occur in history, when great principles are involved, as
> a rule the majority are wrong. The minority are usually right. In every age
> there have been a few heroic souls who have been in advance of their time,
> who have been misunderstood, maligned, persecuted, sometimes put to
> death. Long after their martyrdom monuments were erected to them and
> garlands woven for their graves.[86]

Like Christ, Debs was found guilty. His "Statement to the Court," delivered
at his sentencing, opens with what are probably his most quoted lines:

> Your Honor, years ago I recognized my kinship with all living being, and I
> made up my mind that I was not one bit better than the meanest on earth. I
> said then, and I say now, that while there is a lower class, I am in it, while
> there is a criminal element I am of it, and while there is a soul in prison, I
> am not free.[87]

As a final parallel, Debs forgave his betraying Judas.[88]

Debs was sixty-three years old when he entered prison, but he was
probably perceived as older. Since as early as 1904, Debs had not been in
good health.[89] His schedule had been one "of exhausting, almost orgiastic

speaking tours followed by weeks of collapse in bed," to use Irving Howe's description.[90] The evidence suggests that, however much Debs resented being thought of or referred to as an old man, he was, in fact, perceived and referred to that way.[91] At Debs's trial, remarking on his address to the jury, one of the Justice Department agents reportedly said to a member of the press: "You've got to hand it to the old man. He came through clean."[92] The year of Debs's imprisonment, Upton Sinclair wrote, "The United States has an old man in prison in the Federal Penitentiary of Atlanta. The government regards this old man as a common felon, and treats him as such; shaves his head, puts a prison suit upon him, feeds him upon prison food, and locks him in a steel-barred cell fourteen consecutive hours out of each twenty-four."[93] Debs's age and his apparent frailty served to make him appear harmless and to magnify his suffering. His presidential campaign in 1920 served to spotlight further the fact of his imprisonment. Campaign posters and buttons depict a gaunt, drawn visage in prison attire standing before bars with the inscription, "For President, Convict No. 9653."

With his imprisonment for the second time, the Debs legend achieved a predictable denouement; Debs became Christ crucified. Witter Bynner, a poet currently enjoying renewed attention, wrote the following verse which is typical of much of the sentiment expressed at the time:

> *9653*
> (TO E. V. D.)
> Nine six five three,
> Numbers heard in heaven,
> Numbers whispered breathlessly,
> Mystical as seven,
> Numbers lifted among stars
> To acclaim and hail
> Another heart behind the bars,
> Another God in jail,
> Tragic in their symmetry,
> Crucified and risen,
> Nine six five three,
> From Atlanta Prison.[94]

The comparison, like much of the rhetoric which inspired it, was, of course, hyperbolic. Debs did not lose his life for his beliefs as had Christ and many of the rest of Debs's martyred canon, and, although no one would deny that his times in prison were times of real suffering for him, it is true that Debs, by his own admission, "was never personally mistreated" while in prison: "On the other hand, during my prison years I was treated uniformly with a peculiar personal kindliness by my fellow prisoners, and not infrequently by officials."[95] In fact, in light of historical accounts, Debs's denial that any special favors were ever accorded him seems disingenuous.[96]

Of course, to Debs's disciples it made no difference that his claims to Christhood were greatly exaggerated; they embraced him as their Messiah. As Walter Hurt wrote, "Debs is also intrinsically a hero. None can be a hero or a martyr by design, any more than one can design one's own birth. And it is not necessary to die in order to be either. To insist otherwise were tantamount to declaring that death makes the poet. The fact is that heroism and martyrdom consist in the process of living, and death ends them just as it extinguishes genius."[97]

But to the vast majority of workers for whom Debs claimed to suffer, the image was not persuasive. Most Americans at the turn of the century failed to see industrial employ as slavery, so they could not see Debs as their savior. Progressive reformers like Theodore Roosevelt achieved great popularity precisely because their temperate ideas on reform were viewed as mitigating the appeal of radical programs like socialism.[98] As Samuel Hays has put it, "Twentieth-century Americans slowly learned how to live with a new industrial system that they could not and *did not choose* to destroy."[99]

Saint Gene

We have names for such people as Debs appears to have been: those who devote themselves to flailing at invincible enemies we call quixotic, and those who voluntarily bring suffering upon themselves we term masochistic; both terms suggest pathological states. No one in his right mind would choose inevitable failure or suffering, we contend, but it is precisely the element of choice that Debs wished to deny through his suffering. Presenting himself as a prophetic figure, Debs spoke the language of commitment and duty.

"If I have criticized, if I have condemned, it is because I believed it to be my duty," said Debs to the jury in 1918.[100] In the Canton speech, he told his audience that the socialist movement "has taught me how to serve—a lesson to me of priceless value . . . to realize that, regardless of nationality, race, creed, color or sex, every man, every woman who toils, who renders useful service, every member of the working class without exception, is my comrade, my brother and sister—and that to serve them and their cause is the highest duty of my life."[101] Consistently in his speeches accepting his party's nomination for office, Debs spoke of it as a duty that had been imposed on him: "I can simply say that obedient to your call I respond. Responsive to your command I am here. I shall serve you to the limit of my capacity."[102] Debs's expressed reluctance to assume the burdens of duty is offset by his resignation to duty: "Personally I did not wish the nomination. It came to me unsought. It came as summons to service and not as a personal honor."[103] "The wrongs in labor I knew from having experienced them, and the irresistible appeal of these wrongs to be righted determined my destiny," he claimed. "The high ambition and controlling purpose in my life has been the education, organization and emancipation of the working class. I began to speak and write for them for the same reason. In this there was no altruism, no self-sacrifice, only duty. I could not have done otherwise."[104] Especially in the line regarding the "controlling purpose" of his life, Debs reflects the idea that he was born (or reborn) to serve the cause; amidst the chaos of the industrial revolution in America, Debs's life had meaning.

Debs saw himself as immersed in the suffering of the working class, and he viewed himself as a providential instrument for the relief of that suffering. When serving as an instrument of divine will, the speaker disappears— in Debs's words, he is reduced to a tongue. There is no longer a self-interested ego to engage in subterfuge. The subjective element claims to have absented itself. The message claims to be pure object, sacred Truth.[105] Furthermore, it is the same truth the audience would see if they were not blinded. So to the extent that the Truth concerns the suffering of those in the audience, the speaker becomes representative of them in their true state. It is, in Northrop Frye's description, "the total empathy between poet and audience which arises when the poet is not so much a teacher of his audience or a spokesman for them, as both at once."[106] Insofar as Debs was not blind and was consecrated, he was *in extremis,* but insofar as he represented the true state of the working class, he was in a sense a manifestation of the will of that class. As Debs himself put it, "The working man is the only man in whose presence I take off my hat. As I salute him, I honor myself."[107] "I am simply the tongue of the working class, making this appeal from the working class to the working class." His art of oratory, he maintained, came from consecrating himself to a great cause. "I simply had to speak and make people understand."[108] In another speech, he phrased the sentiment this way: "The Socialist movement is of the working class itself; it is from the injustice perpetrated upon, and the misery suffered by this class that the movement sprang, and it is to this class it makes it appeal. It is the voice of awakened labor arousing itself to action." [109]

As a charismatic leader, Debs also attempted to extend the divine imperative to the movement he led. It is significant that he so often spoke of the "mission" or the "historic mission" of the Socialist Party. [110] As Kraditor has noted, "The concept of mission implies that the purpose of an organization is not determined by its members." This means that the purpose of the movement cannot be invented or determined by the participants, but must be discovered. [111] In other words, the purpose of the movement is not of the participants; it is not reducible to terms of human will; it is separate, sacred; there is a general calling present of which Debs is only an example. Debs had no doubt that in the socialist movement the workingman would find his "true place, and though he be reduced to rags, and tormented with hunger pangs, he will bear it all and more, for he is battling for a principle, he has been consecrated to a cause and he cannot turn back." [112] In the socialist movement there was a call to duty for the workingmen of America and the world. [113]

Duty is the inescapable refrain in Debs's rhetoric. Like Martin Luther, Debs agitated; he could do no other; it was an example of manly self-assertion. Debs tried to ensure that every time the workingman closed his eyes to his duty he would see the image of Debs bearing the cross of labor. As a suffering servant he transcended the role of the individual speaker; he became universal, symbolic. And religious symbols have their power, according to Mircea Eliade, in that they convey their message even when no longer consciously understood in every part. "For a symbol speaks to the whole human being and not only to the intelligence." [114]

In conceiving Debs as symbol, we appreciate the importance of the myth that he helped to foster. Debs's suffering stood as both a measure and a manifestation of the strength of his faith. [115] It was also intended to serve, as with the discourse of the Old Testament prophets, as a pathetic antidote to the prevailing *a-pathos*. Ignoring requirements for detailed, workable proposals, Debs, through his public suffering, sought to make that suffering real to America and to make it the center of debate. A New Orleans reporter once tried to make sense out of the contradictory impressions garnered in attending a Debs speech. On the one hand, the reporter noted that the full audience "listened with intensity and applauded with passion," but on the other hand, he also sensed that there were few converts to socialism in the room when the speech was over. He wrote, "It was not so much that they cared for what he said, but that they cared that he cared for them—if this does not confuse the point."[116]

Debs's rhetoric was a rhetoric of sympathy, an idea associated with the rhetorical theory of Adam Smith, a product of the same time and the same school of thought as George Campbell. And while it is unlikely that Debs ever studied Smith or Campbell, he did take as his models those orators who had been shaped by the writings of the Scottish Common Sense philosophers of the late eighteenth century, orators like Wendell Phillips and Robert Ingersoll. Debs entered the twentieth century with the rhetorical conventions of the nineteenth.

Today, Debs's speeches seem somewhat quaint, a bit naive. Irving Howe has termed them "wilted flowers from the garden of nineteenth-century eloquence."[117] As a suffering servant, Debs produced a highly personal, highly ethical rhetoric, a rhetoric unabashed at its own *pathos,* a rhetoric often at odds with what Richard Gregg has noted is "the idealized kind of problem discussion we like to see on the public stage."[118] Gregg sees in much of this discourse an expressive function, an assertion of the self. But we are years removed from Debs's world of high collars and straw hats for summer, perhaps too far removed to consider seriously his claim of selflessness; our cynicism smiles at the idea that Debs would suffer as the representative of a class. We deny the altruism in favor of an a fortiori ulterior motive. In his own time, however, Debs's sincerity was almost unquestioned. Even those who could not accept the programs praised the *ethos.* Stephen Reynolds wrote of the situation in Terre Haute that "many here would like to hang his ideas, but the man, the strong personality, the gentleness and cordiality of his greeting when he meets his neighbors and fellow-citizens, disarm all prejudice."[119] On the occasion of Debs's death, an article in the *Terre Haute Post* related the following anecdote:

The late Anton Hulman, senior, founder of the Hulman company, one of the largest wholesale grocery concerns in Indiana, was attending a meeting of coffee growers in New York. One morning at one of the sessions a coffee wholesaler mentioned the fact that Debs was in jail in Chicago for his part in the Pullman railroad strike.

"That is where he ought to be," said this man. "Such a wild-eyed menace ought to be hanged."

Hulman was on his feet in an instant and in his quiet way said:

"I have known Gene Debs since he was a tiny boy. I was a lifelong friend of his father and no better man did I ever know. I think if you knew Eugene Debs as I know him you would neither say that he ought to be in jail nor that he ought to be hanged. I do not agree with all that Gene Debs says or thinks. But I would trust him with every dollar I had."[120]

The acceptance of the Debs *ethos* and the simultaneous rejection of his social vision was a characteristic response among Debs's opponents. Arthur Schlesinger, Jr., has noted that "Men and women loved Debs even when they hated his doctrines. His sweetness of temper, his generosity and kindliness, his sensitivity to pain and suffering, his perfect sincerity, his warm, sad smile and his candid gray eyes were irresistible."[121] Walter Hurt, eschewing hero worship in the socialist ranks, nonetheless recognized that the value of Debs's personality to the socialist movement was "inestimable": "He is a loadstone of popularity that attracts to Socialism thousands whom its philosophy would at first repel."[122]

The Debs legend does not stand careful scrutiny—no mortal life could sustain the weight of adulation that Debs's admirers have lavished on him— but to ask this is to misunderstand the function and value of the legend. However fragile and desperate for reassurance the man behind the myth, he projected an image that was strong and generous; the emphasis on the ethical side of persuasion renewed a confidence in the capacity of the individual human being to shape his world. Like his radical predecessors, Debs was concerned with possibilities, but his reforms always had a human scale. Walter Hurt tied Debs to the vanishing tradition of Emerson when he wrote, " 'Self-trust,' says Emerson, 'is the essence of heroism.' Debs believes in himself because he believes in mankind, of which he is a part."[123]

There is a very real sense, of course, in which it was already too late; the agrarian myth with all its overtones of self-reliance simply failed to reflect the realities of the modern world. The year after Debs's death in 1926, John Dewey published *The Public and Its Problems* in which he wrote, "The Great Society created by steam and electricity may be a society, but it is no community. The invasion of the community by the new and relatively impersonal and mechanical modes of combined human behavior is the outstanding fact of modern life."[124] Debs's insistence on virtue, looking backward as it did to the melodramatic language of Balzac, Dickens, and Hugo, all of whom Debs adored, could not compel assent in the world of *This Side of Paradise*. To say, however, that Debs was too late or that he opposed the inevitable does not make his effort less laudable or the ideals he held less desirable. Debs attempted to revivify a myth that had helped create community in America, and in doing so he attempted to give

Dewey's lost public a common voice. Of course, Debs did not understand his crusade as a reactionary one; for him the values he espoused were universal and eternal.

One measure of the appeal of Debs's atavism is the degree to which the Debs legacy has survived even today. In 1955, on the centennial of Debs's birth, Norman Thomas wrote, "One of the purposes of a centennial celebration of Gene Debs' birth is to remind ourselves of a unique human being, one of those rare spirits whose life on earth was an outstanding blessing to his fellows by reason of what he was as well as by reason of what he did." [125] More recently, David A. Shannon wrote,

> Dead for half a century, Debs continues to be the nation's foremost radical hero, the most popular leader of a Marxist movement, the Left's most beloved personality. Neither his successor as leader of the Socialist Party, Norman Thomas, nor any of the Communist leaders since World War I, nor the often colorful and sometimes bizarre characters of the New Left of the 1960's and early 1970's even approach Debs as a radical heroic figure. [126]

Nelson Algren gave Debs a place alongside Theodore Dreiser and John Peter Altgeld as one of "the great Lincolnian liberals, the ones who stuck out their stubborn necks in the ceaseless battle between the rights of Owners and the rights of Man, the stiff-necked wonders who could be broken but couldn't be bent." [127] As late as 1976, the Socialist Party was still prominently billing itself as "the party of Eugene Debs"; the Eugene V. Debs local of the United Steelworkers, a local for builders at the Pullman railroad car plant and one of the early locals in the CIO organization, was until 1985, three years after the closing of the plant, a living tribute to Debs and his vision of industrial unionism—workers standing up for themselves. [128] Radio station WEVD in New York City continues to broadcast programming in Yiddish and in the languages of recent immigrant groups, serving populations very much like those Debs sought to serve in his lifetime, and the Eugene V. Debs Foundation, which purchased the Debs home in Terre Haute in 1962 and has restored it as a library and memorial, is dedicated to perpetuating Debs's vision.

Debs had an appreciation for the adoration of posterity; his emphasis on the afterlife of martyrs in the memories of the people attests to this and there is no question but that Debs hoped to be honored in the same way, to have "monuments built" and "garlands woven" for his grave rather than face the mortality of the "respectable but forgotten" grave of anonymity. Louis Untermeyer suggested that Debs's garland would be a crown of thorns,[129] and Debs would surely have taken comfort in the words of Isaiah, often read as a prognostication of Christ:

> He is despised and rejected of men; a man of sorrows, and acquainted with grief; and we hid as it were *our* faces from him; he was despised, and we esteemed him not. Surely he hath borne our griefs, and carried our sorrows: yet we did esteem him stricken, smitten of God, and afflicted. . . . He shall see of the travail of his soul, *and* shall be satisfied: by his knowledge shall my righteous servant justify many; for he shall bear their iniquities. Therefore will I divide him *a portion* with the great, and he shall divide the spoil with the strong; because he hath poured out his soul unto death: and he was numbered with the transgressors; and he bare the sin of many, and made intercession for the transgressors.[130]

Part II

6

The Word in Darkness

We see not our signs: *there* is no more any prophet: neither is *there* among us any that knoweth how long.   —Psalms 74:9

Son of man, prophesy against the prophets in Israel that prophesy, and say thou unto them that prophesy out of their own hearts, Hear ye the word of the Lord; Thus saith the Lord God; Woe unto the foolish prophets, that follow their own spirit, and have seen nothing! O Israel, thy prophets are like the foxes in the deserts.   —Ezekiel 13:2–4

And I heard, but I understood not: then said I, O my Lord, what shall be the end of these *things?* And he said, Go thy way, Daniel for the words *are* closed up and sealed till the time of the end. Many shall be purified, and made white, and tried; but the wicked shall do wickedly: and none of the wicked shall understand; but the wise shall understand.   —Daniel 12:8–10

Among the ways that prophetic rhetoric distinguishes itself from the Graeco-Roman model is its transgression of classical genres. As the law in ancient Hebrew culture was given, the deliberative function of prophecy may be truncated. Still, there is a strong element of future concern, characteristic of deliberation, of the consequences of adhering or not adhering to the law, and the *rîb* pattern at the center of prophecy provides a clear judicial element. But even more essential than this judicial function, it might be argued, is the epideictic function of prophecy, not only in the celebration and encouragement of common values, but in the sense that epideictic both depends upon and recreates community.[1] Indeed, it is only in the presence of a viable community that the declaratory impulse in prophecy has adequate credibility to insist on engagement. In the absence of such a community, it is easily dismissed as lunatic rant. Prophecy is, in James Boyd White's terms, a language, and it is by languages, "shared conceptions of the world, shared manners and values, shared resources and expectations and procedures for speech and thought," he insists, "that communities are in fact defined and constituted."[2]

It is not necessary to become embroiled in the debates over the nature and precise temporal location of postmodernity to borrow from that body of literature certain insights about the decay of community in contemporary America. Barry Smart notes that, over and above the fractiousness collected under postmodern scholarship, "there appears to be a shared sense that significant cultural transformations have been taking place in Western societies during the period since the end of the Second World War and further that the term 'postmodernism' may be appropriate, for the time being at least, to describe some of the implied shifts in 'sensibility, practices and discourse formations.' "[3] There is also considerable agreement that these "cultural transformations" involve dislocation, alienation, uncertainty, and atomization. Smart describes postmodern forms of sociology as forms "which place emphasis upon the tenuous, negotiable, meaningful, interpretive, and sociolinguistically constituted character of social life, upon the fragile 'tacit understandings' which constitute the insecure foundation of social life."[4] David Harvey is more bluntly critical of these same tendencies, seeing not a reconstitution of social life, but the destruction of its possibility:

> Postmodernist philosophers tell us not only to accept but even to revel in the fragmentations and the cacophony of voices through which the dilemmas of the modern world are understood. Obsessed with deconstructing and delegitimating every form of argument they encounter, they can end only in condemning their own validity claims to the point where nothing remains of any basis for reasoned action.[5]

"There is, in postmodernism," he notes elsewhere, "little overt attempt to sustain continuity of values, beliefs, or even disbeliefs."[6]

Postmodernism is a reaction to the disintegration of the Enlightenment project of the grand narrative, the regularity of prediction and control, and the stability of common sense. The American Revolutionaries, Wendell Phillips, and Eugene Debs were able to capitalize on a common belief structure, the roots of society in their respective times. Their radicalism, like that of the Old Testament prophets, was essentially reactionary. Challenging not root beliefs but contemporary understandings, they demanded a realization of orthodoxy through the excision of corrupt practice.[7] But the career of Eugene Debs, I have claimed, marked the end of an era. Already in Debs's time there were the unmistakable signs of a dissolution of consensus in American society, a trend catalyzed by the First and Second World Wars. Postmodernism is a term that suggests the unraveling of that faith that sustained radical thought for the Revolutionaries, Phillips, and Debs, an abrogation of the "vital center," the decline of the common language necessary not only to consensus, but to apostasy as well.[8] Postmodernism is the recognition of the fragmentation of the national community against which the radical seeks definition; it is impossible to stand in opposition to fog.[9] As Hal Foster expresses it, "Pluralism is a condition that tends to remove, art, culture and society in general from the claims of criticism and change."[10] Nor is what President Jimmy Carter termed our "national malaise" merely the fashionable fetish of sociologists, literary critics, and philosophers, indulged in recondite treatises in obscure journals. Postmodernism is not, as David Harvey puts it, "an autonomous artistic current. . . . Its rootedness in daily life is one of its most patently transparent features."[11] It reveals itself, however inarticulately, even in our most ostensibly "mindless," low culture entertainments.[12]

In such an environment, the prophet is not possible. Prophecy is an ineluctably social phenomenon. It is inconceivable that one should serve as God's spokesperson in a world where God, the common bond, the *religio,* is dead.[13] But the impulses that give rise to prophecy, the need for authority, judgment, and meaning, are tenacious. The appetites of the ersatz *polis* do not disappear in a postmodern, postreligious world. The competition for and the need to apportion scarce resources, the substance of politics, continues, as does the need for forms of discourse through which these decisions can be negotiated. Even more important than the persistence of political necessities, the desire for cohesion, for unity, for community does not die either.

A theory of prophetic discourse in American radical reform, if it is to have genuine utility, should provide critical touchstones by which prophets can be judged against their professions and nonprophets can be judged against the prophetic standard. It should be illuminating not only of those discourses that conform to its outlines, but should also provide a perspective against which to read discourses that fall under the traditional shadow of prophecy but that lack the social-rhetorical resources to sustain the convergence of speaker, audience, and sacred truth that prophecy demands. In other words, a theory of prophetic discourse should illuminate, and provide some means for evaluating, the dynamic when prophecy fails. This is the purpose of the three case studies here in part II. Three broad rhetorical responses to the need for judgment in a world without God are illustrated:

apocalyptic, the attempt to carry forward the prophetic authority in a world where God is no longer hegemonic; poetic, the attempt to carry forward the appearance of prophetic authority by an imitation of its outward form; and thoroughly secular rhetoric, the capitulation to the postmodern world and the abandonment of the prophetic.

Apocalypticism

Stephen O'Leary is certainly correct to argue that anomie is inadequate as an explanation of apocalyptic, even the presence of apocalyptic, much less its particular shape and logic,[14] and it is certainly the case that there have been important displays of apocalyptic discourse in America prior to the conclusion of the Second World War, though many scholars, including, at times, O'Leary himself, consistent with their purposes, have not bothered to distinguish apocalyptic from prophetic, collapsing both under the rubric "millennialism."[15] Yet it is equally true, I will argue, that the exhaustive anomie characteristic of the postmodern era vitiates the possibility of prophecy and makes tenable the move of apocalyptic to the political main stage in a way unprecedented in American history. Never, before the 1950s, was an apocalyptic rhetoric able to define the national agenda, not so long as a viable civil religion could maintain the ultimate triumph of the national will. My reading of American history is entirely consistent with those who find the philosophical roots of the postmodern disintegration of the social fabric in the late nineteenth century,[16] as the conclusion of the previous chapter suggests and as subsequent discussion will elaborate, but that reading also indicates an obstinate belief in the national covenant that gave definition to a people and provided a platform for radical dissent. The abolitionists and Eugene Debs deeply influenced the national conversation, leaving their imprint on their respective rhetorical epochs and on subsequent history, in ways that O'Leary's Millerites could never aspire to. As an instrument of definition, the national covenant marginalized those who did not operate within its fundamental assumptions.

Paramount among those assumptions is the positive outcome of history. The putative view of the jeremiad as a speech of woe notwithstanding, prophetic religion is profoundly optimistic. It was, after all, a vehicle of reform among the Jews of the Old Testament, and in American radicalism it has been consistently associated with perfectionist thinking and hopes for the millennium.[17] In the Old Testament, the optimism of prophecy was sustained by faith in the omnipotence of Yahweh as the sole creator of heaven and earth and the controller of history. The belief in a single omnipotent God as the author of history ensured a unity of motive in the world and allowed the coherence of vision evident in prophecy; the essential monotheism of the Old Testament did not allow that Yahweh should coexist with deities of sufficient power to exercise effective influence in opposition to His justice.[18] In the cosmology of the Old Testament, there were only two powers, God's will and human will, the latter a gift of God, malleable, and finally nugatory. Human will influenced but could not control the course of history. In such a world, human beings made their fate in accordance with the terms of the covenant.

To emphasize the optimism of prophecy is not to deny the gravity of the threat in the prophetic message. But as the product of a loving God, the threat was intended to instruct, to discipline, and was always conditional. It was posed in the hope that retribution might be averted. The "demonic" side of Yahweh might punish His people or test them, but only in accordance with the revealed truths of the covenant, the knowledge of God revealed to all but the willfully blind. For Yahweh, unique among ancient gods, was a moral god; He acted not on caprice but in accordance with established principle.[19] As evidenced in earlier chapters, the rules of the covenant bound Yahweh as much as they did the peoples of Israel and Judah. Implicit in the threat was a restatement of boundaries and order. However unwelcome the prophetic word may have been in other respects, as the continuing testimony to the undeviating covenant it did provide assurance of Yahweh's presence in history, the integrity of His rule(s), and the inevitability of His justice. The prophetic word, as illustrated in the previous cases, offers escape from chaos.

Prophecy, however, does not suggest the end of history. The escape it provides is not a stable state. The natural entropy of the world constantly assails the fragile mythos. Because it contains what von Rad has called a "tension of history,"[20] the prophetic faith is a strenuous one; each new event must be evaluated and the people held to account. The greater the calamities that arise, the greater the effort required to avert them, and the greater the guilt when reform fails. In the religion of the Old Testament prophets, responsibility was always a matter between the people and Yahweh. When the events of history reach inhuman and incomprehensible proportions, theories of human culpability are no longer adequate. New causes commensurate with the terror of the perceived effects must be sought. In the history of the ancient Jews, this time was the end of the sixth century B.C.E., the time of the Babylonian Exile. The Exile was a crisis of unmatched intensity, involving as it did the burning of Jerusalem, the surrender of self-government for the Jewish people, and the end of the Davidic succession. Constrained to work within the here and now of events, prophetic theology demanded that Yahweh reveal Himself in this world through a correspondence between causes and effects. At the time of the Exile, the guilt required to account for events was unbearable, opening Yahweh's control of history to question.[21]

It has been suggested that prophecy at this juncture was no longer able to sustain the burden of history.[22] The crisis of meaning was of such enormity that the organization necessary to hierarchy was impossible. In such an environment, "the absence of persons who are acknowledged by members of their society as performing the role of the prophet"[23] is merely a symptom of the larger social chaos and a harbinger of democracy in the worst sense of the word. Instead of the univocal response that would have been required to give the illusion of order, prophecy during the Babylonian and early Persian periods was given over to bitter divisions that seemed only to reflect earthly chaos. The false prophets who were so savagely denounced by Ezekiel and Zepenaiah retreated from the hard terms of the covenant. Their message was one of acquiescence. False prophets provided absolution rather than judgment.[24]

Scholars have traditionally held that Persian doctrines of dualism were influential in corrupting the prophetic word.[25] Rather than rationalize evil as an aspect of God's will, as did the ancient peoples of Israel and Judah, or suggest that, while God did not cause evil, He allowed it to happen as a condition of the freedom of human beings, the basic position maintained by Christianity, ancient Persians held evil to be independent of and opposed to forces of good. Dualism does not limit evil to the exercise of venal human will, the mistreatment of widows and orphans, displays of covetousness, anger, lust, gluttony, vanity, sloth, and pride; evil is a cosmic force rivaling God. According to Georges Bataille, violence in a dualistic world loses its constructive potential, its ability to restore intimacy, and becomes purely destructive, a threat to the established order.[26] Only an evil of such magnitude is capable of serving as the responsible agent for otherwise unaccountable grief.

Frightening as the thought of a puissant evil may be, it enjoys the advantage of deflecting responsibility from the self. The agon of history in a dualistic cosmology is not principally between God and His people, but between God and evil, a contest in which the people are but the hapless prize.[27] The fullest expression of these tendencies can be seen in apocalyptic, a response to chaos which, in opposition to prophecy, tended to remove the battle from the human realm of history to a superordinate realm of cosmic forces.[28] Faced with hardships of a magnitude that the drama of God and people could not contain, the apocalyptist restores balance by reaching outside history for both causes and consequences. As Paul Hanson has noted, while prophecy affirms the historical realm as

> a suitable context for divine activity from the cosmic level to the level of the politico-historical realm of everyday life, . . . the visionaries, disillusioned with the historical realm, disclosed their vision in a manner of growing indifference to and independence from the contingencies of the politico-historical realm, thereby leaving the language increasingly in the idiom of the cosmic realm of the divine warrior and his council.[29]

In contrast to prophecy, apocalyptic is profoundly deterministic and pessimistic. Although the apocalyptist assures the ultimate triumph of God's will, the world as it exists is incorrigible; justice will require not an enforcement of the terms of the covenant, to which evil is not subject, but a destruction of evil itself. Evil cannot be reformed. The day of judgment requires the end of the drama of good and evil, the end of history.[30] The rhetorical consequences of this position are difficult to calculate. The violent and excessive language in apocalyptic might inspire readers to enlist in God's holy war, but the emphasis on human helplessness in the face of the supernatural would seem to call for passivism.[31] In either case, the language of instruction becomes superfluous because the world is understood to be beyond redemption; all one can do is to align oneself with God and wait or participate in the holocaust. The issue is an important one, because it suggests a judgment of the humanistic and moral status of apocalyptic based on the audience it implies.[32]

Unfortunately, apocalyptic texts offer little clarification in resolving this question. The determinism in apocalyptic lies at the end of history. There lies the locus of judgment. Current history is surrendered to chaos. Apocalyptists announce the imminence of judgment, but they do not judge; they pledge the restoration of order, but they are not its vehicle. Premillennial apocalyptic in particular makes bearable the iniquitousness of history by pointing to signs of the end and promising restitution in the next world for what is unjustly suffered in this one, but it is not responsible for either suffering or salvation.[33]

Extension of the discursive realm beyond history provides a nebulous point of focus for new expectations. The end of history may be determined, but when is it? As might be expected of a theology that could be so easily discredited by lack of fulfillment, apocalyptic shrouds its forecasts in mystery and ambiguity. The language of apocalyptic is highly metaphorical and symbolic, as is appropriate for the description of a supernatural world. John Collins, extending the work of Paul Ricoeur, has argued that "mystery and indeterminacy" constitute much of "the 'atmosphere' of apocalyptic literature," and suggests "that the text may on occasion achieve its effect precisely through the element of uncertainty."[34]

If the text of apocalyptic is too amorphous to judge, perhaps we can look to its author. In the case of prophecy, I have argued that the prophet lives the text, that he strives to realize the demands of his message in the flesh. But apocalyptic, as it fractures history, also shatters the identity of its author. The characteristic use of the pseudonym in apocalyptic presents us with three personae behind the message: God as the author of the vision; the purported transcriber of the vision, usually an eminent historic figure; and the actual author of the book.[35] The use of the pseudonym is consistent with the apocalyptic view of history: it reinforces the idea that history was determined from the beginning by allowing the people to find in their current circumstance the fulfillment of predictions ostensibly from an earlier time,[36] and it diminishes chronology as a source of order by locating the author simultaneously in the past, the present, and the future, that is, in eternity.

Apocalyptic, then, responds to crisis by retreating into another world. It does not seek to make the current world morally legible. Apocalyptic is an admission that the old rules no longer hold if, indeed, they ever did; it abolishes the identity of persons and makes a farrago of history; it leaves no stable points of reference. Apocalyptic does not order by division. It dissolves all divisions in the present, relieving human tension not in righteousness but in helplessness. Apocalyptic surrenders this world in the hope of a better one hereafter.

In the modern world, the Second World War stands out as a crisis that threatened not just a particular orthodoxy, but the foundations of value. It is this event that provides our American analog to the sixth century B.C.E. Exile of the Jews. Richard Weaver, in his postwar polemic *Ideas Have Consequences*, wrote, "Our feeling of not understanding the world and our sense of moral helplessness are to be laid directly to an extremely subversive campaign to weaken faith in all predication."[37] Weaver's description, if not entirely idiosyncratic, is an apt description of the conditions of apocalyptic.

If Weaver is correct in his assessment of the ominous doubts that besieged Americans following the Second World War, the argument would lead us to expect a failure of the liberal rhetoric of prophecy among radicals and the ascendancy of something resembling apocalyptic, a discourse that can hold in the balance both terror and passivism. As perhaps the most prominent extremist of the postwar era in America, Senator Joseph R. McCarthy provides an obvious subject for study. Producing a rhetoric that some mistook for radical, McCarthy could not impose order or provide a bright outcome because there was no fixed and received basis for judgment. There were no longer any unchallenged first premises that could sustain a prophetic discourse. The line between light and darkness, God's first division in the ordering of creation, is amorphous and fluid in McCarthy's rhetoric. McCarthy's discourse reflects the irresolution and confusion that ties the modern, apparently secular, genre of the fantastic to the ancient genre of apocalyptic.

Poetry

A second response of moral discourse in a world where God has died is the reification of the form of sacred discourse in the hope that the counterfeit will be accepted as genuine and have the desired effect, perhaps even offered under the delusion that the form is the genuine article. Such a process codifies the extraordinary and converts it to ritual, an aestheticized, rationalized representation of the divine where the tendency is always for technique to usurp inspiration. Historically, poetry has been the formulary vehicle for prophecy, and it is the rules of poetry that enable the creation of a simulacrum of the prophetic sans the divine motive.

At least since publication of Bishop Lowth's *Praelectiones Academicae de Sacra Poesi Hebraeorum* in 1741, the literature of the Old Testament and of the prophets in particular has been recognized as a great poetic achievement.[38] This recognition is based on both the outward form of prophecy — its rhythm, its musicality, its artful structures, its highly stylized vocabulary — and on the claim of the prophetic to inspiration, literally an inbreathing of the divine word. About the function of poetry for the ancient peoples of Israel and Judah, Bruce Vawter has written,

> In modern society poetry is largely a literary exercise removed from the rough-and-tumble of everyday life, but this was not so in antiquity when national sagas, the utterances of the sages, and the epics of the past were

invariably treasured up in poetry. Poetry, by its rhythm and distinctive vocabulary, was better suited for arresting oral communication than was prose.[39]

The function of the poem as a song, the primary vehicle for the preservation and dissemination of a culture in preliterate societies, seems almost universal.[40] But poetry, like most preservatives, is also astringent or tonic.

The poem is an appropriate vehicle for prophecy because it allows radical perspectives to emerge through renaming. From at least the time of Isocrates on, it has been recognized in Western culture that poetic is granted certain license with language beyond that granted to rhetoric or prose.[41] The poet is a "maker" from the Greek *poiein*, to make; in producing poetry, the poet reproduces the act of creation[42]—the poem is an act of re-creation; it creates a new language—and in so doing, realizes the potential for social criticism. In renaming, re-creating the elements of his society, the poet may challenge the established and accepted relationships of the status quo. Theophil Spoerri recognizes the power of poetry in its conservative side: "It is poetry which watches over all changes in language. Not only was poetry the mother tongue of mankind in the beginnings of history, but it remains so through the ages. It is the protectress of life and the guardian of equilibrium."[43] Walter Brueggemann, on the other hand, recognizes in this power a subversive function:

> Poetic imagination is the last way left in which to challenge and conflict the dominant reality. The dominant reality is necessarily in prose, but to create such poetry and lyrical thought requires more than skill in making rhymes. I am concerned not with the formal aspects of poetry but with the substantive issues of alternative prospects that the managed prose around us cannot invent and does not want to permit.[44]

Both Spoerri and Brueggemann recognize in poetry the power to name and thus to structure or define significant realities. Prophetic poetry defines the comfortable and convenient as a violation of sacred law. As Melvin Lasky has noted of the highly metaphorical language of radical reform: "The imaginative extension of political ideas and their embellishment by myth and metaphor induce an ideological atmosphere in which men, beginning with more ordinary and even humdrum social concerns, come to think of their activities in terms of the life-and-death purposes of mission and destiny."[45] Thus, American radicals have consistently sought to define their audiences as sinners and slaves.

In setting themselves against what Brueggemann has called the "dominant reality," poets run the risk of being dismissed as mad, thus mitigating their threat to the status quo.[46] Only by some claim on the divine does the poet-prophet achieve any credibility in his critique of the officially sanctioned version of reality. Plato, in the *Phaedrus,* admitted the madness of both poets and prophets, but found the madness of the latter to be a "heaven-sent madness" superior to "man-made sanity."[47] In most cultures, there is no division between the types of madness Plato presents, his distinction being based on a division of labor among the Greek gods, and the madness of poets is not distinguished from the madness that inflames the prophet.[48]

The conflation of poetic and prophetic inspiration is illuminating with regard to the function of language in prophecy. Language not only serves as the vehicle for a radical renaming, but also as evidence of the divine source of that renaming. Nora Chadwick emphasizes the prophetic requirement that divine knowledge be expressed in extraordinary language: "Great prominence is usually given to poetic diction and skill in the pedantic use of phrase and artificial language (rhetoric). Always skill in language is stressed."[49] In the tradition of Old Testament prophecy, the link between poetic diction and divine afflatus is quite direct. David Freedman contends that for the ancient Hebrews, the poem itself, as a transcendent medium, served as evidence of divine inspiration,[50] and R. B. Y. Scott writes, "The gift of such language is to the prophets a gift indeed, the gift by Yahweh of a vessel to contain his word."[51] In its most extreme form, the inspired demonstrates transcendence by speaking in a tongue, sometimes a foreign language, which in normal life he is supposed to be incapable of speaking.[52] Poetic diction, then, serves a very special function for the prophet; it is not an accessory, but a necessary sign of *charism.*[53]

Throughout the preceding chapters, the interaction of this claim of the prophet to inspired knowledge and the prophet's message has been the focus of attention. The link between prophecy and poetry provides a means of articulating characteristics of the message that serve to communicate the character of the speaker. Many of the characteristics of the prophetic message are commonly thought of as characteristics of poetry. In particular, the fact that poetry, because it is often conceived as having a divine source or at least to emanate from genius, is thought to be concerned with universal and transcendent truths, the mimetic, truths that cannot easily be accommodated to the needs or desires of a particular audience, and the suggestion that poetic emphasizes *pathos* over *ethos* or *logos.*[54] In suggesting that prophecy is poetic, I am not denying the obvious rhetorical qualities that I have claimed both for Old Testament prophecy in the Bible or as it has influenced American radicals. Rather I recognize, with the majority of contemporary writers on rhetoric and poetic, the practical inseparability of these two modes of discourse. Prophecy, I would claim, is to be located in what Donald Bryant has described as "that area of discourse where the intellect and the emotions bestir each other in the exploration of opinion, judgment, of social action . . . the characteristic common ground of literature and politics."[55]

Form, though, is in itself inadequate to the task of reconstituting the religious community. It is ironic that invariance is both key to the power of form (witness the Roman Catholic mass prior to Vatican II) and also betrays it as a lifeless anachronism lacking continuing inspiration. It is this invariance that allows the form to be imitated and endlessly replicated, a process akin to what Weber would view as the routinization of charismatic authority, and this replication occurs at the moment that authority shifts from prophet to priest, the latter laying claim to authority "by virtue of his service in a sacred tradition," rather than by "personal revelation and charisma."[56] The danger lies not in the derivative nature of the presentation, but in the potential for such derivations, being divorced from essences and stemming only from surfaces, to become caricatures. Hal Foster recognizes this failing in postmodern art when it attempts to quote tradition: "Today, artists and architects only *seem* to prise open history . . . to redeem specific moments; in fact, they only give us hallucinations of the historical, masks of these moments. In short, they return to us our historically most cherished form—as kitsch."[57] Robert Welch, I will argue in chapter 8, falls prey to just such criticism. Attempting to revive a radical tradition in the absence of common root principles, Welch reached for the techniques of poetry. Welch believed that he heard the voice of God in the echo of Emerson, but his absolutism was absorbed into an ecumenical world that reduced all absolutes to the partial truths of a pluralistic universe.

Economic Rationalization

A third possible response of rhetoric to the death of God is conformity to the pressures of secularization. Beginning with the American Revolutionary leaders, this analysis of the rhetoric of American radicalism has focused on the voice of God (nature, the absolutely and objectively true) delivering His prohibitions through His spokesmen considered as American prophets. The men whose discourse has been examined spoke on behalf of the dispossessed, claiming for them certain inherent and inalienable rights based on ideas of the right. The rhetorical posture of the radicals follows Aristotle's dictum that wrongs committed in the name of the state are properly appealed to the court of higher law for redress. I have tried to demonstrate in radical rhetoric a consistent denigration of the idea that political and economic power is necessarily connected to righteousness.[58]

It is possible to take a cynical view of Aristotle's advice and to see in it no more than the exercise of those resources which best serve the case. But it is equally plausible to see, as I have argued is the case with prophecy, an inviolable and uncompromisable moral claim in the higher law, especially as Aristotle solemnly asserts in another place: "For there really is, as every one to some extent divines, a natural justice and injustice that is binding on all men, even on those who have no association or covenant with each other."[59] Within a philosophy of natural or divine law, all the arrangements of humankind are subject to evaluation by criteria that cannot be abrogated by considerations of political expedience or majority will. *"Because it functions as an absolute standard for testing positive law,"* writes Kathleen Jamieson, "natural law [God's law] is the obvious rhetorical appeal to be employed when confronting tyranny or injustice."[60] At the same time, as Jamieson goes on to recognize, the potency of the appeal is "tied to the audience's ability to believe that a knowable moral norm correctly articulated by the rhetor inheres in all men."[61] Natural law most effectively warrants the argument "when the audience is willing, because of utility or commonality of belief structure, to grant that the posited law or right may function as an unchallenged first premise."[62]

It is the acceptance of the partiality of the world that marks the residue of nineteenth-century liberalism in twentieth- century thought, a profound and unfettered individualism.[63] The consequences for argument are far-reaching. In contrast to the moral stance described by Jamieson and manifested in prophecy, Irving Horowitz describes the rhetorical possibilities in pluralism: "The more one emphasizes the fragmentation of the world, the more one must insist on the pragmatic values of men, the less can an argument be made for action as good in itself."[64] What Horowitz describes is the antithesis of prophecy and has substantial implications for the rhetorical options of those movements of social reform that acknowledge the partiality of the world, that recognize the death of God, the decay of natural law.

Max Weber described modern societies as tending toward differentiation, specialization, and increasing bureaucratization. S. N. Eisenstadt claims

that Weber found in modern societies "a growing differentiation and autonomy of various centers, growing demands for access to them, and for
participation in them, culminating in tendencies toward the obliteration of
the symbolic difference between center and periphery."[65] John Dewey's
analysis of American society in the wake of the industrial revolution cor-
roborates this general view. Dewey wrote,

> The ramification of the issues before the public is so wide and intricate, the
> technical matters involved are so specialized, the details are so many and so
> shifting, that the public cannot for any length of time identify and hold itself.
> It is not that there is no public, no large body of persons having a common
> interest in the consequences of social transactions. There is too much public,
> a public too diffused and scattered and too intricate in composition.[66]

Both Dewey and Weber make their observations in the context of
discussions of social change, and Weber's conclusion that society, in this
process of diffusion and participation, becomes "demystified" is particularly
revealing. In Eisenstadt's reading of Weber, the sum of these centrifugal
tendencies is "to dissociate one's predisposition to the charismatic from the
societal centers and from the traditions of the larger culture and to associate
it more and more only with the sphere of private, face-to-face relations and
activities—and even here to emphasize tendencies toward secularization,
negation of purity, and dissociation of seriousness and any normative commitment."[67] A world where there is no center, where there is no division
between the center and the periphery, is a world without the mystery and
separation necessary to the sacred. And where there is no externalization of
truth, there is no principle that commands assent except self-interest, and
there is thus no community.[68]

Jürgen Habermas, following both Weber and Dewey, extends the analysis
of the demystification or rationalization of society to the "scientization of
politics," finding that "rationalizing tendencies" come both from above and
from below. From below, there is a demand for some compensatory value
to replace that meaning and order that are lost in modern society. Typically,
the succedaneum is economic, as this is the value that characterizes capitalist
societies. From above, there is a recognition that the mythologies—"the
public religion, the customary rituals, the justifying metaphysics, the un-
questionable tradition"—must be converted to a more negotiable form;
they must become secularized.[69]

Peter Berger finds the origins of secularization in the industrial revolution. Like Weber and Habermas, Berger sees secular tendencies moving

outward from some centrally located sector in society, creating a homogeneous familiarity. The scientific logic that made the industrial revolution possible asserts itself as "an autonomous, thoroughly secular perspective on the world," making what was formerly sacred and mysterious continuous with the mundane world of everyday existence.[70] "A sky empty of angels becomes open to the intervention of the astronomer and, eventually, of the astronaut," writes Berger.[71] Religion is relegated to the marketplace, where it presents itself as a balm in the lives of private individuals.[72] Again, the focus turns from the transcendent to the immanent and the atomic, the self. It is from this position that the antireligious nature of pluralism, defined by Berger as "a social-structural correlate of the secularization of consciousness,"[73] can be most clearly seen.

In *The Brothers Karamozov*, Dostoevsky presents the potentialities of a world where God is absent. "When there is no God, everything is permitted," is Ivan's refrain. If there is no God, no absolute truth, there is no law, no ordonnance, no basis for prohibition.[74] The consequences are at once liberating and terrifying. On the one hand, it appears that those whom the old morality has oppressed are given license, since the moral and legal justifications for oppression are sundered. On the other hand, the oppressed lose all moral claims on the oppressor. At first glance, it may seem that the absence of moral claims on either side is no more static than are moral claims in competition. The critical difference, though, lies in the fact that the absence of moral claims forecloses the possibility of moral debate completely. Moral claims at a point of stasis presume a tension that may be broken or resolved. Secular argument is flaccid and inert.

Negotiation, as opposed to the proclamation of prophecy, is the form of secular debate. Secular debate reflects the economic values of its time by assuming the form of the so-called "rational exchange model" or "game theory."[75] Unlike the absolutisms of moral argument, all positions in rational economic argument are bargainable; the old ethic of exclusion and prohibition is replaced by tolerance. As Robert Paul Wolff has written,

> Tolerance in a society of competing interest groups is precisely the ungrudging acknowledgment of the right of opposed interests to exist and be pursued. The economic conception of tolerance goes quite naturally with the view of human action as motivated by interests rather than principles or norms. It is much easier to accept a compromise between competing interests—particularly when they are expressible in terms of a numerical scale like money—than between opposed principles which purport to be objectively valid.[76]

In the transition from what was in a profound sense a religious society, a society that had a sense of transcendental authorship and purpose, to a society based on pluralistic tolerance, we have changed from a society based on authority to a society based on economics. In Robert Bellah's phrase, we have broken the sacred covenant.[77] Ivan Karamozov's grand inquisitor makes the following solemn diagnosis of the human condition: "There are three forces, the only three forces that are able to conquer and hold captive for ever the conscience of these weak rebels for their own happiness — these forces are: miracle, mystery, and authority."[78] For this we have sought to substitute a utilitarian calculus. Reason is no longer the faculty by which the truth is apprehended, as it was for Thomas Paine. Reason is today understood to be the rules for computing the advantages and disadvantages of particular strategies.[79] "The voices of reason" in the contemporary world, writes Robert Paul Wolff, are arrayed "against the passion of intolerant faith."[80] Reason, in the modern view, makes no moral demands, for such demands are in themselves discredited. Reason offers some evidence of resources convertible to economic terms in exchange for privilege; it does not demand rights. In this world, there are no prophets; only madmen talk to God.

In an earlier analysis, I illustrated this retreat from the religious to the economic by contrasting one of the best known speeches of our time, Martin Luther King, Jr.'s "I Have a Dream" speech, widely regarded as religious, to Malcolm X's "The Ballot or the Bullet." Apposed to Malcolm X's much reviled insistence on the inherent nature of human rights, King's discourse is revealing of something fundamental about the preferred modes of appeal in our society. His emphasis on the contractual nature of the Constitution is precisely the converse of the denigration of charter rights by the American Revolutionaries, and his development of the metaphor of the check in the exordium suggests as the basis for rights the very economic rationality identified by Weber, Berger, Habermas, and others as a hallmark of postreligious society.[81] King's rhetoric is entirely consonant with the career of the Civil Rights Act of 1964 for which it implicitly campaigned. It is worth recalling that the Civil Rights Act of 1964 originated in the Senate Commerce Committee and that the act was upheld by the Supreme Court under the power of Congress to regulate interstate commerce, not on the power of Congress, under the Fourteenth Amendment, to promote equality in the private sector.[82] The genetic heritage of the speech manifests itself in the fact that the group protesting at the 1996 Democratic National

Convention in Chicago was not the "I Have a Dream Coalition," but the "Cash the Check Coalition."

The final case study presented here examines a movement for social reform that has carried the logic of negotiable rights to its most complete expression to date, the contemporary movement roughly comprehended under the rubric "gay liberation."

7

A Vision of the Apocalypse

Joe McCarthy's Rhetoric of the Fantastic

> Her prophets *are* light *and* treacherous persons: her priests have pol-
> luted the sanctuary, they have done violence to the law.
> —Zephaniah 3:4

> After this I saw in the night visions, and behold a fourth beast, dread-
> ful and terrible, and strong exceedingly; and it had great iron teeth: it
> devoured and brake in pieces, and stamped the residue with the feet
> of it: and it was diverse from all the beasts that *were* before it; and it
> had ten horns.   —Daniel 7:7

In his time, Joe McCarthy was hailed at the most gifted demagogue ever produced in America.[1] Now, more than forty years after his
censure by his colleagues in the United States Senate, the man and the
phenomenon still cast a pall over political discussion in America. The name
of the great smear campaigner has, in recent years, been hurled at those
whom we wished to discredit and used by the discredited to suggest the
injustice of their trial. Jeremiah Denton was compared to "that ultimate
American witch-hunter, the late Joe McCarthy," and Kurt Waldheim, after
charges were raised regarding his Nazi activities during the Second World
War, claimed that he was the victim of McCarthyism. The Reagan administration's liberal application of the McCarran-Walter Act revived what Arthur Miller referred to as "one of the pieces of garbage left behind by the
sinking of the great scow of McCarthyism."[2] McCarthy's presence was felt
in the 1988 presidential campaign when Democratic candidate Michael
Dukakis, in response to aspersions cast on his patriotism, compared the
tactics of his opponents to the slander of the late senator from Wisconsin.
In one speech, Dukakis expressed his confidence that his Texas audience
could "smell the garbage."[3] One of the highest profile examples of the

revenant McCarthy, eerily evocative of the Army-McCarthy hearings, was Clarence Thomas's televised avowal before the U.S. Senate Judiciary Committee that the use of the U.S. Senate by unscrupulous forces bent on destroying the country was worse than McCarthyism.[4] In 1992, McCarthy made a return visit to presidential politics as the Clinton campaign accused George Bush of McCarthyism for his attacks on Clinton's patriotism. Most recently, "P.C.," or political correctness, has been denounced by its detractors as "McCarthyism of the left" and the war on drugs as "chemical McCarthyism." Perhaps it is inevitable that the activities of Alfonse D'Amato's Whitewater investigative committee should have been compared to the activities of McCarthy's committees in the 1950s.[5] More than forty years after his death, his lingering aura betrays how far we are from any satisfactory understanding of Joe McCarthy. Indeed, it is as if in not understanding him, we have not really buried him. McCarthy, by some power we still fail to comprehend, made himself one of the most prominent symbols of a decade of American life. The residual fear of that unidentified power still haunts the cloakrooms of American politics.

As a rhetorical phenomenon, McCarthyism has received surprisingly slight attention. Our moralistic revelations of his lapses of logic, his shameless unoriginality, his torturing of evidence, his half-truths, his ugly barbarisms, and his unforgivable uncouthness have been more dyslogic than critical and have revealed more about our own good intentions and our ideal rhetoric than they have about the mystery that is Joe McCarthy. Indeed, perhaps in seeking to discredit the substance of McCarthyism we have missed the larger question. Perhaps it is the metaphor of the specter that is appropriate for a discussion not only of McCarthy's continuing influence, but the source of that influence even while he was alive. Perhaps the substance of McCarthyism has remained so elusive and so invulnerable to exposure because there was no substance there at all. As Walt Kelly's Jayhawk, in a cartoon strip of the McCarthy era, responds when asked to prove the existence of the invisible Indians whom he claims raised him, "Bein' invisible they natural don't leave no traces an' to this day, no sign of 'em is ever been found. Sheer proof." "Sheer," affirms Pogo.[6]

McCarthyism, I will argue, represents an apocalyptic rhetoric as a response to the dissolution of community in America. McCarthy did not attempt to resolve the crisis of his time through restoration of the covenant. Rather he capitulated to the widely felt notion that the old rules no longer held. He fled the crisis and accompanied his people into a hazy alterity. McCarthy's rhetoric is characterized by the indeterminacy, mystery, and ambiguity of apocalyptic. It was, I will argue, an amplification of its time, never able to achieve the level of standing in definitive opposition.

A Great Cloud over the 1950s

Contemporary historians and social critics have labored in recent years to rescue from Broadway and television the decade of the 1950s as it has been sanitized, idealized, and popularly associated with *I Love Lucy,* hula hoops, enormous gaudy automobiles, gauche fashions, and a congenial prosperity. The Fifties, in fact, were no more fabulous than the 1890s were gay, and its apparently frivolous entertainments reveal, just beneath the surface, the same desperate seriousness that fueled the Roaring Twenties. The celebration of material well-being as the ultimate good reflected, as had been the case at the turn of the nineteenth century, the desuetude of any other form of value, and it concealed gross inequalities in the distribution of wealth. The frenetic pace of spending and the enlargement of the credit culture suggests an interior voice murmuring "Eat, drink, and be merry, for tomorrow we die." Even our current nostalgia for the family of the Fifties, a family that seems, in shows like *Leave It to Beaver, Father Knows Best,* and *Ozzie and Harriet,* to have reached a state of beatitude, overlooks the degree to which these shows themselves reflected the nostalgic yearning of an anxious time for a presumably simpler and perhaps saner past. The Fifties simply cannot be adequately understood without recognizing World War II as their immediate predecessor and the "Great Fear" as much of their present.[7]

The horror of the Second World War, the second in as many generations, was certainly unsettling to Americans. Everything was on a scale that made a profanity of human beings—Hitler, the scope of the war, the new technologies of war, the bomb. Weaver called it "a marvelous confusion of values."[8] If the war itself was unsettling, the aftermath was even more so. There was no return to "normalcy" as there had been after the First World War. For all our victory parades and celebrations of the end of the war, there was an inconclusiveness about World War II. We could not simply disarm and return to a peacetime economy when it was over. America had new responsibilities in a world that had gotten smaller since the First World War. We had to help rebuild Europe and to maintain a cold war with the Soviet Union, formerly our ally.[9] Korea was symbolic of many of our frustrations and anxieties. In August 1950, a Gallup poll found 57 percent of Americans believing that our involvement in Korea was the beginning of World War III.[10]

The 1949 announcement that the Soviet Union had exploded an atomic bomb exacerbated tensions. In 1947, Americans ranked the "A bomb" second behind electric lights and appliances as the greatest invention in history.[11] In 1949, following Truman's announcement of evidence that the Soviet Union had exploded a nuclear weapon, 45 percent of Americans thought war was more likely as a result.[12] Between 1947 and 1954, Americans consistently reported, by large majorities, that they believed it was the intention of the Soviet Union to achieve dominance over the world.[13] The prevention of war was ranked as the most important problem facing the candidates in the 1950 elections,[14] and a 1951 poll revealed that 50 percent of Americans would not feel safe in their cities or communities in the event of an atomic attack.[15] Churchy La Femme, in Walt Kelly's comic strip "Pogo," complained of "these modern day disasters what consists of ten years of worry an' ten seconds of boom an' wango," and lamented days spent "scannin' the sky—not knowin' when—wonderin' whether to wear pajamas that night so's to be found decent—wonderin' whether to take a bath—whether to pack a light lunch."[16] William Faulkner, accepting the Nobel Prize for Literature, lamented, "Our tragedy today is a general and universal physical fear so long sustained by now that we can even bear it. There are no longer problems of the spirit. There is only the question: when will I be blown up?"[17]

For a country that had grown up in the faith that they were God's Chosen People, destined to work His will on this earth, such power in the hands of an enemy nation could only mean that America's select status had been decisively annulled, either by an angry God or by a rival one; there seemed to be little difference. But there is a very great difference between a God who uses calamity to His preordained ends and a God who competes with Satan for control over history, as the distinction between apocalyptic and prophecy suggests.

W. H. Auden's 1947 poem "The Age of Anxiety" provided a convenient label for the time and gave eloquent expression to much that we could not or would not articulate. Auden wrote of "Lies and Lethargies" policing the world, and went on to develop a nightmare scenario around "The fears that we fear [when] We fall asleep. . . . Nocturnal trivia, torts and dramas. . . . Moulds and monsters on memories stuffed With dead men's doodles, dossiers written In lost lingos," and he recognized that, even in wakefulness, "athwart our thinking the threat looms, Huge and awful as the hump of

Saturn Over modest Mimas, of more deaths And worse wars, a winter of distaste To last a lifetime." Our age, he mourned, was one "Infatuated with her former self Whose dear dreams though they dominate still Are formal facts which refresh no more."[18]

An autopsy on America's "dear dreams" of "her former self," the "formal facts" for which we now longed, revealed that they had been dead for some time. America finally faced an epistemological crisis that had its roots in the nineteenth century, the product of such diverse thinkers as Comte, Freud, Einstein, Nietzsche, Kierkegaard, Pierce, and James. The works of the existentialists, in particular, ignored for half a century, not merely in popular venues, but by professional philosophers, suddenly became the concern of "even the weekly news magazines."[19] Nineteen forty-eight saw the publication of the English translation of Albert Camus's *The Plague* wherein Father Paneloux assured his congregation that God, after looking on the people of Oran with compassion for a long while, had grown weary of waiting: "His eternal hope was too long deferred, and now He has turned His face away from us. And so, God's light withdrawn, we walk in darkness, in the thick darkness of the plague."[20]

Camus's was not an American voice, but he and Sartre and other existentialists spoke to our anxieties. J. Ronald Oakley, in his history of the Fifties, notes that "much of the fiction of the day was concerned with individual alienation that led to despair, suicide, murder, rape, and other desperate acts of lonely individuals in mass society."[21] Like Father Paneloux's congregation, Americans faced with crisis returned to the church in increasing numbers. The reason most commonly provided as an explanation for this religious revival, given by almost one third of the respondents in a 1954 Gallup poll, was "Fear, unrest, uncertainty of future."[22] Richard Niebuhr called it part "of a rather frantic effort of the naturally optimistic American soul to preserve its optimism in an age of anxiety."[23] In 1949, Arthur Schlesinger, Jr., wrote, "Western man in the middle of the twentieth century is tense, uncertain, adrift. We look upon our epoch as a time of troubles, an age of anxiety. The grounds of our civilization, of our certitude, are breaking up under our feet, and familiar ideas and institutions vanish as we reach for them, like shadows in the falling dusk."[24]

Behind much of the angst of the Fifties and providing it with a kind of coherence was modern science. There was the obvious fact of the bomb, but the more important questions were the subtle ones about what it meant. There is a certain irony in the fact that Hiroshima and Nagasaki were the products of a theory that both taught us the limits of our knowledge and laid the foundation for harnessing the greatest power known to humankind. The philosophically limited, pragmatic success of the atomic bomb granted the theory that made it possible considerable credibility in its claim that we could not know in any transcendent sense.[25] It also suggested that such knowledge was superfluous.

The explosion of the atomic bomb, then, was the zenith of industrialization, a process that had steadily decayed the half-life of God. It was, in the words of social historian Paul Boyer, an event of such magnitude that it seems to have become "one of those categories of Being, like Space and Time, that, according to Kant, are built into the very structure of our minds, giving shape and meaning to all our perceptions."[26] By 1950, left with a God who was no longer immanent in the world, who was both unknowable and unnecessary, history became at best inscrutable, at worst meaningless.[27] The foundation of the Common Sense philosophy that had sustained the American Revolutionaries, Wendell Phillips, and Eugene Debs had been thoroughly eroded. The unraveling of national community that had its roots in turn-of- the-century industrialization, though covered over by two world wars and a depression, was now exacerbated by developments in technology and society. It was in this era, the era in which Daniel Bell saw "the end of ideology," the end of "secular religion"[28] that Joe McCarthy claimed a place in the spotlight of American politics.

Photostats and Fantasy

Joe McCarthy understood the feeling of moral arrest in his audience. He called it

> an emotional hang-over . . . a temporary moral lapse which follows every war. . . . It is the apathy to evil which people who have been subjected to the tremendous evils of war feel. As the people of the world see mass murder, the destruction of defenseless and innocent people, and all of the crime and lack of morals which go with war, they become numb and apathetic. It has always been thus after war.[29]

The prophet's mandate in such times of crisis, as exampled in the cases of the American Revolution, Wendell Phillips, and Eugene Debs, is to judge. The prophet measures the conduct of the people against the law of God and exhorts the people to obey God's will. He counters apathy with suffering, and demands an assertion of virtue. However distasteful the prophet's demand may be, it abolishes all doubt in its appeal to absolute righteousness. Joe McCarthy's response to chaos was not certitude, but bewilderment.

McCarthy looked upon the postwar world and found it fantastic. "Strangely, however, after the arrest of six suspects in that case of treason, there was an unusual sequence of events, resulting in a most fantastic finale," said McCarthy, referring to the government's fumbled case against *Amerasia* magazine.[30] Concerning the same case, McCarthy produced a letter from T. A. Bisson, a member of the *Amerasia* board. Bisson's letter was "a fantastic document if ever there was one."[31] In a second reference, the letter from Bisson was called "a rather fantastic document coming from the man whom Mr. Jessup used to initiate the smear campaign—a rather fantastic document coming from a man high up in the State Department, but not too fantastic, however, when coming from a man who worked under Frederick Vanderbilt Field on *Amerasia*."[32] According to McCarthy, Owen Lattimore was able to beguile audiences with "fantasies and untruths,"[33] attempting to sell the American people "a rather fantastic bill of goods."[34] The failure of the Tydings Committee to call a witness suggested by McCarthy was "the most fantastic situation conceivable, something unheard of in any Senate or House Committee; unheard of even in a kangaroo court."[35] The alleged raping of State Department personnel files before committee members were allowed access to them was "the most fantastic project I have ever heard of."[36] And orders concerning the mission of the Seventh Fleet during the Korean war were termed "the most incredibly fantastic order that has ever existed in war or peace." "Impossible, yes! Unbelievable, yes! But it is all a matter of cold record."[37]

McCarthy's reaction to the fantasy he discovered was, appropriately, amazement and incredulity. Our foreign policy was an "amazing failure";[38] the "picture of treason which I carried in my briefcase to that Caucus room [for the opening hearing of the Tydings Committee] was to shock the nation."[39] A State Department document revealed the "astounding position of the Secretary of State," and McCarthy had no doubt that Senator Knowland of California would find much in it that would "shock him also."[40] "Even in normal times," McCarthy said, his evidence would be "shocking." "Today, however, it is doubly shocking."[41] Dean Acheson's failure to read some communist documents regarding China was "disturbing in the extreme. . . . Incredible. Incredible."[42] And the failure of the Truman administration to expedite the delivery of economic and military aid to Chiang Kai-Shek was "one of the most shocking subversions of the will of the Congress by an administration that our history will show." [43] Owen Lattimore's discussion of the China problem in the *Sunday Compass* of New York, July 17, 1949, was "astounding," [44] and the testimony of Secretary of State George Marshall "and his palace men" before the Russell committee was one of "self-satisfied shocking revelations." [45] Any attempt to understand one of Secretary of State Marshall's statements on China was certain to leave McCarthy's colleagues "dumbfounded." [46] McCarthy's picture of Communist infiltration in America was "amazing . . . disturbing . . . incredibly unbelievable." [47]

McCarthy's posture, beginning in astonishment, is entirely appropriate for an age of uncertainty, and it could be the basis for a shared *pathos* with his audience. Yet, in order for McCarthy to emerge as a prophetic leader, he would have needed to transcend this shared anxiety and articulate the true quality of events as measured against a shared moral code. The incipient sense of outrage in McCarthy's remarks, though, never moves beyond the moment of wonder, and it finally leaves the audience in a phantasmagorical world, paralyzed by a fragile sense of the real and a lack of fixed criteria for choosing among the constantly shifting scenes.

McCarthy's charges frustrate judgment by their bewildering lability. Even as he proclaimed the incredible nature of his discoveries, McCarthy insisted on their authenticity. Tzvetan Todorov has found a similar tension at the heart of the genre of the fantastic — the hesitation between belief and rejection, that moment suspended between the marvelous (the extraordinary but ultimately credible) and the uncanny (the bizarre and ultimately untrue), [48] and Rosemary Jackson, building on Todorov's work, writes, "A characteristic most frequently associated with literary fantasy has been its obdurate refusal of prevailing definitions of the 'real' or 'possible,' a refusal amounting at times to violent opposition." [49] McCarthy's astonishment that the rules have been broken even as he continues to believe in their binding force, his confrontation with the "anti-expected," signals the presence of the genre of the fantastic, [50] a celebration of ambiguity, something indefinite, a moment of hesitation and indecision. When we encounter an extraordinary event, for the interval that we cannot decide whether we are hallucinating or witnessing a miracle, we are participants in the fantastic. It is a moment of epistemological uncertainty. The literary fantastic, while it raises emotions and exploits attitudes, stubbornly refuses to render final judgments that would allow us to direct them. As Eric Rabkin puts it,

"The wonderful, exhilarating, therapeutic value of Fantasy [for Rabkin, the genre most characterized by the fantastic] is that it makes one recognize that beliefs, even beliefs about Reality, are arbitrary."[51]

The conception of the fantastic in literary studies stands in sharp contrast to uses common in communication studies, where fantasy or the fantastic is examined for its constitutive force.[52] The fundamental uncertainty of the literary fantastic refuses the epistemological grounds on which community might be (re)constructed. Rather than ordering the chaos of the world propaedeutic to judgment, the fantastic is a capitulation that merely reflects our confusion back to us. In this respect, it can be argued that the fantastic is a modern analog to biblical apocalyptic, now divorced from a specific theology. The parallel to apocalyptic reminds us that, while Rabkin emphasizes the liberating, "exhilarating" aspects of literary fantasy, its terrifying aspects—the incipient chaos, a kind of epistemological freefall—must not be forgotten. Alice's adventures are filled with horrific moments. The effect is even more unsettling when the fantastic insinuates itself into politics.

In order to give direction in such a setting, McCarthy had to find some anchor, some stable axiom on which to build. McCarthy understood that he was not charismatic; however colorful a figure he may have been, he recognized that he was not blessed with the divine. He never claimed a transcendent insight, and he never made the prophet's "of a truth the Lord hath sent me" his claim to the credence of his audiences.

Against the incredible, McCarthy pitted the completely secular epistemology of his time, the objective, the verifiable, the political equivalent of scientific facts: "I have in my hand," "The file shows," "I have nothing completely ready at this time, and must refer to the documents before me," "There is a memorandum in the file," "A report dated July 16, 1947, states," "I have before me several documents." "I have before me another document." "I have a copy of it in my hand." "I have a photostat of the letter." "I have before me an affidavit." "I hold in my hand two photostats." "Since that time I have dug up additional photostats." "I have before me a copy." "Mr. President, I have a file which I desire to insert in the *Record* today, containing photostats." "I hold in my hand the testimony." "Here are photostats of official letterheads." "I have complete unchallengable documentation." "I hold in my hand the official record."[53] These are the phrases McCarthy used throughout his speeches to create an objective reality credible enough to balance his claims on the marvelous.

Barnet Baskerville termed McCarthy a "brief-case demagogue."[54] The ever-present, overstuffed briefcase was a repository of the objective, the facts, photostatic reproductions, the record. Richard Rovere saw in it McCarthy's desire to have "the dust of the archives clinging to him."[55] The briefcase was external to McCarthy; it was not subjective. McCarthy only produced the evidence and invited the audience to share in his incredulity. McCarthy's speeches in the Senate are an endless request for unanimous consent to have articles, letters, memoranda, and other materials printed in the *Congressional Record*. *McCarthyism: The Fight for America* is similarly filled with photographs, photostatic copies of documents, letters, and articles, and appeals to published testimony by other sources, that is, the public record. In the Army-McCarthy hearings, two of the most dramatic confrontations occurred over a cropped photograph and a document, purportedly a carbon copy of a letter from J. Edgar Hoover, which Army counsel Joseph Welch derided as "a copy of precisely nothing,"[56] thus contributing to the sense of unreality.

McCarthy's heavy dependence on documentation was, in a sense, crippling; it betrayed his own doubts about the credibility of the picture he presented to his audiences and made judgment impossible. There is no affirmation in McCarthy's discourse, only hesitation. As Jackson has put it, "By foregrounding its own signifying practice, the fantastic begins to betray its version of the 'real' as a relative one, which can only deform and transform experience, so the 'real' is exposed as a category, as something articulated by and constructed through the literary or artistic text."[57] In a similar vein, Rabkin notes, "In the transcendent reality of the fiction, the fictional becomes real; and then we are reminded that the real is itself fictional. This self-reflection is fantastic."[58] The effect is circular and inescapable. A dialectic is created in which each element undermines the other, making the synthesis absurd. Every time he presented evidence, McCarthy, with equal vigor, discredited it, making it impossible for his audience to decide which part of the claim to accept. In placing so much weight on evidence that he had termed questionable, McCarthy called into question, not just the particulars of his case, but the integrity of evidence itself. Like a magician exposing the pedestrian mechanics of his tricks, McCarthy suggested the illusory nature of all demonstration.

McCarthy could not lead for he had no direction, and he could not judge for he had no standard. Joe McCarthy was not part of the sacred. He was not a transcendent being who bore the understanding of God's will. He was just Joe, a skunk hunter from a small farm community in the Midwest, and he was just as amazed as the rest of us.

In creating, but not resolving, a tension between the uncanny and the marvelous, the real and the incredible, McCarthy subverted his own efforts at persuasion. But his Faustian exchange also broached untold possibilities. By implicitly denying the compelling power of his evidence, he called into question its theoretical basis. "Presenting that which cannot be, but *is,* fantasy exposes a culture's definitions of that which can be: it traces the limits of its epistemological and ontological frame," writes Jackson.[59] This is the significance of McCarthy's posture—"Inconceivable? Yes. But it is true."[60]

Unhampered by the laws of the everyday world, McCarthy was free to take his audience into a domain in which unpleasant judgment could be withheld indefinitely.[61] As Rabkin puts it, "This function of the fantastic is educational in the root sense: . . . it creates in the mind a diametric reversal and opens up new and fantastic worlds."[62] Americans were not looking for a Father Paneloux to tell them that their sinfulness was responsible for their sorry state, but a Father Paneloux who could hold marvelous evil forces in a balance with our culpability, commanding our assent to neither, this Father Paneloux had promise for America in the Fifties.

The world McCarthy fashioned was a dark creation where things were not always what they seemed to be, a world where evil forces worked behind a veil of secrecy.

> How can we account for our present situation unless we believe that men high in this Government are concerting to deliver us to disaster? This must be the product of a great conspiracy, a conspiracy on a scale so immense as to dwarf any previous such venture in the history of man. A conspiracy of infamy so black that, when it is finally exposed, its principals shall be forever deserving of the maledictions of all honest men.[63]

Reflecting the hyperbolic tendencies of the fantastic, the conspiracy McCarthy described was of superhuman, supernatural proportions.[64] Populated with evil geniuses and sinister cabalists in unholy alliance, parading as newspapermen, honored generals, secretaries of state, and presidents, all meeting in richly paneled but outwardly innocent looking barns, pouring over secret documents, engaged in secret plots involving spies, espionage, and infiltration, with the ultimate aim of destroying Western civilization, McCarthy's world was a nightmare. He intimated "hidden and undisclosed forces," "dark forces," "chicanery," the "mysterious" disappearance of incriminating documents, secret contracts, and secret trials, and secret parleys, "treachery," and "lies."[65] Metaphorically, McCarthy introduced octopi, snakes, and spiders into the dream: the hoax being perpetrated was "monstrous"; "the Communist party—a relatively small group of deadly conspirators—has now extended its tentacles to that most respected of American bodies, the United States Senate"; a "world-wide web" of conspiracy had been spun from Moscow; Drew Pearson and fellow travelers were venomous; "the Truman Democratic Administration was crawling with Communists"; Dean Acheson was elegant and alien.[66] Homosexuals, too, figured prominently in McCarthy's fantasy world, yet another perversion of the rules of everyday life.[67]

Even more threatening than the ability of the enemy to assume malevolent forms was its ability to assume no form at all, to become invisible: "One knows that traitors are at work. One sees the political fingerprints of the Communists on every document drafted. One can see the footprints of Communist betrayals down every path they travel."[68] In a metaphor that might have recalled the contemporaneous film *The Invisible Man*, McCarthy claims to see the signs of communist presence, but not the communists themselves.

The idea of invisibility recalls the metaphors of vision discussed earlier. McCarthy's use of this set of metaphors reveals basic epistemological differences between himself and his radical precursors. In the discourse of the American Revolution, Wendell Phillips, and Eugene Debs, there is an emphasis on awakening to a new dawn, a new day of work and exertion. Sleep is a personal condition; it is restful and comfortable. Ideological sleep is an indulgence, an avoidance of confrontation and judgment, a failure of virtue. The same holds true for willful blindness. It is an incapacity of the individual, subjective, not objective. When awakened the truth is irresistible; the dawn, the new day, is inexorable, reminding us again of the origin of the term revolution.

McCarthy, on the other hand, dwells on darkness, things done in the night. Darkness is not a personal incapacity; it is imposed from without. In a discussion of the rhetorical uses of archetypal metaphor, Michael Osborn finds that darkness brings "fear of the unknown, discouraging sight, making one ignorant of his environment—vulnerable to its dangers and blind to its rewards. One is reduced to a helpless state, no long able to control the world about him. Finally, darkness is cold, suggesting stagnation and thoughts of the grave."[69] Osborn's description resonates remarkably with the description of the anxieties of the Fifties presented above, and is an apt characterization of the darkness metaphor as used by McCarthy. Sleep is no longer a personal indulgence, but something induced by evil forces so that they might do their work undetected. McCarthy suggested that the American people had been given sleeping tablets by the president and the State Department in order to lull them into a false sense of security,[70] and that Truman was persuaded to fire MacArthur "in the dead, vast, and middle of the night."[71] "I awake each morning in the fear that overnight, in some secret chamber of the United Nations, the enemies of the United States, with Britain and India at their head, have made a secret deal—a new Yalta."[72]

As nocturnal creatures, McCarthy's enemies have kinship with witches, vampires, bats, rats, and wolves. "The enemies of our civilization, whether alien or native, whether of high or low degree, work in the dark," he warned. "They are that way more effective."[73] "The pattern of Communist conquest has been the same in every country over which the stygian blackness of Communist night has descended."[74]

It is McCarthy's expressed intention to expose the communists, to subject them to the searching light of truth, but they are powerful and his success is not guaranteed: "If, after all is said and done, this unholy alliance should have its way, then I propose the premise that holds it together—that vigorous anti-communism is more dangerous than communism—as a fitting epitaph on the grave of American civilization."[75]

That McCarthy could allow for the death of civilization, that he could, in his rhetoric, acknowledge the possibility of failure, is a phenomenon absent from the preceding chapters. The basically optimistic prophetic faith seen heretofore does not allow for the final triumph of an "unholy alliance." There are only two sources of power in that simple world: God and human will. One is either awake and acts in accordance with God's will or one is asleep or willfully blind and acts in accordance with human will. But human will is insignificant compared with the will of God, and in the end, God's purpose will be served. The evil confronted by earlier radical movements was merely the venal exercise of the human will: George III as a symbol of England, the plantation owners of the South, and the industrialists of the turn of the century shared a common sin in their rejection of God's justice, the justice of natural law, in favor of their personal luxury. More importantly, the people shared in the sin by their complicity in a corrupt system; the judgment is addressed to them. The audience of the prophet is second-person plural. Such evil is human scale and ultimately ineffectual.

McCarthy presents a different theology. It is not the optimistic theology of prophecy, but the pessimistic theology of apocalyptic, given sophisticated treatment in McCarthy's time in works like Reinhold Niebuhr's *Children of Light, Children of Darkness.* McCarthy did not crusade against the failure of human virtue; his holy war was against evil. In his famous speech at Wheeling, West Virginia, in 1950 he drew the lines of battle:

> Today we are engaged in a final, all-out battle between communistic atheism and Christianity. The modern champions of communism have selected this as the time. And, ladies and gentlemen, the chips are down—they are truly down.[76]

Two years later, in another famous speech wherein he accused Adlai Stevenson of aiding the communist cause, McCarthy averred,

> We are at war tonight—a war which started decades ago, a war which we did not start, a war which we cannot stop except by either victory or death. The Korean war is only one phase of this war between international atheistic communism and our free civilization.[77]

The earthly war in Korea is insignificant; it is merely a symptom of the all-consuming cosmic war that would determine our fate. Human history is inadequate to contain forces of this magnitude. In 1954, just before his censure by the Senate, McCarthy sang the same refrain: "At the risk of boring you with some repetition, I repeat, the world is in an ideological struggle, and we are on one side and the Iron Curtain countries are on the other."[78] From the time he took up the anticommunist cause until the virtual end of his career, McCarthy consistently warned of the imminence of the Armageddon.

McCarthy capitalized on, but did not create, the radical *agon* reflected in these excerpts. The appellation "the Cold War" testifies to the ubiquity of such thinking, even among relative moderates. Upon assuming the presidency for a second term in 1957, Dwight Eisenhower spoke of a divided world: "The divisive force is international communism and the power that it controls. The designs of that power, dark in purpose, are clear in practice."[79] It was a modern variant of the old Persian dualism. But McCarthy's reaction was notable. While Eisenhower and others continued to talk of "unconquerable will," "firm and fixed purpose[s]," "hope,"[80] McCarthy warned of failure.

In representing a battle of such epic proportions, McCarthy again stretches credulity and suggests something of the nexus between apocalyptic and fantasy. Paul Hanson has found in the transition between prophetic and apocalyptic eschatology a shifting of the relative weights of the elements of the real and the mythic, the mundane and the visionary. Hanson illustrates a reintroduction of the mythic into prophetic discourse in Deutero-Isaiah

51:9–11, a call for God to awaken and exercise again the power by which He slew Ra'hab, the dragon of chaos.[81] The scale and theme are common to McCarthy's discourse, apocalyptic, and fantasy.

The scale of McCarthy's war is matched by the power of his warriors. Fantasy is a completely determined world; happenstance is abolished; the regnant powers control events to the most minute detail. Todorov calls it "pan-determinism": "everything," he writes, "down to the encounter of various causal series (or 'chance') must have its cause, in the full sense of the word, even if this cause can only be of a supernatural order."[82]

The obvious language for the expression of such power is the language of conspiracy. Conspiracies are not accidental; they are, literally, "a breathing together"; they are contrived. As McCarthy expressed it,

> The people, Mr. President, recognize the weakness with which the administration has replaced what was so recently our great strength. They are troubled by it. And they do not think it accidental. They do not believe that the decline in our strength from 1945 to 1951 just happened. They are coming to believe that it was brought about, step by step, by will and intention. They are beginning to believe that the surrender of China to Russia, the administration's indecently hasty desire to turn Formosa over to the enemy and arrive at a ceasefire in Korea instead of following the manly, American course prescribed by MacArthur, point to something more than ineptitude and folly.[83]

McCarthy's Republican colleagues had hoped that such declarations were simply enthusiastic displays of partisan politics and that the election of Eisenhower would curb McCarthy's zeal. They were dismayed when this was not the case, but McCarthy's controversial attacks on Eisenhower were perfectly consistent with what has been argued here. In McCarthy's fantasy world, the election of a Republican administration was simply a change in human personnel. The real battle was elsewhere.

The tandem concept to pan-determinism in fantasy is "pan-signification."[84] The world of fantasy is a highly structured drama. Every event contributes to the advancement of the plot. In apocalyptic fantasy, all events are filled with foreshadowings of the end, all of which must be attended to and interpreted. McCarthy's world was just such a world, groaning with meaning: "At first blush the policy as set forth in the above document would appear disorganized and without clear point. It was not pointless, however. Those who drafted it understood very clearly the over-all plan being advanced."[85] "You need not seek far to find the real reason lurking behind this avowed one."[86] Pan-signification is the continuing testimony to the awesome powers at work in the world of fantasy; to exercise such control that every action infallibly works toward a predetermined end is precision on a terrifying scale:

> To fit this incident into the global picture, let me remind you, these prisoners have been held by the Chinese for two years, so their selection of a time of announcement was, of course, a deliberate act. In fact, we have—we find little evidence in all of the actions of the Communist states that indicates any haphazard actions on their part. Everything they do is deliberate and well-thought out.[87]

Superhuman intelligence is ascribed to the enemy, thus the "evil genius" theme so prominent in McCarthy's rhetoric.[88] Evil genius—"twisted-thinking intellectuals"—has the power not only to execute its designs, its "blueprint for disaster," but also the power to conceal its design by corrupting the judgment of the American people, tricking them into believing false interpretations of traitorous objectives.[89] Like McCarthy's world, the monistic world of the prophet is heavily invested with meaning, but the interstices are left to the exercise of human frailty, and human frailty is not an effective causal agent. As suggested in the previous chapter, monism implies one design for the world and one meaning for events. One is either asleep (blind) or awake, but not mistaken.

In a dualistic cosmology, there are two designs for the world, equally powerful in their plausibility. One may be asleep (blind) or awake, and if awake, one may be confronting truth or illusion, good or evil.[90] The power of evil is often portrayed as that of the seductress exercising hypnosis or enchantment, casting spells that cause us to act, not in accordance with our own will, but not in accordance with the good either. Evil has both the power to conceal its influence and to parade as the good.

It is this powerful evil that McCarthy presented to his audiences. McCarthy talked of Alger Hiss's exercising a "Svengali-like influence over Secretary of State Stettinius" at Yalta, and of Marshall and Acheson's having a "hypnotic influence" over Truman.[91] "I regard as the most disturbing phenomenon in America today the fact that so many Americans still refuse to acknowledge the ability of Communists to persuade loyal Americans to do their work for them." The American people must be alerted to the fact "that this vast conspiracy possesses the power to turn their most trusted servants into its attorneys-in- fact."[92] "It is," said McCarthy, "the clandestine enemy which taxes our ingenuity."[93]

McCarthy presented America with Tamino's choice and no clear criteria by which to make it. Sometimes he appeared to offer the lifeline of "just good, everyday American horse sense."[94] For example, when identifying communists, he simply looked for people and policies that reflected the Communist Party line "right down to the dotting of every 'i' and the crossing of every 't' ": "As one of my farmer friends once said, if a fowl looks like a duck and quacks like a duck and eats like a duck we can assume it is a duck."[95] Such confidence in appearances, however, was undermined by those like the former communist and professional government witness Louis Budenz in his testimony on Owen Lattimore. In a performance that would have made Lewis Carroll proud, Budenz refused to assent to any stable criteria:

> Wasn't it true, asked Morgan, that Lattimore's *Solution in Asia* had been condemned by the *Daily Worker?* Yes, Budenz replied, but the Party often protected its members by criticizing them, "that is to say, that is, to damn them with faint praise—rather, to praise them with faint damns, is the way I want to put it." And hadn't Lattimore publicly opposed the Soviet invasion of Finland? True enough, said Budenz, but Party members were sometimes given "exemptions" in order to disguise their real purpose.[96]

In the world of fantasy, it is not obvious what things mean. The rules have been subverted and are no longer dependable. McCarthy, his appeals to common sense notwithstanding, understood this; he understood that he could not merely show, he had to interpret: "Do Senators follow me?" "Do Senators follow this?" "Do Senators get the picture?" he queried again and again.[97] "I wonder whether Senators get the awfulness of that picture."[98] "Now what does this mean, my good friends, what does this mean to the 150,000,000 American people?" he asked his television audience.[99] "I digress to explain the significance of that utterance."[100] "In order to recognize the significance of these two documents, it might be well for me to digress for a minute."[101] "In other words . . ."[102]

In other words, the documents he held in his hand were not enough; they did not carry their own self-evident meaning. Sometimes they required translation. After presenting a quotation that noted that General Stilwell, Secretary of State Marshall's choice to command the U.S. Army in China, did not like Chinese officialdom but had a great regard for the Chinese people, McCarthy offered the following interpretation:

> As we all know, "people" in Communist parlance has a special meaning. It does not mean all the people in our sense. It is a catchword, an occult word,

clear to the initiates, meaning Communists. They use it in a special sense to designate all their political organs. We all recall the various people's fronts organized to promote the Communist cause throughout the world. More specifically the Chinese Communist army was referred to in Communist parlance as the people's army.[103]

"People" is one of the most generic and colorless terms available to denote an aggregate of human beings. McCarthy recognizes this when he contrasts the communist "special meaning" with "our sense," innocent and inclusive. The communist "people," according to McCarthy, who freights the usage in this context with sinister implications, is only a ruse, an attempt to pass beneath the threshold of signification. The achievement of discerning a particular significance is secondary to the achievement of recognizing that there is a significance to be discerned.

McCarthy's struggle to separate the significant from the insignificant is unremitting. Figure-ground discriminations are not clear in the dark world of the fantastic: "Note those words, Mr. President." "Mr. President, listen to this." "I call the Senate's attention to this statement." "Listen to this if you will."[104] In a complex, relativistic world, all events require interpretation; nothing is unworthy of our attention.

I have concentrated on how McCarthy used his evidence to create tensions between belief and doubt in his audiences, but none of McCarthy's evidence would ever have been given a forum had it not been for the power of his office. There is no doubting that much of the credence given McCarthy's claims resulted from his status as a U.S. senator. As David Oshinsky has phrased the question that had to be raised by McCarthy's charges, "Would a United States senator go this far out on a limb without hard evidence?"[105] Millard Tydings knew very well that as a senator, McCarthy was more likely to be believed than someone standing "on the corner of 9th and G streets who is carrying on a casual conversation,"[106] and Walter Lippman recognized the power of the office when he argued that McCarthy's charges, because he was a senator, were news and had to be treated as such, however reluctantly; McCarthy could not be suppressed by the media.[107]

Though the institutions of the media could not, without the benison of the Senate, themselves author McCarthy's undoing, the representational power of the media, especially television, did serve a critical enabling function when the Senate finally decided that McCarthy had overstepped the bounds of allowable conduct. And it is consistent with the thesis argued here that, in the instances where the media authored its own scripts, some of the most influential among them employed an ironic mode.[108] Irony forgoes the head-on attack and unsettles its object indirectly. There is a sense in which, just as the fantastic simultaneously demands our assent and dismisses such a demand, irony also mounts its criticism and is able to retreat to a posture of "all in fun" or of having been misread.

Even television, though, had to await a certain revocation of sanctuary before it could exercise its power against Wisconsin's junior senator. As a senator, McCarthy spoke from the temple, and was provided, not only the sanctuary of congressional immunity, but even a certain amount of support in the reluctance of the Senate to disavow one of its own. Because Republicans, in fact, were eager to use McCarthy in the pursuit of their own political ends, McCarthy received the blessing of the Tafts, the Lodges, and other party scions who personally found him and his methods distasteful.[109]

Nowhere is McCarthy's dependence on the positive sanction of the Senate clearer than in the course of his career after his censure in 1954. The censure, although it did not materially affect McCarthy's standing in the Senate, did serve notice that he no longer participated in the collective *ethos* of that body; the Senate had admitted that McCarthy had said discreditable things, and in doing so, it broke the spell of the fantastic. Alice awoke from the dream and was left with only reflections on the uncanny. Because McCarthy had built his case on the collective *ethos* of the Senate, he had tacitly ceded to it the effective power to discredit him as a part of itself. The effect of the censure on the press and the public was immediate and unmistakable: it was no longer necessary to pay attention to Senator McCarthy.[110]

McCarthy had an unfailing apprehension of the epistemological crisis of the Fifties with its "key terms": "irony, paradox, ambiguity, and complexity,"[111] and he exploited that apprehension ruthlessly. McCarthy apprehended the crisis because he participated in it. His discourse does not indicate that he ever transcended it. His audience was not the prophetic "you," but the inclusive "we." Within that crisis, McCarthy struck a delicate balance that avoided judgment, and in avoiding judgment, he left his audience in disarray. As frightening as chaos was, it seems that it may have been preferable to the terrible truths that threatened America after the Second World War. By offering a discourse that did not command assent, McCarthy allowed America to contemplate some of its most dreadful monsters at a distance. The delicate equilibrium that he maintained for almost four years was wrecked when the hierarchical power bestowed on him by his seat in the Senate was symbolically revoked. The scale fell abruptly on the side of the uncanny, and Americans were left to wonder at how bizarre it had all been.

Evaluating the Dream

McCarthyism has been termed a national nightmare.[112] By taking the metaphor literally, we are in a position to understand some of the contradictions that still occupy the attentions of McCarthy's biographers, students of McCarthyism, and historians of the period. The underlying debate in all the biographical works on McCarthy devolves on the question of sincerity.[113] Beginning with Rovere's biography at the end of the McCarthy decade, and continuing through Oshinsky's, currently regarded as definitive, everyone who has focused on the man has felt compelled to look at the sources of McCarthy's anticommunism; a series of conflicting impressions regarding the sometimes playful attitude he took toward his crusade in private, his apparent lack of passionate involvement with the topic, his childish delight in spy games, and his nonchalant attitude toward particular cases; his documented fondness for lying; his statement to Jack Anderson that this was the real thing; and his willingness to endure censure rather than back down. Much of the evidence divides along the lines of a Jekyll and Hyde public presentation versus private behavior. McCarthy's willingness to excoriate a political opponent or a member of the press for the crowd and then to turn and throw a friendly arm around his victim is a source of constant perplexity to his chroniclers.[114]

To find conflict in these apparent oppositions is to assume a stable set of rules, and fantasy has no such rules. It is, writes Jackson, "founded on contradictions."[115] And not just a single set of contradictions, but "the continuing diametric reversal of the ground rules within a narrative world."[116] Fantasy embraces both fear of the demonic and a sense of play. Fantasy cannot find stable reference points. If it did the moment of hesitation would be lost, and it would no longer be fantasy. McCarthy's failure to display a commitment to his individual cases may not have been an effective method of exposing communists, but it was sublimely effective in prolonging the moment of hesitation.

Finally, having sundered all other unities, all other sources of stability, fantasy shatters the unity of the individual.[117] In a reversal of the apocalyptist's pseudonymity, McCarthy went beyond the bounds of ghostwriting to appropriate materials never intended for his use. "America's Retreat from

Victory" is the most prominent example. McCarthy did not digest the materials provided by others and make them his own, he simply gave them voice. "McCarthyism" absorbed the identity of Joe McCarthy into the much larger phenomenon he represented.

Fantasy often signals the dissolution of identity with a narrative voice confused between first and third person singular.[118] McCarthy reveals the same split persona in his speeches and writings. He informs his audience, "The smear attacks on *McCarthy* are no longer being made with the hope that they can thereby force *me* to give up this fight to expose and get Communists out of government."[119] "On that day the President of the Newspaper Guild, Harry Martin, attacked *McCarthy* and made it clear to the membership that any favorable coverage of *my* fight against Communists was taboo."[120] "Even *my* bitterest enemy will admit, if he is honest, that these matters would not have been given a second thought if someone other than *McCarthy* were involved."[121] Between the two McCarthys, it seems likely that all his biographers are right in the main. Their mistake is in trying to find a nonexistent resting place. McCarthy's manic levels of activity are a metaphor for his world, which was in constant disequilibrium.

Does this leave us anything to say about the McCarthy *ethos,* fragmented and disjointed as it is? Certainly it can be said that McCarthy was no prophet: he was guided by no self-evident truths, no sacred canon; he did not offer judgment in time of crisis. All his cries of "smear" notwithstanding, the evidence overwhelmingly indicates that McCarthy did not suffer the burden of his commitments (at least not until after censure), but reaped the personal rewards of his message—notoriety, money, and political power. Nor did McCarthy confront his society with a radical position, for fantasy cannot posit. What was mistaken for radicalism by some of McCarthy's contemporaries was really just the hyperbolic, irrational discourse of fantasy parading as politics. Even as fantasy, McCarthy's was not very extraordinary by the standards of the period. Films of the Fifties shared many of the same themes and uncertainties we find in McCarthy's discourse. McCarthyism as a fantasy was little more than a shameless amalgam of *The Court Martial of Billy Mitchell* and *Invasion of the Body Snatchers.*[122] And radio programs such as "I Was a Communist for the FBI" provided audiences with an atmosphere of multiple reversals and subterfuges that made the convolutions of McCarthy's stories commonplace. A nation willing to join in the search for Bridey Murphy was not shaken by McCarthy's rejection of the traditional unities of narrative.

In failing to challenge his audience with the radical values of their society, McCarthy stood as a symbol of the deterioration of those values. Rather than reconstituting his audience, he left it in a state of dissolution. Richard Rovere has written,

> McCarthy, though a demon himself, was not a man possessed by demons. His talents as a demagogue were great, but he lacked the most necessary and awesome of demagogic gifts—a belief in the sacredness of his own mission. A man may go a long way in politics—particularly in democratic politics—without much in the way of convictions, but to overcome adversity he needs the strength that can be drawn either from belief in an idea or from a sense of his own righteousness. If he has no convictions, he can scarcely draw courage from them.[123]

Perhaps it is for this reason, rather than for its actual prohibitions, that Ellen Schrecker finds the legacy of McCarthyism to be one of absences: "McCarthyism's main impact may well have been in what did not happen rather than in what did—the social reforms that were never adopted, the diplomatic initiatives that were not pursued, the workers who were not organized into unions, the books that were not written, and the movies that were never filmed."[124]

McCarthy was plagued by demons and bereft of gods. He created a momentary audience out of common fears, but he could not provide it or himself with a sustaining cause. The swaggering, loutish Marine hero was a cripple, and we watched him toss away his crutches in an evangelical fever and fall on his face—pitiable and for that reason all the more despicable. McCarthy never assumed a radical heroic stand against the overwhelming uncertainties of his day; his faith lacked the necessary substance. The notable absence of historical references in his speeches reveals the shallowness of his response to the world. He had nothing to draw upon but the resources of his own profane experience. McCarthy could worship nothing larger than himself, only fear it.

McCarthy the man, we must probably conclude, was a tragic figure. He participated in the epistemological chaos of his time to the point of psychosis.[125] McCarthy's fantasy world was his poor response to fear, and it is only when we recognize fantasy as a form of spiritual impoverishment that we can properly evaluate what McCarthy wrought. Building her case on the work of Sartre, Foucault, and Frederic Jameson, Jackson finds in fantasy human compensation for a failure of the transcendent.[126] She quotes Maurice Levy's assertion that: "The fantastic is a compensation that man provides for himself, at the level of imagination, for what he has lost at the level of faith."[127] The compensation that humankind can provide for itself, however, is insufficient to replace what has been lost, for fantasy is hollow at its core:

> Unlike marvelous secondary worlds, which construct alternative realities, the shady worlds of the fantastic construct nothing. They are empty, emptying, dissolving. Their emptiness vitiates a full, rounded, three-dimensional visible world, by tracing in absences, shadows without objects. Far from fulfilling desire, these spaces perpetuate desire by insisting upon *absence,* lack, the non-seen, the unseeable.[128]

Fantasy, framed as a literary event, provides a temporary escape. It may even, as Sade claims of *Eugenie de Franval* and *Justine, or Good Conduct Well Chastised,* provide moral guidance.[129] When it is transposed without warning into the quotidian realm of politics and business, devoid of artistic boundaries, it is paralyzing.

For a time in the Fifties, America played Joseph K. at Joe McCarthy's court. Like the man in the enigmatic parable at the end of *The Trial,* we sat outside and waited for the law. What McCarthy presented to America in the Fifties was just such a world. We wanted him to execute judgment, to banish our demons, to provide us with a vision, a standard under which to march, and an enemy to march against. But McCarthy did not slay Ra'hab, the dragon of chaos, he only goaded it. We were left without gods or devils, heroes or villains, only the haunting suspicion that both existed. No clear, stable dramatic structure emerged, and the rules for judgment were systematically subverted. In emphasizing the darkness of the postwar world, McCarthy concentrated on what was unseeable and thereby unknowable. His promises notwithstanding, he never turned on the light. Rather he insinuated the lurking presence of "things that go bump in the night." There is no salvation here, only the articulation of anxiety. As soon as the show was over, the audience, as an audience, largely disintegrated, the residuum remaking itself on the edges of the politics of the 1960s as the John Birch Society. Only the McCarthy persona survives, precisely because of its insubstantiality, a ghost lurking about the dark places of American politics.

8

Prophecy as Poetry

The Romantic Vision of Robert Welch

And thou shalt speak my words unto them, whether they will hear, or whether they will forbear: for they *are* most rebellious. But thou, son of man, hear what I say unto thee; Be not thou rebellious like that rebellious house: open thy mouth, and eat what I give thee. And when I looked, behold, an hand *was* sent unto me; and, lo, a roll of a book *was* therein.   —Ezekiel 2:7–9

Then said I, Ah, Lord God! behold, I cannot speak: for I *am* a child. But the Lord said unto me, Say not, I *am* a child: for thou shalt go to all that I shall send thee, and whatsoever I command thee thou shalt speak. Be not afraid of their faces: for I *am* with thee to deliver thee, saith the Lord. Then the Lord put forth his hand, and touched my mouth. And the Lord said unto me, Behold, I have put my words in thy mouth.   —Jeremiah 1:6–9

From the time of its founding in 1958 until the mid-1960s, the John Birch Society and its founder Robert Welch were the most prominent features in the landscape of the political far right in America. Seymour Martin Lipset and Earl Raab suggest that Welch and his organization "took the center of the right-wing stage in America for close to a decade,"[1] and Benjamin Epstein and Arnold Forster termed the John Birch Society the "spearhead of the Radical Right movement."[2]

Granting these assessments, it must still be remembered that Welch never achieved anything like the influence that Joe McCarthy, often seen as Welch's predecessor, achieved. In fact, Welch's close identification with McCarthy made it easy for liberal intellectuals, shamed over their timidity in the McCarthy affair, to expiate their guilt by deriding McCarthy's heir apparent.[3] Writing in the *New York Times Magazine* in 1961, George

Barrett, pointing to the increasing ridicule of the society and its founder as evidence for his assessment, found the Birchers to be overrated as the source of a renascent McCarthyism.[4] In 1964, an article in the *New Republic* was entitled "Little Old Pink Man Who Called Ike Red."[5] Robert Welch was not the aggressive, hard-hitting, reckless bully that McCarthy had been. Welch was "little," diminutive; "old," frail, feeble, weak, impotent; "pink," silly, frivolous, toothless as a newborn animal, perhaps even effeminate; and finally, the sneering reference to one of Welch's most famous pronouncements concerning Eisenhower's alleged service to the communist cause indicates how far we were from taking Welch seriously. Other treatments were more direct in their assessment. A 1964 *Newsweek* article on Welch was entitled "Sick, Sick, Sick,"[6] and a 1966 article in *Time* suggested that Welch was "touched in the head":

> Since he founded the John Birch Society nearly ten years ago, Robert Welch has displayed one of the most fertile imaginations in American politics. Though his fascinating statement that Dwight Eisenhower had consciously served the "Communist conspiracy for all his adult life" will probably remain its foremost figment, his mind has lost none of its youthful fancy with advancing years.[7]

The quantity of ridicule directed at Welch, and its violence and energy, combine to belie the easy confidence suggested by its jocular condescension. Liberals of the early Sixties were certain that Welch was not a real threat, but they wanted to ensure that others understood this as well. Rather than paint him as a ruthless demagogue, then, those who opposed Welch dismissed him as a clown, a crackpot, a kook. That they felt it necessary to acknowledge Welch at all is testament to a perception of his potential power. That Welch never succeeded in realizing this power is the product of complex forces, some of which will be examined here.

Robert Welch as an Artist in Words

> O Freedom! If to me belong
> Not mighty Milton's gift divine,
> Nor Marvell's wit and graceful song,
> Still with a love as deep and strong
> As theirs, I lay, like them, my best gifts on thy shrine!
> —John Greenleaf Whittier, *Proem*

Against the popular portrait of Welch as a raving lunatic, he presented himself as a conscientious craftsman of language, a wordsmith, a poet. In *The Politician,* Welch informed the reader that it was an "unfinished manuscript,"[8] and bemoaned the pressures that led to its "premature publication."[9] In works intended for publication, Welch used vivid vocabulary, antithesis, parrhesia, triadic structures, polysyndeton, alliteration, anaphora, hyperbaton, metaphor, and allusion as favorite stylistic devices.

Some samples from Welch's writings include the assertion that we were moving deeper into an era of "darkness, slavery, and treason,"[10] and that the Birchers had suffered a "torrent of smear,"[11] in spite of which the Birch program persisted "with all of its dreams and ideals and aspirations."[12] Welch was semiapologetic that *The Blue Book* should appear somewhat dated to readers in 1961, but he explained, "There is no instant at which the shutter may be snapped so the print will remain true."[13] He warned his audience that the truth he brought "is simple, incontrovertible, and deadly . . . unless we can reverse forces which now seem inexorable in their movement."[14] A speech reprinted in *The Blue Book,* entitled "Look at the Score," uses an extended game metaphor to describe communist incursions on the free world,[15] occurring "with ever-increasing spread and speed,"[16] as we can see by the light of "the lamp of experience."[17]

Western Europe could not be depended on, for it was "either dying before our eyes, or is already dead. For the vigor of its muscles and the strength of its whole body have been sapped beyond recovery by the cancer of collectivism."[18] Yet there was hope in the persons of the "really true believers still left. We honor them. We need their steadying adherence to the rock of reverence, and their aspiration of unwavering obedience to ancient and divine commandments. We desperately need their unshakable confidence in absolutes, in eternal principles and truths, in a world of increasing relativity and transitoriness in all things. We admire them."[19] This, however, was not to be understood as a plea for fundamentalism. An attempt to enforce such an overly concrete and simplistic view of the world in our day and age "would be like trying to tie the waves of the ocean together with ropes, or to confine them with fishing nets."[20]

Not content with the entailments of the disease metaphor, Welch portrayed communism not only as a cancer but also as an octopus:

> so large that its tentacles now reach into all of the legislative halls, all of the union labor meetings, a majority of the religious gatherings, and most of the schools *of the whole world.* It has a central nervous system which can make its tentacles in the labor unions of Bolivia, in the farmer's cooperatives of

Saskatchewan, in the caucuses of the Social Democrats of West Germany, and in the classrooms of the Yale Law School, all retract or reach forward simultaneously. It can make all of these creeping tentacles turn either right or left, at the same time, in accordance with the intentions of a central brain in Moscow or Ust'-Kamenogorsk. The human race has never before faced any such monster of power which was determined to enslave it. There is no reason for underrating its size, its efficiency, its determination, its power, or its menace.[21]

Our proper attitude toward the enemy, whether octopus or disease, is conveyed by the war metaphor. We were, in Welch's mind, engaged in a pitched battle against the communist conspiracy.[22] To succeed in this battle, we needed to profit from all human experience, "but we shall make our own amalgam of the organizational metals forged by that experience with the mercury of our own purpose."[23] To make this amalgam Welch sought to reconstruct faith, which must be the "foundation of our new dream." He sought to unite various religious views under a faith "so true that neither our hearts nor our reasons can deny it, so broad that it takes in without violation the faith of our fathers, and so deep that it can inspire martyrdom at need."[24] In attempting to meld his new alloy, Welch alluded to the poem "God, the Architect" by Harry Kemp, the last stanza of which is

> But, chief of all thy wondrous works,
> Supreme of all thy plan,
> Thou hast put an upward reach
> In the heart of man.[25]

Welch hoped that this concept of God having put an upward reach in the heart of man would serve as an umbrella concept, transcending individual creeds and uniting his hearers. It was Welch's position on religion that made the John Birch Society the least sectarian of the extreme right-wing organizations.

There are many other examples of literary (self-)consciousness in Welch's writings. In closing his pamphlet "To the Negroes of America," Welch alluded to Lincoln's message to Congress of December 1, 1862: "This is our America. It is your country and mine, and the last best hope of all mankind."[26] It is not happenstance that Welch attempted to echo Lincoln in an appeal to blacks. "A Letter to Khrushchev" contains an extended metaphor comparing the Soviet world plan and their success with Sputnik. Welch compared the stages of the communist encroachment on the free world with the stages of the rocket ship.[27]

Certainly one of Welch's most artistic speeches is "More Stately Mansions."[28] In the title of this speech, he alludes to Oliver Wendell Holmes's poem "The Chambered Nautilus." The snail becomes the master metaphor for the speech. Welch found it an appropriate symbol for his cyclical view of history and an appropriate model for organizing the speech. "More Stately Mansions" spirals outward through a historical discourse and ultimately circles back around on itself. If we look to the sermon for an analog, Welch began with an implied "text" which he made explicit at the end of the speech, thus returning to his starting point. The chambered nautilus illustrated the moral of Welch's sermon, that individualism can be gained only through collectivism. The snail builds chambers, but those chambers grow successively larger until they become so expansive that they are no longer confining or restrictive. The final chamber is a transcendence. To conclude the speech, Welch quotes the last stanza of Holmes's poem:

> Build thee more stately mansions, O my soul,
> As the swift seasons roll!
> Leave thy low-vaulted past!
> Let each new temple, nobler than the last,
> Shut thee from heaven with a dome more vast,
> Till thou at length are free,
> Leaving thine outgrown shell by Life's unresting sea!

In "More Stately Mansions," whatever our evaluation of Welch's success, we must recognize the attempt to produce a well-made poem, a poem wherein "everything is formed, and hence rendered poetic (whatever it may have been in itself), by virtue simply of being made to do something definite in the poem or to produce a definitely definable effect, however local, which the same materials of language, thought, character-traits, or actions would be incapable of in abstraction from the poem, or the context in the poem, in which they appear."[29]

It was Welch's study of poetry, no doubt, that influenced the poetic qualities in his discourse. There are numerous quotations from poems and references to poems throughout Welch's speeches and writings. His favorite poets included James Russell Lowell, Holmes, Shelley, Whittier, Cowper, and Tennyson. In addition, there is some evidence in the speeches that Welch kept company with poets. He refers to Alfred Noyes as "my good friend," and the Harry Kemp quoted by Welch was a Massachusetts resident when he died in 1960. That Welch may have seen himself as part of a community of poets is further suggested by the fact that, in addition to his political discourses, he wrote what we commonly conceive to be poetry. His sonnet "To Alfred Noyes" appears in both *The Blue Book*[30] and in "Through the Days to Be."[31]

Welch is not alone among the figures examined here in exhibiting a poetic consciousness. Some of the enduring prose of the American Revolution and of Wendell Phillips and the abolitionists reveals the same qualities claimed here for Welch. John Greenleaf Whittier was, in fact, an active writer for the abolitionist cause. Phillips was fond of quoting Whittier, Pope, Milton, Carlyle, Elizabeth Barrett Browning, and Isaac Watts,[32] among others. With Eugene Debs in particular, Robert Welch shared a poetic heritage. Debs, who always expressed his indebtedness to Victor Hugo's *Les Misérables*, considered Walt Whitman "his good friend," and was a drinking buddy of James Whitcomb Riley, often quoted poetic sources in his speeches, including the works of Longfellow, Holmes, and Whitman, and sometimes achieved poetic quality in his own right.[33]

That radical discourse should consistently seek poetic forms may be seen as corroboration for some of the ideas expressed in chapter six concerning poetry and social order. But left here, the argument is incomplete. Thus far I have merely argued that Welch was a stylist, a conscientious craftsman of language. That claim may be surprising, but it is in itself relatively insignificant. It suggests that the relationship of Robert Welch to his discourse is more complex than the popular image of Welch as a lunatic would suggest—interesting, but trivial. If this claim is to be significant, some relationship between Welch's diction and his ideology must be posited.

I have already observed that poetic diction has, in many cultures throughout history, served as evidence of divine election. With Welch, this idea is particularly appealing. Welch was reared in the Southern Baptist Church, a tradition heavily infused with the radical poetry of evangelical hymnody.[34] When he left the Baptist Church, he became a Unitarian, a sect that has produced some of the most distinguished American hymnists, some of whom were also among Welch's favorite poets—Longfellow, Bryant, Emerson, Holmes, and Whittier.[35]

Both Baptism and Unitarianism have their roots in the tradition of eighteenth- and nineteenth-century evangelicalism, from the Greek *angelos* or "messenger." There are clearly strong parallels between the office of the evangel as a messenger of God and the calling of the prophet. That evangelical hymns replaced the singing of biblical psalms (including the words of the prophets) in evangelical worship services is a significant statement as to the perceived status of those hymns.[36] The "Behold!" of the evangel signals the same apodeictic discourse found in prophecy, a discourse that rests on, indeed is, the word of God.

Given the connections among poetry, song, and divine commission, and the facts of Welch's heritage, it seems not unreasonable to speculate that Welch's metaphors, anaphoras, and the like, if truly a reflection of this tradition, are more than ornamental blossoms plucked from Peacham's *Garden of Eloquence*. It seems more likely that they signal something essential about his self-concept. The question remains as to whether or not the substance of his discourse will bear out the thesis that Welch was a man possessed of a divine mission. With that end in mind, I turn to Welch's obsession with the nineteenth century and its poets.

Welch as Social Sage

> And how can man die better
> Than facing fearful odds
> For the ashes of his fathers
> And the Temples of his Gods.
> —Thomas Babington Macaulay, "Horatius"

> The sign and credentials of the poet are that he announces that which no man foretold. He is the true and only doctor; he knows and tells; he is the only teller of news, for he was present and privy to the appearance which describes. He is a beholder of ideas and an utterer of the necessary and causal. For we do not speak now of men of poetical talents, or of industry and skill in metre, but of the true poet.
> —Ralph Waldo Emerson, "The Poet"

That Welch's favorite poets are from the nineteenth century is not happenstance. The nineteenth century was a glorious time in history as Welch saw it, particularly American history. But the special appeal of the poets of this period for Welch was based on more than their location in time. The poets of the nineteenth century had a conception of themselves and their craft that Welch saw as necessary to rescue the America of the twentieth century from ruin. Welch is best understood through an understanding of his icons and their self-proclaimed role as social prophets.

It is a commonplace that reactionaries desire radical change in the sense that they wish to move backward in time. For Welch, backward was the nineteenth century.[37] Of the nineteenth century he said: "In my amateurish opinion, the last half of the nineteenth century A.D., like the first half of the sixth century B.C. before it, was the high water mark up to its time of human civilization, accomplishment, and hope for the future."[38] In "Republics and Democracies," Welch rhapsodized, "Throughout all of the nineteenth century and the very early part of the twentieth, while America as a republic was growing great and becoming the envy of the whole world, there were plenty of wise men, both in our country and outside it, who pointed to the advantages of a republic, which we were enjoying, and warned against the horrors of a democracy, into which we might fall."[39] It was during the nineteenth century that we experienced "the highest level to which man has yet climbed in his struggle to reach an enlightened and humane life,"[40] and the middle of the nineteenth century was "the very apex of the enlightenment achieved by the Western European Civilization."[41] At the close of his lecture on the first day of the founding meetings of the John Birch Society, Welch demonstrated his affinity for nineteenth-century America by quoting the last stanza of "The Battle Hymn of the Republic." Written by a fellow Unitarian, this hymn has been called "the most symbolic song" of the nineteenth century, one that reflects "the quintessence of Evangelical consensus that dominated nineteenth-century American culture."[42]

The poets Welch so admired and liberally quoted were both cause and consequence of this cultural attainment. Beginning with the publication of *Lyrical Ballads* in 1792 by Wordsworth and Coleridge, a new conception of poetry began, a poetry with a strong kinship to philosophy. Nineteenth-century poets looked upon eighteenth-century empiricism and found it wanting. Although they believed in the empirical world, the nineteenth-century poets, under the spell of Hegel, tended to be neo-Platonists in their belief in an ideal world that provided the underlying unity for the world of everyday life.[43] As it was for biblical prophets, history became an important vehicle for revealing the meaning of human events, an organic process with its source in universal moral law.[44] Because of its organic nature, poets like Carlyle could view history as potentially instructive: "Properly told, it teaches men their own true nature and how they should live," said Carlyle, "it reveals to them how the world they live in is organized."[45]

History, then, was a sacred story, and it was the duty of the poet to ensure that it was "properly told." According to Northrop Frye, poets of the nineteenth century saw themselves as central figures in civilization. They were able to claim this role because of an emerging view of humanity as the creative agent in its own world. Consequently, the poet's purpose as a serious writer was not primarily to please, but to enlighten the public and to expand its consciousness. Frye claims that "the Romantic poet often feels, even more oppressively than his predecessors, that his calling as a poet is a dedication, a total way of life, and that a commitment to it has an importance to society beyond poetry itself."[46] Shelley, for example, held that all the great authors of revolutions in the world's history were poets: "The most unfailing herald, companion, and follower of the awakening of a great people to work a beneficial change in opinions or institutions is poetry."[47] Thus it is that in the nineteenth century, Blake decried the black smoke emanating from the chimneys of England; Byron became physically involved in the struggle for Greek liberty; and Walt Whitman had his social vision. The masses are unable to articulate and thus mobilize against the moral torpor of the time; the poet must become their spokesperson.[48] In the words of Emerson,

> The great majority of men seem to be minors, who have not yet come into possession of their own or mutes, who cannot report the conversation they have had with nature. . . . Every man should be so much an artist that he could report in conversation what had befallen him. Yet, in our experience, the rays or appulses have sufficient force to arrive at the senses, but not enough to reach the quick and compel the reproduction of themselves in speech. The poet is the person in whom these powers are in balance, the man without impediment, who sees and handles that which others dream of, traverses the whole scale of experience, and is representative of man, in virtue of being the largest power to receive and to impart.[49]

The view expressed by Emerson and held by many of his contemporaries is comprehended in John Holloway's summary of the poetic activity of the late nineteenth century. Holloway writes, "For their own time they performed an activity which has an enduring place in human life: the activity, we might call it, of the sage."[50]

In the United States, it was "the mind of New England," to use Vernon Parrington's phrase, that dominated nineteenth-century thought. Parrington narrates the origins of the Romantic ascendancy in New England as a struggle of liberal Unitarian tendencies against the oppressive weight of Calvinism.[51] By Parrington's account, the mind of New England had a tremendous ethical impetus, and the ascendancy of Unitarianism over Calvinism may be described as the expansion of that ethical impetus to include a "warm social sympathy" or social conscience.[52] Ultimately, of course, Unitarianism plowed the ground in which the seeds of transcendentalism flourished, carrying the capacity of humankind to still greater heights and, using the ideal world as a standard by which to judge the extant one, carrying criticism to more stringent lengths than either Unitarianism or Puritanism before it.

This social impulse in nineteenth-century poetry is the impulse of the prophet, "the man without impediment, who sees and handles that which others dream of, traverses the whole scale of experience, and is representative of man, in virtue of being the largest power to receive and to impart." For Emerson, whom Harold Bloom practically equates with American Romanticism and whom Welch refers to as "the most profound of all Americans,"[53] the master metaphor was the "transparent eyeball." It is again the metaphor of vision, critical to the prophet in his role as seer. James Cox has argued, "If the metaphor did not cause Emerson to be what he was, it nonetheless reveals to us, in the light of what he turned out to be, *who* he was."[54] And Emerson was a prophet.

Among nineteenth-century poets, Emerson was not alone in his conception of his calling. Aaron Kramer writes, "Most poets believe that what their seraph-touched eyes behold *is* the Truth, and that their sacred mission is to transmit the Truth effectively enough for the listener to share."[55] This idea was particularly prominent in the nineteenth century. Kramer continues, "In the main . . . the enunciation of a truth is treated by the poet as a solemn duty and privilege. For a world in danger, he prophesies. For a world in darkness, he glows. He claims direct kinship with the inspired singers of all ages, all lands; these are his idols, their flame he holds aloft."[56] Finally, Kramer notes, American poets of the nineteenth century evidence a strong self-consciousness of their kinship to the prophets of the Old Testament as well as to their pre-Romantic forebears.[57]

As a prophet, the poet is circumscribed from making a "pretty tale" for "pretty people in a nice saloon." The poet must present the truth.[58] Emerson's speech "The American Scholar" is a benchmark example of the prophetic stance, although much of Emerson's discourse would be equally illustrative. Herbert Wichelns's description of Emerson's relationship to his audience is revealing in this context:

> Perhaps because of the manuscript, from which he seldom departed long, Emerson's auditors generally felt that he was not in direct communication with them. A public monologist, rather than a lecturer, one of his English

hearers styled him, and though the earnestness and simplicity of the speaker bespoke sympathy and respect, yet always there was a distance between the speaker and his hearers.[59]

It is indeed the manuscript that caused this distance, but it is the manuscript in a metaphoric as well as a literal sense. Emerson spoke from the manuscript of truth. John Sloan, who has noted the same distance between Emerson and his audiences that Wichelns has described, suggests that it is the result of a strong philosophical commitment that the speaker must speak the truth as he sees it, and that the truth cannot be compromised for the audience.[60]

This may have seemed a rather long digression away from our subject, Robert Welch, but it is actually the shortest route to Welch's essential character. To understand the nature of nineteenth-century poetry is to understand the nature of Welch's discourse.

Like the nineteenth-century poets and their predecessors the prophets, Welch begins with a vision of woe:

> Unless we can reverse the forces which now seem inexorable in their movement, you have only a few more years before this country in which you live will become four separate provinces in the world-wide Communist dominion rule by police-state methods from the Kremlin.[61]

> In summary, gentlemen, we are losing, rapidly losing, a cold war in which our freedom, our country, and our very existence are at stake.[62]

Not only did Welch have a vision, he was exceptional in having it. America was oblivious to the pending disaster; the communist conspiracy was taking place right under our very noses;[63] Welch constantly exhorts his audiences to "wake up."[64]

At first it is not clear whether Welch used the metaphors of vision, sleep, and conspiracy in a way similar to McCarthy or if his idea of sleep was more like that of Debs, Phillips, and the American Revolutionaries. There is in Welch's discourse the idea that a simple awakening is redemptive, an idea common to prophecy and genuinely radical American discourses. There is also the idea, seen in the rhetoric of McCarthy, of an evil conspiracy capable of magnificent deceptions, suggesting that a simple awakening may not be sufficient. Welch provides us with a clue in his admittedly odd description of a camouflage operation. Referring to one of Eisenhower's agreements regarding U.S. involvement in the International

Atomic Energy Agency, Welch said, "We think it was camouflaged but deliberate treason; and that camouflage consisted primarily of our unwillingness to use the senses God gave us and look squarely at plain facts."[65]

On the surface, the charge resembles those made against the Truman and Eisenhower administrations by McCarthy—"camouflaged but deliberate treason"—but for Welch, culpability rests ultimately with the American people for failing to use gifts provided by an omnipotent God to confront an inexorable truth—"to use the senses God gave us and look squarely at the facts." There is no suggestion here that evil has the power ultimately to confound God's will without our complicity; the facts, looked at squarely, are incorruptible. It is this fundamental faith that marks a critical difference between Welch and McCarthy and that qualifies Welch as a would-be prophet. Welch had a vision of the true.

The vision of the Old Testament prophets was a direct revelation from Yahweh. The vision of the nineteenth-century poets came from an acute sensitivity to their world. For both, history was the testament to the superordinate meaning of events in the world. Welch, too, found his vision in history. He was particularly enamored of Oswald Spengler's theory of history as cyclical, a theory of history resembling those prominent in the nineteenth century. About Spengler's theory (itself not far removed from the nineteenth century), Welch said, "Basically, when you dig through the chaff and the dressing in Spengler enough to get at his thought, he held that a societal development which we ordinarily classify as a civilization is an organic culture, which goes through a life cycle just the same as any of the individual organisms which we see whole and with which we are more familiar."[66] Welch went on to compare the lives of cultures to the lives of human beings in an analogy strikingly similar to one made by Emerson in his essay entitled "History."[67]

For Welch, as for Carlyle, the organic nature of history allowed it an instructive function, what Carlyle termed "didactic destiny." Welch's concern was that forces of evil, by their collectivist nature, had been better able to use the lessons of history than had the forces of good,[68] so he often opened his speeches with a "history lesson" designed to reveal the relevance of his message to his audience.[69]

History, for Welch, functioned, as it did for the prophets, as the arena in which God's purpose is revealed; it stood as an antidote to the twentieth-century tendency for man to see himself "as no longer responsible to a Divine Being, but as merely a living accident, not connected in any way with cosmological purpose."[70] "The keystone to my own religious belief," wrote Welch in *The Blue Book*, "I think, was best delineated by Tennyson in just one great line: 'For I doubt not through the ages one increasing purpose runs.' " And Welch went on to establish that that purpose is God's.[71] History was revelatory for Welch; it does not conceal or distort; it is "true" and "objective"; in history, if we do not "close our eyes" to the "difficult parts," we "see clearly."[72]

In Welch's faith in history, we find the optimistic side of his message, a faith in the possibility of salvation as part of God's divine plan. Dark and threatening as the picture of communist incursion may be, Welch had no doubt that "truth and honor and hope for the future, and everything that really counts in human life, are all on our side."[73] In a speech in 1969, Welch quoted a passage from *The Blue Book*, "still true today," that reveals his fundamental faith:

> We do not have to be too late, and we do not have to lose the fight. Communism has its weaknesses, and the Communist conspiracy has its vulnerable points. We have many layers of strength not yet rotted by all of the infiltration and political sabotage to which we have been subjected. Our danger is both immense and imminent; but it is not beyond the possibility of being overcome by the resistance that is still available. *All we must find and build and use, to win, is sufficient understanding.* Let's create that understanding and build that resistance, with everything mortal men can put into the effort—while there still is time.[74]

"The only thing which can possibly stop the Communists is for the American people to learn the truth in time," he wrote in *The Blue Book*.[75] "To feel that we cannot win . . . is a form of pessimism to which I, for one, shall never yield."[76]

The rhetoric appropriate to Welch's epistemology is a rhetoric now familiar from previous chapters, a rhetoric of education or demonstration. There was an irrepressible didacticism in the rhetoric of Wendell Phillips, and "education" was touted as the sole strategy of the Socialist Party. "The campaign of the Socialist Party is and will be wholly educational," declared Eugene Debs repeatedly.

> To arouse the consciousness of the workers to their economic interests as a class, to develop their capacity for clear thinking, to achieve their solidarity industrially and politically is to invest the working class with the inherent power it possesses to abolish the wage system and free itself from every form of servitude, and this is the mighty mission of the socialist movement.[77]

Unless the worker had a profound understanding of the true reasons underlying it, any "reform" at the political level was, for Debs, mere window
dressing; understanding of the socialist principle was necessary before genuine reform could be effected: "It is the value of the socialist principle that
is taught and emphasized, and if this is not understood and approved, the
vote is not wanted."[78]

As distant as they are politically, Welch shares with Debs a common faith
rooted in nineteenth-century epistemology, and his discourse reflects this
common heritage:

> Nowhere do these people know, nor will they believe, what is happening to
> them, until it is too late. And one reason is that the fundamentally decent
> human mind simply refuses to believe that any sizable clique of other human
> beings can become so totally evil. When you have a system of tyranny which
> depends on, and comprises within its methods of self-aggrandizement, every
> foulness known to man, a system which nobody wants, then one simple and
> straightforward fact should be as obvious as a sunrise. This is that all it
> would take to stop the advance of Communism would be the sufficient
> understanding of Communism — of its purposes, its methods, and its prog-
> ress — by the people over whom it is surreptitiously weaving its infinite lines
> of power.[79]

The threat of evil is great, but it is only made possible by the reluctance of
the people to confront it, a willful blindness. The truth, when acknowledged, is omnipotent and sufficient to dispel the threat. The proper means
for gaining acknowledgment of the truth is, according to Welch, education:

> For we regard education as the means, and political action as only the
> mechanics, for bringing about improvements in government. The mechanics
> of change will automatically be used when sufficient education has prepared
> the way. We mean it quite literally, therefore, when we say that education is
> our total strategy, and truth is our only weapon. Or when we say, as made
> clear throughout The Blue Book and emphasized on its last page, that our
> gigantic task is simply to create understanding.[80]

Welch's metaphor of the truth as weapon echoes Wendell Phillips's "God
has given us no weapon but the truth, faithfully uttered, and addressed,
with the old prophet's directness, to the conscience of the individual
sinner."[81] In the discourse of Phillips, we have the nineteenth-century
doctrine of perfectionism in full flower, a doctrine in which Debs also
shared. Perfectionism involved the ability of human beings to partake of
divine truth and to order their lives accordingly. Welch's frequent allusion

to the "upward reach" that God has placed in the heart of man, along with his faith in the ability of God's truth to touch humanity, reflects his devotion to the same idea.

John L. Thomas has described the nineteenth-century perfectionist's view of reform in a way that illuminates Welch's faith and his strategy: "Deep and lasting reform," writes Thomas, "meant an educational crusade based on the assumption that when a sufficient number of individual Americans had seen the light, they would automatically solve the country's social problems."[82] Welch could hardly have expressed it better when he said:

> The John Birch Society believes that simple truth is the very core of morality; and that when we can persuade enough people to make truth the prerequisite to all statements and the accepted guide to all actions, at least half of the world's problems will rapidly disappear.[83]

From this perspective, it is difficult to escape the vision of Welch as the avatar of the nineteenth-century "educator-prophet," the "true reformer" who "studied man as he is from the hand of the Creator, and not as he is made by the errors of the world."[84] Welch's faith lay in the potential of uncorrupted human nature.

It is in the distance between the potential of uncorrupted human nature and its actual fallen state that the tension of Welch's message lies. Welch spoke to a world in which "all faith has been replaced, or is rapidly being replaced, by a pragmatic opportunism with hedonistic aims."[85] In this atmosphere, it was far too easy, in Welch's view, for an American

> to make decisions about his own life and actions entirely on the basis of his temporal comforts and the earthly desires of his own personality. If he is the kind of man that wants financial success for the ease, or leisure and travel, or the prestige which it supposedly brings (and sometimes does), he is not going to buck Communist pressures in any way that will endanger that success or handicap his progress. If he is imbued with ambition for power, he is more readily inclined to get on the Communist bandwagon, if that seems to be the surest road to power (as it certainly does to a great many Americans today).[86]

Welch's indictment of such selfishness is related to his praise of the American republic of the nineteenth century. Republican virtue, the very same as that valorized by the Revolutionaries, Phillips, and Debs, stands at odds to such placing of the self above the community. Welch's derogation of "ease" and "leisure" recalls the rhetoric of strength and sacrifice of the American radical tradition.

In an atmosphere of moral laxity, Welch came to make judgment and to resurrect the terms of the American covenant:

> We must oppose falsehoods with truth, blasphemy with reverence, foul means with good means, immorality and amorality with more spiritual faith and dedication, rootlessness and chaos with tradition and stability, relativity with absolutes, pragmatism with deeper purposes, hedonism with a more responsible pursuit of happiness, cruelty with compassion, and hatred with love.[87]

Inaugurating the John Birch Society in 1958, Welch quoted Emerson to the effect that "every mind must make its choice between truth and repose. . . . It could not have both." He continued, "Today you have left your choice somewhat in my hands. And I am not only bringing you truth instead of comfort, but truth which may shatter a lot of the comfort you already feel."[88] The history lesson with which he began was "tedious and perhaps even painful,"[89] but his perennial rationale was "We must not only know the truth, but face the truth, if it is to set us free or to keep us so."[90]

Welch's task, then, was not always welcome or pleasant, but he had been called, and he felt the weight of his mission in the same manner as Frye suggests the nineteenth-century poets felt the weight of their divinations. In the rhetoric of Welch, as in the rhetoric of those who preceded him, we hear the call of duty:

> Not only are we a part of some mighty purpose beyond our understanding, and not only do we have a clear duty to be true to that purpose to the fullest extent that we are allowed to grasp its workings and its direction; but all human experience shows that the total happiness of any generation and of its posterity is directly tied to the respect of that generation for the "upward reach" in man's nature.[91]

Welch allowed no choice in his mission, and he asserted "that there is no force and no discouragement which could make me quit or even put less of my life and energy into the struggle."[92] Welch "offers himself" as a "personal leader" in the fight against communism:

> The only thing which can possibly stop the Communists is for the American people to learn the truth in time. It is to contribute my small bit to such an awakening that I have given up most of my business responsibilities and most of my income, in order through my magazine and speeches to bring some inkling of the truth to as many people as I can reach. I do not expect nor deserve any slightest applause or sympathy for this sacrifice. I mention it at

all for just one reason only—which is to show how deadly serious the situation appears to me.[93]

In other places, Welch noted how "we" have been smeared, how "we" have suffered, how "we" have been slandered, but duty demanded that there be no deterrent. As he introduced the problem to the group gathered at the organizational meeting of the John Birch Society, it was a question of duty:

> Nobody in this group was selected because he would be coming to the meeting for personal pleasure, and I am sure nobody has done so. The ultimate reason that brought each man here was a sense of patriotic duty, and deep concern for the future of his family and his country.[94]

The theme of martyrdom and self-sacrifice is one Welch shares not only with the American Revolutionaries, Wendell Phillips, and Eugene Debs, but also with the poets of the nineteenth century. Aaron Kramer notes that nineteenth-century poets developed a complete tradition of martyrdom replete with a canon of martyred poets of the past and predictions of continued torture for the future.[95] "That the true men must pay for their truths is terribly clear,"[96] writes Kramer, but they persist because "almost all of them couple the expectation of martyrdom with a sense of privilege at being chosen, and confidence in the ultimate triumph of their integrity."[97] The martyred canon represents a kind of great hereafter for those who have dared to stand against the comfortable consensus of their time.

The question of duty or calling is inextricably bound to Welch's relationship to his message and to his audience. The message, for Welch and for his progenitors, was primordial and could not be compromised to the demands of the audience or situation. The audience must be molded to the message. Compare the following descriptions of Welch's speaking style to Wichelns's description of Emerson quoted earlier:

> Welch wore a black business suit and looked like a traveling shoe salesman. He was unaware of his audience, and spoke from carefully prepared note cards, looking up only when he wanted to extemporize a point. He hesitated every time someone booed or laughed or shouted disapproval, but plodded on through his accusations.[98]

> Mr. Welch seems to be unaware of his audience, talking to his lecture cards and keeping almost word-for-word to the same ninety-minute speech in each town. He is touchy, however; if there is a shuffle in the audience he hesitates, and looks up suspiciously.[99]

Welch was not of his audience; he was consecrated, separate. His rectitude was not a matter of their approval, and his success was not subject to earthly measure. He bore witness to God's truth. Welch, in short, conceived of himself as a prophet, a sacred messenger.

It may be objected that it is not necessary to view Welch as a nineteenth-century poet in order to account for the characteristics in his discourse noted here, but it is the case that evidence of Welch's kinship with nine-teenth-century poetry is ubiquitous. It also appears that the epigraph to *The Blue Book,* and used again for "What Is the John Birch Society?" may be read as a poetic statement of Welch's conception of his mission. It reads as follows:

> But on one man's soul it hath broken,
>   A light that doth not depart;
> And his look, or a word he hath spoken
>   Wrought flame in another man's heart.

And it is certainly the case that Welch, no less than the nineteenth-century poets themselves, held much of nineteenth- century poetry to be holy writ. In *The Blue Book* Welch wrote,

> And gentlemen, lest some of you think there is anything blasphemous or even too secular in my repeated reference to the poets in this discussion, let me point out to you that the men who wrote many of the books of the Old Testament, and those who wrote most of the books of the New Testament, were the poetic spirits of their respective ages. Theirs were the minds on which their contemporaries and successors depended to interpret and phrase man's most profound thoughts, most permanent beliefs, and deepest faith. Those same interpretations and recordings and expressions of man's devel-oping experiences, beliefs, and faith do not come to us today as further books added to our Bible; but they are being given to us, with greater and easier understanding than we might otherwise achieve, by the same kind of reverent and poetic minds.[100]

Welch evidenced a strong consciousness of the role of the nineteenth-century poets and of their relationship to the Old Testament prophets. It seems clear that these poets were Welch's models.

There are additional comparisons that might be drawn between Welch and his nineteenth-century preceptors, particularly between Welch and Emerson. Welch often expressed his admiration for Emerson, calling him "the most profound of all Americans," and quoting him often. Not only was Emerson an individualist and staunchly antisocialist—themes very important to Welch—he was also the first truly American philosopher. Lewis Mumford has characterized Emerson as "the father of American literature;"[101] Harold Bloom has called him simply "Mr. America";[102] Oliver Wendell Holmes called Emerson's 1837 Phi Beta Kappa address at Harvard "an American intellectual Declaration of Independence,"[103] and other sources credit Emerson's era with production of the first distinctively American literature.[104] Emerson's "Americanism," to use the label Welch adopted for his own philosophy, must have been terribly appealing to a man who believed himself to be profoundly American. In addition to references in Welch's writings, we also know that Welch left his childhood religion to become a Unitarian, the sect in which Emerson preached, and that Welch chose to headquarter the John Birch Society just outside Emerson's home city of Boston. These conjectures are interesting, but they are ultimately no more than that. Welch was always quite closed regarding his personal life, and it is not likely that he would confess in print that he modeled his life after that of Emerson.[105]

Such a confession, however, is unnecessary to the argument that Robert Welch was a poet-prophet. His attention to style is part of a tradition in which eloquence is equated with vision. Imitating his nineteenth-century models, Welch sought to lay claim to a vision common to nineteenth-century poets and the prophets of the Old Testament. To make this identification is not to make an evaluation, however. Unlike McCarthy, there is no question that Welch was a man possessed of a positive faith. The question remains as to whether Welch may have been one of the many well-intentioned but deceived who have believed they spoke with the authority of divine truth.

Robert Welch and the Poetry of Imitation

> Conservatism makes no poetry, breathes no prayer, has no invention; it is all memory. —Ralph Waldo Emerson, "The Reformer"

> Talk not of genius baffled. Genius is master of man. Genius does what it must, and Talent does what it can.
> —Owen Meredith, "Last Words of a Sensitive Second-Rate Poet"

The crisis Robert Welch confronted in the late 1950s and early 1960s was a crisis of faith more than it was any temporal threat from communism.

Communism itself was only a symptom of the larger moral paralysis. Welch's view of the decline of faith closely parallels the decline of nineteenth-century modes of belief outlined in chapter 6. Welch praised the nineteenth century and the first half of the twentieth for their moral strength, but he noted in 1958 that "For the last fifty years our age has been a dream that was dying. . . . The basic reason why the old age is dying, as I tried to make clear yesterday, is that the faith which was the core of its strength no longer commands the unquestioning loyalty of enough of its devotees. For the dream of any nation or any people must depend on faith." [106]

The faith Welch sought to restore is the faith expressed in a poem by Tennyson that Welch quotes:

> Our little systems have their day;
>   They have their day and cease to be:
>   They are but broken lights of Thee,
> And Thou, O Lord, art more than they.[107]

Tennyson's faith was an admirable one, in Welch's view, but as a framework of belief it "could not withstand the sheer facts and convincing rationalizations of the scientific revolution." [108] To the faith expressed in Tennyson's poetry, Welch contrasted "the cynical flippancy of a current gem":

> A life force afflicted with doubt,
> As to what its own being was about,
>   Said: "The truth I can't find,
>   But I'm creating a mind,
> Which may be able to figure it out.[109]

It is instructive that Welch used poetry as his benchmark in comparing the age of faith to the age of cynicism, skepticism, and nihilism in which he found himself. Tennyson's poem, in its form, reflects the striving toward order and stability in his era. It is characterized by regular and predictable schemes of rhyme and meter; its form is reassuring. The second poem quoted by Welch expresses twentieth-century sentiments, but it is still essentially conservative in its tenacious adherence to the old forms. Welch could easily have pointed to the changed form (or formlessness) of twentieth-century poetry to make his case. The poetry of e. e. cummings is a convenient and prominent example in which patterns of rhyme and meter are discarded along with the rules of punctuation and the conventions of grammar. The form of much of twentieth-century poetry reflects the chaos about which the poem quoted by Welch only talks. The music of Wolpe, a contemporary of Welch, provides an example of the same tendencies on the musical side of poetic form. Welch's longing for the order of traditional forms was reflected in his own use of the sonnet for his eulogy "To Alfred Noyes." Welch provided the prescribed fourteen lines of iambic pentameter with the rhyme scheme abba, cddc, efefef.[110]

Welch's emphasis on form is consistent with the formal aspects of the nineteenth-century philosophy upon which it was based, and his prophecy seems, finally, to reduce to a reification of form, a ritualistic performance of the poem. It is liturgical. Liturgy and ritual are antithetical to prophecy. Ritual reassures; it confirms the regnant order. Prophecy challenges. Ritual suggests continuity; prophecy is a response to crisis. Ritual is often the cosmetic illusion of order painted over the anguished face of chaos; beneath the mask, it is hollow. Welch's ritual, too, was an empty one. It is the calcified shell that is left when the living organism has died. It is only the outward appearance of the organism. Welch's ritual was empty because, as he correctly observed, the epistemology of the late twentieth century would not support it.

Welch held the founding meeting of the John Birch Society almost a decade after McCarthy gave his famous speech at Wheeling, West Virginia. The acute dislocation the American people had felt in 1952 had, by late 1958, subsided to the status of a dull ache. The late Fifties and early Sixties were prosperous times in America, and material well-being served as an effective salve for our epistemological wounds. There was a period after the American withdrawal from Korea and prior to a general awareness of our involvement in Viet Nam when the world seemed peaceful and nonthreatening. In 1960, America chose as its new president the youthful and liberal John Kennedy over that old communist-hunter Richard Nixon. Kennedy both reaffirmed our faith in America's strength against communism in the Cuban missile crisis and consorted with Martin Luther King, Jr., a man whom J. Edgar Hoover, the most unimpeachable source of the McCarthy era, had called a "liar." Kennedy's election serves to indicate the degree to which America was ready to accept the post–Second World War corporate-liberal alliance, an alliance characterized by an outlook that has been termed "pluralistic." Many of the men associated with the Kennedy cabinet were the architects of this new consensus.

Pluralism was, of course, not created in the post–Second World War world; it has had various forms throughout the history of philosophy. Of particular interest here is William James's turn-of-the-century campaign for a pluralistic philosophy as against a then-predominate nineteenth-century "absolute idealism." James savaged Hegel, on whose philosophy of history so much nineteenth-century poetry was based, and he gently chided Emerson for yielding himself "to the perfect whole."[111] James's was a philosophy that reflected, in Richard Bernstein's words, the "untidiness of experience and the cosmos itself: . . . He leaves us with as many questions to be asked as he has answered. It is impossible to rest content with James's philosophy, and he would be the first to insist upon this."[112] James himself said of pluralism's poor show against monism,

> Whether materialistically or spiritualistically minded, philosophers have always aimed at cleaning up the litter with which the world apparently is filled. They have substituted economical and orderly conceptions for the first sensible tangle; and whether these were morally elevated or only intellectually neat, they were at any rate always aesthetically pure and definite, and aimed at ascribing to the world something clean and intellectual in the way of inner structure. As compared with all these rationalizing pictures, the pluralistic empiricism which I profess offers but a sorry appearance. It is a turbid, muddled, gothic sort of an affair, without a sweeping outline and with little pictorial nobility. Those of you who are accustomed to the classical constructions of reality may be excused if your first reaction upon it be absolute contempt—a shrug of the shoulders as if such ideas were unworthy of explicit refutation. But one must have lived some time with a system to appreciate its merits.[113]

By 1960, Americans had lived with James's pluralism for half a century, although most would not have been able to identify the source. That we had kept it locked in the attic like a retarded child for much of that time while we clung tenaciously to the old order, proved to be an insufficient interdiction against it. And if pluralism was not a comfortable philosophy, it was at least pragmatic. In James's description of the classical conception of the world, on the other hand, we see both its essentially generous spirit and its false promise. Welch came to the debate fifty years too late to be of aid to Emerson.

The generally complacent atmosphere of the early 1960s in America betrayed Welch's claim to the existence of a crisis of faith. It appears that there was, at worst, a personal discomfort, which Welch shared with a relatively small number of Americans. Genuine radicalism cannot project a purely personal vision. If it attempts to do so, it fails to engage the society to which it is addressed. Even the notion of extremism suggests a relation to society. The purely personal vision does not. The willingness of most

Americans to accept "a pluralistic universe" weakened the root or charismatic terms over which Welch sought to engage us. The one had fractured into the many, and the potential army had been left scattered across the ideological landscape; transcendence and absolutism are not adequate rallying cries in a pluralistic world.

Welch at one point attributes to Emerson the sentiment that "it is the outlook of genius to feel that what is true of yourself is also true of all mankind." Welch modestly claims not to have genius but only to imitate it.[114] Here we have two keys to Welch's ultimate failure as a prophet. First, Welch attempted to give a common voice to America at a time when the idea of the common voice had been discredited. Second, the voice with which Welch spoke was not his own or even of his own time, but an imitation, a pale memory of voices from the past. It seems somehow appropriate that the harshest criticism of Welch should be found in the words of one of the poet-prophets he most admired. There is a sense both of Emerson's genuine prophetic power and of Welch's lack as Emerson reaches across a century to scold his epigone:

> Every man has his own voice, manner, eloquence, and, just as much, his own sort of love and grief and imagination and action. Let him scorn to imitate any being, let him scorn to be a secondary man, let him fully trust his own share of God's goodness, that, correctly used, it will lead him on to perfection which has no type yet in the universe, save only in the Divine Mind.[115]

Robert Welch came to the audience of the mid-twentieth century with the vision and vocabulary of the nineteenth. Barely more than a decade after his death we see the man who dominated the political right in America in the 1960s in sepia tones framed by brittle edges. Welch did not speak to our time. Coleridge would have called him a pedant, one who uses words "unsuitable to the time, place, and company."

Poetry has changed dramatically in the twentieth century. Of the two tendencies prevalent in nineteenth-century poetry—the tendency toward introspection and the urge to create socially significant poetry—it is the tendency toward the self which, not surprisingly, survives in our pluralistic culture. In a book published in 1960, Archibald MacLeish discussed the withdrawal of poetry from public life and mused that "poetry was never a house cat before."[116] Small wonder that we did not recognize Robert Welch; he had been dead for over half a century.

Welch's failure has its parallel in Old Testament prophecy. The prophet, writes Abraham Heschel, "is a person who knows what time it is."[117] The classical prophets of the eighth century B.C.E. knew what time it was and knew God's purpose for that time, but, as James Crenshaw has argued, there was a nascent decay of prophecy in the tensions within prophecy itself.[118] By the sixth century B.C.E., great gaping cavities are evident in the foundations of prophecy. The post-Exilic prophets proclaimed themselves to be the messengers of Yahweh to an individualistic, syncretistic world. In such a world, it is not the particular truth that the prophet tells that finds no support, but the idea that there is a truth at all; Yahweh must take His place as one among many. The epistemological structure of the time could not support the tremendous weight of prophecy, only its empty shell. In my final case study, I turn to a movement so thoroughly secular that not even the forms of prophecy are available to it.

9

Secular Argument and the Language of Commodity
Gay Liberation and Merely Civil Rights

> Stay yourselves, and wonder; cry ye out, and cry: they are drunken,
> but not with wine; they stagger, but not with strong drink. For the
> Lord hath poured out upon you the spirit of deep sleep, and hath
> closed your eyes: the prophets and your rulers, the seers hath he cov-
> ered.   —Isaiah 29–9–10

> Behold, the days come, saith the Lord God, that I will send a famine
> in the land, not a famine of bread, nor a thirst for water, but of hear-
> ing the words of the Lord: And they shall wander from sea to sea, and
> from north even to the east, they shall run to and fro to seek the word
> of the Lord, and shall not find *it*.   —Amos 8:11–12

It is in the post–World War II, postmodern world that the
movement for homophile liberation in America first made its appearance.
Only since 1948 has there been a sustained effort on behalf of gay and
lesbian rights in the United States. Such a movement had to await the
dissolution in the postwar period of various sources of authority, sources of
authority that had supported an ideology puissant enough to secure the
denigration of the homosexual self. Indeed, according to the most commonly told version of the story, it was not until 1969 that homosexuals in
the United States rallied and sustained a strong enough sense of self-worth
to demand rights. Historically, religion, science, and the law concurred in
holding homosexuals to be pariahs. As Edmund White has put it, "At that
time [1969] we perceived ourselves as separate individuals at odds with
society because we were 'sick' (the medical model), 'sinful' (the religious
model), 'deviant' (the sociological model) or 'criminal' (the legal model).

Some of these words we might have said lightly, satirically, but no amount of wit could convince us that our grievances should be remedied or our status defended. We might ask for compassion but we could not demand justice."[1] As long as such an ideology could be effectively maintained, it precluded any possibility of organization of behalf of gay rights. Before homosexuals could organize for rights, there had to be a significant dereliction of this orthodoxy.

The church, medical science, and the law are viewed by gay and lesbian activists as three parts of a mutually reinforcing system of social control.[2] Religion and science, with their shared assumptions about the objectivity of the world and the ability to know it in absolute terms, have tended to treat the world they reveal as external to humanity, something separate, sacred. Science profanes the temple by exposing its innermost chambers and by using the forces of nature to its own ends, but it cannot alter the basic substance; it cannot make man and nature coequal.[3] Both religion and science find normative implications in the worlds they reveal, and both have used the law to enforce these norms in human society. Considered another way, the law has used both religion and science as justification for its strictures. In the interplay among religion, science, and law is the collocation, "the laws of nature and of nature's God." As evidenced in the statement above by Edmund White and countless others like it, gay men and lesbians in America share a profound understanding of our status as violators of this monolithic law.

The hegemonic quality of this ideological construction is not what is most remarkable here. What is remarkable is the degree to which it illustrates how the oppressed become coconspirators in their own oppression. Mort Crowley's *The Boys in the Band* is the classic presentation of gay self-loathing and the hopelessness of redemption. Homosexuals are not authorized to speak with the voice of righteousness. Until quite recently, homosexuals as a group willingly prostrated ourselves before the awesome certainty of our illness;[4] concluded, as Bruce Bawer did, that there "was no way to be both gay and Christian;"[5] and, having repudiated access to moral argument either by self-condemnation or excommunication, were quiescent in the face of oppressive laws, for behind the laws lay the incontrovertible justice of natural law as revealed by religion and science.[6] For as long as a significant consensus held the univocality of these three institutions regarding homosexuality, homosexuals were left without any moral claims against oppressive laws.[7]

The rhetorical poverty of the gay rights position is revealed when compared to the requirements of Patricia Schmidt's paradigm for social change. Based on her study of Lord Ashley and the Ten Hours Factory Act, Schmidt concludes, "Support for a new policy in a moral age requires that morally-based justifications be established over time by individuals who are perceived to be motivated by moral considerations."[8] The American radicals examined in this study consistently attempted such a moral stance in their various crusades, but homosexuals have been decisively excluded from assuming such a position. In an age that subscribes to the morality presented here, it is preposterous to believe that God would favor the violation of His law.

If an issue can be placed in the moral realm, it is at the same time removed from the political. In the preceding chapters, American radicals have been shown consistently to place themselves and their causes above and beyond politics. If an issue can not only be placed in the moral realm, but also condemned, it is moribund. There is no radical potential in sin or in sickness. A society may work to cure or to exorcise sickness or moral failing, and in doing so it transforms the problem into a problem of the individual rather than one of the social order. Social protest is not an option where such a transformation has been successful. In this way, deviant groups are made politically marginal. The sick and the fallen, like lost sheep, await the shepherd who will lead them back into the fold or to the slaughterhouse.[9]

Liberation through Tolerance

If gay men and lesbians could not command the recognition of God-given rights, there was at least hope that, in the absence of God, certain rights might be granted. Although Dennis Altman, like Edmund White and many others who write on the homophile movement in America, tends to discount the activity of "homophile rights" organizations prior to the Stonewall Rebellion in 1969, what he says about the character of the movement is revealing: "Because gay liberation opposes so many of the basic assumptions around which society is organized, because it repudiates both the expectations of the straight world and the guilts and hostilities that these have produced in the gay world, it could only emerge amidst conditions of flux and considerable uncertainty about traditional moral values."[10] The aftermath of the Second World War saw the efflorescence of uncertainties that had been germinating since the turn of the century, and it was in this atmosphere of confused permissiveness that homophile liberation organizations were at last able to take root.[11]

The two world wars and the Great Depression had focused America's attention for a time on our common devils, granting us the illusion of community, but as soon as the devils were vanquished and we had the opportunity to look again to ourselves, we discovered that we had no common God. William Lee Miller provides a chiaroscuro of the tensions by tracing the development of religious "neo-orthodoxy" in the period between the world wars. Neo-orthodoxy was an attempt to restore a sacred code in the void left by "liberal Protestantism," which Miller characterizes as " 'tolerant' and inclined to deprecate creedal- doctrinal distinctions[,] . . . 'democratic' and humanistic in ethics and strongly inclined to reduce religion to ethics[,] . . . optimistic and progressive, taking a sanguine view of man and society: in all this it fits very well into American ideas."[12] But neo-orthodoxy had contradictions of its own, suffered an infection of liberal pluralism, and was itself reduced to rules of etiquette, a truly civil religion, charming but impotent.[13]

The ethic of tolerance, however, was more than an ethic of default; tolerance was seen as a positive good. In 1962, Arthur M. Schlesinger, Jr., looked upon the American landscape and eulogized a twentieth-century view of freedom that had long shed itself of its nineteenth-century companion, moral absolutism: "Freedom implies humility, not absolutism; it implies not the tyranny of the one but the tolerance of the many. Against the monolithic world, the American intellectual tradition affirms the pluralistic world. Against the world of coercion, it affirms the world of choice."[14] "Freedom," the God term of the American Revolution, Wendell Phillips's abolitionist rhetoric, and Eugene Debs's labor agitation here has a strange harmonic; its tone is no longer colored by the counterpoint of "duty," "right," and "judgment." Edwin Schur provides an incisive characterization of the modern view of freedom when he writes, "Unless one subscribes to some thoroughgoing conception of natural law, it would seem that the realities of life in a culturally (and morally) pluralistic world should cause one to be extremely cautious about implying a basis for moral certitude."[15] Schur pinpoints exactly the missing element of the new freedom; liberty is no longer a right endowed by nature, but a permission.

In an atmosphere of permissiveness, Alfred Kinsey's *Sexual Behavior and the Human Male* was merely another symptom of the "scientization" and "demystification" of the world and the rationalization of sexual mores, not a causal factor of moral crisis as Edward Sagarin insinuates.[16] The first so-called "Kinsey report" and the almost simultaneous genesis of homophile liberation groups were both made possible, not only by the evanescence of sacred prohibitions, but by the active encouragement of a new enlightenment.

As a part of this enlightenment, the 1948 Kinsey report represented an important shift in the focus of science where sexual mores were concerned. Left to support the weight of an otiose moral code, the medical and social sciences found themselves divided. Deprived of a common faith, they were left with nothing but their own profession of impartiality and objectivity as a guide. Recognizing that "whatever beneficent results medicine might promise, by the mid-twentieth century it had in fact branded homosexual men and women with a mark of inferiority no less corrosive of their self-respect than that of sin and criminality," John D'Emilio goes on to make the following observation:

> Yet to a certain extent physicians also subverted the earlier approaches. Once homosexual behavior entered the realm of science, it became subject to careful investigation. No matter how solid the consensus that homosexuality was a disease, the accumulation of empirical evidence could inspire dissenting theories, whereas Christian teachings rested on the immutable words of the Bible. Unlike moralists and law enforcement officials, doctors had a vested interest in naming, describing, and classifying the "unmentionable vice" in all its forms. . . . The medical model introduced a dynamic element into discussions of same-sex eroticism that could serve the interests of reformers.[17]

In the postwar period, science found itself incapable of enforcing proscriptions in the name of nature and of nature's God that religion was unwilling to make. The diminuendo of God's "Thou shalt not . . ." following the Second World War represents a very real change for sexual mores in general and for homosexuals in particular. The dereliction of natural law allowed for a new ethic of permissiveness. It is in this sense of permission that homophile liberation is best understood.

Deprived of the authority of religion and science, the law stood exposed as a very fragile creation. Grant Gilmore, in the 1974 Yale Law School Storrs Lectures on Jurisprudence, argued that American law over the first half of this century suffered the loss of the nineteenth-century ideal of one true law in the Platonic sense, eternal and unchanging, and yielded to a pluralistic legal realism. Gilmore describes the law, not as holy writ, but as something "designed to insure that our institutions adjust to change, which is inevitable, in a continuing process which will be orderly, gradual, and, to the extent that such a thing is possible in human affairs, rational. The function of the lawyer is to preserve a skeptical relativism in a society hell-bent for absolutes. When we become too sure of our premises, we necessarily fail in what we are supposed to be doing."[18] Like latter-day Hobbesians, legal realists assume no law behind the law. The law is not something that is found, but something that is, in Gilmore's word, "designed." Consequently, Gilmore finds a great increase in statutory law in the twentieth century, for there is no conception of an unwritten law that governs those cases not explicitly redacted.[19]

When the sacred is demystified, it is reduced to the pedestrian. When Toto drew back the curtain and revealed the Wizard, we discovered that he was really just a displaced Kansan, a man like ourselves against whom our demands could be boldly pressed. The vulnerability of the law and its power, stripped of any countervailing claims, to provide the sanction of legality, if not righteousness, was not lost on homosexuals. One of the most important products of the movement toward legal realism is the Model Penal Code of the American Law Institute. Reflecting the best impulses in twentieth-century pluralism, the Model Penal Code, among its other provisions, decriminalized homosexual behavior between consenting adults. From the time of its publication in 1955, the Model Penal Code provided an opportunity for a movement that heretofore had been purely defensive to take the offensive by opening laws to criticism based on twentieth-century notions of the reasonable, a criticism that could never have impugned the sacred.[20]

Recently, Andrew Sullivan has defined separate argumentative fields for religion and politics, which, while each may influence the other, are held to incommensurable standards of judgment. "One of the first principles of liberal societies, as they have emerged from the theocracies and dictatorships of the past, is that the religious is not the same as the political; that its very discourse is different; and that the separation of the two is as much for the possibility of vibrant faith as it is for the possibility of a civil polity."[21] Sullivan disqualifies arguments based on religious authority alone from participation in the civil realm because they are unanswerable and insists that "religiously based civil reasons," susceptible to judgment by the rules of reason and open to discussion, "are an essential part of any liberal polity."[22]

Most recently, an editorial on *Romer v. Evans* made clear that the issues at stake were constitutional and legal, not moral:

It [Colorado's Amendment 2] is an attempt by the majority to prohibit the participation of a particular minority in the political process. In other words, the amendment says that if you happen to be in a group out of favor with the majority, your rights can be curtailed or even eliminated. For that reason, Amendment 2 is far more than just an attack on gays and lesbians. It is a very real threat to the civil rights of all citizens.[23]

Colorado's Amendment 2 is misguided, not in its violation of transcendent and immanent principle, but in its violation of the U.S. Constitution. The distinction is made clear in a letter to the editor on the facing page: "This case should not concern a moral issue, but rather a constitutional issue. It is *only* a question as to whether constitutional rights apply to all this country's citizens."[24] Further, the consequences of a judgment upholding Amendment 2 will have its consequences in the civil sphere defined by the U.S. Constitution: such a verdict, it is feared, would serve to encourage the activity of "those who seek to control the basic civil rights of any other group."[25] Because there is no figurative court of appeal beyond the Constitution, and no literal court of appeal beyond the U.S. Supreme Court, there is no suggestion that the Court's ruling might be rejected or resisted. Gays appear helpless before the law.

The rhetorical posture assumed in these and other gay protests reflects an acceptance of what Stuart Scheingold has termed "the myth of rights": "The myth of rights rests on a faith in the political efficacy and ethical sufficiency of law as a principle of government."[26] Ronald Dworkin relates this belief in the ethical sufficiency of the law to the overall intellectual climate here traced, labeling the belief "legal positivism," the understanding "that individuals have legal rights only insofar as these have been created by explicit political decisions or explicit social practice."[27] Consistent with this outlook, gay rights activists have repeatedly waged their most important and visible battles in the legislative or judicial arenas, attempting to change their status through changes in the law and its interpretation.[28] It is a strategy that would have made no sense to the American Revolutionaries who proclaimed precisely that statutory law could not alter their fundamental and inalienable rights. Nor would it have made sense to Wendell Phillips, who would no doubt have found the idea of petitioning the legislature for rights that were in truth granted by God a grand farce, to Eugene Debs who felt obligated to suffer the consequences of illegal behavior rather than act against the mandate of the higher law, or to Robert Welch, who waged much of his crusade against the idea that the state could make right by decree. In subscribing to a positivistic conception of the law, gays and lesbians reflect the tendencies toward scientization and demystification discussed by Weber, Dewey, and Habermas rather than the natural rights philosophies of the American radical tradition.

The distance between gay rights activists and their radical forebears is perhaps best illustrated in the features of gay rights contests during the past two decades. Two seminal contests defined the basic outlines of much of the subsequent discourse: the 1977 drive to rescind an action by the Metropolitan Commission for Dade County, Florida, banning discrimination in employment and housing based on affectional or sexual preference, and the 1981 campaign that led to Wisconsin's becoming the first state to guarantee gays and lesbians equal protection in employment, housing, and public accommodations.[29]

The Miami struggle quickly expanded to a national struggle and is comparable to recent battles in Oregon, Cincinnati, and Colorado. These engagements represent a defensive reaction on the part of the movement against a right-wing grassroots effort to revoke gains by or on behalf of the movement's constituents. The primary characteristics of these campaigns include the definition of the argumentative ground by religious fundamentalists and the attempt of gays and lesbians to respond with appeals to tolerance. In Miami, Anita Bryant and her forces exercised an exclusive claim on the vocabulary of moral commitment. It was Bryant who sought to establish charismatic authority: "This is not my battle, it's God's battle."[30] It was Bryant who crusaded on behalf of righteousness: "God says there are some things that are evil and some things that are good. That's simple enough for even a child to understand. Certain things are right; other things are wrong. But they are right or wrong because God says so. We are right when we do God's will; we are wrong when we do not."[31] And it was Bryant who rejected the power of legal reformulation in opposition to God's law.[32] Ronald Fischli's criticism of Bryant's misology is correct in its characterization, but Fischli's own pluralist preference for "reasoned and flexible dialogue," "self-criticism," and "the democratic process" neglects the power of Bryant's implacable absolutism, the coercive power of absolute duty.[33] If there was a rhetoric imitative of the American radical tradition in Miami, it was the rhetoric of Anita Bryant, not that of gay rights activists. And it is this tradition that is carried forward by the "radical right" in recent conflicts as, for example, when Kevin Tebedo, executive director, Colorado for Family Values, proclaims, "Jesus Christ is king of kings and lord of lords. All power and authorities are given unto him. That's political. Jesus Christ sets the standard. If you don't want to live by it, that's your choice, but it's his standard, not ours."[34] Tebedo makes clear the presence of the sacred in the separation of Christ's standards, untouchable and immutable, from the human realm.

It may appear that Bryant and Tebedo contradict the large claim that the postmodern age in America is characterized by a failure of moral community, but they are more likely the exception that proves the rule. Bryant and her political kin are widely viewed as the contemporary "radical right." Despite its clamorousness, the New Christian Right is still viewed as politically marginal, the last recourse of the estranged. It represents, in large part, a reaction against the very tendencies that have succeeded in making pluralism the political center in America, tendencies that are viewed by the right as symptoms of moral desuetude. Spectacular victories like those in Miami and Colorado notwithstanding, the last twenty years have seen the "Moral Majority" thwarted by a born-again president, held at arm's length by a president who had been their bright hope of salvation, spurned by an American public who saw it at close range on television when it took control of the 1992 Republican National Convention, and denied strong antiabortion language and a place at the podium for the 1996 GOP convention. The unpopularity of gay rights among Americans has allowed Christian fundamentalists and their allies to create an aura of power that is largely illusory.[35] The New Right has been notably less successful in its campaigns against women's rights, birth control, and its crusades for the teaching of creationism and the restoration of prayer in public schools. Whatever their attitudes toward homosexuals, Americans do not seem ready to return the country to "the rule of God and the Bible" strictly interpreted.

Even the cause of gay rights has made some modest gains in the years since Miami,[36] and where it has been rejected, there is some evidence to indicate that it may not be on the moral grounds held by the New Christian Right. The potent language of "special rights" has more to do with inequality and the perception, in a time of scarcity, that others may be gaining unfair advantage than it does with morality.[37] Indeed, it is widely believed that, Kevin Tebedo notwithstanding, the insistence in Colorado that the debate was about "civil rights and the fairness issue,"[38] versus the Oregon campaign's resolution that homosexuality be held "abnormal, wrong, unnatural, and perverse,"[39] largely accounts for the success at the polls of the former and the defeat of the latter.

The Wisconsin campaign is in many respects, the mirror image of Dade

County, Colorado, and other defensive struggles. Like those that established civil rights for gays and lesbians in localities around the country, the operation in Wisconsin represented gays and lesbians on the offensive, working through legislative channels, employing the techniques of lobbying, often, as in the case of Columbus, Ohio, largely out of public view.[40] The argumentative ground in these instances carefully separates the legal and the religious spheres, avoiding a direct confrontation with moral issues, and emphasizes "civil rights." Many mainline churches have been willing to support this separation, allowing that, regardless of the moral status of gay and lesbian behavior (the distinction between the condition and the act is important in contemporary religious thinking), gays and lesbians should not be subject to discrimination in the civil sphere. Arguments in instances such as these can be fairly characterized by the fact that they center on the legal arena, either the courts or the legislature, and rather than radically confronting society on its own God terms, homosexuals and supporters prefer to define the legal arena very narrowly, circumventing confrontation on fundamentals. By emphasizing diversity and individuality, gay rights argument attempts to mitigate the coercive force of duty. Without clashing over questions concerning the validity of certain sacred truths, gays and lesbians simply ask to be excluded from their purview. It is a passive conception of liberty,[41] one that reveals its weaknesses when its opponents charge that it is merely libertinism.

The rhetoric of gay rights does not challenge the *polis*, singular, because it does not recognize the root necessary to ground the *polis*. Liberty conceived as "freedom from" operates to loosen the bonds that obligate us to the welfare of the community. Gay rights rhetoric is almost apolitical, perhaps even antipolitical, in that it addresses the multitude as a mass of individuals, not as a political unity. Its appeal is not to *de cive* but to each person as the maker of his or her own destiny. It is a rhetoric of disengagement. In all this, the rhetoric of gay rights establishes itself, not as a rhetoric of judgment, but as a rhetoric of nonjudgment. There is no potential for radical commitment in such a discourse.[42]

Economics and the Negotiation of Civil Rights

Rather than challenge contemporary understandings of root issues, gays and lesbians have tended instead to market ourselves to private consumers. In 1989, Marshall Kirk and Hunter Madsen received notice in *Time* magazine as well as in other venues for their proposal for a gay/lesbian self-marketing campaign. Such a strategy, they argued, modeled on advertising, would be "practical," "sensible," scientifically grounded, "completely unobjectionable," "hitched" to "pre-existing standards of law and justice," "expedient," and narrowly positivistic.[43] Though presented as a startling change of direction, it was, in fact, more of the same. Splits between radicals and moderates are endemic to the nature of social movements and are very much in evidence in American social movements, including the Revolution, abolitionism, and early labor. The split between assimilationism and separatism is more recent, accompanying the rise of identity politics. Madsen and Kirk provide only what may be a particularly extreme version of the assimilationist ethic that has largely characterized the gay liberation movement. The practical outcome of Madsen and Kirk's version would be the disappearance of gays and lesbians,[44] that is, we would become indistinguishable from straight people. There is no hint in this goal that there has been either progress or interruption of strategy since the early direct actions by the Mattachine Society of Washington, D.C., described by David Jernigan as "direction action" by "small groups of 'appropriately groomed' gay men (in coats and ties) and lesbians (in skirts) picketing in front of the White House, or at Independence Hall in Philadelphia every Fourth of July."[45] Kirk and Madsen have, apparently, been at least personally successful in their efforts to be lost in the suburbs, but their cause is currently being carried forward by Bruce Bawer and others collectively known as the "gay neo-con[servative]s."[46]

Urvashi Vaid's controversial book *Virtual Equality: The Mainstreaming of Gay and Lesbian Liberation* is the most sustained and most critical statement of this position; her only error lies in discerning some fundamental change in direction and tactics with the rise of gay neo-conservatism.[47] Vaid has, like many, been seduced by a romantic vision of the late 1960s and, especially for gay and lesbian rights, early 1970s, a vision I once described of ourselves "in bright red cloches storming the barricades,"[48] a vision that transforms the period into the normative standard against which all political activity must be judged. Such is the perspective in a bit of nostalgia delivered at the 1996 Pride March in Northampton, Massachusetts, by Warren J. Blumenfeld, one of the founders in the early 1970s of the Gay Liberation Front. Blumenfeld reminisces that the early movement was characterized by members' insistence "on the freedom to explore new ways of living as part of a radical transformation of society . . . as we went along, inventing new ways of relating." And he concludes somewhat ruefully,

Looking back over the years, as our visibility has increased, as our place within the culture has become somewhat more assured, much certainly has been gained, but also, something very precious has been lost. That early excitement, that desire—though by no means the ability—to fully restructure the culture, as distinguished from mere reform, seems now to lay dormant in many sectors of our community.[49]

The late 1960s and early 1970s, however, were never the norm, certainly not in post–World War II America. Against the backdrop of the postmodern era, the activism of those years was an exceptional moment, the bright flare of the utopian idealism of the Port Huron Statement extinguishing itself in a marvelous pyrotechnic display, and never included more than a tiny minority. At the very moment that Blumenfeld was involved with the GLF reinventing the world, John Reid (significantly, a pseudonym) was finding a wide audience with his autobiographical account of how he had slipped, undetected, into the corporate culture of IBM and made his way in society at large.[50] It is Reid's (and Madsen and Kirk's) well-mannered, clean-cut, collegiate image that we prefer to put before the public. The Fall 1993 issue of *Momentum,* the newsletter for members of the Human Rights Campaign Fund, included in its "Action Plan for the Future" the following goals: "advertising and broadcasting our message, *along with positive images about lesbian and gay people,* to the American public" (3, emphasis added). And in what do these "positive images" consist? Consider films like *Making Love* and *Longtime Companion,* characterized by Todd Haynes, director of *Poison,* as "films with gay subjects that are formally very straight and don't challenge the dominant ways of representing the world."[51] Or compare Candace Chellew's appeal to 1996 readers to the earlier description of Mattachine, Washington, D.C.'s "direct actions":

> For a few marches in the coming years, why don't we try to look like everyday people on gay pride day? Or better yet, let's dress in our professional clothes so people will know we come from all walks of life. And for heaven's sake, no floats or bare chests—male or female. If that doesn't make a big impact on how we are perceived, then break out the chiffon, party all you want, and equal rights be damned. But I believe you'll be hearing Middle America scream, "Those can't be queers; they look like regular people!" Then we'll be on the road to winning our rights.[52]

Finally, recall that one of the biggest and most publicized gay rights issues in recent years has been over the right to disappear, to be, literally, in uniform, the debate over gays and lesbians in the military.

This celebration of the normative is the language, not of sacred principle, but the language of accountancy. The mode is a statistical concept, and its use as a standard to guide politics is the precise inversion of radical ideals from the exalted to the common. Business and professional clothing, in this reading, serve as a grand metonymy, unifying ideas of respectability, civility, invisibility, and financial power. There is more than a trace of paradox in the combination. The language of money operates in such a way as to accommodate, and thus to make superfluous, the conflict in which its power might be exercised. As David Harvey writes,

> The common material languages of money and commodities provide a universal basis within market capitalism for linking everyone into an identical system of market valuation and so procuring the reproduction of social life through an objectively grounded system of social bonding.[53]

"Money unifies precisely *through* its capacity to accommodate individualism, otherness, and extraordinary social fragmentation," Harvey concludes,[54] thus the phrase "common currency." In this way, money poses as succedaneum for the political. Contemporary observers have often noted that the contemporary town square is a shopping mall.

Lee Goodman, writing in the *GPU News* (Milwaukee) in the fall following the Miami defeat, makes the connection quite explicitly:

> Where the system has worked (and worked well), it has done so precisely to the extent that the constituencies, minorities, and pressure groups have acted with full and deliberated cognizance of the limitations and tensions which are internal to the political order. Good intentions, while often necessary, have seldom been sufficient; calculation, understanding, and rational assessment of means, ends, and costs are the payoff factors.[55]

Goodman's economic justification for business-suit tactics, with its emphasis on rationality, calculation, and "payoff factors" suggests an implicit faith in the mechanical integrity of process, an exchange model of social reform. It is the process above all else that must be respected, for the denial of absolute truth has obviated the possibility that any given content could challenge the supremacy of the reasonable. It also demonstrates how the economic can be *exchanged* for the political, how money as a civil and rational mode of exchange usurps civility understood as a characteristic of *de cive*.

Twenty years later, Stephen Miller is among the devil's barkers, hawking a measure of heterosexual tolerance in exchange for our collective soul. Miller quotes approvingly from, appropriately, the *Economist,* an editorial praising the rise of "ordinary homosexuality, . . . the gay New Yorker who is more interested in bringing his lover to the company's Christmas party than in overturning corporate capitalism. He neither menaces the social order, as generations of priests and headmasters maintained, nor tartly flouts it, as generations of gay rebels have done. He is, you could say, sexually left-handed: that is all."[56] The source of this editorial and its prominent concern with the health of corporate capitalism are notable in a discussion of the reduction of politics to economics. Close attention should be paid to the rewards that good behavior will purchase: the right to bring one's lover to the company Christmas party at the price of disappearing, "assimilating," the rest of the year. Contra Miller, Scott Tucker protests, "Our lives are not negotiable."[57]

Tolerance is a specious attainment; it has nothing to pose against the declaratory stance of the opposition. It is always supplicant, consisting as it does of the goodwill of the powerful. Tolerance, as Thomas Paine well understood, is no substitute for rights: "Toleration is not the *opposite* of Intolerance, but is the *counterfeit* of it. Both are despotisms. The one assumes to itself the right of withholding Liberty of Conscience, and the other of granting it."[58] At its best, tolerance provides, in Christopher Isherwood's phrase, "annihilation by blandness." At its worst, tolerance "serves the cause of oppression."[59] Tolerance too easily becomes senescent and indiscriminate; ultimately, its impartiality can be extended to include even prevailing intolerance and oppression.[60]

Louis, in Tony Kushner's *Angels in America*, recognizes the fraudulence of tolerance: "*Power* is the object, not being tolerated. Fuck assimilation."[61] In a society that has abandoned principle to futility, all hierarchies are hierarchies of power, and in our postmodern society, that power is economic or quasi-economic. Politics in such an environment, naturally if lamentably, becomes a contest over money. Debates over campaign financing and the setting of new records for spending in every election year are only the surface. Parallels between the politics of today and *fin de siècle* political bosses, the Hannas, the Tammanys, the Tweeds, are misguided. The current situation signals, not the corruption of politics by corporate interests, but the reduction of politics to a subset of economics. The great robber barons exerted their power over politics to some end external to it, even to extralegal ends. The assimilation required of gays and lesbians to acquire the power of influence, on the other hand, becomes an end in itself and obviates the very cause that it was marshaled to support.

One significant feature of politics in which it differs from corporate sales campaigns is that politics can often reach its goals as well by buying as by selling. Vote buying is only the most unvarnished example of this. This distinction has not been lost on the gay rights community. In a 1995 article in the Politics section of the *Advocate* entitled "Money Talks," John Gallagher reviews arguments for and against getting cozy with the Republican-dominated Congress. Proponents argue for a more "buttoned-down image," and the use of professional consultants and lobbyists with ties to the Republican Party. In Gallagher's article, Mike Isbell, deputy executive director for public policy at Gay Men's Health Crisis, is quoted as saying with regard to the different arguments appropriate to Republicans versus Democrats, "One of the things we find is, whereas earlier we were able to rely solely on a humanitarian argument, in many Republican offices the most compelling argument is cost effectiveness."[62] Not only has the community created its own political action committees, most notably the Gay and Lesbian Victory Fund and The Human Rights Campaign Fund PAC (which in 1993 boasted that it was among the top fifty PACs),[63] and contributed heavily, as gays and lesbians, to Clinton's 1992 campaign, but gay rhetoric reveals a broad shift from legislative halls to the marketplace.[64] An early sign, emanating from the system of acronyms used to classify socioeconomic groups in the 1980s, was "DINK," "dual income, no kids," now the name of a gay/lesbian record company. Cheeky, yes, but significantly it features gay and lesbian couples not as sexual activity, a vision offensive to many Americans, but as buying power, a vision both attractive to corporate power brokers and inoffensively sterile, as illustrated by the recent IKEA furniture ads, which feature a clean-cut male couple, young executive types, shopping for furniture (not bedroom furniture). An advertisement in *POZ* equates "Gay Money" and "Gay Power" and urges the reader to "Tap it with *Quotient: The monthly newsletter of marketing to gay men and lesbians.*"[65] Daniel Harris has marked these traits in the host of new magazines he groups as "the new gay glossies," publications, he writes, that "habitually sing the praises of enterprising homosexuals who have clambered to the top of the corporate ladder and now lead prosperous lives as openly gay executives, fashion designers, investment gurus, pulp novelists, and soap-opera stars," that picture gay life as "sanitized . . . scrubbed clean of overt sexuality and unseemly images.[66] Although the editor of *Out* refutes Harris's claims that these magazines ignore political issues, she does reveal something of her publication's assimilationist approach: "Most importantly, *Out* recognizes that our readers live in a context larger than their gayness. Our mission is to make a magazine that speaks to the fullness of our experience and to a vision of gay men and lesbians that goes beyond the clichés."[67] Those men and women in their anonymous but stylish professional attire come immediately to mind, particularly when Ms. Pettit's annihilation of the bonds of stereotype is followed by this concluding line of defense:

> Every month 120,000 readers respond to this mission by picking up *Out* and voting for it with their wallets. *This* is why advertisers have sought out our publication in unprecedented numbers. Perhaps *Harper's* can afford to be glib about its revenue stream, but in the gay press, where magazines have traditionally been overlooked by media buyers and stocked in the porn section, financial viability is nearly a revolutionary act.[68]

Even more telling is a full-page, four-color advertisement from an issue of *POZ* picturing the partners of Christopher Street Financial Incorporated, any one of whom would be interchangeable with either member of the couple in the IKEA ad, or, more significantly, with any of the legions of young, well-dressed MBAs who daily troop to offices on Wall Street, LaSalle Street, and Montgomery Street. The headline copy reads: "The second most important relationship you'll ever have could be with one of these men." By the spring of 1996, this nascent direction is articulated and institutionalized in the Third Annual National Gay and Lesbian Business and Consumer Exposition, including among its sponsors such Forbes 500 corporations as American Express, IBM, American Airlines, and The Prudential.[69] The nexus of the commercial and the political is evident in a press photo released by the New York Mayor's Office: Rudolph Giuliani congratulating expo organizer Steve Levenberg.[70]

The same sort of attention that used to be devoted in media-watch columns to the representation of gays and lesbians on television and in the movies is now spent on gay-friendly advertising campaigns such as the one for Subaru featuring same-sex couples.[71] Even AIDS, called by the *Advocate* "the only disease to have its own gift shop,"[72] has not been immune. *POZ* sponsored a "Life expo," "a quality of life consumer expo for everyone impacted by AIDS and HIV" on May 31–June 1, 1996. Corporate sponsorship was provided by Bristol-Meyers Squibb, Pharmacia & Upjohn, Roche Laboratories, Glaxo Wellcome, LifeWise, Janssen Pharmaceutica, and Abbott Laboratories, among others.[73] That *POZ* has entered into partnership with some of the very same corporations perennially on ACT-UP's hit list at the very least raises questions regarding the balance of commercial and principled motive. But other, more general, corporate interests are served by AIDS as well. Dave Mulryan, a specialist in "inducting corporations into the gay marketplace," remarks, "Larger corporations are looking for a way to get to the gay market, and they're comfortable doing it by some affiliation with AIDS."[74] Such activities as Tanqueray's sponsorship of AIDS Rides are, according to Molryan, vehicles for companies to build entirely unobjectionable goodwill in the gay community.

Though not addressing the real impact of AIDS products on treatment, research, and care related to the disease itself, Paul Varnell adduces several recent campaigns, including the one for Subaru, in an editorial counseling gays and lesbians on the potential advantages of being recognized as a "niche market."[75] Varnell recognizes "that there is little or nothing in this change that is motivated by benevolence or a concern for gay rights," yet he finds the argument from "economic necessity" to be a compelling foil to moral arguments against gay rights. It changes the ground of argumentation and makes the contest one between morals and the bottom line. "In that light, it may be that the next significant jump in gay influence will take place through the economic sphere rather than in the currently stalled political arena," he concludes.[76] Certainly, Bruce Bawer is probably correct in observing that at present, privileges and benefits for same-sex partners are spreading more rapidly in the corporate world than in the legislatures or the courts "or, for that matter, the National Gay and Lesbian Task Force."[77]

Gays and lesbians, then, are being encouraged to recognize their economic clout and have attempted to use it directly as a kind of secondary vote, as economic referenda, following failures in the electoral arena. According to those offering the "Uncommon Clout Card," a Visa card currently being marketed in the gay and lesbian community, every time you use your card "you vote with your dollars to support companies friendly to gays, lesbians, and those with HIV."[78] The proliferation of gay and lesbian yellow pages is another indication of this strategy. The Spring/Summer 1996 edition of the *Alternative Phonebook: Chicago's Lesbigay Yellow Pages* touts itself as a vehicle for "economic empowerment" and urges readers to "spend your gay dollars wisely—fight discrimination and strengthen our community by supporting only those businesses that support us" (2).

Withholding dollars completes the strategy. After the victory at the polls for Amendment 2, gay leaders called for a boycott of Colorado, and the *Advocate* reported that a boycott of Cincinnati following that city's 1993 antigay charter amendment modeled on Amendment 2 had been successful to the tune of $24 million in lost convention business.[79] There is more than a little irony in the placement of an ad for Rivendell Marketing and the National Gay Newspaper Guild between pages of an article admonishing gay activists not to emulate our enemies by the use of economic boycotts.[80] The Rivendell ad, displaying a map with various major U.S. cities and their corresponding gay papers, promises, "With One Ad Buy, You Can Reach One of the Country's Most Affluent Communities: . . . With a combined readership of over 550,000, the National Gay Newspaper Guild can help you target some of the most affluent, well-educated and brand loyal consumers in the country. Find out more about what *The Wall Street Journal* describes as 'the most potentially profitable, untapped market in the U.S. today.' "[81] The advertisement touts a power that the editorial counsels us not to use.

The referendum, whether political or economic, is a symptom of a general failure of principle, a resort to the power of the countinghouse; its values are entirely pragmatic; there is no pretense that positions will succeed or fail based on principle. The referendum is an admission that principle is insufficient. The New Christian Right understands this as well as gay activists and has turned to the referendum, economic and political, as its primary tool against gay rights.[82] Marcuse writes of this symptom of twentieth-century turpitude, "This pure tolerance of sense and nonsense is justified by the democratic argument that nobody, neither group nor individual, is in possession of the truth and capable of defining what is right and wrong, good and bad. Therefore, all contesting opinions must be submitted to 'the people' for its deliberation and choice."[83]

The strategy appears, on its face, to be eminently rhetorical. There is no question that gays and lesbians subscribing to the strategy assent to a common currency with straight society, that they, like Bruce Bawer, believe that "if the heterosexual majority ever comes to accept homosexuality, it will do so because it has seen homosexuals in suits and ties, not nipple clamps and bike pants; it will do so because it has seen homosexuals showing respect for civilization, not attempting to subvert it."[84] In the 1990s, the preferred means of presenting gay men and lesbians in "suits and ties" avoids the heat of Washington, D.C., on the Fourth of July and the hecklers in Philadelphia that Kameny and his followers faced—marches, after all, "hail from a simpler, perhaps simplistic, time when gay politics could be understood in terms of 'us against them.' To march was to set oneself at odds with the system on the assumption that the Establishment was our enemy."[85] In the 1990s, we call from the comfort of our own home and register our ownership of the Lexus, Cuisinart, and Missoni sweater. The Gay Census, conducted by Overlooked Opinions, "the nation's only gay owned and operated survey firm,"[86] though it drapes itself in the language of politics—the American flag, the use of the first three words of the U.S. Constitution—has only a couple of questions on party identification and voting. The greater number of questions concern what publications are read by the subject, recent purchases, consumer activities, and whether or not one believes strongly in supporting advertisers that advertise in gay media.[87]

Syndicated columnist Arlene Zarembka has not only exposed the invalidity of data so collected, she has also addressed its negative political consequences: First, the spurious data are used by those who argue against civil rights protections for gays and lesbians to demonstrate the lack of need. Second, the data are used to fuel a conspiracy theory of gay and lesbian power as represented in the infamous videos *The Gay Agenda* and *Gay Rights, Special Rights.* Zarembka observes: "As economic stress increases in the country, so will scapegoating. Demagogues are playing on the stereotype of wealthy Gay men and Lesbians flying around the world, whipping up powerful resentment against the Gay community."[88] Anyone who would discount Zarembka's claim is directed to Justice Scalia's dissenting opinion in *Romer v. Evans* where he writes,

> The problem (a problem, that is, for those who wish to retain social disapprobation of homosexuality) is that, because those who engage in homosexual conduct tend to reside in disproportionate numbers in certain communities, . . . have high disposable income, . . . and of course care about homosexual-rights issues much more ardently than the public at large, they possess political power much greater than their numbers, both locally and state-wide.[89]

"Gay marketing hype may sell the Gay community to corporate America, but it does so at a heavy price," warns Zarembka. "The selling of the Gay community to corporate America . . . implies that Gay men and Lesbians are valuable only as consumers, insinuating that those without purchasing power are unworthy of concern."[90] Bawer reflects precisely this tendency when he emphasizes that most gay men are "smart, talented people who h[o]ld down respectable jobs in the corporate world or the fashion industry, on Wall Street or Publishers' Row."[91] The cry for gays to be "reasonable" strongly recalls in this context the roots of the term in the language of accountancy. It draws attention away from substance and focuses on the medium and process of exchange. The "gay market" is the ultimate antiessentialist position, focusing, not on the intractable fact of a sexual orientation that divides homosexuals from heterosexuals in the eyes of the law, but on the superficial and ephemeral status of bank accounts. Such a strategy divides the economic self from the affectional/sexual self, and it leaves the latter unredeemed. Justice Scalia's argument that certain kinds of conduct, "murder, for example, or polygamy, or cruelty to animals," or homosexual conduct, are the legitimate targets of "animus" based on "moral disapproval"[92] is left untouched by economic arguments, allayed perhaps by the ability to purchase indulgences, but fundamentally uncontested.

Camille Paglia may scorn the "action" during Pope John Paul II's Mass in Central Park in 1995, but her logic is painfully twisted. On the one hand, she decries the paucity of "ideas," principles, behind the gay protest. On the other hand, the basis of her objection is not substantive, but pragmatic; the protest failed as a public relations appeal:

> Amid heavy media coverage, a major gay protest went virtually unreported, even by the usually obsequiously pro-gay *New York Times*. Six men cleverly invaded Saks Fifth Avenue and unfurled a long white banner from a sixth-floor window facing St. Patrick's Cathedral, where a huge crowd waited for the pope to arrive to recite the rosary. The sign read, CONDOMS SAVE LIVES. Gay newspapers reported a child asking, "What's that, Dad?" and her father replying, "Those are bad people." When police arrested the protesters and tore down the banner, the crowd cheered.[93]

The poor media coverage and the crowd's cheers are evidence of the emptiness of ideas? This is a patent misapplication of causes to effects. Paglia goes on to criticize the "dull, feeble slogan, redolent of reactionary '50s Betty Crocker caretaking."[94] One can only try to imagine what her response might have been to Debs, Phillips, or the American Revolutionaries. There is no consideration here that condoms do, in fact, save lives, that they might save many more were it not for the intransigent opposition of the Roman Catholic Church and its leader, that the demonstration was, perhaps, an example of principled action wherein principle only and not the "payoff" directs. Little wonder, though, that Paglia would not recognize such a curiosity. In a world constrained only by physics and economics, to be arrested, to suffer for a cause, can only be explained by an inadequate credit limit. ACT-UP may be routinely criticized, by Paglia and others, for its failure to win the hearts and minds of the American people,[95] but it remains to be seen whether or not it is possible to buy same, and if bought, what we would have.

The commodification of the gay liberation movement is, of course, not without its dissenters. Jeff Getty of ACT-UP, the first person to be approved for an experimental transplant of bone marrow from baboons as a treatment for HIV, disdains "white-collar AIDS activists" who worry more about protecting their own budgets than about saving people with the disease.[96] "Marc Contefag" and "Michael Homoscarce," introducing a reprint of the leaflet "Queers Read This! I Hate Straights" in their 'zine, protest the co-optation of ersatz gay leadership by white-tie fundraisers:

> Who are the people making decisions for us in Central Ohio? They are the "A" gays, the upper-crust financially elite. What makes them competent and effective leaders? It's certainly not their ability to represent us or form coalitions within the diversity of our community. It's definitely not their work in anti-racism, sexism, and classism. No, it is simply their ability to write a check. This gives them access to boards of directors, this allows them to manipulate and control our representation and decision-making. They sell us out, they attempt to speak for us without even knowing who "we" are. They use their white and class privilege not as a tool for constructive change, but for solidifying their status and power in new ways.[97]

Conte and Scarce's indictment underscores, not only the retreat from activism toward money and respectability, but also the profoundly personal and selfish turn of movement politics. Rejecting money as the basis and measure of legitimate power, Conte and Scarce also reject the assimilationist politics that it serves, as the leaflet they reprint makes clear:

> Being queer is not about a right to privacy; it is about the freedom to be public, to just be who we are. It means everyday fighting oppression; homophobia, racism, misogyny, the bigotry of religious hypocrites and our own self hatred. . . . It's not about the mainstream, profit-margins, patriotism, patriarchy or being assimilated. It's not about executive directors, privilege and elitism. It's about being on the margins, defining ourselves; it's about gender-fuck and secrets, what's beneath the belt and deep inside the heart; it's about the night.[98]

Even as they lodge their protests, however, ACT-UP and Jeff Getty, Queer Nation, Marc Contefag and Michael Homoscarce, and the anonymous author of "I Hate Straights," provide testimony to the connections among money, civility, assimilationism, and power, and they acknowledge the dominance of the nonconfrontational, reasonable, assimilationist model in gay rights protest.

When radical protest does claim the spotlight, as for example ACT-UP's 1988 shutdown of Burroughs-Wellcome's Burlingame, California, distribution center, or the "action" in New York City's Saint Patrick's Cathedral protesting John Cardinal O'Connor's opposition to condom distribution programs and gay rights, it is not only repudiated by the larger part of the gay and lesbian community—the editorial "Doctor ACT UP, or how we learned to stop worrying and grew to love zaps" addresses the deep ambivalence of the community at large toward such radical groups, and is more generous than most[99]—it is also subject to co-optation by the commercial media as spectacle, as ACT-UP activist Scott Tucker recognizes.[100] This recognition is consistent with Guy Debord's vision of the modern spectacle, arriving at its full power within the last twenty years, as "the autocratic reign of the market economy which had acceded to an irresponsible sovereignty, and the totality of new techniques of government which accompanied this reign."[101]

In the world described here, rights are reduced to license and are "civil" only in that they are purchased from the state. The current uproar over same-sex marriages is indicative. Not only is marriage something for which one purchases a license, the right to marry, from the state, but many of the arguments, especially by supporters of same-sex marriage, feature economic considerations: Social Security benefits, Medicare benefits, inheritance laws, communal property laws, income tax status.

Gay liberation is not alone in adopting the language and rationale of economics. The analysis has its roots in the thinking of Debs and W. E. B. DuBois and begins to reveal its current shape in Carmichael and Hamilton's manifesto for black power and Malcolm X's calls for economic self-sufficiency, both in the 1960s. In the 1990s, it has reached its baldest, least varnished form in debates over environmental issues, especially proposals that would allow corporations a certain number of air pollution units. Corporations that could reduce pollution below their allowable limits would be permitted to sell their pollution units to other corporations. These other corporations would then be buying the "right" to pollute in a certain amount in excess of their allotment. Since when does anyone have a "right" to destroy the environment, and whence does this right come? Surely nature does not grant the right to destroy nature. This loose usage of "right" merely provides force to a regulative device created by the state to balance short-term economic interests with the health and long-term interests of the people. It also exposes, particularly well in this case, the great reduction of sacred space in the contemporary world in that nature, formerly an earthly manifestation of the sacred, becomes a commodity.

Returning to the case of gay rights, if there is, as Bawer and others argue, nothing essential in being gay except sexual orientation, then our money would be better spent at Brooks Brothers than with the Human Rights Campaign Fund or the National Gay and Lesbian Task Force. The surfaces need only be brought into conformity with the surface of the culture at large. If, on the other hand, there is something irremediably different about being gay, then, as Mickey Wheatley warns, "Putting on a three- piece suit does not change the fact that we are still largely despised because we represent a major threat to patriarchal culture. Our politics and personalities are as central to us as our sexual orientation, and should be celebrated, not oppressed." [102]

Radicalism has historically stood against chaos with the defining power of principle. The secular argument examined here tends, conversely, toward homogenization in the public realm through the lingua franca of money. Private resources purchase the "right" to pursue their own interests without regard to the common good. Ralf Dahrendorf describes this assault on civil society as occurring when it is posited that "there is no such thing as society, only individuals and government." In opposition to a mentality that says "I have to have at least 40 percent of the market to be viable," Dahrendorf insists on a certain degree of contest, of "untidiness" to provide the creative energy necessary to civil society. Radical debate over principle provides that untidiness. A nation of suits does not.

Rick Moody, in his widely hailed novella *The Ring of Brightest Angels around Heaven* provides a glimpse of a future conformity in which "these people look exactly like other people you know." The story begins in the Ruin, a New York City bar of sorts "decorated in twisted car parts and fruitless conversation and postindustrial clutter, in the collision of strangers and in the flicker of lost opportunities," and follows, for a time, Jorge Ruiz in a world where no distinctions matter and all value has dissipated save "the sight of a balance sheet, the sound of a cash register, or the ebb and flow of ordinary conversation, these were the things that really ruined these patrons, that caused mortal discomfort." Jorge finds himself confronting Times Square: "The neon of the gyro place, the neon of the shoe repair store, they were all the neon of Peep World. Jorge confused the thresholds of these businesses. They were identical. Just like, after a time, strangers and the people he knew were one and the same. The neon that called to him in Times Square was all one sign. It said: follow your itch, hasten your descent. Go ahead, dive."[103] It is not the world that gay and lesbian moderates or Christian Coalition evangelicals are crusading for, but it is very likely the world that denies the possibility for radical voices.

10

The Seraph and the Snake

The Prophets Isaiah and Ezekiel dined with me, and I asked them how they dared so roundly to assert that God spake to them; and whether they did not think at the time that they would be misunderstood, & so be the cause of imposition.

Isaiah answer'd: "I saw no God, nor heard any, in a finite organical perception; but my senses discover'd the infinite in every thing, and as I was then perswaded, & remain confirm'd, that the voice of honest indignation is the voice of God, I cared not for consequences, but wrote."

Then I asked: "Does a firm perswasion that a thing is so, make it so?"

He replied: "All poets believe that it does, & in ages of imagination this firm perswasion removed mountains; but many are not capable of a firm perswasion of any thing."

—William Blake, *The Marriage of Heaven and Hell*

It is commonly argued that America has no genuine radical tradition, that its remarkably nonideological politics precludes the kinds of commitment and enthusiasm characteristic of politics in Europe. With its independence secured in a revolution widely held to have been conservative, America has been stubbornly resistant to various kinds of socialism and sweeping and zealous reform.[1]

But "radical" is one of those terms that threatens to disintegrate from casual overuse. Depending on one's politics and one's position, radicalism is either something to which one eagerly aspires or a term of severest censure. It is both a term of praise and of approbation. It is used loosely to connote terrorism, anarchy, outspokenness, alienism, simple disagreement, and changes on a large scale. It is both a threat and an opportunity. There exists the assumption that we all know radicalism when we see it, a dubious assumption at best. There is even a certain amount of irony in our glib use of the term, for it belies the consensus it is supposed to reflect. Some uses betray their factional origins, while other uses are simply trivial. One suspects that the designation has lost its discriminative ability. As Edwin Black once reminded us regarding "revolutionary," a term that claims a close kinship to the term radical, "Some literature produces convulsions in the world; and some merely wears a *bonnet rouge* to the Rotary meeting."[2]

If we are to talk meaningfully about a radical tradition in America, we must talk in terms of those values that have been capable over the course of our history of engaging Americans in significant ways, of causing genuine convulsions. Radicalism is not to be confused with the *bonnet rouge,* not to be confused with fringe groups no matter how clamorous; it is not frivolous or ancillary. Radicalism is, quite literally, that which involves the roots of a culture. The six preceding studies, all dealing with figures or movements that have been loosely identified as radical eruptions in American politics, have pointed to two central and antithetical themes in American culture. Whatever radical tradition we might claim should probably be explained as part of a continuing dialectic between them.

From seventeenth-century liberalism, particularly Locke, we have received an idea of freedom. The American Revolution successfully defined the right to the autonomous pursuit and preservation of life, property, and happiness, fettered only to the extent necessary to ensure the equal right of others to do likewise, as a central theme in American politics. The vocabulary recurs in the rhetoric of abolitionism, in Debs's rhetoric against wage slavery, in McCarthy's rhetoric against communist domination, in Welch's insistence on the virtues of individualism, and in the rhetoric of gay liberation. That freedom is an essential aspect of the American identity can hardly be argued. Our idea of freedom is the source of our individualism and our pluralism.

But the idea of freedom promulgated by the American Revolutionaries was not simply the absence of strictures or the granting of license. Freedom was, for the Whigs and for those who followed them, not a privilege but an indicator of moral status, and as such, it entailed certain obligations, certain duties. Moral status must be earned. Thus a second theme in American politics has been the theme of duty, of moral compunction, the source of our tendencies toward conformism and absolutism.

It is the curious amalgam of freedom and responsibility in American political thought that has been responsible for what Louis Hartz has termed its "veritable maze of polar contradictions, winding in and out of each other hopelessly: pragmatism and absolutism, historicism and rationalism, optimism and pessimism, materialism and idealism, individualism and conformism."[3] Hartz looks at the American tradition within the context of European liberalism, and though he offers occasional concessions to the religious influences in our heritage, he generally maintains that Americans as reformers have not played the role of "secular prophets," have not been intemperate, and have not been prey to religious enthusiasms.[4] The liberal tradition is antithetical to such postures, and within that tradition, they must be viewed as aberrations and contradictions.

But a view of the American tradition that sees only its mundane and businesslike side, that stresses its origins in the Enlightenment, might be accused of stressing Locke to the exclusion of Calvin, thus providing a confusing and inelegant view of its shape. Our preference for Matthew Arnold's Hellenic ideal risks obscuring the Hebraic side of our culture. The transformation of freedom into a moral concept and its pairing with duty is defalcated and tenuous in Locke. The disciplinarian side of the American character is more readily attributed to our Puritan heritage. It was Calvin who, in the name of freedom of worship, authored one of the most regimented and demanding orthodoxies in the Western world, and it was Calvin who, by his emigration to Holland, began a Puritan exile that provided the foundations for the exodus myth created by his spiritual descendants in America.

The myth of the American exodus, which reached its culmination in the Revolution, unabashedly drew its parallels from the exodus themes in the Old Testament. It captured all the contradiction of freedom and obligation in a powerful synthesis. The example of Moses and the covenant made clear that escape into freedom involved hardship and sacrifice; freedom and discipline became, not antithetical, but complimentary. Furthermore, an escape that is, in part, a sign of the beneficence of a divine being involves, not only a disciplined response to adversity, but also a certain debt.

It was the role of the Old Testament prophets to remind the peoples of Israel and Judah of that debt, to demand an adherence to those terms upon which their continued freedom depended. American Whigs, likewise, argued that the dual nature of the law both provided guarantees and made demands; they depended on the ability to enlist discipline in the service of freedom. Making freedom a sacred concept, early American radicals were able to demand a certain consensus as to its nature and its requirements.

The discourse of the Old Testament prophets continues to provide American radicals with a model even into the twentieth century because it is a highly visible discourse of radical reform that strikes an amenable balance between the contradictory elements of freedom and duty. The rhetoric of the radicals examined here provides testimony as to the sometimes quite self-conscious influence of this model, though the line of influence became more oblique as American radicals, over the course of years, molded these materials into an indigenous prophetic tradition. With the ascension of American prophets to canonical status, the influence of the biblical books was sometimes obscured, but as long as the tradition could be sustained, it bore the marks of its source.

Seeking to articulate those essential marks, I began with the idea that the prophet is somehow alienated from his audience, possessed of a message that is somehow exclusive. At the same time, the prophet engages those premises that are central to the culture. The prophet is simultaneously insider and outsider; he compels the audience, but only by use of those premises to which they have assented as a culture. The discourse is, then, both of the audience and extreme to the audience. It might fairly be said that the prophet shares the ideals of his audience rather than the realities of its everyday life. He reminds his audience of that transcendental side of its culture that makes it larger than our individual wants and needs and aspirations and challenges us toward the achievement of that ideal. That effort requires exertion, sacrifice, and a renunciation of indolence, an exercise of virtue. Prophetic discourse seeks to reshape, to re-create the audience in accordance with a strict set of ideals as commanded by God, revealed in natural law, and assented to in principle but unrealized by the audience.

The attitude of the prophet toward the audience reveals much about the cosmology and epistemology behind his discourse. At the same time that the prophet sets himself apart from his audience, he depends on an understanding that they share the same world with him, thus making them the subjects of his visions. The world as God's creation is considered sacred, substantially immune to alteration by humankind. Properly attended to, it contains directives for living. Alone in the Judeo-Christian cosmos, only humanity has a model of the ideal and the independence of will to deny that ideal. Here is the conflict between freedom and duty at its source: the presence of a free will coterminous with divine dictates. Prophetic discourse seeks to reform the people in accordance with the demands of the ideal.

The belief that the ideal is shared, that there is a common and unquestioned vision of the good, invests prophetic discourse with a fundamental faith in its auditors. From the American Revolution to the time of Debs, radical reformers were profoundly optimistic, optimistic about the possibility of reform and about people as the vehicles for that reform. People, after all, could know the truth if they would only open their eyes to it, and thus knowing, why would they not act in accordance? Such an optimistic view of human nature holds no cautionary tales on the role of passion; there is no dark side of the psyche straining against its chains. Precisely the opposite is the case: it is because man's feelings are asleep, anesthetized, dormant, because man is apathetic, that evil is allowed to exist. The rhetoric in this tradition exhibits an unabashed emphasis on emotional appeal, on awakening the feelings, on speaking to the heart. Prophetic reformers were confident that if the people could simply be made to feel the truth, reform would follow as a necessary consequence.

The American Revolution is unique among the cases included here as the only example among them of a radical movement widely held to have been successful. Its success might be explained by its ability to achieve, for that brief historical moment, a compelling balance of the elements of freedom and duty. By the time of Wendell Phillips, the doctrine of perfectionism had seriously eroded the basis of consent upon which prophecy depended. The path was cleared for legitimate disagreement or at least irresolvable disagreement between persons making equal claims to perfection. Phillips and his compeers were able to prick the conscience of antebellum Americans precisely to the degree that some consensus on transcendental values remained viable, but though that consensus was sufficiently strong to engage Americans in a significant way, it was not strong enough to compel assent. The studies of those who followed Phillips reveal a continuing erosion of the cultural homogeneity necessary to validate prophecy and an increasing incapacity to argue convincingly from premises of obligation. By such a reading of our cultural history, it should have surprised no one when Bill Clinton's "New Covenant" theme, designed in the tradition of FDR's "New Deal," John Kennedy's "New Frontier," and Lyndon Johnson's "Great Society," to sound the vision of a new administration, was allowed to wither ignominiously on the vine.

The failure of obligation is critical, for it is the presence of obligations that allows us to exist as a culture. Unalloyed freedom is anarchy. Obligation is presented by the prophet as an order, and it in turn provides order to a confused world. It is the flight from chaos that provides the fundamental conservatism in American radicalism. The common themes in the rhetorics of the Revolution, Phillips, and Debs represent efforts to preserve some nucleus that orders society, some invariant point of reference. Faced with crises of culture, rhetors in each of these studies in part I sought to restore a vision of structure and clarity to the world. They shaped an American identity from the materials of their Calvinism, their English heritage, their classical Western educations, and their Judeo- Christian ethic. They explored the ramifications of that identity, applied it in their respective situations, innovated where necessary—but always with a respect for the essential and the definitive—and in the process, revivified for succeeding generations a cultural tradition.

Nor is the American prophetic tradition as it developed from the American Revolution, through Phillips, to Debs, and even to some extent to Welch a mere critical hypostatization. Looking to the rhetoric of those who made it, it is evident that it was, quite literally, handed down from one generation of radicals to the next: Wendell Phillips was a student of the American Revolution; Debs was a student of Phillips; and Welch appears to have been a student of nineteenth-century America and of Emerson in particular. Our understanding of these discourses is poorer to the extent that we ignore this lineal influence. Failing to recognize its sources, we misread its intentions and mislocate its aspirations. Radicalism understood as a tradition does not threaten culture, but reaffirms and challenges it.

Conservatism in this sense is not a simple reactionary impulse. The American prophetic tradition is not a retreat into an idealized world in the past. American radicals from Paine and Otis to Phillips to Debs sought to preserve some agreement on goals; they attempted to maintain the sanguine vision which the past had created of the ideal future. The great tradition of American prophets has been unfailingly progressive. Faith, I have argued, has been their great common bond. It has been the "will to believe," as William James once termed it, that has sustained the prophetic impulse. With a "firm perswasion" in the divine sanction of their mission, American prophets have held an almost limitless confidence in the future. It is that confidence that failed in the period following the Second World War.

According to Henry May, the "hegemony" of "Progressive Patriotic Protestantism . . . ended exactly in 1919."[5] Certainly there was evidence of its decay in Debs's time, but it is my argument that the genesis of the decline occurred much earlier and that its full implications were not felt until after the Second World War. Our vivid memories of the Sixties notwithstanding, it is important to remember that of the four decades since the end of the Second World War, three of them have seen movements of the right more prominent than movements of the left in America. As important representatives of this trend, the movements inspired by Joe

McCarthy and Robert Welch are characterized by a lack of faith. They were reactionary not because they wished to move backward in time—in McCarthy's case this is simply inapplicable, and in the case of Welch it is merely a symptom. They were reactionary because they existed only as reactions to threat; they were not positive; they had no direction to offer, no plan, no goals, no god—at least no supremely potent god capable of assuring his will in history. They had only devils to battle. They appealed to a dissolute world, a world without a common faith, unable or unwilling to acknowledge the command of any supreme being so diminished that it could occupy the small spaces of mystery that rationality and technology had left to it. For a people capable of destroying its own world, indeed its own existentially defined universe, there is no sacred space, nothing beyond ourselves.

Left exposed and vulnerable, McCarthy's response was to refuse the shelter of sanctuary; he preferred a bellicose game of hide-and-seek. There is a distorted vestige of American manliness and virtue in his discourse, all bare knuckles and brashness. Welch, on the other hand, responded to chaos with nostalgia. He did not carry the tradition forward; he was overwhelmed by it. There is no innovation in Welch's rhetoric. He recited his poems in praise of a bygone era suggesting that the greatest vision to which we could aspire was one that existed only as a perversion of memory. In a world completely subordinated to our control, the only thing we cannot touch is the past, and even that is an illusion, for those like Welch profane the past by making of it an idyllic fiction. The lack of a common history is one of the symptoms of the break in the tradition of the prophetic voice in America.

What the contemporary right has in common with the prophetic tradition is the impulse to order. The rigid, formal characteristics of prophetic discourse create sense out of confusion. They offer clarity and provide direction. Although they emphasize the negative side of this equation, that those on the right should be so obsessed with plots suggests the same impulse. But there is a considerable difference between an order that derives from compassion, is optimistic, and provides direction for the future and one that derives from fear, is faithless, and retreats into the mythical past. The former may be criticized for its utopian excesses, but the latter is the provenance of fascism. The former emphasizes freedom, the latter discipline. The former emphasizes opportunity, the latter impending foreclosure.

Modern movements of the left are no less spiritually impoverished than those of the right. Many of the radical explosions of the 1960s have been characterized as idealistic, but the stress on the newness of the "New Left" suggests a rupture with the old ideals, and it is telling to note how many of the ideals of the Sixties were imported: religions of the East and Middle East, continental philosophies, and various forms of Marxism were seized upon as sources of transcendental value, changes signaled in discourse by a shift from the rhetorical form of the "Declaration" to that of the "Manifesto." These visions failed to capture the imagination of most Americans, not because of any inherent defect, but because radicalism is cultural, and these ideals were not of our culture. In fact, that radicals should have turned to them is suggestive of how moribund our own ideals had become. Except perhaps for recollections of the Declaration of Independence, Thoreau on civil disobedience, or other signature documents recited either as liturgy or as evidence of hypocrisy, there was little evidence of historical awareness in the rhetoric of the Sixties, and no evidence that the spiritual sources that fueled the radicalism of the past were considered either viable or relevant.

As an extreme manifestation of these tendencies, such social movements as gay liberation have abandoned transcendental ideals altogether. Gay liberation has, in fact, been decisively excluded from claims on the divine. Some segments of the movement may profess belief in some higher order, and certainly individuals might, but as a social movement, gay liberation is characterized by an overwhelming emphasis on the individual, the freedom side of the freedom/discipline equation. A commanding transcendental presence is antithetical to a policy of "live and let live."

Gay liberation efforts have largely been characterized by Arnold's ideal of "sweetness and light," a campaign for *civil rights.* As congenial as that may be, it also contains clear defects and limitations. By adhering to the rules of "reasonable discourse," gay liberation leaders reinforce the underlying ideas regarding the nature of reasons and truth; they provide tacit assent to the claim that their cause may not be right, and they deny the integrity of reasons that might compel concordance with their cause. "Reasons" are both enthymematic and compelling of reform only as long as there exists the assumption of widespread agreement on what should be. In a pluralistic world, reasons can be only that to which the audience is willing to assent, something to be negotiated. In short, gay liberationists have no faith in their own righteousness.

Faith is a nonempirical idea. As such, its compass is not restricted to the narrow world of the observable and the quantifiable; its only limits are those of the human imagination. Freed from the chains of the quotidian and the pedestrian, faith reflects itself in the grandeur and spaciousness of our mythologies. As Northrop Frye describes it, we live in two worlds. For the objective world, the world we are actually in, we develop "a logical language of fact, reason, description, and verification." For the "potentially created world," the ideal civilization we are trying to build or maintain, we develop "a mythical language of hope, desire, belief, anxiety, polemic, fantasy, and construction."[6] It might be said that we can judge a culture by the quality of the stories it tells about itself, by its mythical language.[7] The stories of the Greek golden age still capture the imagination, and the achievement of the Old Testament has been its ability to anchor a cultural identity for three millennia. Such stories solicit our continuing admiration because they remind us of what humanity can achieve when it strains to reach beyond itself into the sacred, all the while recognizing its own finitude.

About such stories, Matthew Arnold, in his essay "The Proof from Prophecy," wrote,

> That men should, by help of their imagination, take short cuts to what they ardently desire, whether the triumph of Israel or the triumph of Christianity, should tell themselves fairy-tales about it, should make these fairy-tales the basis for what is far more sure and solid than the fairy-tales, the desire itself— all this has in it, we repeat, nothing which is not natural, nothing blameable. Nay, the region of our hopes and presentiments extends, as we have also said, far beyond the region of what we can know with certainty. What we reach but by hope and presentiment may yet be true; and he would be a narrow reasoner who denied, for instance, all validity to the idea of immortality, because this idea rests on presentiment mainly, and does not admit of certain demonstration. In religion, above all, *extra-belief* is in itself no matter, assuredly, for blame. The object of religion is conduct; and if a man helps himself in his conduct by taking an object of hope and presentiment as if it were an object of certainty, he may even be said to gain thereby an advantage.[8]

Stories at this level are more than the products of a single author; they represent a common voice, a cooperative effort to define our highest ideals and aspirations, our most elevated visions. Arnold recognized them as part of a cultural urge to perfection, and Nietzsche admired the Old Testament precisely because he found therein a people. That some single prophet may become the spokesperson for the mass does not negate the communal nature of the story, for without engagement the story remains inert and sterile.

Borrowing from the stories of the Old Testament, the American prophets examined here at least began with visions that were both noble and exalted, stories that dared to gamble on presentiment alone. But just as Old Testament prophecy was unable to sustain itself, the exodus myth fashioned by the leaders of the American Revolution contained within it tensions that allowed it to devolve first to melodrama, then to melodramatic passion play, then to fantasy, until there was nothing left but the formal trappings of poetry, and finally, a renunciation of the transcendent story altogether in favor of the temporal and prosaic utterances of economics. It seems quite appropriate here to speak of a degenerative genre,[9] a failure of imagination. There is an increasing tendency over the course of these studies to substitute literary conventions for a consensus absent at the spiritual level.

Yet it must be said in defense of those who created the stories of the Revolution, of the slave power conspiracy, of the rights of workers, of the communist conspiracy, of the need to recognize the equal rights of all, that they at least had the courage to recognize and acknowledge things larger than themselves, though some were defeated in the process. In doing so, they have added color and character to our heritage. That their closest kin are found in imaginative literature suggests the reach of their thought. But unlike the authors of novels, plays, and poems, our visionaries cannot be dismissed as idle speculators; they do not allow us to isolate their fictions from the realities of our everyday world. They insist on being taken as renderings of the possible.

That efforts to create grand mythologies have an element of foreignness and extravagance for us reflects how far we are estranged from the faith that motivates them. We have adopted the constricted logic of empiricism, a logic that reduces all things to our level, puts all things on our terms. It replaces commitment with method. It is a logic that demands little of us either in belief or in consequence.[10] A strictly empirical worldview does not reshape human beings; through the achievements of science and technology, it accommodates them; it reshapes the environment, and its success in doing so is prima facie evidence of its veracity. We thus assume a position of passivity and seek to absolve ourselves of responsibility for our decisions. Matthew Arnold, though he sought to temper what he viewed as the excessive Hebraism of his day, warned against such a misplaced faith in the external, in "machinery." The "elegant Jeremiah" understood that culture must properly be a "harmonious perfection," a "totality," "fire and strength" as well as "sweetness and light." In "Dover Beach" he lamented the "melancholy, long, withdrawing roar" of the "Sea of Faith," "Retreating, to the breath Of the night wind, down the vast edged drear And naked shingles of the world." The world, he continued,

> Hath really neither joy, nor love, nor light,
> Nor certitude, nor peace, or help for pain;
> And we are here as on a darkling plain
> Swept with confused alarms of struggle and flight,
> Where ignorant armies clash by night.

That Arnold's poem, originally intended as a criticism of political excess, sounds equally appropriate in a time characterized by diffidence is a striking testament to the soundness of his instinct for balance and a lesson in deference and responsibility. Had he been a thoroughgoing Hellenist, his idea of balance might have resembled the golden mean wherein everything is trimmed of excess and reduced to the palatable, but Arnold finally preferred a more dynamic and athletic notion of homeostasis, less an average than an offsetting of opposing elements. Much as he celebrated "sweetness and light," he was unwilling to renounce those expressions of faith characterized by "fire and strength," which he recognized as having their own value in a culture.

In contrast to Arnold's time, we have erred on the side of Hellenism. We are plainly uncomfortable with the unverifiable and the extraordinary. We prefer the blandness of the bureaucrat to the supernal vision of the seer. Our cynicism prevents us from crediting claims on the divine. We view the prophetic tradition as remarkably naive in its faith in ultimate goodness. We prefer to look for the snake lurking behind every purported angel. Our distrust of prophets is really a reflection of a profound distrust of ourselves and our ability to tell true from false. We take no chances; we hide behind a timorous notion of reason, worn like sensible shoes.

This is, finally, the failing of so many current prescriptions for the national malaise. On the one hand, those on the right would retreat to rigid orthodoxies as sources of order. On the other hand, those who count themselves liberals place their faith in the processes of reason without content.[11] Both responses embrace an idea of civility, but neither comprehends the role of continuing radical opposition in maintaining cultural definition, the need to aerate the roots of society by means that involve some violence to the soil. And the question must be raised as to whether we have not lost some of the richness of our traditions by condescending to the faith on which they were based. We have lost twice, because we can neither fully appreciate the motives that impelled some to speak as prophets, which alienates us from our history, nor can we expect a renascence of prophetic activity in a world that cannot warrant its fundamental assumptions, which alienates us from the possibility of a prophetic future. It is on the recovery of this abandoned faith, this native radicalism, I suggest, that the revival of a compelling social vision and the discourse that would be its vehicle depends.

Notes

NOTES TO CHAPTER I

1. Congressional Record, 104th Cong., 2d sess., May 7, 1996, E720–21.

2. Todd Gitlin, *The Twilight of Common Dreams* (New York: Metropolitan Books, 1995).

3. Gertrude Himmelfarb, *On Looking into the Abyss: Untimely Thoughts on Culture and Society* (New York: Vintage, 1995).

4. *Miss Manners Rescues Civilization from Sexual Harassment, Frivolous Lawsuits, Dissing, and Other Lapses in Civility* (New York: Crown, 1996).

5. Todd Gitlin, "The Uncivil Society," *New Perspectives Quarterly* (Spring 1990), 47.

6. Gitlin, "The Uncivil Society," 48.

7. Jack Newfield, *New York Times* (December 29, 1968), III, 3.

8. Abe Fortas, "Justice Fortas Defines the Limits of Civil Disobedience," *New York Times Magazine* (May 12, 1968), 28 + .

9. Richard M. Nixon, "First Inaugural Address" (January 20, 1969) as printed in James R. Andrews and David Zarefsky, *Contemporary American Voices: Significant Speeches in American History, 1945–Present* (White Plains, NY: Longman, 1992), 258.

10. Bruce Lincoln, *Discourse and the Construction of Society: Comparative Studies of Myth, Ritual, and Classification* (New York: Oxford University Press, 1989), 3.

11. Robert N. Bellah, Richard Madsen, William M. Sullivan, Ann Swidler, and Steven M. Tipton, *Habits of the Heart: Individualism and Commitment in American Life* (Berkeley and Los Angeles: University of California Press, 1985).

12. Lee C. Bollinger, *The Tolerant Society* (New York: Oxford University Press, 1986), 9.

13. Additional examples include: William Barrett, *Rhetoric and Civility: Human Development, Narcissism, and the Good Audience* (Albany: State University of New York Press, 1991); Neil Postman, *Amusing Ourselves to Death: Public Discourse in the Age of Show Business* (New York: Penguin, 1986); Thomas Shachtman, *The Inarticulate Society: Eloquence and Culture in America* (New York: Free Press, 1995).

14. Franklyn S. Haiman, "The Rhetoric of 1968: A Farewell to Rational Discourse," in Wil A. Linkugel, R. R. Allen, and Richard L. Johannesen, eds.,

Contemporary American Speeches, 3d edition (Belmont, CA: Wadsworth, 1972), 133–47.

15. Mary Ann Glendon, *Rights Talk: The Impoverishment of Political Discourse* (New York: Free Press, 1991).

16. See also: Wayne C. Booth, *Now Don't Try to Reason with Me: Essays and Ironies for a Credulous Age* (Chicago: University of Chicago Press, 1970).

17. Jean Bethke Elshtain, *Democracy on Trial* (New York: Basic Books, 1995), 2, 11, 19, 77.

18. Elshtain, *Democracy on Trial,* 95.

19. Thomas Cole, *The Origins of Rhetoric in Ancient Greece* (Baltimore: Johns Hopkins University Press, 1991), 47–54.

20. Robert Hariman, "Decorum, Power, and the Courtly Style," *Quarterly Journal of Speech* 78 (1992), 156.

21. Charles Walter Brown, *The American Star Speaker and Model Elocutionist* (Chicago: M. A. Donohue & Co., 1902), 20–21.

22. James Boyd White, *When Words Lose Their Meaning: Constitutions and Reconstitutions of Language, Character, and Community* (Chicago: University of Chicago Press, 1984), xi.

23. Kenneth Burke, *A Rhetoric of Motives* (Berkeley and Los Angeles: University of California Press, 1969), 39.

24. For a complete dissertation on the relationship of communication, order, authority, hierarchy, organization, integration, and mystification, see: Hugh Dalziel Duncan, *Communication and Social Order* (New York: Oxford University Press, 1968).

25. For a discussion of relevant issues and literature, see Karlyn Kohrs Campbell and Kathleen Hall Jamieson, "Form and Genre in Rhetorical Criticism: An Introduction," in Karlyn Kohrs Campbell and Kathleen Jamieson, eds., *Form and Genre: Shaping Rhetorical Action* (Annandale, VA: Speech Communication Association, [1978]), 9–32.

26. See Russell Hanson, *The Democratic Imagination in America: Conversations with Our Past* (Princeton: Princeton University Press, 1985), 22–25.

27. Campbell and Jamieson, "Form and Genre in Rhetorical Criticism," 24–25.

28. Classic studies of America's sacred self-conception include Perry Miller, *Errand into the Wilderness* (Cambridge: Belknap Press of Harvard University Press, 1956); and Ernest Lee Tuveson, *Redeemer Nation: The Idea of America's Millennial Role* (Chicago: University of Chicago Press, 1968).

29. For example: James Turner Johnson, ed., *The Bible in American Law, Politics, and Political Rhetoric* (Philadelphia: Fortress Press; Chico, CA: Scholars Press, 1985); and Ernest R. Sandeen, ed., *The Bible and Social Reform* (Philadelphia: Fortress Press; Chico, CA: Scholars Press, 1982).

30. See especially Sacvan Bercovitch, *The American Jeremiad* (Madison, WI: University of Wisconsin Press, 1978).

31. Bercovitch, *The American Jeremiad,* 32–33, 34, 37, 44, 45, 80.

32. Bercovitch, *The American Jeremiad,* xiv, 4, 79.

33. Matthew Arnold, *Culture and Anarchy,* J. Dover Wilson, ed. (Cambridge: Cambridge University Press, 1960).

34. Arnold, *Culture and Anarchy,* 131.

35. See Isaac Rabinowitz, "Pre-Modern Jewish Study of Rhetoric: An Introductory Bibliography," *Rhetorica* 3 (1985), esp. 137–38.

36. Michael V. Fox, "The Rhetoric of Ezekiel's Vision of the Valley of the Bones," *Hebrew Union College Annual* 51 (1980), 5. Heschel provides a particularly good introduction to differences between Greek thought and Hebrew thought in the ancient world and as they have evolved and influenced our culture. Abraham Heschel, *The Prophets,* 2 vols., Colophon edition (New York: Harper and Row, 1962), esp. v. 2, chap. 3. See also: Isaac Rabinowitz, "Towards a Valid Theory of Biblical Hebrew Literature," in Luitpold Wallach, ed., *The Classical Tradition: Literary and Historical Studies in Honor of Harry Caplan* (Ithaca, NY: Cornell University Press, 1966), 315–28.

37. For example, see: James H. Billington, *Fires in the Minds of Men: Origins of the Revolutionary Faith* (New York: Basic Books, 1980); Samuel D. Clark, J. Paul Grayson, and Linda M. Grayson, eds., *Prophecy and Protest: Social Movements in Twentieth-Century Canada* (Toronto: Sage Educational Publishing, 1975); Maurice Cranston, ed., *Prophetic Politics* (New York: Simon and Schuster, 1970); Hans Kohn, *Prophets and Peoples: Studies in Nineteenth Century Nationalism* (New York: Collier, 1961); Leon Festinger, Henry W. Reicken, and Stanley Schacter, *When Prophecy Fails,* Torchbook edition (New York: Harper and Row, 1964).

38. George Bernard Shaw, "Preface," *Saint Joan,* Penguin edition (Baltimore: Penguin, 1951), 41–42.

39. Kenneth Burke reminds us that the word "persuasion" comes from the Latin *suadere,* which shares its roots with "suavity," "assuage," and "sweet." *A Rhetoric of Motives,* 52.

40. Robert N. Bellah and Phillip E. Hammond, *Varieties of Civil Religion* (San Francisco: Harper and Row, 1980), 126, passim.

41. Bellah and Hammond, *Varieties of Civil Religion,* 36, passim.

42. Kenneth Burke, *A Grammar of Motives* (Berkeley and Los Angeles: University of California Press, 1969), 112, passim. Burke also talks of money emancipating men "from a belief in any spiritual power but money itself and its psychoses." *A Rhetoric of Motives,* 135. There will be more on this theme in chapter 9.

43. William A. Gamson, *Power and Discontent* (Homewood, IL: Dorsey Press, 1968), 83–84. See also: Charles Tilly, *From Mobilization to Revolution* (Reading, MA: Addison-Wesley, 1978).

44. For an overview of the social-scientific idea of radicalism, see: Egon Bittner, "Radicalism," in David Sills, ed., *International Encyclopedia of the Social* Sciences, 18 vols., v. 13 (New York: Macmillan and Free Press, 1968), 294–300.

45. Todd Gitlin, "Postmodernism: Roots and Politics," in Ian Angus and Sut Jhally, eds., *Cultural Politics in Contemporary America* (New York: Routledge, 1989), 353.

NOTES TO CHAPTER 2

1. Aristotle, *Rhetoric,* W. Rhys Roberts, trans., in *The Basic Works of Aristotle,* Richard McKeon, ed. (New York: Random House, 1941), 1356a1–3.

2. James Turner Johnson, "Introduction," in James Turner Johnson, ed., *The Bible in American Law, Politics, and Political Rhetoric,* (Philadelphia: Fortress Press; Chico, CA: Scholars Press, 1985), 1.

3. According to Claus Westermann, "The most important result for the history and understanding of prophetic speech in the Old Testament is that the character of the prophetic speeches as messengers' speeches is now fully confirmed by the religio- historical background shown in the Mari letters. There is thus no longer any reason for disputing the definition of the prophetic speech introduced by Lindblom and Kohler which assumes its character to be the speech of a messenger." Claus Westermann, *Basic Forms of Prophetic Speech,* Hugh Clayton White, trans. (Philadelphia: Westminster Press, 1967), 128. See also: R. B. Y. Scott, *The Relevance of the Prophets,* revised edition (New York: Macmillan, 1968), 92, 126–27. Scott describes the prophets as Yahweh's voices "speaking in the first person on his behalf, whether or not their oracles as they have come down to us are prefaced by the messenger's introductory formula, 'Thus saith the Lord.' What they proclaimed was a Word from Yahweh—definite, relevant, urgent." See also Bruce Vawter, C. M., *The Conscience of Israel: Pre-Exilic Prophets and Prophecy* (New York: Sheed and Ward, 1961), esp. 38–39, 47–50.

4. Abraham J. Heschel, *The Prophets,* Colophon edition, v. 2 (New York: Harper and Row, 1962), esp. 138–39. See also: Scott, *Relevance of the Prophets,* 90, 99; Burke O. Long, "Prophetic Authority as Social Reality," in George W. Coats and Burke O. Long, eds., *Canon and Authority: Essays in Old Testament Religion and Theology* (Philadelphia: Fortress Press, 1977), 7.

5. Ezekiel 3:14.

6. Jeremiah 20:9.

7. Amos 3:8. See also: Sheldon Blank's description of Jeremiah's speech as not "automatic, nevertheless it is beyond his power to refrain from speech. He is possessed with a sense of inevitability." Sheldon H. Blank, " 'Of a Truth the Lord Hath Sent Me': An Inquiry into the Source of the Prophet's Authority," in Harry M. Orlinsky, ed., *Interpreting the Prophetic Tradition: The Goldenson Lectures 1955–1966* (Cincinnati: Hebrew Union College Press; New York: KTAV Publishing House, 1969), 13.

8. Margaret D. Zulick, "The Agon of Jeremiah: On the Dialogic Invention of Prophetic Ethos," *Quarterly Journal of Speech* 78 (1992), 137.

9. Zulick, "The Agon of Jeremiah," 137.

10. On the messenger formula, see: Westermann, *Basic Forms*. See also Helmer Ringgren, "Prophecy in the Ancient Near East," in Richard Coggins, Anthony Phillips, and Michael Knibb, eds., *Israel's Prophetic Tradition: Essays in Honour of Peter R. Ackroyd* (Cambridge: Cambridge University Press, 1982), 1.

11. Heschel, *The Prophets*, v. 2, 206; Michael V. Fox, "The Rhetoric of Ezekiel's Vision of the Valley of the Bones," *Hebrew Union College Annual* 51 (1980), 8.

12. Vawter, *Conscience of Israel*, 16–17.

13. Scott, *Relevance of the Prophets*, 130ff, 142ff; Heschel, *The Prophets*, v. 1, 70ff, 159–86, 190.

14. Heschel, *The Prophets*, v. 1, 169.

15. Scott, *Relevance of the Prophets*, 144.

16. Ezekiel 12:2.

17. Amos 6:4–6.

18. Heschel, *The Prophets*, v. 2, 146.

19. Isaiah 29:11–12.

20. Amos 2:4.

21. Isaiah 28:7.

22. Jeremiah 5:21.

23. See: Richard Ohmann's remarks on the relationship between stylistic choices and epistemology. "Prolegomena to the Analysis of Prose Style," reprinted in Howard S. Babb, ed., *Essays in Stylistic Analysis* (New York: Harcourt Brace Jovanovich, 1972), 35–49.

24. Westermann, for example, uses the term *apodictic* to describe the law with which the prophets were concerned. *Basic Forms*, 172.

25. Heschel, *The Prophets*, v. 1, 22.

26. Westermann describes the accusation in the prophetic speech as a recitation of facts (*Basic Forms*, 132, 144, 145, 146) and describes the combination of the accusation and the announcement stemming from it as "self-evident." *Basic Forms*, 153, cf. 187–88. Anthony Phillips discusses the concern of the prophets with "natural law . . . a breach of which any rational man ought to have been able to discern for himself." Anthony Phillips, "Prophecy and Law," in Coggins, Phillips, and Knibb, *Israel's Prophetic Tradition*, 223–24.

27. Chaim Perelman and L. Olbrechts-Tyteca, *The New Rhetoric: A Treatise on Argumentation*, John Wilkinson and Purcell Weaver, trans. (Notre Dame, IN: University of Notre Dame Press, 1969), 3.

28. Richard Weaver, *The Ethics of Rhetoric*, Gateway edition (Chicago: Henry Regnery Co., 1965), 166, passim.

29. Blank, " 'Of a Truth the Lord Hath Sent Me,' " 9.

30. W. D. Hudson, "What Makes Religious Beliefs Religious?" *Religious Studies* 13 (1977), esp. 230–31.

31. Blank, " 'Of a Truth the Lord Hath Sent Me,' " 17.

32. Walter Brueggemann, *The Prophetic Imagination* (Philadelphia: Fortress Press, 1978), 66; see also: Thomas W. Overholt, *Channels of Prophecy: The Social Dynamics of Prophetic Activity* (Minneapolis: Fortress Press, 1989).

33. A. S. Van der Woude clarifies this complex relationship of consensus and opposition: "None of the writing prophets seem to have denied these traditions [the normative theological traditions of Israel] as such but they have drawn different conclusions from them than their contemporaries." A. S. Van der Woude, "Three Classical Prophets: Amos, Hosea and Micah," in Coggins, Phillips, and Knibb, *Israel's Prophetic Tradition,* 40. Bruce Vawter's comments closely parallel Van der Woude's. Vawter, *Conscience of Israel,* 16–17.

34. Chronicles 11:1–3. See also: Heschel, *The Prophets,* v. 2, 254ff; Vawter, *Conscience of Israel,* 176ff.

35. Jeremiah 23:10. Kenneth Burke finds the secular covenant along with the fall from grace implied in the sacred covenant of creation, thus establishing a cycle from order to disobedience to guilt to victimage to redemption in a new order. Kenneth Burke, *The Rhetoric of Religion: Studies in Logology* (Berkeley and Los Angeles: University of California Press, 1970).

36. Isaiah 1:23–26.

37. Heschel, *The Prophets,* v. 1, 159ff.

38. See, in particular: Phillips, "Prophecy and Law," 217–32.

39. Vawter, *Conscience of Israel,* 47.

40. Westermann, *Basic Forms,* 133–36, 199.

41. Joseph Blenkinsopp, "The Prophetic Reproach," *Journal of Biblical Literature* 90 (1971), 267–78.

42. Egon Bittner, "Radicalism," in David Sills, ed., *International Encyclopedia of the Social Sciences,* 18 v., v. 13 (New York: Macmillan and Free Press, 1968), 294.

43. See, in particular: Aaron D. Gresson, "Minority Epistemology and the Rhetoric of Creation," *Philosophy and Rhetoric* 10 (1977), 244–62; Parke G. Burgess, "The Rhetoric of Moral Conflict: Two Critical Dimensions," *Quarterly Journal of Speech* 56 (1970), 120–30; Kathleen Jamieson, "The Rhetorical Manifestations of Weltanschauung," *Central States Speech Journal* 27 (1976), 4–14.

44. On the nature of the sacred as separate, see Mircea Eliade, *The Sacred and the Profane: The Nature of Religion,* Willard R. Trask, trans. (New York: Harcourt, Brace and World, 1959). See also Fox, "The Rhetoric of Ezekiel's Vision," 8.

45. Emile Durkheim, *Sociology and Philosophy,* D. F. Pocock, trans. (New York: Free Press, 1974), 25.

46. Heschel, *The Prophets,* v. 1, 16. See also: Burke, *Rhetoric of Religion,* 35ff, esp. 37–38; Peter L. Berger, *The Sacred Canopy: Elements of a Sociological Theory of Religion,* Anchor edition (Garden City, NY: Doubleday, 1969), 87f.

47. The term "identification" is associated with Kenneth Burke as a key term in rhetoric, but it has been pointed out on more than one occasion that one factor that hinders traditional Aristotelian criticisms of radical discourse is that traditional

rhetoric is an "insider's rhetoric." See, in particular: Herbert W. Simons, "Persuasion in Social Conflicts: A Critique of Prevailing Conceptions and a Framework for Future Research," *Speech Monographs* 39 (1972), 227–47.

48. Westermann stresses the situational nature of prophetic discourse, in *Basic Forms*, esp. 131, 153; see also: Fox, "The Rhetoric of Ezekiel's Vision," 4.

49. Heschel, *The Prophets*, v. 2, 188. Simon John de Vries holds, "The basic conflict [in prophecy] is always between covenant integrity and political opportunism." *Prophet against Prophet* (Grand Rapids, MI: Wm. B. Eerdmans, 1978), 148.

50. See, for example, DeWitte Holland, ed., *Preaching in American History* (Nashville: Abingdon Press, 1969); Barbara A. Larson, *Prologue to Revolution: The War Sermons of the Reverend Samuel Davies*, Bicentennial Monograph (Falls Church, VA: Speech Communication Association, 1978); Robert N. Bellah, *The Broken Covenant: American Civil Religion in Time of Trial* (New York: Seabury Press, 1975), 12f.

51. Robert N. Bellah, "The Revolution and the Civil Religion," in Jerald C. Brauer, ed., *Religion and the American Revolution* (Philadelphia: Fortress Press, 1976).

52. Leon I. Feuer places special emphasis on the occurrence of the prophet in a "time of trouble." Leon I. Feuer, "Prophetic Religion in an Age of Revolution," in Orlinsky, *Interpreting the Prophetic Tradition*, 181, 183, 198, passim. See also: Overholt, *Channels of Prophecy*, esp. 81, 112–14.

53. Scott, *The Relevance of the Prophets*, 95f.

54. Jürgen Habermas, *Legitimation Crisis*, Thomas McCarthy, trans. (Boston: Beacon Press, 1975), 3.

55. Berger, *The Sacred Canopy*, 21ff.

56. John E. Smith, *Experience and God* (New York: Oxford University Press, 1968), 59.

57. Westermann, *Basic Forms*, 26–27. Westermann's view is corroborated by many other Old Testament scholars. For example, see: Blenkinsopp, "The Prophetic Reproach," 267–78, esp. 268; J. Begrich, *Studien Zu Deuterojesaja*, cited in Yehoshua Gitay, *Prophecy and Persuasion: A Study of Isaiah 40–48* (Bonn: Linguistica Biblica, 1981), 7–8; Phillips, "Prophecy and Law," 217–32.

58. Westermann, *Basic Forms*, 177ff.

59. Westermann, *Basic Forms*, 172–73.

60. Westermann, *Basic Forms*, 176.

61. Blenkinsopp, "The Prophetic Reproach," 268.

62. Micah 2:1–4.

63. Nietzsche would find here the institutionalization of a "pathos of distance" in the contractual relationship between debtor and creditor. Nietzsche, *The Genealogy of Morals*, in *The Birth of Tragedy and The Genealogy of Morals*, Anchor books edition, Francis Golffing, trans. (Garden City, NY: Doubleday, 1956).

64. Heschel, *The Prophets*, v. 2, xvii–86.

65. Vawter, *Conscience of Israel*, 128.

66. Northrop Frye, *The Critical Path: An Essay on the Social Context of Literary Criticism,* Midland edition (Bloomington: Indiana University Press, 1973), 53.

67. Heschel, *The Prophets,* v. 2, 64.

68. Brueggemann, *The Prophetic Imagination,* 44–61; see also: Heschel, *The Prophets,* v. 1, 32–36, passim. The special relationship of the prophet to the powerless is also a central theme in James Limburg, *The Prophets and the Powerless* (Atlanta: John Knox Press, 1977).

69. Leo Strauss, *Natural Right and History* (Chicago: University of Chicago Press, 1953), 74.

70. Heschel, *The Prophets,* v. 1, 24, 26, 38, 87.

71. Ohmann, "Prolegomena to the Analysis of Prose Style," 47.

72. Jeremiah 21:12.

73. Malachi 3:2–7.

74. Lundbom attempts to make the case that Jeremiah can be read as persuasive discourse which finds its center in the audience, but he is often reduced to acknowledging the intent of the prophetic word to "shatter" or "break" the people so that they can be remolded. Jack R. Lundbom, *Jeremiah: A Study in Ancient Hebrew Rhetoric* (Missoula, MT: Society of Biblical Literature and Scholars Press, 1975), 40f, 42, 56, 58, 73, 77, 90, 95, 116f; Cf. 79, 91, 92.

75. Frye, *The Critical Path,* 120.

76. Heschel, *The Prophets,* v. 2, 185. See also: Scott, *The Relevance of the Prophets,* 44–45. In his review of the literature regarding the office of the prophet, Westermann finds *nabi* to be historically associated with the office of the messenger as opposed to the office of the seer. Some scholars see the two offices becoming conflated in late Old Testament prophecy. Westermann, *Basic Forms,* 14–80. Vawter's review of the meaning of *nabi* is consistent with Heschel and Westermann in that Vawter finds *nabi* becoming *prophetes* in the Greek Septuagint. This would be consistent with the view that the *nabi* is one who is called to speak for another. Vawter, *The Conscience of Israel,* 34ff.

77. Jeremiah 20:7–9.

78. Heschel, v. 1, 113. Clines and Gunn take issue with Heschel's rendering, preferring to translate *pittîtanî* as "persuasion." D. J. A. Clines and D. M. Gunn, " 'You Tried to Persuade Me' and 'Violence! Outrage!' in Jeremiah XX 7–8," *Vetus Testamentum* 28 (1978), 20–27. Nonetheless, they come to the conclusion that Jeremiah's rage is directed against Yahweh for compelling him, through persuasion, to speak as a prophet. von Rad, too, would argue that the prophet is a free agent, but he also concedes that "the prophets themselves felt that they had been compelled by a stronger will than theirs." Gerhard von Rad, *The Message of the Prophets,* D. M. G. Stalker, trans. (New York: Harper and Row, 1965), 37, 50–59.

79. Scott, *The Relevance of the Prophets,* 99. Similarly, Heschel notes the metaphor of the hand of God used by the prophets to express "the urgency, pressure,

and compulsion by which he is stunned and overwhelmed." *The Prophets,* v. 2, 224.

80. Jeremiah 1:5.

81. Isaiah 49:5.

82. William James, *The Varieties of Religious Experience* (New York: New American Library, 1958), 143.

83. James, *Varieties of Religious Experience,* 157.

84. See: Berger, *The Sacred Canopy,* 56.

85. Kenneth Burke defines martyrdom as "the idea of total voluntary self-sacrifice enacted in a grave cause before a perfect (absolute) witness. It is the fulfillment of the principle of mortification, suicidally directed, with the self as scapegoat (in contrast with homicidal use of an external scapegoat as purificatory victim)." Burke, *The Rhetoric of Religion,* 248. And William James clarifies the relationship between self-sacrifice and mortification by noting that obedience to God represents the sacrifice of intellect and will; to the extent that the prophet is obedient to his call, he is mortified. James, *Varieties of Religious Experience,* 53, 245; Eliade, *The Sacred and the Profane,* 196–201.

86. R. B. Y. Scott expresses the nature of the calling in terms of being set apart. Scott, *The Relevance of the Prophets,* 99, 100. Edgar Magnin finds the physical separation of the prophets' "pulpit" from the temple to be symbolic of this sacredness. Edgar F. Magnin, "The Voice of Prophecy in This Satellite Age," in Orlinsky, *Interpreting the Prophetic Tradition,* 103–21. The sense of separateness is also implied in theories of prophetic ecstasy, which means "to put out of place." Robert R. Wilson, "Prophecy and Ecstasy: A Reexamination," *Journal of Biblical Literature* 98 (1979), 321–37.

87. Zulick, "The Agon of Jeremiah," 135.

88. von Rad, *The Message of the Prophets,* 37.

89. Jeremiah 20:14–18.

90. Nietzsche, *The Genealogy of Morals,* 221, emphasis Nietzsche's. For James's criticism of Nietzsche, see: *Varieties of Religious Experience,* 286–87.

91. Overholt, *Channels of Prophecy,* 163–83.

92. Long, "Prophetic Authority as Social Reality," 8.

93. James Crenshaw, *Prophetic Conflict* (Berlin: Walter de Gruyter, 1971), 38. Sheldon Blank makes the same point when he notes that Jeremiah's strongest argument for his authenticity was not an argument at all, but the simple affirmation that God had sent him. Blank, " 'Of a Truth the Lord Hath Sent Me,' " 9.

94. George Bernard Shaw, *Saint Joan,* Penguin edition (Baltimore: Penguin, 1951), 122.

95. Shaw, *Saint Joan,* 123.

96. Crenshaw, *Prophetic Conflict,* 94. See also: Magnin, "The Voice of Prophecy in This Satellite Age," 118.

97. Shaw, *Saint Joan*, 158.

98. Max Weber, "The Prophet," in S. N. Eisenstadt, ed., *Max Weber on Charisma and Institution Building: Selected Papers* (Chicago: University of Chicago Press, 1968), 253.

99. Weber, "The Prophet," 254. Heschel writes of the prophet as anthropotropic (God turning toward man) while priests were theotropic (man turning toward God): "The prophet speaks and acts by virtue of divine inspiration, the priest performs the ritual by virtue of his official status." Heschel, *The Prophets,* v. 2, 221.

100. Vawter, *Conscience of Israel,* 20. On prophecy as charismatic, see also: Heschel, *The Prophets,* v. 2, 139; Overholt, *Channels of Prophecy,* 24, 70, passim.

101. In J. E. T. Eldridge, ed., *Max Weber: The Interpretation of Social Reality* (New York: Charles Scribner's Sons, 1971), 229.

102. This is clear in Weber's writings where charismatic authority is contrasted with rational forms like bureaucratic authority, and it is the focus of William H. Swatos, Jr., "The Disenchantment of Charisma," *Sociological Analysis* 42 (1981), 119–36. See also: George P. Boss, "Essential Attributes of the Concept of Charisma," *Southern Speech Communication Journal* 41 (1976), 300–13.

103. von Rad, *The Message of the Prophets,* 206, 218–28. On interpretations of the servant songs, see Colin G. Kruse, "The Servant Songs: Interpretive Trends since C. R. North," *Studia Biblica et Theologica* 8 (1978), 3–27.

104. Isaiah 50:4.

105. Kenneth Burke, *A Rhetoric of Motives* (Berkeley and Los Angeles: University of California Press, 1969), 222.

106. F. G. Bailey, *The Tactical Uses of Passion* (Ithaca, NY: Cornell University Press, 1983), 38. Burke Long writes: "Even events of conspicuous hardship and failure could be interpreted so as to support claims of authority (Jeremiah 1:18–19; 15:19–20)." Long, "Prophetic Authority as Social Reality," 15.

107. von Rad discusses the use of "martyrdom" to describe pre-Christian sufferings and finds that examples from the Old Testament prophets approach very closely Christian martyrdom, "for even in Israel it became more and more apparent that loyalty to Yahweh logically would lead to suffering." von Rad, *The Message of the Prophets,* 276f.

108. James, *Varieties of Religious Experience,* 32. Shaw notes, "The test of sanity is not the normality of the method but the reasonableness of the discovery." "Preface," *Saint Joan,* 14.

109. James, *Varieties of Religious Experience,* 37.

110. James, *Varieties of Religious Experience,* 207. Writing of Saint Joan, Shaw says, "For us to set up our condition as a standard of sanity, and declare Joan mad because she never condescended to it, is to prove that we are not only lost but irredeemable." "Preface," 18.

111. Swatos, "The Disenchantment of Charisma," 124; Long, "Prophetic Au-

thority as Social Reality," 4. Overholt treats this as something of a revelation in his discussion of "social dynamics." Overholt, *Channels of Prophecy*, 143, 157, 181.

112. von Rad, *The Message of the Prophets*, 223.

113. James, *Varieties of Religious Experience*, 290.

114. Zulick, "The Agon of Jeremiah," 142.

115. Comparisons of Debs and Lincoln are especially common. For example, see: John Swinton, "Lincoln, 1860—Debs, 1894," reprinted in *Debs: His Life, Writings, and Speeches* (Chicago: Charles H. Kerr and Company, 1908), 501–4; Walter Hurt, "Eugene V. Debs: An Introduction" (Williamsburg, OH: Progress Publishing Co., n.d.), 15; Charles Erskine Scott Wood, "Debs Has Visitors," in Ruth Le Prade, ed., *Debs and the Poets* (Pasadena, CA: Upton Sinclair, 1920), 84–88. On the general phenomenon of comparing Debs and Lincoln, see: Bernard J. Brommel, "Eugene V. Debs: Spokesman for Labor and Socialism," unpublished dissertation, Indiana University, 1964, 168f, 226.

NOTES TO CHAPTER 3

1. Stephen Hopkins, "An Essay on the Trade of the Northern Colonies," in Merrill Jensen, ed., *Tracts of the American Revolution* (Indianapolis, IN: Bobbs-Merrill, n.d.), 16–17.

2. Clinton Rossiter, *The Political Thought of the American Revolution* (New York: Harcourt, Brace and World, 1963), 17ff.

3. Second Continental Congress, in Richard Hofstadter, ed., *Great Issues in American History from the Revolution to the Civil War, 1765–1865* (New York: Vintage, 1958), 49–50.

4. Bernard Bailyn, *The Ideological Origins of the American Revolution* (Cambridge, MA: Harvard University Press, 1967), 1.

5. Bailyn, *Ideological Origins*, 19.

6. Thomas J. Archdeacon, "American Historians and the American Revolution: A Bicentennial Overview," *Wisconsin Magazine of History* 63 (1980), 290.

7. Gordon S. Wood, "Rhetoric and Reality in the American Revolution," *William and Mary Quarterly*, 3d series, 23 (1966), 2.

8. Martin Howard, Jr., "A Letter from a Gentleman at Halifax," in Jensen, *Tracts*, 73.

9. Thomas Bolton, "An Oration," in David Potter and Gordon L. Thomas, eds., *The Colonial Idiom* (Carbondale and Edwardsville: Southern Illinois University Press, 1970), 301.

10. See: Dickinson's Letter no. 3, reprinted in Forrest McDonald, ed., *Empire and Nation* (Englewood Cliffs, NJ: Prentice-Hall, 1962), 15–20.

11. [Daniel Leonard], "Massachusettensis," December 19, 1774, in Jensen, *Tracts*, 283–84.

12. [Leonard], "Massachusettensis," December 26, 1775, in Jensen, *Tracts*, 287.

13. Joseph Galloway, "A Candid Examination of the Mutual Claims of Great Britain and the Colonies," in Jensen, *Tracts,* 351.

14. Galloway, in Jensen, *Tracts,* 398.

15. *Samuel Johnson's Dictionary: A Modern Selection,* E. L. McAdam, Jr. and George Milne, eds. (New York: Pantheon, 1964); Thomas Paine, "Common Sense," in Jensen, *Tracts,* 405; see also Charles Howard McIlwain, *The American Revolution: A Constitutional Interpretation,* paperback edition (Ithaca, NY: Cornell University Press, 1958), 163, on the identification of the law of reason and the law of nature.

16. Max Weber, "Natural Law," in S. N. Eisenstadt, ed., *Max Weber on Charisma and Institution Building: Selected Papers,* (Chicago: University of Chicago Press, 1968), 100–102; Melvin J. Lasky, *Utopia and Revolution* (Chicago and London: University of Chicago Press, 1976), 251ff; Leo Strauss, *Natural Right and History* (Chicago: University of Chicago Press, 1953).

17. Jay Fliegelman, *Declaring Independence: Jefferson, Natural Language, and the Culture of Performance* (Stanford, CA: Stanford University Press, 1993), 36–37.

18. Fliegelman, *Declaring Independence,* 40, 42–44, 48, 58, 75–76, 88–90, 96–98, 103.

19. Peter Thatcher, in Potter and Thomas, *The Colonial Idiom,* 277.

20. John Dickinson, "Speech against the Petition to Change the Form of Government," in Potter and Thomas, *The Colonial Idiom,* 182.

21. Fliegelman, *Declaring Independence,* 24.

22. Fliegelman, *Declaring Independence,* 43.

23. Fliegelman, *Declaring Independence,* 37, 65.

24. Lloyd Bitzer, "The Rhetorical Situation," *Philosophy and Rhetoric* 1 (1968), 1–14.

25. Stephen E. Lucas, *Portents of Rebellion: Rhetoric and Revolution in Philadelphia, 1765–76* (Philadelphia: Temple University Press, 1976), 60–66. See also: Charles Lomas, *The Agitator in American Society* (Englewood Cliffs, NJ: Prentice-Hall, 1968), 152.

26. Egon Bittner, "Radicalism," in David Sills, ed., *International Encyclopedia of the Social Sciences,* 18 v., v. 13 (New York: Macmillan and Free Press, 1968), 294.

27. Lucas, *Portents of Rebellion,* 77ff.

28. For broad characterizations of some of the issues, see: Edmund S. Morgan, "Don't Tread on Us," *New York Review of Books* (March 21, 1996), 17; Gordon S. Wood, *The Radicalism of the American Revolution* (New York: Vintage, 1993), 3–8; Theodore Draper, *A Struggle for Power: The American Revolution* (New York: Times Books, 1996), xiii; John Phillip Reid, "The Irrelevance of the Declaration," in Hendrik Hartog, ed., *Law in the American Revolution and the Revolution in the Law* (New York: New York University Press, 1981), 46–89; Stephen E. Lucas, "Justifying America: The Declaration of Independence as a Rhetorical Document," in

Thomas Benson, ed., *American Rhetoric: Context and Criticism* (Carbondale and Edwardsville: Southern Illinois University Press, 1989), 123–24, n44.

29. Robert N. Bellah, *The Broken Covenant: American Civil Religion in Time of Trial* (New York: Seabury Press, 1975); Sacvan Bercovitch, *The American Jeremiad* (Madison, WI: University of Wisconsin Press, 1978), 3, 14, 42–44, 92, 93ff, 114.

30. Ernest Lee Tuveson, *Redeemer Nation: The Idea of America's Millennial Role* (Chicago: University of Chicago Press, 1968). See also: Mark A. Noll, "The Bible in Revolutionary America," in James Turner Johnson, ed., *The Bible in American Law, Politics, and Political Rhetoric* (Philadelphia: Fortress Press; Chico, CA: Scholars Press, 1985), 39–60.

31. Ernest Wrage, "Public Address: A Study in Social and Intellectual History," *Quarterly Journal of Speech* 33 (1947), 455–56.

32. Lucas, *Portents of Rebellion*, 126–51.

33. Jensen, "Introduction," in *Tracts*, liii–liv.

34. First Continental Congress, "Declaration and Resolves, October 14, 1774," in Hofstadter, *Great Issues*, 26–31.

35. James Otis, in Jensen, *Tracts*, 24.

36. [Goddard?], in Jensen, *Tracts*, 89.

37. [Samuel Adams?], in Jensen, *Tracts*, 239.

38. McIlwain, *The American Revolution*, 171–85.

39. The following discussion is heavily indebted to George H. Sabine's classic work *A History of Political Theory*, 4th edition, revised by Thomas L. Thorson (Hinsdale, IL: Dryden Press, 1973); and Strauss, *Natural Right and History*. See also: Paul K. Conkin, *Self-Evident Truths* (Bloomington: Indiana University Press, 1974); Carl L. Becker, *The Declaration of Independence: A Study in the History of Political Ideas*, Vintage edition (New York: Vintage Books, 1942); Staughton Lynd, *Intellectual Origins of American Radicalism* (New York: Pantheon, 1968); and Lasky, *Utopia and Revolution*.

40. See also: Locke's description of the state of nature as a state of war. John Locke, *Second Treatise*, III, in Peter Laslett, ed., *Two Treatises on Civil Government*, Mentor edition (New York: New American Library, 1963). Calvin's view was similar. See: Michael Walzer, *The Revolution of the Saints: A Study in the Origins of Radical Politics* (Cambridge, MA: Harvard University Press, 1965), esp. 41.

41. Carl L. Becker, *The Heavenly City of the Eighteenth-Century Philosophers* (New Haven and London: Yale University Press, 1932).

42. See: Rossiter, *Political Thought of the American Revolution*, 115ff for further discussion of this relationship and quotations from pertinent documents.

43. Samuel West, "Election Day Sermon," in Potter and Thomas, *The Colonial Idiom*, 582–83.

44. See: Locke, *Second Treatise*, XIII, 149:20–33.

45. For the connection between the Levellers and the Whigs, see: Bailyn,

Ideological Origins, 34ff; Bernard Bailyn, "The Central Themes of the American Revolution," in Stephen G. Kurtz and James H. Hutson, eds., *Essays on the American Revolution* (Chapel Hill: University of North Carolina Press for the Institute of Early American History and Culture, 1973), 7–8; Becker, *The Declaration of Independence,* 79.

46. [Samuel Adams?], in Jensen, *Tracts,* 235–38.

47. [Samuel Adams?], in Jensen, *Tracts,* 235–38.

48. In Jensen, *Tracts,* 239–40.

49. Lucas, "Justifying America," 83.

50. Galloway, in Jensen, *Tracts,* 366.

51. Daniel Dulany, "Considerations on the Propriety of Imposing Taxes in the British Colonies for the Purpose of Raising a Revenue by Act of Parliament," in Jensen, *Tracts,* 106–7.

52. See, for example: Draper, *A Struggle for Power,* 35–36.

53. Locke refers to the function of the legislature as an "Umpirage . . . for the ending [of] all Differences, that may arise amongst any of them." *Second Treatise,* XIX, 212: 3–9; VII, 88: 10–27. On "affirmative law" vs. "new law" and Parliament's role, see: McIlwain, *The American Revolution,* 66, 72f.

54. Edmund Burke, "On Conciliation with the Colonies," in *Speeches and Letters on American Affairs by Edmund Burke,* Everyman's Library (London: J. M. Dent and Sons; New York: E. P. Dutton and Co., 1908), 117.

55. Burke, "On Conciliation with the Colonies," 121.

56. Thomas Paine, *The Rights of Man,* Introduction by Eric Foner (New York: Penguin, 1984), 165.

57. Otis, in Jensen, *Tracts,* 39.

58. On Calvin's uncomfortable vacillation on the question of legitimacy in government, see: Walzer, *The Revolution of the Saints,* 41, 58f, passim.

59. Locke, *Second Treatise,* XI, 135: 32–38.

60. As opposed to arbitrary laws, e.g., *Second Treatise,* XI, 137: 2.

61. Otis, in Jensen, *Tracts,* 29.

62. For example, see: Hopkins, 48; [Goddard?], 84, both in Jensen, *Tracts.* See: Pauline Maier, *From Resistance to Revolution* (New York: Vintage, 1974), 149ff.

63. West, "Election Day Sermon," in Potter and Thomas, *The Colonial Idiom,* 587.

64. Bailyn, "The Central Themes of the American Revolution," 8.

65. Thomas Jefferson, in Jensen, *Tracts,* 274.

66. Locke, *Second Treatise,* XVIII, 199: 1–11.

67. Jeremiah 23:10.

68. Hopkins, in Jensen, *Tracts,* 54. Cf. Locke, "For I have truly no *Property* in that, which another can by right take from me, when he pleases, against my consent." *Second Treatise,* XI, 138: 13–15.

69. John Adams, "Novanglus, January 30, 1775," in Jensen, *Tracts,* 315.

70. Burke, "On Conciliation with the Colonies," 90–91.

71. On "God terms" and "devil terms" see: Richard Weaver, *The Ethics of Rhetoric,* Gateway edition (Chicago: Henry Regnery, 1965), 211ff.

72. [Goddard?], in Jensen, *Tracts,* 83.

73. Micah 1:10.

74. Locke, *Second Treatise,* XIII, 155: 15–19.

75. Adams, "Novanglus, January 23, 1775," in Jensen, *Tracts,* 301. On the historical connection between planetary and political revolution, see: Lasky, *Utopia and Revolution,* 227ff; James H. Billington, *Fire in the Minds of Men: Origins of the Revolutionary Faith* (New York: Basic Books, 1980), 17. For a summary statement of the rhetorical and psychological appeals of natural law, see: Kathleen M. Jamieson, "Natural Law as Warrant," *Philosophy and Rhetoric* 6 (1973), 235–46.

76. [Goddard?], in Jensen, *Tracts,* 88.

77. Abraham J. Heschel, *The Prophets,* Colophon edition, v. 1 (New York: Harper and Row), 108ff. Although prophetic predictions were conditional, when the conditions had been fulfilled the consequences were inexorable.

78. Jacob Duché, in Jack P. Greene, ed., *Colonies to Nation, 1763–1789: A Documentary History of the American Revolution* (New York: W. W. Norton, 1975), 263. On Adams's reaction to the sermon, see: Emory Elliott, "The Dove and the Serpent: The Clergy in the American Revolution," *American Quarterly* 31 (1979), 188.

79. Duché, in Greene, *Colonies to Nation,* 264.

80. See: Lucas, "Justifying America," 75–76, on the significance of "necessity" in the argot of eighteenth-century politics.

81. Morton White, *The Philosophy of the American Revolution* (New York: Oxford University Press, 1978), 229ff, emphasis White's. See also: Rossiter, *The Political Thought of the American Revolution,* 141–42, 145.

82. "Declaration of the Stamp Act Congress," in Greene, *Colonies to Nation,* 64.

83. Otis, in Jensen, *Tracts,* 22.

84. Wood, *Radicalism,* 204. Leo Strauss provides some insight into the relationship between right, duty, and virtue in Hobbes, Locke, Rousseau, and Burke. Strauss, *Natural Right and History,* 145, 181ff, 255ff, 281, 298.

85. Aristotle, *Nicomachean Ethics,* W. D. Ross, trans., in *The Basic Works of Aristotle,* Richard McKeon, ed. (New York: Random House, 1941), esp. 1094a1, 1095a13, 1097b22–1098a17, 1102a5, 1104b13, 1106a10; Aristotle, *Rhetoric,* W. Rhys Roberts, trans., in *Basic Works,* McKeon, ed., 1332a9–10, 1360b4–18.

86. Aristotle, *Politics,* Benjamin Jowett, trans., in *Basic Works,* McKeon, ed., 1289a26–44.

87. Aristotle, *Politics,* 1260a12.

88. Aristotle, *Politics,* 1288a39.

89. Aristotle, *Politics,* 1301a40–1301b1.

90. Robert N. Bellah, "The Revolution and the Civil Religion," in Jerald C.

Brauer, ed., *Religion and the American Revolution* (Philadelphia: Fortress Press, 1976), 69; see also: Bellah, *The Broken Covenant*, 23–25.

91. "Brutus," "On the Promise of the Nonimportation Associations," June 1, 1769, in Greene, *Colonies to Nation*, 157. Regarding the need of human nature to be governed by men of virtue in a "disinterested" manner, see: Jack P. Greene, "An Uneasy Connection: An Analysis of the Preconditions of the American Revolution," in Kurtz and Hutson, *Essays on the American Revolution*, 54.

92. Paine, *Rights of Man*, 236.

93. Second Continental Congress, in Hofstadter, *Great Issues*, 51.

94. Greene, "An Uneasy Connection," 59–60.

95. Isaiah Berlin, "Introduction," in Isaiah Berlin, ed., *The Age of Enlightenment* (New York: New American Library, Mentor Books, 1956), 14.

96. Berlin, "Introduction," 28.

97. See: Garry Wills's challenge to Carl Becker in Garry Wills, *Inventing America: Jefferson's Declaration of Independence* (New York: Vintage Books, 1979); Becker, *The Declaration of Independence*. For a good critique of Wills's book, see: John Hamoway, "Jefferson and the Scottish Enlightenment: A Critique of Garry Wills's *Inventing America: Jefferson's Declaration of Independence*," *William and Mary Quarterly* 36 (1979), 503–23.

98. On intuition as the foundation for American Revolutionary beliefs, see: White, *Philosophy of the American Revolution*. On the role of feeling in eighteenth-century thought in general, see: John D. Boyd, S.J., *The Function of Mimesis and Its Decline*, 2d ed. (New York: Fordham University Press, 1980), esp. chap. 2, 51, 75. On the rational elements in the eighteenth-century idea of feeling, see: A. D. Lindsay, "Introduction," David Hume, *A Treatise on Human Nature* (New York: Dutton, 1911), II, x; T. H. Irwin, "Aristotle on Reason, Desire, and Virtue," *Journal of Philosophy* 72 (1975), 567–80; and Edward M. Galligan, "Irwin on Aristotle," *Journal of Philosophy* 72 (1975), 579.

99. Joseph Warren, in Potter and Thomas, *The Colonial Idiom*, 252.

100. On the relationship of some of these developments and the characteristics and functions of "basic truths," see: Stephen Toulmin, *Knowing and Acting* (New York: Macmillan, 1976), esp. 143ff.

101. William James, "The Will to Believe," in *The Will to Believe and Other Essays in Popular Philosophy* (1897; reprint, New York: Dover Publications, 1956), 14–15.

102. John Locke, *An Essay Concerning Human Understanding*, II, i, 25; II, ii, 2; in Berlin, *The Age of Enlightenment*, 43, 45.

103. Locke, *Second Treatise*, XIX, 230: 18–20.

104. Hume, *A Treatise of Human Nature*, I, iii, 7, 94ff; David Hume, *An Inquiry Concerning Human Understanding*. On Hume's distance from Descartes in his refutation that beliefs can ultimately be justified by reason, see: Barry Stroud, *Hume* (London: Routledge and Kegan Paul, 1977), 11ff.

105. Thomas Reid, *An Inquiry into the Human Mind,* Timothy J. Duggan, ed. (Chicago: University of Chicago Press, 1970), 30; Thomas Reid, *Essays on the Intellectual Powers of Man,* Baruch Brody, ed. (Cambridge, MA: M.I.T. Press, 1969), 304–5.

106. In Greene, *Colonies to Nation,* 35.

107. Jefferson, in Jensen, *Tracts,* 258.

108. Jefferson, in Jensen, *Tracts,* 275.

109. [Leonard], "Massachusettensis," December 26, 1775, in Jensen, *Tracts,* 296.

110. [Adams], "Novanglus," January 23, 1775, and [Adams], "Novanglus," January 30, 1775, both in Jensen *Tracts,* 297, 312.

111. Otis, in Jensen, *Tracts.*

112. Charles Inglis, in Hofstadter, *Great Issues,* 63.

113. Second Continental Congress, "Declaration of the Causes and Necessity of Taking up Arms," in Hofstadter, *Great Issues,* 47.

114. Paine, in Jensen, *Tracts,* 418.

115. James Chalmers, in Jensen, *Tracts,* 447–88. For further discussion of eighteenth-century epistemology in colonial thought, see: White, *Philosophy of the American Revolution,* 3–141.

116. Weber, "Natural Law," in Eisenstadt, *On Charisma and Institution Building,* 100–102; Margaret Macdonald, "Natural Rights," in Jeremy Waldron, ed., *Theories of Rights* (London: Oxford University Press, 1984), 25f; Becker, *The Declaration of Independence,* 61, 66.

117. Locke, *Second Treatise,* II, 11: 24–25.

118. Locke, *Second Treatise,* II, 6: 6–9.

119. Hobbes, *Leviathan,* I, i, 1.

120. Reid, *Inquiry,* 88.

121. R. Hazelton, "Believing is Seeing: Vision as Metaphor," *Theology Today* 35 (1979), 405.

122. White, *Philosophy of the American Revolution,* 18, 23f, 105.

123. Paine, *Rights of Man,* 159.

124. [Leonard], "Massachusettensis," December, 26, 1775, in Jensen, *Tracts,* 296. Emphasis added.

125. [Goddard?], in Jensen, *Tracts,* 89, 82.

126. [Leonard], "Massachusettensis," January 9, 1775, in Hofstadter, *Great Issues,* 35.

127. Paine, *Rights of Man,* 157.

128. Paine, *Rights of Man,* 184.

129. Heschel, *The Prophets,* v. 1, 16.

130. White, *Philosophy of the American Revolution,* 7, passim. White makes a similar argument regarding elitism in a moral sense, 131ff.

131. John Dickinson, "Letters from a Farmer," II, in Hofstadter, *Great Issues,* 24.

132. Chalmers, in Jensen, *Tracts,* 478.
133. Paine, in Jensen, *Tracts,* 418.
134. Paine, in Jensen, *Tracts,* 426.
135. Paine, "Common Sense," in Jensen, *Tracts,* 405.
136. White, *Philosophy of the American Revolution,* 14.
137. Isaiah 40:6.
138. Elizabeth Cady Stanton, "Introduction" to *The Woman's Bible,* in Alice S. Rossi, ed., *The Feminist Papers: From Adams to de Beauvoir* (New York: Columbia University Press, 1973), 404.
139. Locke, *Second Treatise,* XIX, 242.
140. Becker, *The Declaration of Independence,* 15.
141. In "Justifying America" Lucas makes the argument that, in many respects, the *Declaration* reflects the common rhetorical practices of the time.
142. [Samuel Adams?], "A State of the Rights of the Colonists," in Jensen, *Tracts,* 233–55.
143. Henry Laurens, in Jensen, *Tracts,* 185–206.
144. James Bowdoin, Dr. Joseph Warren, and Samuel Pemberton, "A Short Narrative of the Horrid Massacre in Boston," in Jensen, *Tracts,* 207–32.

NOTES TO CHAPTER 4

1. James Stewart, *Wendell Phillips: Liberty's Hero* (Baton Rouge: Louisiana State University Press, 1986), 34.
2. See also: Richard Hofstadter, *The American Political Tradition and the Men Who Made It* (New York: Vintage, 1974), 181. James Redpath, ed., "Publisher's Advertisement," in Wendell Phillips, *Speeches, Lectures, and Letters,* First series (Boston: Lee and Shepard, 1894), pagination uncertain; Irving Bartlett, *Wendell Phillips: Brahmin Radical* (Boston: Beacon Press, 1961); Irving H. Bartlett, "The Persistence of Wendell Phillips," in Martin Duberman, ed., *The Antislavery Vanguard: New Essays on the Abolitionists* (Princeton, NJ: Princeton University Press, 1965), 107–11; Irving H. Bartlett, "Wendell Phillips and the Eloquence of Abuse," *American Quarterly* 11 (1959), 509–20; Willard Hayes Yeager, "Wendell Phillips," in William Norwood Brigance, ed., *A History and Criticism of American Public Address,* v. 1 (New York: McGraw-Hill, 1943), 329–62; Louis Filler, "Introduction," in *Wendell Phillips on Civil Rights and Freedom* (New York: Hill and Wang, 1965), x–xi.
3. Stewart, *Liberty's Hero,* 327.
4. Hofstadter, *The American Political Tradition,* 175. Rhetorical critic Ernest Bormann reflects this traditional view in his influential essay, "The Rhetoric of Abolition," in Ernest G. Bormann, ed., *Forerunners of Black Power: The Rhetoric of Abolition* (Englewood Cliffs, NJ: Prentice-Hall, 1971). Aileen Kraditor, *Means and Ends in American Abolitionism: Garrison and His Critics on Strategy and Tactics, 1834–1850* (New York: Vintage Books, 1970), is particularly critical of traditional inter-

pretations of abolitionism. Lewis Perry and Michael Fellman, eds., *Antislavery Reconsidered: New Perspectives on the Abolitionists* (Baton Rouge: Louisiana State University Press, 1979), provides essays that attempt to balance wholesale condemnation and blind, reactionary defense.

5. Bartlett, "The Persistence of Wendell Phillips," 111; Bartlett, "The Eloquence of Abuse," 516. The phrase is Robert C. Winthrop's.

6. E. L. Godkin, "Wendell Phillips as a Whipper-In," *The Nation* (February 8, 1866), 166, quoted in Winona L. Fletcher, "Knight-Errant or Screaming Eagle? E. L. Godkin's Criticism of Wendell Phillips," *Southern Speech Journal* 29 (1964), 217.

7. See: "The Lost Arts," in Ashley Thorndike, ed., *Modern Eloquence,* revised edition in 15 vols., v. 13 (New York: Lincoln Scholarship Fund, 1929), 281. See also: Hofstadter, *The American Political Tradition,* 182.

8. Phillips, *Speeches, Lectures, and Letters,* 282.

9. S. N. Eisenstadt, ed., "Introduction," in *Max Weber on Charisma and Institution Building: Selected Papers* (Chicago: University of Chicago Press, 1968), xix.

10. Donald M. Scott, "Abolition as a Sacred Vocation," in Perry and Fellman, *Antislavery Reconsidered,* 51–74.

11. Timothy L. Smith, "Righteousness and Hope: Christian Holiness and the Millennial Vision in America, 1800–1900," *American Quarterly* 31 (1979), 30.

12. Perry Miller, *The Life of the Mind in America from the Revolution to the Civil War* (New York: Harcourt, Brace and World, 1965), 6, 7.

13. Joseph R. Gusfield, *Symbolic Crusade: Status Politics and the American Temperance Movement,* paperback edition (Urbana, IL: University of Illinois Press, 1966), 31. On parallels between abolitionism and temperance, see: Gusfield, *Symbolic Crusade,* 54; Scott, "Abolition as a Sacred Vocation," 66f. On Phillips's own involvement with temperance, see: Stewart, *Liberty's Hero,* 217–18, 259–61, 283, 285, 302, 327.

14. David Brion Davis, "Slavery and Sin: The Cultural Background," in Duberman, *The Antislavery Vanguard,* 3, passim; David Brion Davis, *The Problem of Slavery in Western Culture* (Ithaca, NY: Cornell University Press, 1966); David Brion Davis, *The Problem of Slavery in the Age of Revolution, 1770–1823* (Ithaca, NY: Cornell University Press, 1975).

15. Scott, "Abolition as a Sacred Vocation," 68.

16. James B. Stewart, "Heroes, Villains, Liberty, and License: The Abolitionist Vision of Wendell Phillips," in Perry and Fellman, *Antislavery Reconsidered,* 169ff. Ronald G. Walters, "The Erotic South: Civilization and Sexuality in American Abolitionism," *American Quarterly* 25 (1973), 177–201.

17. Scott, "Abolition as a Sacred Vocation," esp. 66ff.

18. "John Brown and Harper's Ferry," in Filler, *Civil Rights and Freedom,* 107.

19. "In Defense of Lovejoy," in Filler, *Civil Rights and Freedom,* 9.

20. "The Boston Mob," in Filler, *Civil Rights and Freedom,* 12.

21. "The Boston Mob," in Filler, *Civil Rights and Freedom*, 26.

22. *The Constitution a Pro-Slavery Compact* (New York: Negro Universities Press, 1969), 6.

23. Review of Lysander Spooner's Essay on the Unconstitutionality of Slavery Reprinted from the "Anti-Slavery Standard" with Additions (Boston: Andrews and Prentiss, 1847).

24. George V. Bohman notes this speech along with Lincoln's speech at Cooper Union as contributing to an increasingly tense political discussion in the spring of 1860. George V. Bohman, "Owen Lovejoy on 'The Barbarism of Slavery,' April 5, 1860," in J. Jeffrey Auer, ed., *Anti-Slavery and Disunion, 1858–1861: Studies in the Rhetoric of Compromise and Conflict* (New York: Harper and Row, 1963), 115.

25. "The Argument for Disunion," in Filler, *Civil Rights and Freedom*, 116. Note again the allusion to Isaiah.

26. "John Brown and Harper's Ferry," in Filler, *Civil Rights and Freedom*, 97. See also: Lewis Perry, *Radical Abolitionism: Anarchy and the Government of God in Antislavery Thought* (Ithaca, NY: Cornell University Press, 1973) on abolitionist views of the Constitution, esp. 163–66. Davis, *Slavery in the Age of Revolution*, tirelessly traces the Revolutionary legacy as received by the abolitionists with all its tensions and contradictions, esp. 164–212, 255–342.

27. "Philosophy of the Abolition Movement," in Filler, *Civil Rights and Freedom*, 41.

28. *Liberator*, May 16, 1845, as quoted in Bartlett, *Brahmin Radical*, 130.

29. "Philosophy of the Abolition Movement," in Filler, *Civil Rights and Freedom*, 65–66.

30. See: Perry's account of "come-outerism" in *Radical Abolitionism*, esp. 92–128. See also: Bartlett, *Brahmin Radical*, 94ff.

31. For an account of the role of the Bible in debates over slavery, see: Davis, *Slavery in the Age of Revolution*, 523–56.

32. See: Bartlett, *Brahmin Radical*, 96ff.

33. "Philosophy of the Abolition Movement," in Filler, *Civil Rights and Freedom*, 49.

34. "Philosophy of the Abolition Movement," in Filler, *Civil Rights and Freedom*, 52.

35. "Against Idolatry," in Filler, *Civil Rights and Freedom*, 86.

36. "The Argument for Disunion," in Filler, *Civil Rights and Freedom*, 115.

37. "Philosophy of the Abolition Movement," in Filler, *Civil Rights and Freedom*, 38.

38. Isaiah 42:18.

39. "Philosophy of the Abolition Movement," in Filler, *Civil Rights and Freedom*, 71.

40. Hofstadter, *The American Political Tradition*, 178, emphasis Hofstadter's.

41. "Harper's Ferry," 274; "The Boston Mob," 225, both in *Speeches, Lectures, and Letters.*

42. "Philosophy of the Abolition Movement," in Filler, *Civil Rights and Freedom*, 43.

43. Murray Edelman, *Political Language: Words That Succeed and Policies That Fail* (New York: Academic Press, 1977), 45.

44. Sacvan Bercovitch, *The American Jeremiad* (Madison, WI: University of Wisconsin Press, 1978), 62.

45. Bercovitch, *The American Jeremiad*, passim.

46. Scott, "Abolition as a Sacred Vocation."

47. Scott, "Abolition as a Sacred Vocation," 64.

48. See: Bartlett, *Brahmin Radical*, 9–11; Oscar Sherwin, *Prophet of Liberty: The Life and Time of Wendell Phillips* (New York: Bookman Associates, 1958), 18, 32; Stewart, *Liberty's Hero*, 9, 16.

49. "The Boston Mob," in Filler, *Civil Rights and Freedom*, 21–22.

50. "The Boston Mob," in Filler, *Civil Rights and Freedom*, 22.

51. Wilson identifies the problem of vocational relevance in antebellum America. R. Jackson Wilson, *In Search of Community: Social Philosophy in the United States 1860–1920*, Galaxy books edition (London: Oxford University Press, 1970), 19–21.

52. Max L. Stackhouse, "Jesus and Economics: A Century of Reflection," in James Turner Johnson, ed., *The Bible in American Law, Politics, and Political Rhetoric* (Philadelphia: Fortress Press; Chico, CA: Scholars Press, 1985), 117.

53. Stackhouse, "Jesus and Economics," 147 n4.

54. Stackhouse, "Jesus and Economics," 147 n4.

55. Ronald Walters, *American Reformers, 1815–1860* (New York: Hill and Wang, 1978), 81–82.

56. Walters, *American Reformers, 1815–1860*, 81.

57. See: Anne C. Loveland's "Evangelicalism and 'Immediate Emancipation' in American Antislavery Thought," *Journal of Southern History* 32 (1966), 172–88. See also: Gilbert Hobbes Barnes's classic, *The Antislavery Impulse, 1830–1844* (New York: American Historical Association, 1933); Louis Filler, *The Crusade Against Slavery* (New York: Harper and Row, 1960); James B. Stewart, *Holy Warriors* (New York: Hill and Wang, 1976); and Scott, "Abolition as a Sacred Vocation."

58. "John Brown and Harper's Ferry," in Filler, *Civil Rights and Freedom*, 98, 102, 103.

59. "John Brown and Harper's Ferry," in Filler, *Civil Rights and Freedom*, 105.

60. Bartlett, "Wendell Phillips and the Eloquence of Abuse," 516.

61. David Brion Davis, "The Emergence of Immediatism in British and American Antislavery Thought," *Mississippi Valley Historical Review* 49 (1962), 219–23. Emphasis Sharp's.

62. In *The Constitution a Pro-Slavery Compact*, 106.

63. Letter reprinted from the Blagden papers in Irving H. Bartlett, *Wendell and Ann Phillips: The Community of Reform, 1840–1880* (New York: W. W. Norton, 1979), 239. Emphasis Garrison's.

64. See: Filler, *Civil Rights and Freedom*, 64, 71, 109, 125, 131, 132, 138, 145, 146.

65. "Philosophy of the Abolition Movement," in Filler, *Civil Rights and Freedom*, 50.

66. Letter of 21 April, 1861 from the Blagden papers, reprinted in Bartlett, *Wendell and Ann Phillips*, 239.

67. *Liberator*, January 24, 1851, quoted in Stewart, *Liberty's Hero*, 66.

68. Quoted in Bartlett, *Brahmin Radical*, 133.

69. For consideration to this effect, see Bartlett, *Brahmin Radical*, 42–52.

70. "The Right of Petition," in Filler, *Civil Rights and Freedom*, 24.

71. "In Defense of Lovejoy," in Filler, *Civil Rights and Freedom*, 1–9.

72. Kenneth Burke, *Counter-Statement*, Campus edition (Berkeley and Los Angeles: University of California Press, 1968), 184.

73. *The Constitution a Pro-Slavery Compact*, 110.

74. "The War for the Union," in Filler, *Civil Rights and Freedom*, 138.

75. Bartlett, *Brahmin Radical*, 22; Stewart, *Liberty's Hero*, 30–31.

76. See, for example: his speeches "The Philosophy of the Abolition Movement," 65f; "Against Idolatry," 84; "John Brown and Harper's Ferry," 110; and "The Argument for Disunion," 128; all in Filler, *Civil Rights and Freedom*.

77. "John Brown and Harper's Ferry," in Filler, *Civil Rights and Freedom*, 101.

78. See, for example: "The Boston Mob," 18; "The Argument for Disunion," 122, 136, both in Filler, *Civil Rights and Freedom*. For a summary view of the natural rights legacy in abolitionism, see: Dwight L. Dumond, "The Controversy over Slavery," in Arthur M. Schlesinger, Jr. and Morton White, eds., *Paths of American Thought*, Sentry edition (Boston: Houghton Mifflin, 1970), 93–96.

79. Bartlett, *Brahmin Radical*, 3–16, passim; Sherwin, *Prophet of Liberty*, esp. 13–17.

80. "In Defense of Lovejoy," in Filler, *Civil Rights and Freedom*, 3.

81. "Phillips never doubted that the revolutionary fathers were on his side." Bartlett, "The Persistence of Wendell Phillips," 105. See also: Dwight L. Dumond, *Antislavery: The Crusade for Freedom in America* (Ann Arbor, MI: University of Michigan Press, 1961).

82. "The Argument for Disunion," in Filler, *Civil Rights and Freedom*, 120.

83. Smith, "Righteousness and Hope," 21–45.

84. "The Boston Mob," in Filler, *Civil Rights and Freedom*, 14.

85. Irving H. Bartlett, *The American Mind in the Mid-Nineteenth Century* (New York: Thomas Y. Crowell, 1967), 18f, passim. See also: Miller, *The Life of the Mind in America*, 25, 65, 69f, 141; Smith, "Righteousness and Hope," 34.

86. "Philosophy of the Abolition Movement," in Filler, *Civil Rights and Freedom*, 62, emphasis Phillips's.

87. "Philosophy of the Abolition Movement," in Filler, *Civil Rights and Freedom*, 55.

88. "Philosophy of the Abolition Movement," in Filler, *Civil Rights and Freedom*, 52.

89. "Philosophy of the Abolition Movement," in Filler, *Civil Rights and Freedom*, 38.

90. Abraham Heschel, *The Prophets*, Colophon edition, v. 2 (New York: Harper and Row, 1962), 92.

91. "Philosophy of the Abolition Movement," in Filler, *Civil Rights and Freedom*, 71.

92. Heschel, *The Prophets*, v. 2, 38.

93. Edwin Black, *Rhetorical Criticism: A Study in Method* (Madison, WI: University of Wisconsin Press, 1978), 138f.

94. Black, *Rhetorical Criticism*, 142. See also: Bailey's analysis of hortatory discourse. F. G. Bailey, *The Tactical Uses of Passion: An Essay on Power, Reason, and Reality* (Ithaca, NY: Cornell University Press, 1983), esp. 131.

95. Black, *Rhetorical Criticism*, 143f.

96. "Philosophy of the Abolition Movement," in Filler, *Civil Rights and Freedom*, 35.

97. Stewart, "The Abolitionist Vision of Wendell Phillips," 171, passim. See also: Stewart, *Liberty's Hero*, 25, 61, 150.

98. David Hume, *A Treatise of Human Nature*, edited with an introduction by A. D. Lindsay (New York: Dutton, 1911), Bk. II, pt. 3, sec. iii.

99. George Campbell, *The Philosophy of Rhetoric*, Lloyd F. Bitzer, ed. (Carbondale, IL: Southern Illinois University Press, 1963); Lloyd F. Bitzer, "Hume's Philosophy in George Campbell's *Philosophy of Rhetoric*," *Philosophy and Rhetoric* 2 (1969), 139–66. Campbell's *Philosophy of Rhetoric* would have been one of the texts Phillips studied under Edward T. Channing at Harvard. On Phillips as Channing's student and Channing's texts, see Dorothy I. Anderson and Waldo W. Braden, "Introduction," in Edward T. Channing, *Lectures Read to the Seniors in Harvard College* (Carbondale, IL: Southern Illinois University Press, 1968), xi, xix.

100. Channing, *Lectures Read to the Seniors in Harvard College*, 80.

101. Campbell's treatment of rhetoric was not atypical on this issue. Whately's *Elements of Rhetoric* arbitrated the dispute between Campbell and Aristotle on the appropriate use of the passions generally in Campbell's favor. Richard Whately, *Elements of Rhetoric*, Douglas Ehninger, ed. (Carbondale and Edwardsville: Southern Illinois University Press, 1963), 176–77ff. Adam Smith's theory of rhetoric was also based on the idea of sympathy, *sym-pathos*.

102. Thomas Mann, *The Magic Mountain*, H. T. Lowe-Porter, trans., Vintage Books edition (New York: Random House, 1969), 603.

103. Hazel Catherine Wolf, *On Freedom's Altar: The Martyr Complex in the Abolition Movement* (Madison, WI: University of Wisconsin Press, 1952).

104. Kraditor, *Means and Ends,* 37 n44.

105. For example, see: Filler, *Civil Rights and Freedom,* 20, 26, 27, 38, 71, 85, 119, 141.

106. "The Boston Mob," in Filler, *Civil Rights and Freedom,* 21f.

107. "In Defense of Lovejoy," 6; and "John Brown and Harper's Ferry," 107, both in Filler, *Civil Rights and Freedom.*

108. "Philosophy of the Abolition Movement," in Filler, *Civil Rights and Freedom,* 60.

109. "Philosophy of the Abolition Movement," in Filler, *Civil Rights and Freedom,* 57.

110. Merton L. Dillon, *The Abolitionists: The Growth of a Dissenting Minority,* Norton edition (New York: W. W. Norton, 1979); Merton L. Dillon, "The Failure of the American Abolitionists," *Journal of Southern History* 25 (1959), 159–77.

111. Louis Filler writes that it was only his "unbridled and habitual radicalism" that "saved him from downright popularity." Filler, *Civil Rights and Freedom,* 95.

112. Peter Brooks, *The Melodramatic Imagination: Balzac, Henry James, Melodrama, and the Mode of Excess* (New Haven, CT: Yale University Press, 1976), 14f, 43ff.

113. Peter Brooks, "The Melodramatic Imagination: The Example of Balzac and James," in David Thorburn and Geoffry Hartman, eds., *Romanticism: Vistas, Instances, Continuities* (Ithaca, NY: Cornell University Press, 1973), 211; Brooks, *The Melodramatic Imagination,* 43.

114. Brooks, "The Melodramatic Imagination," 203.

115. John Cawelti, *Adventure, Mystery, and Romance* (Chicago: University of Chicago Press, 1976), 45–46; Brooks, "The Melodramatic Imagination," 198–220.

116. Brooks, *The Melodramatic Imagination,* 15.

117. Brooks, "The Melodramatic Imagination," 212; see also: Brooks, *The Melodramatic Imagination,* 43.

118. Brooks, "The Melodramatic Imagination," 212.

119. Quoted in Brooks, "The Melodramatic Imagination," 207.

120. Brooks, "The Melodramatic Imagination," 208; see also: 219.

121. Nathaniel Hawthorne, *The Blithedale Romance,* v. 3 of The Centenary Edition of the Works of Nathaniel Hawthorne, © 1964, Ohio State University Press, 10–11.

NOTES TO CHAPTER 5

1. Kenneth Burke, *A Grammar of Motives* (Berkeley and Los Angeles: University of California Press, 1969), 122–23, passim.

2. I. A. Richards, "Doctrine in Poetry," reprinted in W. J. Bate, ed., *Criticism:*

The Major Texts, enlarged edition (New York: Harcourt Brace Jovanovich, 1970), 586.

3. Sidney Lens, *Radicalism in America,* Apollo edition (New York: Thomas Y. Crowell, 1969), 197.

4. Charles A. Madison, *Critics and Crusaders: A Century of American Protest* (New York: Henry Holt, 1947), 487.

5. Irving Howe, "In the American Grain," *New York Review of Books* (November 10, 1983), 18; see also: Bernard J. Brommel, *Eugene V. Debs: Spokesman for Labor and Socialism* (Chicago: Charles H. Kerr, 1978), 221.

6. Charles Lomas, "Urban Mavericks and Radicals," in Paul H. Boase, ed., *The Rhetoric of Protest and Reform, 1870–1898* (Athens, OH: Ohio University Press, 1980), 49.

7. Bert Cochran, "The Achievement of Debs," in Harvey Goldberg, ed., *American Radicals: Some Problems and Personalities,* Modern Reader edition (New York: Modern Reader Paperbacks, 1969), 163.

8. Richard L. McCormick, "Public Life in Industrial America," in Eric Foner, ed., *The New American History* (Philadelphia: Temple University Press, 1990), 112.

9. Ronald Lee and James Andrews, "A Story of Rhetorical- Ideological Transformation: Eugene V. Debs as Liberal Hero," *Quarterly Journal of Speech* 77 (1991), 20–37.

10. Herbert G. Gutman, *Work, Culture, and Society in Industrializing America: Essays in American Working-Class and Social History* (New York: Alfred A. Knopf, 1976), 13, 33.

11. Robert G. Gunderson, "A Setting for Protest and Reform," in Boase, *Rhetoric of Protest and Reform,* 1; Samuel P. Hays, *The Response to Industrialism, 1885–1914* (Chicago: University of Chicago Press, 1957), 1–3; Gutman, *Work, Culture, and Society,* 80; McCormick, "Public Life in Industrial America," 93.

12. Robert H. Wiebe, *The Search for Order, 1877–1920* (New York: Hill and Wang, 1967), 12.

13. Gutman, *Work, Culture, and Society,* 15f, passim.

14. Richard Hofstadter, *The Age of Reform: From Bryan to F. D. R.* (New York: Vintage Books, 1955), 24ff; Hays, *The Response to Industrialism,* 83.

15. Edward Bellamy, *Looking Backward,* Signet edition (New American Library, 1960), 189.

16. "Unity and Victory," in Arthur Schlesinger, Jr., ed., *Writings and Speeches of Eugene V. Debs* (New York: Heritage Press, 1948), 9; Gutman, *Work, Culture, and Society,* details some of these changes in the work atmosphere.

17. Wiebe, *The Search for Order,* 148, 150–51.

18. "Unionism and Socialism," in Schlesinger, *Writings and Speeches of Eugene V. Debs,* 124; see also: "The Canton Speech," in Jean Y. Tussey, ed., *Eugene V. Debs Speaks* (New York: Pathfinder Press, 1972), 271.

19. Gutman has detailed the degree to which the industrial order conflicted with older modes of work, in *Work, Culture, and Society*. See also: Wiebe, *The Search for Order*, 20, 47; Milton Meltzer, *Bread and Roses: The Struggle of American Labor, 1865–1915*, Mentor edition (New York: New American Library, 1967), 3–12.

20. See: Michael Kammen on the association of "liberty" and "order" in the Gilded Age, especially with regard to decisions regarding the rights of labor to form unions and to strike. *Spheres of Liberty: Changing Perceptions of Liberty in American Culture* (Madison: University of Wisconsin Press, 1986), esp. 102–10.

21. Hofstadter, *The Age of Reform*, 209.

22. "Revolutionary Unionism," in *Debs: His Life, Writings and Speeches* (Chicago: Charles H. Kerr, 1908), 435.

23. Quoted in *The Tribune of Labor*, a pamphlet celebrating a speaking tour Debs made of the West Coast; no publication data.

24. "Watch Your Leaders, Says Debs to Workers," campaign flyer, no publication data. That the flyer is from the 1920 campaign is deduced from Debs's references to Cox and Harding as the major party candidates.

25. Our word "virtue" comes from the Latin for "manliness." In Debs's day, women may have been considered guardians of the moral order, but virtue was still largely talked about in terms of manliness and manhood. See: Mark C. Carnes and Clyde Griffen, eds., *Meanings for Manhood: Constructions of Masculinity in Victorian America* (Chicago: University of Chicago Press, 1990).

26. "Declaration of Revolt," *Appeal to Reason* (January 7, 1911), 1.

27. Richard Weaver, *The Ethics of Rhetoric*, Gateway edition (Chicago: Henry Regnery, 1965), 227–32.

28. "Liberty," in Schlesinger, *Writings and Speeches of Eugene V. Debs*, 8.

29. "Industrial Unionism," in *Debs: His Life, Writings and Speeches*, 446; see also: "Unity and Victory," in *Debs: His Life, Writings and Speeches*, 28.

30. "The Federal Government and the Chicago Strike," in *Debs: His Life, Writings and Speeches*, 204–5; see also: the speech given on Debs's return to Terre Haute after the successful Great Northern strike in *Debs: His Life, Writings and Speeches*, 10.

31. "Liberty," speech given upon his release from Woodstock Jail, November 22, 1895, in Schlesinger, *Writings and Speeches of Eugene V. Debs*, 6. See also: Bernard J. Brommel, "The Pacifist Speechmaking of Eugene V. Debs," *Quarterly Journal of Speech* 52 (1966), 150; Ray Ginger, *The Bending Cross: A Biography of Eugene Victor Debs* (New Brunswick, NJ: Rutgers University Press, 1949), 25, 65, 192, 202, 230, 301, 331, 369, 462.

32. Nick Salvatore, *Eugene V. Debs: Citizen and Socialist* (Urbana: University of Illinois Press, 1982), 229.

33. "Address to the Jury," in Tussey, *Debs Speaks*, 283–84; "Master of the Machine," quoted in Brommel, *Spokesman for Labor and Socialism*, 93.

34. Aileen S. Kraditor, *The Radical Persuasion, 1890–1917: Aspects of the Intellectual*

History and Historiography of Three American Radical Organizations (Baton Rouge: Louisiana State University Press, 1981), 223.

35. "Revolutionary Unionism," in Schlesinger, *Writings and Speeches of Eugene V. Debs,* 220. As Salvatore and Kraditor both make very clear, Debs had a profound ambivalence toward the rank and file; a fundamental fear of their baser natures and consequent contempt counterbalanced whatever mystic faith he may have had in them. Salvatore, *Citizen and Socialist,* esp. 46, 48, 96f; Kraditor, *Radical Persuasion,* 125–34, 261.

36. Ginger, *Bending Cross,* 10; Brommel, *Spokesman for Labor and Socialism,* 17; Salvatore, *Citizen and Socialist,* 11; For examples of direct allusion to biblical sources in Debs's speeches, see: "Prison Labor," 32, 33; "The Western Labor Movement," 85; "Industrial Unionism," 124; "Homestead and Ludlow," 218, all in Tussey, *Debs Speaks.*

37. In *Debs: His Life, Writings and Speeches,* 61–63.

38. On Marxism as religion, see: Joseph Schumpeter, *Capitalism, Socialism, and Democracy* (New York: Harper and Brothers, 1947), chapter 1, "Marx the Prophet"; Karl Jaspers, *Reason and Anti-Reason in Our Time,* Stanley Godman, trans., reprint edition (Hamden, CT: Archon Books, 1971), 7–17.

39. Quoted in Ginger, *Bending Cross,* 334f. On the alliance of these appeals, see: Kraditor, *Radical Persuasion,* 205–47.

40. "How I Became a Socialist," in Tussey, *Debs Speaks,* 47.

41. "Working Class Politics," in Tussey, *Debs Speaks,* 173f.

42. "Unionism and Socialism," 114. See also: "Unionism and Socialism," 122; "Craft Unionism," 188; "You Railroad Men," 255; "The Issue," 303, all in Schlesinger, *Writings and Speeches of Eugene V. Debs.*

43. "Industrial Unionism," in Tussey, *Debs Speaks,* 127.

44. "The Canton Speech," in Tussey, *Debs Speaks,* 257–58.

45. "Industrial Unionism," in Tussey, *Debs Speaks,* 134.

46. "The Canton Speech," in Tussey, *Debs Speaks,* 245.

47. "What's the Matter with Chicago?" in Tussey, *Debs Speaks,* 70.

48. "Danger Ahead," 180; "The Socialist Party's Appeal (1904)," 106, both in Tussey, *Debs Speaks.*

49. "The Outlook for Socialism," in Tussey, *Debs Speaks,* 66.

50. "You Railroad Men," in Schlesinger, *Writings and Speeches of Eugene V. Debs,* 243. See also: Bernard J. Brommel, "Eugene V. Debs: The Agitator as Speaker," *Central States Speech Journal* (1969) 209.

51. "How I Became a Socialist," in Tussey, *Debs Speaks,* 47.

52. Lomas says of Debs's efforts before Pullman: "Debs had four solutions in five years as he moved at the end of the century from militant unionism to Bryanism to utopianism to social democracy." Lomas, "Urban Mavericks and Radicals," 38. But Lomas also notes that Debs's later career, after helping found the Socialist Party, was more consistent (48).

53. "How I Became a Socialist," in Tussey, *Debs Speaks,* 48–49.

54. Pamphlet published by the Rand School Press, New York, n.d.

55. Louis Kopelin, *The Life of Debs,* 4th edition (Girard, KS: Appeal to Reason, n.d.), 21.

56. Herbert M. Morais and William Cahn, *Gene Debs: The Story of a Fighting American* (New York: International Publishers, 1948), 54.

57. Upton Sinclair, *The Jungle,* Signet edition (New York: New American Library, 1960), 322.

58. "Debs the Statesman of the Masses," *National Rip-Saw* (November 1921), 12.

59. Stephen Marion Reynolds, "Life of Eugene V. Debs," in *Debs: His Life, Writings and Speeches,* 2.

60. Salvatore, *Citizen and Socialist,* esp. 149–55.

61. "The Outlook for Socialism," in Tussey, *Debs Speaks,* 60–61.

62. Salvatore, *Citizen and Socialist,* 64.

63. Quoted in Ginger, *Bending Cross,* 266.

64. Ginger, *Bending Cross,* 291.

65. "Serving the Labor Movement," in Schlesinger, *Writings and Speeches of Eugene V. Debs,* 443.

66. "How I Became a Socialist," in Tussey, *Debs Speaks,* 44–45.

67. See: "Martin Irons, Martyr," 42; "The Issue," 297–98; "The Knights of Columbus," 388, all in Schlesinger, *Writings and Speeches of Eugene V. Debs.*

68. "The Issue," in Schlesinger, *Writings and Speeches of Eugene V. Debs,* 297f.

69. See: "The Martyred Apostles of Labor," 20–24; "Martin Irons, Martyr," 41–42; "Mother Jones," 285–86; "Thomas McGrady," 286–91; "Tom Money Sentenced to Death," 403–5; "John Swinton: Radical Editor and Leader," 409–17, all in Schlesinger, *Writings and Speeches of Eugene V. Debs.*

70. "John Brown: History's Greatest Hero," in Schlesinger, *Writings and Speeches of Eugene V. Debs,* 281.

71. Henry Keys, "Eugene V. Debs Honored, But Not by His Home Folks," *Terre Haute Tribune* (Sunday, June 7, 1908), 17.

72. Reynolds, "Life of Eugene V. Debs," in *Debs: His Life, Writings and Speeches,* 3.

73. John Spargo, "Eugene V. Debs, Incarnate Spirit of Revolt," in *Debs: His Life, Writings and Speeches,* 507.

74. Ruth Le Prade, "The Martyrdom" in *Debs and the Poets,* Ruth Le Prade, ed. (Pasadena, CA: Upton Sinclair, Publisher, 1920), 50.

75. *The Heritage of Debs—The Fight against War* (Chicago: Socialist Party National Headquarters, 1935).

76. See, for example: Robert Hunter, "A Companion to Truth," in *Debs: His Life, Writings and Speeches,* 509f. For some of the elements which went into making the "Debs legend," see Bernard J. Brommel, "Eugene V. Debs: Spokesman for

Labor and Socialism," unpublished dissertation, Indiana University, 1964, 166f; Ginger, *Bending Cross,* 12–14, 82, 267, 270, 288–89, 292–94.

77. Salvatore, *Citizen and Socialist,* 155.

78. Salvatore, *Citizen and Socialist,* 155.

79. Mark Shorer, *Sinclair Lewis: An American Life* (New York: McGraw Hill, 1961), 337, quoted in Brommel, "Eugene V. Debs," dissertation, 226.

80. Letter of May 16, 1926. Copy in files of Bernard Brommel.

81. Copy in files of Bernard Brommel.

82. *National Rip-Saw* (November 1921), 14.

83. Kopelin, *The Life of Debs,* 33.

84. Walter Hurt, *Eugene V. Debs: An Introduction* (Williamsburg, OH: Progress Publishing Co., n.d.), 36.

85. As related in Brommel, *Spokesman for Labor and Socialism,* 92; Ginger also notes the incident and writes: "Such an incident was unusual but not unique." Ginger, *Bending Cross,* 267; see also: the poem Ginger reprints on Debs as a Messiah, 265.

86. "Address to the Jury," in Tussey, *Debs Speaks,* 283.

87. "Statement to the Court," in Schlesinger, *Writings and Speeches of Eugene V. Debs,* 437.

88. It was Clyde Miller, a reporter for the *Cleveland Plain-Dealer,* who was largely responsible for initiating proceedings against Debs and who was one of the prosecution's chief witnesses at Debs's trial. On Debs's forgiveness, see Ginger, *Bending Cross,* 379–80. According to Brommel, Miller later admitted that he had falsely testified at Debs's trial. Brommel, "Pacifist Speechmaking," 154. See also: Miller's account in Clyde R. Miller, "The Man I Sent to Prison," *The Progressive* (October 1963), 33–35. Miller does not here admit to false testimony. In fact, he recounts that Debs found his testimony "accurate and clear."

89. Ginger, *Bending Cross,* 237.

90. Howe, "In the American Grain," 18; see also: Ginger, *Bending Cross,* 262. Ginger reports that in 1908 before beginning a marathon sixty-five-day speaking tour involving five to twenty speeches a day, Debs had been widely rumored to be "half dead."

91. See Ginger, *Bending Cross,* 268, 317, 347, 403.

92. Ginger, *Bending Cross,* 371.

93. Upton Sinclair, "Introduction," in Le Prade, *Debs and the Poets,* 5.

94. Witter Brynner, "9653," in Le Prade, *Debs and the Poets,* 3. See also poems by Edmund Vance Cooke, John Cowper Powys, Clement Wood, Miriam Allen De Ford, Sara Bard Field, John Milton Scott, and Charles Erskine Scott Wood in the same volume, on 9, 18, 19, 25, 29, 33, 38, 90ff. See also Salvatore, *Citizen and Socialist,* 310–12.

95. From *Walls and Bars,* as excerpted in Tussey, *Debs Speaks,* 295–96.

96. From *Walls and Bars,* as excerpted in Tussey, *Debs Speaks,* 296.

97. Hurt, *Eugene V. Debs: An Introduction,* 11.

98. Hofstadter, *The Age of Reform,* 238f; Richard Hofstadter, "Theodore Roosevelt: The Conservative as Progressive," in *The American Political Tradition and the Men Who Made It* (New York: Vintage, 1974), 266–307; see also: Stephen E. Lucas, " 'The Man with the Muck Rake': A Reinterpretation," *Quarterly Journal of Speech* 59 (1973), 452–62.

99. Hays, *The Response to Industrialism,* 47, emphasis added. See, for example: the letter from a worker opposing clemency for Debs, quoted in Salvatore, *Citizen and Socialist,* 302.

100. "Address to the Jury," in Tussey, *Debs Speaks,* 285.

101. "The Canton Speech," in Tussey, *Debs Speaks,* 258; see also: 244.

102. "Speech of Acceptance," in Schlesinger, *Writings and Speeches of Eugene V. Debs,* 73, 75.

103. "Speech of Acceptance," 361; see also: "The Issue," 294, both in Schlesinger, *Writings and Speeches of Eugene V. Debs;* "Letter of Acceptance," in Tussey, *Debs Speaks,* 234–35.

104. Quoted in Bernard J. Brommel, "Eugene V. Debs: Blue- Denim Spokesman," *North Dakota Quarterly* (Spring 1973), 13; see also: Ginger, *Bending Cross,* 161, 189, 266.

105. For a variation on this theme, the divine self as nonself, see: F. G. Bailey, *The Tactical Uses of Passion: An Essay on Power, Reason, and Reality* (Ithaca, NY: Cornell University Press, 1983), 50.

106. Northrop Frye, *The Critical Path: An Essay on the Social Context of Literary Criticism,* Midland edition (Bloomington: Indiana University Press, 1973), 40.

107. "Labor Day Greeting," in *Debs: His Life, Writings and Speeches,* 289.

108. Quoted in Brommel, "The Agitator as Speaker," 200; Brommel, *Spokesman for Labor and Socialism,* 99, 226.

109. "Unionism and Socialism," in Schlesinger, *Writings and Speeches of Eugene V. Debs,* 120.

110. For example, see: "The American Movement," 95; "Unionism and Socialism," 120; "The Socialist Party and the Working Class," 137; "An Ideal Labor Press," 161; "Craft Unionism," 185; "Revolutionary Unionism," 212; "Speech of Acceptance," 366, all in Schlesinger, *Writings and Speeches of Eugene V. Debs.*

111. Kraditor, *Radical Persuasion,* 231.

112. "Unionism and Socialism," in Schlesinger, *Writings and Speeches of Eugene V. Debs,* 120.

113. See: "The Socialist Party's Appeal (1908)," 164, 167. See also: "The Gunmen and the Miners," 227; "The Canton Speech," 267, 279, all in Tussey, *Debs Speaks.*

114. Mircea Eliade, *The Sacred and the Profane: The Nature of Religion,* Willard R. Trask, trans. (New York: Harcourt, Brace and World, 1959), 129; see also: 211.

115. On the connection between emotion, faith, and suffering, see: Bailey, *Uses of Passion,* 38–40.

116. Quoted in Salvatore, *Citizen and Socialist,* 232.

117. Howe, "In the American Grain," 19.

118. Richard B. Gregg, "The Ego-Function of the Rhetoric of Protest," *Philosophy and Rhetoric* 4 (1971), 85; cf. Harold Barrett, *Rhetoric and Civility: Human Development, Narcissism, and the Good Audience* (Albany: State University of New York Press, 1991).

119. Reynolds, in *Debs: His Life, Writings and Speeches,* 72.

120. *Terre Haute Post* (October 21, 1926), 1.

121. Schlesinger, "Introduction," in Schlesinger, *Writings and Speeches of Eugene V. Debs,* ix; see also: Brommel, "Eugene V. Debs," dissertation, 162; J. H. Hollingworth, *Eugene V. Debs: What His Neighbors Say of Him,* pamphlet, no publication data.

122. Hurt, *Eugene V. Debs: An Introduction,* 10.

123. Hurt, *Eugene V. Debs: An Introduction,* 16.

124. John Dewey, *The Public and Its Problems,* reprint edition (Chicago: Swallow Press, 1954), 98.

125. Norman Thomas, "Socialism Since Debs," *Socialist Call,* 23, Debs Centennial Issue (October 1955), 7.

126. David A. Shannon, Foreword to Brommel, *Spokesman for Labor and Socialism,* 5.

127. Nelson Algren, *Chicago: City on the Make* (Chicago: University of Chicago Press, 1987), 66.

128. I am grateful to Ed Sadowlsky of the United Steelworkers subdistrict #3 office for this information on local #1834.

129. Louis Untermeyer, "The Garland for Debs," in Le Prade, *Debs and the Poets,* 14.

130. Isaiah 53: 3–4, 11–12.

NOTES TO CHAPTER 6

1. Walter H. Beale, "Rhetorical Performative Discourse: A New Theory of Epideictic," *Philosophy and Rhetoric* 11 (1978), 221 = 246; Bernard K. Duffy, "The Platonic Functions of Epideictic Rhetoric," *Philosophy and Rhetoric* 16 (1983), 79–93.

2. James Boyd White, *When Words Lose Their Meaning: Constitutions and Reconstitutions of Language, Character, and Community* (Chicago: University of Chicago Press, 1984), 193; see also: Robert N. Bellah, *Beyond Belief: Essays on Religion in a Post-Traditional World* (New York: Harper and Row, 1970), 47 n13, on the relationship of language and religion.

3. Barry Smart, *Postmodernity* (London: Routledge, 1993), 16.

4. Smart, *Postmodernity,* 75; see also: p. 63.

5. David Harvey, *The Condition of Postmodernity: An Inquiry into the Origins of Cultural Change* (Cambridge, MA: Blackwell, 1990), 116.

6. Harvey, *The Condition of Postmodernity,* 56.

7. For an overview of the evolution of America's national religion, see: Henry F. May, "The Religion of the Republic," in *Ideas, Faiths and Feelings: Essays on American Intellectual and Religious History, 1952–1982* (New York: Oxford University Press, 1983), 163–86; see also: Bellah, *Beyond Belief.*

8. On the problems of rhetoric in a postmodern world, see Michael Calvin McGee, "Text, Context, and the Fragmentation of Contemporary Culture," *Western Journal of Speech Communication* 54 (1990), 274–89; J. Robert Cox, "On 'Interpreting' Public Discourse in Post-Modernity," *Western Journal of Speech Communication* 54 (1990), 317–29.

9. See: Peter L. Berger and Thomas Luckmann, *The Social Construction of Reality: A Treatise in the Sociology of Knowledge,* Anchor edition (Garden City, NY: Doubleday, 1967) on the function of the symbolic universe in delineating the "day side" and the "night side" of reality, 97–98.

10. Hal Foster, "Against Pluralism," in *Recodings: Art, Spectacle, Cultural Politics* (Port Townsend, WA: Bay Press, 1985), 26.

11. Harvey, *The Condition of Postmodernity,* 63.

12. G. Thomas Goodnight, "The Firm, the Park and the University: Fear and Trembling on the Postmodern Trail," *Quarterly Journal of Speech* 81 (1995), 267–90.

13. Thomas W. Overholt, *Channels of Prophecy: The Social Dynamics of Prophecy* (Minneapolis: Fortress Press, 1989). On the status of *religio* today, see: Michael Harrington, *The Politics at God's Funeral: The Spiritual Crisis of Western Civilization* (New York: Penguin, 1985).

14. Stephen O'Leary, *Arguing the Apocalypse: A Theory of Millennial Rhetoric* (New York: Oxford University Press, 1994), 11.

15. For example, see: Paul Boyer, *When Time Shall Be No More: Prophecy and Belief in Modern American Culture* (Cambridge, MA: Belknap Press of Harvard University Press, 1992).

16. Smart, *Postmodernity,* 18–19.

17. Irving Lewis Horowitz, *Ideology and Utopia in the United States, 1956–1976* (London: Oxford University Press, 1977), 166f.

18. On the essential monotheism in the Old Testament, see: James A. Sanders, "Hermeneutics in True and False Prophecy," in George W. Coats and Burke O. Long, eds., *Canon and Authority: Essays in Old Testament Religion and Theology* (Philadelphia: Fortress Press, 1977), 40. See also: James L. Crenshaw, *Prophetic Conflict: Its Effect Upon Israelite Religion* (Berlin: Walter de Gruyter, 1971), 88. Crenshaw notes that the monistic orientation helped to make demons "superfluous."

19. Bruce Vawter, C. M., *The Conscience of Israel: Pre-Exilic Prophets and Prophecy* (New York: Sheed and Ward, 1961), 39–40.

20. Gerhard von Rad, *The Message of the Prophets,* D. M. G. Stalker, trans. (New York: Harper and Row, 1965), 280.

21. von Rad, *The Message of the Prophets,* 229.

22. Crenshaw, *Prophetic Conflict,* 106; D. S. Russell, *The Method and Message of Jewish Apocalyptic* (Philadelphia: Westminister Press, 1964), 73–82.

23. Overholt, *Channels of Prophecy,* 159.

24. Crenshaw, *Prophetic Conflict;* Sanders, "Hermeneutics in True and False Prophecy."

25. Russell, *The Method and Message of Jewish Apocalyptic,* 105, 235ff; Hanson is critical of oversimple attributions to any source of apocalyptic including Persian dualism. Paul D. Hanson, *The Dawn of Apocalyptic* (Philadelphia: Fortress Press, 1975), 5ff. Collins reviews the argument over Persian and other influences and finds much still valid after accounting for dissenting points of view. John J. Collins, *The Apocalyptic Imagination: An Introduction to the Jewish Matrix of Christianity* (New York: Crossroad Press, 1984), 15, 16, 21–28.

26. Georges Bataille, *Theory of Religion,* Robert Hurley, trans. (New York: Zone Books, 1992), 76.

27. Russell, *The Method and Message of Jewish Apocalyptic,* 93, 265.

28. Russell, *The Method and Message of Jewish Apocalyptic,* 88ff, 106. Although Hanson criticizes Russell's argument that apocalyptic is continuous with post-Exilic prophecy, there is agreement on this point. Hanson, *The Dawn of Apocalyptic,* 11–12.

29. Hanson, *The Dawn of Apocalyptic,* 12.

30. von Rad, *The Message of the Prophets,* 273f.

31. O'Leary, *Arguing the Apocalypse,* 12; Barry Brummett, "Premillennial Apocalyptic as a Rhetorical Genre," *Central States Speech Journal* 35 (1984), 85; Adela Yarbro Collins, *Crisis and Catharsis* (Philadelphia: Westminster Press, 1984), 152–60.

32. See: Edwin Black, "The Second Persona," *Quarterly Journal of Speech* 56 (1970), 109–19.

33. John Collins marks this as a distinction between what he calls "historical" apocalyptic and prophecy. Collins, *The Apocalyptic Imagination,* 9. See also: Crenshaw, *Prophetic Conflict,* 107.

34. Collins, *The Apocalyptic Imagination,* 13.

35. Russell, *The Method and Message of Jewish Apocalyptic,* 127ff; Collins, *The Apocalyptic Imagination,* 30f.

36. Collins, *The Apocalyptic Imagination,* 30; Russell, *The Method and Message of Jewish Apocalyptic,* 231.

37. Richard Weaver, *Ideas Have Consequences,* Midway Reprint edition (Chicago: University of Chicago Press, 1976), v, 168.

38. For the influence of Lowth's lectures, see: Abraham J. Heschel, *The Prophets,* v. 2, Colophon edition (New York: Harper and Row, 1975), 155f. Freedman has written: "Bishop Lowth, while not the first to make this observation [the observation that Old Testament prophecy is prophetic], nevertheless marked a turning point in the study of the prophetic literature and the poetry of the Bible generally." David Noel Freedman, "Pottery, Poetry, and Prophecy: An Essay on Biblical Poetry," *Journal of Biblical Literature* 96 (1977), 5 n3. Modern biblical scholars are universally agreed upon the status of the prophets as poets. Robert Carroll, "Poets Not Prophets," *Journal for the Study of the Old Testament* 27 (1983), 26; Crenshaw, *Prophetic Conflict.*

39. Vawter, *The Conscience of Israel,* 49–50.

40. For some interesting anthropological evidence on this point, see: N. Kershaw Chadwick, *Poetry and Prophecy* (Cambridge: Cambridge University Press, 1942).

41. See, for example: G. M. A. Grube, *The Greek and Roman Critics* (Toronto: University of Toronto Press, 1965), on Isocrates, 42–43; on Aristotle, 83. See also: Aristotle's *Rhetoric,* 1404a28–1405b7, where Aristotle asserts several times that the rhetorician has less latitude with language than does the poet. Aristotle, *Rhetoric,* W. Rhys Roberts, trans., in *The Basic Works of Aristotle,* Richard McKeon, ed. (New York: Random House, 1941).

42. Burke repeats the observation of Coleridge that the writing of a poem is "a dim analogue of creation." Kenneth Burke, *The Rhetoric of Religion* (Berkeley and Los Angeles: University of California Press, 1970), 8.

43. Theophil Spoerri, "Style of Distance, Style of Nearness," Corinna Babb, trans., in *Essays in Stylistic Analysis,* Howard S. Babb, ed. (New York: Harcourt Brace Jovanovich, 1972), 68.

44. Walter Brueggemann, *The Prophetic Imagination* (Philadelphia: Fortress Press, 1978), 45. On the power of writers, poets, artists, and others whose work "is not dependent upon dominant economic and political interests" to "immure themselves . . . from official interpretations of reality," see: Claus Mueller, *The Politics of Communication: A Study in the Political Sociology of Language, Socialization, and Legitimation* (London: Oxford University Press, 1973), esp. 146.

45. Melvin Lasky, *Utopia and Revolution* (Chicago: University of Chicago Press, 1976), 520.

46. On the use of insanity as a label used to neutralize those who express a "commitment to an officially forbidden image or definition of 'reality,' " see: Thomas Szasz, *Ideology and Insanity* (Garden City, NY: Anchor Books, 1970), 6, passim. See also: Thomas Szasz, "The Mental Health Ethic," in Richard T. De-George, ed., *Ethics and Society: Original Essays on Contemporary Moral Problems* (Garden City, NY: Anchor Books, 1968), 85–110.

47. *Phaedrus,* 244a–245a, R. Hackforth, trans., in *Plato: The Collected Dialogues*

Edith Hamilton and Huntington Cairns, eds., (Princeton, NJ: Princeton University Press, 1961).

48. Chadwick, *Poetry and Prophecy,* 14.

49. Chadwick, *Poetry and Prophecy,* 48; see also: 41, 58.

50. Freedman, "Pottery, Poetry, and Prophecy," 20, 21, 22, 26.

51. R. B. Y. Scott, *The Relevance of the Prophets,* revised edition (New York: Macmillan, 1968), 103.

52. Chadwick, *Poetry and Prophecy,* esp. 18–19.

53. See: debate between A. Graeme Auld, "Prophets Through the Looking Glass: Between Writings and Moses," *Journal for the Study of the Old Testament* 27 (1983), 3–23, and Carroll, "Poets Not Prophets," 25–31.

54. See: John D. Boyd, S.J., *The Function of Mimesis and Its Decline,* 2d edition (New York: Fordham University Press, 1980); James L. Kinneavy, *A Theory of Discourse,* Norton edition (New York: W. W. Norton, 1980); Bernard Weinberg, "Formal Analysis in Poetry and Rhetoric," in Donald C. Bryant, ed., *Papers in Rhetoric and Philosophy* (Iowa City: University of Iowa Press, 1965); A. W. Staub and G. P. Mohrmann, "Rhetoric and Poetic: A New Critique," reprinted in Douglas Ehninger, ed., *Contemporary Rhetoric* (Glenview, IL: Scott Foresman, 1972), 108–15.

55. Donald C. Bryant, "Literature and Politics," in Don M. Burks, ed., *Rhetoric, Philosophy, and Literature: An Exploration* (West Lafayette, IN: Purdue University Press, 1978), 103.

56. Max Weber, in S. N. Eisenstadt, ed., *On Charisma and Institution Building: Selected Papers* (Chicago: University of Chicago Press, 1968), 254.

57. Foster, *Recodings,* 76.

58. Aristotle, *Rhetoric,* 1375a25–1375b7. See also: Aristotle, *Politics,* where Aristotle writes: "Unlawful it certainly is to rule without regard to justice, for there may be might where there is not right." Aristotle, *Politics,* Benjamin Jowett, trans., in *The Basic Works of Aristotle,* Richard McKeon, ed. (New York: Random House, 1941), 1324b27.

59. Aristotle, *Rhetoric,* 1373b6.

60. Kathleen M. Jamieson, "Natural Law as Warrant," *Philosophy and Rhetoric* 6 (1973), 236, emphasis added. David Lyons in his article "Utility and Rights," reprinted in Jeremy Waldron, ed., *Theories of Rights* (Oxford: Oxford University Press, 1974), 110–36, writes: "Moral rights are not merely *independent of* social recognition and enforcement but also provide *grounds for appraising* law and other social institutions. If social arrangements violate moral rights, they can be criticized accordingly." P. 114, emphasis Lyons's.

61. Jamieson, "Natural Law as Warrant," 236.

62. Jamieson, "Natural Law as Warrant," 242 n7.

63. Horowitz, "The Pluralistic Bases of Modern American Liberalism," in *Ideology and Utopia in the United States,* 169.

64. Horowitz, *Ideology and Utopia in the United States,* 169.

65. S. N. Eisenstadt, "Introduction," in *Max Weber on Charisma and Institution Building,* liv.

66. John Dewey, *The Public and Its Problems,* Swallow Press edition (Chicago: Swallow Press, 1954), 137.

67. Eisenstadt, "Introduction," in *Max Weber on Charisma and Institution Building,* lv.

68. Berger and Luckmann, *The Social Construction of Reality,* develop the idea of externalization of reality and its role in society. Wolff makes the telling remark that "The very essence of social constraint is that one feels it as objective, external, unavoidable, and hence genuinely a limit beyond which one's desires may not extend." Robert Paul Wolff, "Beyond Tolerance," in Robert Paul Wolff, Barrington Moore, Jr., and Herbert Marcuse, *A Critique of Pure Tolerance,* paperback edition (Boston: Beacon Press, 1969), 34.

69. See particularly: Jürgen Habermas, *Toward a Rational Society: Student Protest, Science, and Politics,* Jeremy J. Shapiro, trans. (Boston: Beacon Press, 1970), passim, esp. 68, 98; Jürgen Habermas, *Legitimation Crisis,* Thomas McCarthy, trans. (Boston: Beacon Press, 1975).

70. Peter L. Berger, *The Sacred Canopy: Elements of a Sociological Theory of Religion* (New York: Viking Books, 1969), 129; see also: 107, passim.

71. Berger, *The Sacred Canopy,* 112–13.

72. Berger, *The Sacred Canopy,* 138–47.

73. Berger, *The Sacred Canopy,* 127.

74. The interrelation between morality and law is a complex one. As example, see: statements by philosophical opponents H. L. A. Hart and Ronald Dworkin, both stressing the connection between the moral and the legal. H. L. A. Hart, "Are There Any Natural Rights?" in Waldron, *Theories of Rights,* 79. Ronald Dworkin, *Taking Rights Seriously* (Cambridge, MA: Harvard University Press, 1977), 147, passim. See also: Bataille, *Theory of Religion,* 67–68.

75. For critical discussions of game theory and rational exchange models of conflict, see: Thomas M. Steinfatt and Gerald R. Miller, "Communication in Game Theoretic Models of Conflict," in Gerald R. Miller and Herbert W. Simons, eds., *Perspectives on Communication in Social Conflict* (Englewood Cliffs, N.J.: Prentice-Hall, 1974), 14–75. See also: Fred E. Jandt, "Communication and the Simulation of Social Conflict," in Miller and Simons, *Perspectives on Communication,* 76–89; Herbert Simons's review essay, "Changing Notions About Social Movements," *Quarterly Journal of Speech* 62 (1976), 425–30.

76. Wolff, "Beyond Tolerance," 27.

77. Robert N. Bellah, *The Broken Covenant: American Civil Religion in Time of Trial* (New York: Seabury Press, 1975).

78. Compare Berger's similar comment that "the three most ancient and most

powerful concomitants of the sacred" are "mystery, miracle, and magic." Berger, *The Sacred Canopy*, 111.

79. Almost all discussion of rights today centers around attitudes toward utilitarianism. See: the readings in Waldron, *Theories of Rights;* see also: for example, H. L. A. Hart's "Between Utility and Rights," and Richard Wollheim's "John Stuart Mill and Isaiah Berlin: The Ends of Life and the Preliminaries of Morality," both in Alan Ryan, ed., *The Idea of Freedom: Essays in Honour of Isaiah Berlin* (Oxford: Oxford University Press, 1979); and Dworkin, *Taking Rights Seriously.*

80. Wolff, "Beyond Tolerance," 20.

81. James Darsey, "Vessels of the Word: Studies of the Prophetic Voice in American Public Address," unpublished dissertation, University of Wisconsin, Madison, 1985, 446–49.

82. Richard D. Mohr, *Gays/Justice: A Study of Ethics, Society, and Law* (New York: Columbia University Press, 1988), 145.

NOTES TO CHAPTER 7

1. Richard H. Rovere, *Senator Joe McCarthy*, Meridian Books edition (Cleveland: World Publishing Co., 1960), 3.

2. William A. Henry III, "An Admiral from Alabama," *Time* (June 8, 1981), 20; Arthur Miller, "The Interrogation of Angel Rama," *Harper's* (July 1984), 11–12.

3. Robin Turner, "Dukakis Likens G.O.P. Attacks to McCarthy's," *New York Times* (September 10, 1988), 8. See also: "Reagan Backs Bush in Assailing Dukakis Over Issue of Pledge," *New York Times* (September 21, 1988), A30; "Transcript of First TV Debate Between Bush and Dukakis," *New York Times* (September 26, 1988), A16–A19.

4. National Public Radio, special live broadcast, October 11, 1991, 10–11pm, EST.

5. National Public Radio, "Morning Edition," June 18, 1996.

6. Walt Kelly, *Potluck Pogo* (New York: Simon and Schuster, 1954–55), 28.

7. I. F. Stone, *The Haunted Fifties: 1953–1963* (Boston: Little, Brown and Co., 1963); Lary May, ed., *Recasting America: Culture and Politics in the Age of the Cold War* (Chicago: University of Chicago Press, 1989); Douglas T. Miller and Marion Nowak, *The Fifties: The Way We Really Were* (Garden City, NY: Doubleday, 1977); Paul A. Carter, *Another Part of the Fifties* (New York: Columbia University Press, 1983); S. Coontz, *The Way We Never Were: American Families and the Nostalgia Trap* (New York: Basic Books, 1992); and J. Ronald Oakley, *God's Country: America in the Fifties* (New York: Dembner Books, 1986).

8. Richard Weaver, *Ideas Have Consequences,* Midway Reprint edition (Chicago: University of Chicago Press, 1976), 179.

9. Erling Jorstad, *The Politics of Doomsday: Fundamentalists of the Far Right* (Nash-

ville: Abingdon Press, 1970), 45. On the climate of the Fifties in America, see: Eric F. Goldman, *The Crucial Decade—And After: America, 1945–1960* (New York: Vintage Books, 1960); Talcott Parsons, "Social Strains in America (1955)," in Daniel Bell, ed., *The Radical Right* (Garden City, NY: Anchor, 1964), 209–29.

10. George H. Gallup, *The Gallup Poll: Public Opinion, 1935–1971*, 3 vols. (New York: Random House, 1972), v. 2, 933.

11. Gallup, *The Gallup Poll*, v. 1, 625.

12. Gallup, *The Gallup Poll*, v. 2, 869.

13. Gallup, *The Gallup Poll*, v. 1, 682; v. 2, 925, passim. See also: Goldman, *The Crucial Decade*, 262.

14. Gallup, *The Gallup Poll*, v. 2, 922.

15. Gallup, *The Gallup Poll*, v. 2, 967.

16. Kelly, *Potluck Pogo*, 103.

17. Nobel Prize Acceptance Speech, in Houston Peterson, ed., *A Treasury of the World's Great Speeches*, revised and enlarged edition (New York: Simon and Schuster, 1965), 815.

18. W. H. Auden, *Collected Longer Poems* (New York: Random House, 1969), 268–70; Leonard Bernstein's symphony "The Age of Anxiety" received its world premiere in 1949.

19. Henry D. Aiken, ed., *The Age of Ideology*, Mentor edition (New York: New American Library, 1956), 202, 225. See also: Herbert Marcuse, *Reason and Revolution: Hegel and the Rise of Social Theory*, esp. 267ff.

20. Albert Camus, *The Plague*, Stuart Gilbert, trans., Vintage edition (New York: Vintage, 1972), 90–91.

21. Oakley, *God's Country*, 318–19.

22. Gallup, *The Gallup Poll*, v. 2, 1293.

23. Richard Niebuhr, quoted in Oakley, *God's Country*, 324.

24. Arthur M. Schlesinger, Jr., *The Vital Center: The Politics of Freedom* (Boston: Houghton Mifflin, 1949), 1.

25. See: Paul Johnson, *Modern Times: The World from the Twenties to the Eighties*, Colophon edition (New York: Harper and Row, 1985), 1–5, on the impact of Einstein's theory.

26. Paul Boyer, *By the Dawn's Early Light: American Thought and Culture at the Dawn of the Atomic Age* (New York: Pantheon, 1985), xvii.

27. Nisbet's work on the decline in the twentieth century of the idea of progress, one of the grand narratives of the Enlightenment, is relevant here. Robert Nisbet *History of the Idea of Progress* (New York: Basic Books, 1980), 317ff, esp. 332.

28. Daniel Bell, *The End of Ideology: On the Exhaustion of Political Ideas in the Fifties*, rev. ed. (New York: Free Press, 1962), 400.

29. Joseph R. McCarthy, "First Speech Delivered in Senate by Senator Joe McCarthy on Communists in Government; Wheeling Speech," in *Major Speeches*

and Debates of Senator Joe McCarthy Delivered in the United States Senate, 1950–1951, Reprint from the Congressional Record (Washington, DC: United States Government Printing Office, n.d.), 14. This volume is an odd one. It is obviously a McCarthy campaign document—the title page tells us that it was not printed at government expense, but it has none of the accessibility or popular appeal of Senator Joe McCarthy, *McCarthyism: The Fight for America* (New York: Devin-Adair, 1952).

30. "Information on Lattimore, Jessup, Service, and Hanson Cases," in *Major Speeches,* 66.

31. "Information on Lattimore," in *Major Speeches,* 92.

32. "Information on Lattimore," in *Major Speeches,* 109.

33. "Information on Lattimore," in *Major Speeches,* 98.

34. "Information on Lattimore," in *Major Speeches,* 102.

35. "Information on Lattimore," in *Major Speeches,* 144.

36. "Statement of Four Individuals on State Department Personnel Files; Analysis of Senator Tydings' Statement to Press Regarding State Department Files," in *Major Speeches,* 147.

37. "The Great Betrayal," in Ernest J. Wrage and Barnet Baskerville, eds., *Contemporary Forum: American Speeches on Twentieth-Century Issues,* Washington Paperback edition (Seattle: University of Washington Press, 1962), 297. McCarthy used the same stock phrases over and over. See: "American Foreign Policy (March 14, 1951)," 203; "America's Retreat from Victory; the Story of Gen. George C. Marshall," 217, 257, 258, both in *Major Speeches.*

38. McCarthy, *McCarthyism: The Fight for America,* vii.

39. McCarthy, *McCarthyism: The Fight for America,* 1.

40. "Information on Lattimore," in *Major Speeches,* 121.

41. "Statement of Four Individuals," in *Major Speeches,* 153.

42. "American Foreign Policy (March 14, 1951)," in *Major Speeches,* 190.

43. "America's Retreat from Victory," in *Major Speeches,* 298. This speech is an important one in McCarthy's career. It is agreed that McCarthy was not the principal author, yet the speech reflects his point of view and is embellished with enough pure McCarthy as to become his own. The speech was reprinted many times on its own, including once sometime after 1979 by the Senator Joseph R. McCarthy Educational Foundation, Inc., of Milwaukee, WI. Except for Foundation President Thomas J. Bergen's "Updated Memoranda," which serves as preface to this edition, there is no publication data.

44. "America's Retreat from Victory," in *Major Speeches,* 299.

45. "America's Retreat from Victory," in *Major Speeches,* 303.

46. "America's Retreat from Victory," in *Major Speeches,* 284.

47. "Text of Senator McCarthy's Speech Accusing Truman of Aiding Suspected Red Agents," *New York Times* (November 25, 1953), 5.

48. Tzvetan Todorov, *The Fantastic: A Structural Approach to a Literary Genre,*

Richard Howard, trans., Cornell paperback edition (Ithaca, NY: Cornell University Press, 1975).

49. Rosemary Jackson, *Fantasy: The Literature of Subversion* (London: Methuen, 1981), 14.

50. Eric S. Rabkin, *The Fantastic in Literature* (Princeton, NJ: Princeton University Press, 1976), 10, passim.

51. Rabkin, *The Fantastic in Literature*, 218. Rabkin, though he claims to be in "serious disagreement" with Todorov "in many regards," nonetheless notes how Todorov's work complements his own, especially in viewing the epistemological status of what is presented in the fantastic as liberating because unstable. For Rabkin, the essence of the fantastic is "the continuing diametric reversal of the ground within a narrative world." 118, 73; see also: 4, 8, 12, 14, 28, 41, 120, 213.

52. Ernest G. Bormann, "Fantasy and Rhetorical Vision: The Rhetorical Criticism of Social Reality," *Quarterly Journal of Speech* 58 (1972); Dan Nimmo and James E. Combs, *Mediated Political Realities* (New York: Longman, 1983). Nimmo and Combs further confuse fantasy with melodrama, which is, in fact, a political and constitutive moral genre, as I argue in chapter 4.

53. For these examples, see: "Wheeling Speech," 12, 18, 51, 52; "Information on Lattimore," 66, 67, 86, 104, 105, 111; "Lattimore Letter on Chinese Employed by OWI; Additional Information on Philip Jessup," 133; "Challenge to Senator Tydings to Play Recording of Wheeling Speech," 155; "Statement on David Karr and Drew Pearson," 175; "Explanation of Why Names Were Made Public; Statement on Suspended State Department Officials Under Investigation Being Allowed Access to Secret Files," 323, 324, all in *Major Speeches*; "Text of Address by McCarthy Accusing Governor Stevenson of Aid to Communist Cause," *New York Times* (October 28, 1952), 26–27.

54. Barnet Baskerville, "Joe McCarthy, Brief-Case Demagogue," *Today's Speech* 2 (1954), 8–15.

55. Rovere, *Senator Joe McCarthy*, 168.

56. Both these incidents are included in Emile de Antonio's film of selections from the Army-McCarthy hearings, *Point of Order* (New York: Sterling Productions, 1954).

57. Jackson, *Fantasy*, 84.

58. Rabkin, *The Fantastic in Literature*, 166.

59. Jackson, *Fantasy*, 23.

60. "Explanation of Why Names Were Made Public," in *Major Speeches*, 316.

61. See: Jackson, *Fantasy*, 34; Todorov, *The Fantastic*, 25.

62. Rabkin, *The Fantastic in Literature*, 25.

63. "America's Retreat from Victory," in *Major Speeches*, 305.

64. On the hyperbolic in fantasy, see: Todorov, *The Fantastic*, 77–82, 93.

65. For a sampling of these themes, see: McCarthy, *McCarthyism: The Fight for America*, vii, 2, 3, 5, 7, 8, 31, 39, 46, 47, 48, 54, 61, 75, 81, 82, 85, 91, 92, 99;

"Wheeling Speech," 8, 50; "Information on Lattimore," 121; "Lattimore Letter on Chinese," 125, 142; "American Foreign Policy (December 6, 1950)," 159, 160; "Statement on Drew Pearson," 173, 174; "American Foreign Policy (March 14, 1951)," 189, 192, 204; "America's Retreat from Victory," 216, 217, 231, 242, 264, 277, 285, 333, all in *Major Speeches*.

66. "America's Retreat from Victory," 290, 297, 307, 288, 218, in *Major Speeches;* "McCarthy's Speech Accusing Truman," *New York Times* (November 25, 1953), 5; "Text of McCarthy Speech for Delivery Today in Censure Debate," *New York Times* (November 10, 1954), 18.

67. For McCarthy on "perverts," see, for example: McCarthy, *McCarthyism: The Fight for America*, 14–15. For the relationship between homosexual themes and fantasy, see: Todorov, *The Fantastic*, 131–32. For the fear of homosexuality in the Fifties and McCarthy's association of them with those in the State Department who practiced diplomacy with perfumed handkerchiefs, see: David Riesman and Nathan Glazer, "The Intellectuals and the Discontented Classes (1955)," in Bell, *The Radical Right*, 119.

68. "American Foreign Policy (March 14, 1951)," 189. Edelman's comments on the nature of dangerous enemies are relevant here. Murray Edelman, *Political Language: Words That Succeed and Policies That Fail* (New York: Academic Press, 1977), 34.

69. Michael Osborn, "Archetypal Metaphor in Rhetoric: The Light-Dark Family," *Quarterly Journal of Speech* 53 (1967), 240–41. On the importance of the vision and darkness metaphors to fantasy, see: Todorov, *The Fantastic*, esp. 120–23; Jackson, *Fantasy*, 49.

70. *McCarthyism*, 59; "American Foreign Policy (March 14, 1951)," 204; "America's Retreat from Victory," 302, both in *Major Speeches*.

71. "America's Retreat from Victory," in *Major Speeches*, 216.

72. "America's Retreat from Victory," in *Major Speeches*, 303.

73. "America's Retreat from Victory," in *Major Speeches*, 307.

74. "McCarthy's Speech Accusing Truman," *New York Times* (November 25, 1953), 5.

75. "Excerpts from Transcript of First Day of Senate Hearings on Censure of McCarthy: Senator McCarthy's Statement," *New York Times* (September 1, 1954), 14. See also: *McCarthyism*, vii, 101; "Text of McCarthy Speech for Delivery Today in Censure Debate," *New York Times* (November 10, 1954), 18; "McCarthy Insists on Red Trade Ban," *New York Times* (December 4, 1953), 2.

76. "Wheeling Speech," in *Major Speeches*, 8.

77. "Address Accusing Stevenson," *New York Times* (October 28, 1952), 26.

78. "Texts of Statement by McCarthy and Some Replies," *New York Times* (December 8, 1954), 10.

79. "The Price of Peace," second inaugural address, in Wrage and Baskerville, *Contemporary Forum*, 314.

80. "The Price of Peace," in Wrage and Baskerville, *Contemporary Forum*, 313–14.

81. Paul D. Hanson, *The Dawn of Apocalyptic* (Philadelphia: Fortress Press, 1975), 16–27, esp., 24–25.

82. Todorov, *The Fantastic*, 110.

83. "America's Retreat from Victory," in *Major Speeches*, 305. See also: "Text of McCarthy Speech for Delivery Today in Censure Debate," *New York Times* (November 19, 1954), 18; "Text of Senator McCarthy's Speech Accusing Truman," *New York Times* (November 25, 1953), 5. To dismiss accident, folly, or naiveté as a cause of action in favor of malign deliberation and plotting was a favorite McCarthy refrain. See: "America's Retreat from Victory," in *Major Speeches*, 216, 219, 251, 290, 307.

84. Todorov, *The Fantastic*, 112.

85. "America's Retreat from Victory," in *Major Speeches*, 260.

86. "America's Retreat from Victory," in *Major Speeches*, 295.

87. "Texts of Statement by McCarthy and Some Replies," *New York Times* (December 8, 1954), 10. In the text of McCarthy's speech for delivery in the censure debate as it was published by the *New York Times*, there is a long section built around anaphora and antithesis which follows this general pattern: "It is not significant that the Communists. . . . But it is frighteningly significant that they have succeeded." *New York Times* (November 10, 1954), 18.

88. For example, see: the chapter "The Evil Genius," in *McCarthyism: The Fight for America*, 99–100. Owen Lattimore and others are dangerous precisely because they are brilliant. See, for example: "Information on Lattimore," 85–86; "America's Retreat from Victory," 235, 264, both in *Major Speeches*.

89. See: "American Foreign Policy (December 6, 1950)," 159; "Statement of Time Magazine," 333; "America's Retreat from Victory," 302, 305, 292, 293, 267, 254, 253; "American Foreign Policy (March 14, 1951), 208, 204, all in *Major Speeches*.

90. On the demonic and dualism in the fantastic, see: Jackson, *Fantasy*, esp., 54–55, 58, 131.

91. "American Foreign Policy (March 14, 1951)," 190; "America's Retreat from Victory," 285, both in *Major Speeches*.

92. "Text of McCarthy Speech for Delivery Today in Censure Debate," *New York Times* (November 10, 1954), 18.

93. "America's Retreat from Victory," in *Major Speeches*, 307.

94. "Information on Lattimore," 113; "Statement of Four Individuals," 153, both in *Major Speeches*.

95. "Wheeling Speech," 46; "Information on Lattimore," 112; "Lattimore Letter on Chinese," 134, all in *Major Speeches*.

96. From David M. Oshinsky, *A Conspiracy So Immense: The World of Joe McCarthy* (New York: Free Press, 1983), 151. For a similar statement by McCarthy,

see: *McCarthyism: The Fight for America,* 89. Referring to the Madison, Wisconsin *Capital Times,* a paper "consistently paralleling the editorial line of the Communist *Daily Worker,*" McCarthy said, "They, of course, criticize Communism generally to obtain a false reputation of being anti-Communist. They then go all-out to assassinate the character and destroy the reputation of anyone who tries to dig out the really dangerous under-cover Communists."

97. For example, see: "Wheeling Speech," in *Major Speeches,* 18, 50, 74.

98. "America's Retreat from Victory," in *Major Speeches,* 236.

99. "Address by McCarthy Accusing Stevenson," *New York Times* (October 28, 1952), 26.

100. "America's Retreat from Victory," in *Major Speeches,* 259.

101. "Information on Lattimore," in *Major Speeches,* 111.

102. "America's Retreat from Victory," in *Major Speeches,* 281.

103. "America's Retreat from Victory," in *Major Speeches,* 253. See also: *McCarthyism: The Fight for America,* 86, where McCarthy translates the phrase "progressive persons."

104. See: "Information on Lattimore," 92; "Lattimore Letter on Chinese," 144; "Statement of Four Individuals," 151; "Statement of David Karr and Drew Pearson," 176, all in *Major Speeches.*

105. Oshinsky, *A Conspiracy So Immense,* 112.

106. Millard Tydings, quoted in Oshinsky, *A Conspiracy So Immense,* 170.

107. See: Oshinsky, *A Conspiracy So Immense,* 187. The prerogative of office is the great unspoken assumption in Edwin R. Bayley, *Joe McCarthy and the Press* (Madison, WI: University of Wisconsin Press, 1981).

108. Thomas Rosteck, "Irony, Argument, and Reportage in Television Documentary: See It Now versus Senator McCarthy," *Quarterly Journal of Speech* 75 (1989), 277–98.

109. These themes are developed in all the major sources on McCarthy. The most systematic development is in Robert Griffith, *The Politics of Fear: Joseph R. McCarthy and the Senate* (Lexington, KY: University Press of Kentucky, 1970).

110. Rovere, *Senator Joe McCarthy,* 232ff; Thomas C. Reeves, *The Life and Times of Joe McCarthy: A Biography* (New York: Stein and Day, 1982), 665ff; Oshinsky, *A Conspiracy So Immense,* 495ff. The televised Army-McCarthy hearings are widely credited with being the event which made censure possible. Even here, McCarthy's failing was a failing of credibility rather than any conclusive judgment against him, for the hearings did not provide the latter. See: Orville A. Hitchcock's contribution to Frederick W. Haberman et al., "Views on the Army-McCarthy Hearings," *Quarterly Journal of Speech* 41 (1955), 14.

111. Bell, *The End of Ideology,* 300.

112. See, for example: Richard M. Fried, *Nightmare in Red: The McCarthy Era in Perspective* (New York: Oxford University Press, 1990).

113. See: Edwin Black, "The Mutability of Rhetoric," in Eugene E. White,

ed., *Rhetoric in Transition: Studies in the Nature and Uses of Rhetoric* (University Park, PA: Pennsylvania State University Press, 1980), 76–77, for some pertinent comments about sincerity and rhetoric. The linking of sincerity, Freud, and Sade is particularly revealing in the present context.

114. See, for example: Rovere, *Senator Joe McCarthy*, 54–55; Griffith, *The Politics of Fear*, 14; Oshinsky, *A Conspiracy So Immense*, 14–15.

115. Jackson, *Fantasy*, 21.

116. Rabkin, *The Fantastic in Literature*, 73.

117. Jackson, *Fantasy*, 83f. It is worth noting that Jackson mentions the eighteenth- and nineteenth-century literature that grew out of Common Sense philosophy as having a marked "reluctance to admit of the possible existence of partial or contradictory aspects of the self," in contrast to fantasy. The radical discourses examined in chapters 3 to 5 were based on the same philosophy.

118. Jackson, *Fantasy*, 30f.

119. *McCarthyism: The Fight for America*, 86. Emphasis mine.

120. *McCarthyism: The Fight for America*, 90. Emphasis mine.

121. "Text of McCarthy Speech for Delivery Today in Censure Debate," *New York Times* (November 10, 1954), 18. Emphasis mine. These are obvious cases where McCarthy within a sentence mixed first- and third-person self-references. In larger discourses where the narrator was "I," he often referred to himself in the third person. For example, see: *McCarthyism: The Fight for America*, 88, 94, 95; "Explanation of Why Names Were Made Public," in *Major Speeches*, 316, 317, 318. See also: the Devin-Adair edition of *America's Retreat from Victory* (New York: Devin-Adair, 1951). In his introduction to this volume, McCarthy referred to himself in the third person.

122. Peter Biskind, *Seeing is Believing: How Hollywood Taught Us to Stop Worrying and Love the Fifties* (New York: Pantheon Books, 1983).

123. Rovere, *Senator Joe McCarthy*, 253.

124. Ellen Schrecker, *The Age of McCarthyism: A Brief History with Documents* (Boston: Bedford Books of St. Martin's Press, 1994), 92–93.

125. See: Reeves and Oshinsky, especially the incident reported in Reeves, *Life and Times of Joe McCarthy*, 586; and Oshinsky, *A Conspiracy So Immense*, 412.

126. Jackson, *Fantasy*, 18, 78–79, 158–59, 179.

127. Jackson, *Fantasy*, 18.

128. Jackson, 45; see also: 42, 49, 54, 83.

129. Donatien-Alphonse-François de Sade, "Two Moral Tales," in *The Complete Justine, Philosophy in the Bedroom, and Other Writings*, Richard Seaver and Austryn Wainhouse, eds. and trans. (New York: Grove Press, 1965), 373–743. "To instruct man and correct his morals: such is the sole goal we set for ourselves in this story," writes Sade at the outset of *Eugenie de Franval*, 375.

NOTES TO CHAPTER 8

1. Seymour Martin Lipset and Earl Raab, *The Politics of Unreason: Right-Wing Extremism in America, 1790–1970* (New York: Harper and Row, 1970), 248.

2. Benjamin R. Epstein and Arnold Forster, *The Radical Right* (New York: Vintage, 1967), 3. See also: George Thayer, *The Farther Shores of Politics* (New York: Simon and Schuster, 1967), 174; Seymour Martin Lipset, "Three Decades of the Radical Right: Coughlinites, McCarthyites, and Birchers (1962)," in Daniel Bell, ed., *The Radical Right* (Garden City, NY: Anchor Books, 1964), 373; Alan F. Westin, "The John Birch Society (1962)," in Bell, *The Radical Right,* 240.

3. Welch was one of the wealthy sponsors of the group "Friends of Joe McCarthy" which sponsored a McCarthy comeback campaign after McCarthy's censure by the Senate; he kept a framed picture of McCarthy in his office, and he came to be identified with many "McCarthy themes." Welch often praised McCarthy in his speeches as one whom the communists hounded to death, a great martyr to the communist cause. See: David M. Oshinsky, *A Conspiracy So Immense: The World of Joe McCarthy* (New York: Free Press, 1983), 502; Thayer, *The Farther Shores,* 182; Anthony Hillbruner, "A Night on Bald Mountain or Variations on a theme by McCarthy," *Today's Speech* 10 (1962), 1–4; Robert Welch, "What Is Communism?" (Belmont, MA: American Opinion Reprint Series, 1970), 16; Robert Welch, *The Blue Book of the John Birch Society,* 8th printing (n.p., 1961), 94.

4. George Barrett, "Close-Up of the Birchers' 'Founder,'" *New York Times Magazine* (May 14, 1961), 92.

5. D. Sanford, "Little Old Pink Man Who Called Ike Red," *New Republic* 153 (November 20, 1965), 8.

6. M. Crawford, "Sick, Sick, Sick," *Newsweek* 64 (August 31, 1964), 32.

7. "Touched," *Time* 87 (April 15, 1966), 25.

8. Robert Welch, *The Politician* (Belmont, MA: Robert Welch, 1963), 1.

9. *The Politician,* vii.

10. *The Blue Book,* i.

11. *The Blue Book,* i.

12. *The Blue Book,* iii.

13. *The Blue Book,* 2.

14. *The Blue Book,* 9.

15. *The Blue Book,* 9–39, esp. 10.

16. *The Blue Book,* 29.

17. *The Blue Book,* 27.

18. *The Blue Book,* 50. This is the cancer metaphor discussed by Edwin Black in "The Second Persona," *Quarterly Journal of Speech* 56 (1970), 109–19. Susan Sontag has also explored the radicalism of cancer as metaphor in *Illness as Metaphor* (New York: Farrar, Strauss, and Giroux, 1978), 82, 86.

19. *The Blue Book,* 57–58.

20. *The Blue Book,* 63.

21. *The Blue Book,* 72–73.

22. For example, see: *The Blue Book,* 84–86; Robert Welch, "What Is the John Birch Society?" 1970 edition (Belmont, MA: American Opinion Reprints, 1970), 6, 24. There is, in fact, a close relationship between the cancer metaphor and the military metaphor. See: Sontag, *Illness as Metaphor,* 64–68.

23. *The Blue Book,* 169.

24. *The Blue Book,* 145.

25. *The Blue Book,* 149–50. Harry Kemp, "God, the Architect" was published in James D. Morrison, ed., *Masterpieces of Religious Verse* (New York: Harper and Bros., 1948), #149.

26. Robert Welch, "To the Negroes of America" (n.p., 1967), 8.

27. "A Letter to Khrushchev," in *The New Americanism and Other Speeches and Essays* (Boston: Western Island, 1966), 30–42.

28. "More Stately Mansions," in *The New Americanism,* 15–52.

29. R. S. Crane, *The Languages of Criticism and the Structure of Poetry* (Toronto: University of Toronto Press, 1953), 153.

30. *The Blue Book,* 44.

31. "Through the Days to Be," in *The New Americanism,* 60.

32. See, for example: "The Boston Mob," 17; "Philosophy of the Abolition Movement," 60, 65–66; "Toussaint l'Ouverture," 173; "The Case for Labor," 201; "The Old South Meetinghouse," 212, all in Louis Filler, ed., *Wendell Phillips on Civil Rights and Freedom* (New York: Hill and Wang, 1965).

33. See: various speeches in Arthur Schlesinger, Jr., ed., *Writings and Speeches of Eugene Debs* (New York: Heritage Press, 1948). See also: Bernard J. Brommel, *Eugene V. Debs: Spokesman for Labor and Socialism* (Chicago: Charles H. Kerr, 1978), esp. 103, 208. Debs also tried his hand at "verse." The one most frequently reprinted was the sentimental piece, "Mother."

34. The Baptist Church was among the first to embrace hymns, including collections by Isaac Watts. See: Henry Wilder Foote, *Three Centuries of American Hymnody,* Archon reprint edition ([Hampden, CT]: Archon Books, 1968), esp. 168, 225–29. Reynolds claims that the Baptists were the first sect to introduce congregational hymn singing, in William Jensen Reynolds, *A Survey of Christian Hymnody* (New York: Holt, Rinehart and Winston, 1963), 46. Donald Davie explores the hymnodic tradition, especially that of Isaac Watts and Charles Wesley, with a view toward restoring status to poetry which has been, in Davie's view, discounted by students of poetry because of its liturgical nature. See: Donald Davie, *A Gathered Church: The Literature of the English Dissenting Interest, 1700–1930* (New York: Oxford University Press, 1978), esp. 1–54.

35. On the Unitarian contributions to American hymnody, see: Foote, *Three Centuries of American Hymnody,* esp. 192, 196, 233–54. Whittier cannot really be counted a Unitarian hymnodist in that he was a lifelong member of the Society of

Friends, but he was close to the Unitarians in spirit and some of his poems were appropriated for use in Unitarian hymn books. Foote, *Three Centuries of American Hymnody*, 254–62.

36. On the shift from psalmody to hymnody and its significance, see: Foote, *Three Centuries of American Hymnody*, 3–186; and Reynolds, *A Survey of Christian Hymnody*, 3–65.

37. Conrad makes many arguments (which parallel those I make in the following section) regarding the nineteenth-century roots of the Moral Majority, one of the logical successors to Welch. See: Charles Conrad, "The Rhetoric of the Moral Majority: An Analysis of Romantic Form," *Quarterly Journal of Speech* 69 (1983), 159–70.

38. *The Blue Book*, 48.

39. "Republics and Democracies," in *The New Americanism*, 101. On the significance of republicanism in the nineteenth century, see: Hans Kohn, *Political Ideologies of the Twentieth Century*, 3d edition revised (New York: Harper Torchbooks, 1966), esp. 6, 8, 68, 69.

40. *The Blue Book*, 48.

41. *The Blue Book*, 60.

42. William G. McLoughlin, *Revivals, Awakenings and Reform: An Essay on Religion and Social Change in America, 1607–1977* (Chicago: University of Chicago Press, 1978), 140.

43. R. W. Harris, *Romanticism and the Social Order, 1780–1830* (New York: Barnes and Noble, 1969), 20. See also: "Romanticism," *Princeton Encyclopedia of Poetry and Poetics*, Alex Preminger, Frank J. Warnke, and O. B. Hardison, Jr., eds. (Princeton, NJ: Princeton University Press, 1974). This discussion is also indebted to M. H. Abrams, *The Mirror and the Lamp: Romantic Theory and the Critical Tradition* (London: Oxford University Press, 1953), and Jacques Barzun, *Classic, Romantic, and Modern* (Chicago: University of Chicago Press, 1961).

44. Harris, *Romanticism and the Social Order*, 11; Barzun, *Classic, Romantic, and Modern*, passim. For a description of some of the aspects of the nineteenth-century view of history as it was received from the eighteenth century, see: Stow Persons, "The Cyclical Theory of History in Eighteenth Century America," *American Quarterly* 6 (1954), 147–63.

45. Carlyle, quoted in the chapter "Carlyle as Prophet- Historian," in John Holloway, *The Victorian Sage* (New York: W. W. Norton, 1960), 58.

46. Northrop Frye, *A Study of English Romanticism* (New York: Random House, 1968), 22.

47. Shelley, quoted in Harris, *Romanticism and the Social Order*, 54.

48. For some "political biographies" of some of the English Romantic poets, see: Crane Brinton, *The Political Ideas of the English Romanticists*, reprint edition (New York: Russell and Russell, 1962). See particularly: Wordsworth's idea of poetry in Abrams, *The Mirror and the Lamp*, 330.

49. Ralph Waldo Emerson, "The Poet," in Lewis Mumford, ed., *Essays and Journals* (Garden City, NY: Doubleday, 1968), 248–49.

50. Holloway, *The Victorian Sage,* 2.

51. Vernon L. Parrington, *Main Currents in American Thought,* v. 2, Harvest edition (New York: Harcourt, Brace, and World, 1927), passim, esp. 309–10, 313–15. See also: Sacvan Bercovitch, "Emerson the Prophet: Romanticism, Puritanism, and Auto-American-Biography," in David Levin, ed., *Emerson: Prophecy, Metamorphosis, and Influence: Selected Papers from the English Institute* (New York: Columbia University Press, 1975), 2–6.

52. Parrington, *Main Currents,* v. 2, 264, 331–34.

53. Harold Bloom, "Emerson: The Glory and Sorrows of American Romanticism," in David Thorburn and Geoffrey Hartman, eds., *Romanticism: Vistas, Instances, Continuities* (Ithaca, NY: Cornell University Press, 1973), 155–73; *The Blue Book,* 9.

54. James M. Cox, "R. W. Emerson: The Circles of the Eye," in Levin, *Emerson, Prophecy, Metamorphosis,* 57–81, esp. 59, 61. Emphasis Cox's.

55. Aaron Kramer, *The Prophetic Tradition in American Poetry, 1835–1900* (Rutherford, NJ: Farleigh Dickinson University Press, 1968), 10, passim.

56. Kramer, *The Prophetic Tradition in American Poetry,* 11, passim.

57. Kramer, *The Prophetic Tradition in American Poetry,* 15, passim.

58. The words in quotation marks are Emerson's as quoted in Kramer, *The Prophetic Tradition in American Poetry,* 34. Kramer provides several examples of similar criticisms of the betrayal of mission by other poets. See: 34–35.

59. Herbert A. Wichelns, "Ralph Waldo Emerson," in William Norwood Brigance, ed., *History and Criticism of American Public Address,* v. 2 (New York: Russell and Russell, 1960), 518.

60. John H. Sloan, " 'The Miraculous Uplifting': Emerson's Relationship with His Audience," *Quarterly Journal of Speech* 52 (1966), 10–15.

61. *The Blue Book,* 9.

62. *The Blue Book,* 34.

63. *The Blue Book,* 35.

64. For examples of the awakening metaphor, see: *The Blue Book,* 35, 76; "To the Negroes of America," 1; *The Politician,* 217; "What Is the John Birch Society?" 28.

65. *The Politician,* 255.

66. *The Blue Book,* 44.

67. Emerson, "History," in Mumford, *Essays and Journals,* 79. The replacement of the physics metaphor with the metaphor of biology and the metaphor of the organism is one of the hallmarks of Romanticism. See: Barzun, *Classic, Romantic, and Modern,* 54–55; Abrams, *The Mirror and the Lamp,* 184–213. On the biology metaphor of the nineteenth century and its relation to classical cosmology, espe-

cially that of Plato, see: R. G. Collingwood, *The Idea of Nature,* paperback edition (London: Oxford University Press, 1960). Herbert Spencer's theories of social evolution, which Welch found to be the products of clear-sighted "genius," are the most prominent manifestation of the biology metaphor applied to the social realm. See: *The Blue Book,* 48.

68. For example, see: "More Stately Mansions," 136–37.

69. For example, see: "What Is Communism?" 4. See also: "Look at the Score," in *The Blue Book,* esp. 10–18. Other examples include "More Stately Mansions" and "The New Americanism," both in *The New Americanism and Other Essays.*

70. *The Blue Book,* 64.

71. *The Blue Book,* 72, 71, 28, 77, 24.

72. *The Blue Book,* 146.

73. "What Is Communism?" 22. In *The Blue Book,* 73, Welch wrote: "Truth, reality, human instinct, and the overwhelming weight of human desire are on our side." See also: "A Letter to Khrushchev," in *The New Americanism,* 47.

74. "What Is Communism?"; *The Blue Book,* 174. Emphasis added.

75. *The Blue Book,* 35.

76. *The Blue Book,* 73.

77. "The Socialist Party's Appeal (1904)," in Jean Y. Tussey, ed., *Eugene V. Debs Speaks* (New York: Pathfinder, 1972), 106.

78. "The Socialist Party's Appeal (1904)," in Tussey, *Debs Speaks,* 107.

79. "What Is Communism?" 19. Note the presence of the optimistic sunrise metaphor here.

80. "What Is the John Birch Society?" 6.

81. "Philosophy of the Abolition Movement," in Filler, *Civil Rights and Freedom,* 35.

82. John L. Thomas, "Romantic Reform in America, 1815–1865," *American Quarterly* 17 (1965), 659.

83. "What Is the John Birch Society?" 30.

84. Bronson Alcott, quoted in Thomas, "Romantic Reform in America," 663–64

85. *The Blue Book,* 60.

86. *The Blue Book,* 64.

87. "What Is the John Birch Society?" 31.

88. *The Blue Book,* 9.

89. *The Blue Book,* 10.

90. *The Blue Book,* 60.

91. *The Blue Book,* 152.

92. *The Blue Book,* 170.

93. *The Blue Book,* 35.

94. *The Blue Book,* 4. On John Birch as a martyr symbol, see: Philip C. Wander,

"The John Birch and Martin Luther King Symbols in the Radical Right," *Western Speech* 35 (1971), 4–14. Welch himself expressed his willingness to die for the cause. For example, see: "A Letter to Khrushchev," in *The New Americanism*, 49, 50, 51.

95. Kramer, *The Prophetic Tradition in American Poetry*, 37–38.

96. Kramer, *The Prophetic Tradition in American Poetry*, 36.

97. Kramer, *The Prophetic Tradition in American Poetry*, 39.

98. Sanford, "Little Old Pink Man Who Called Ike Red," 8.

99. Barrett, "Close-Up of the Birchers' 'Founder'," 89.

100. *The Blue Book*, 148.

101. Mumford, *Essays and Journals*, 10.

102. Harold Bloom, *New York Review of Books* (November 22, 1984), 19.

103. Oliver Wendell Holmes, quoted in Irving Bartlett, *The American Mind in the Mid-Nineteenth Century* (New York: Thomas Y. Crowell, 1967), 95.

104. Bartlett, *The American Mind in the Mid-Nineteenth Century*, 95–96.

105. For the second printing of *The Blue Book* in 1959, Welch did reluctantly provide a very sketchy one-page biography. In explaining why no such biography or personal information about the "personal leader" of the John Birch Society had been forthcoming before this time, Welch explained that it was due to his "distaste for anything in the nature of personal publicity." *The Blue Book*, 178–79.

106. *The Blue Book*, 144.

107. *The Blue Book*, 60.

108. *The Blue Book*, 61.

109. *The Blue Book*, 60.

110. Quoted both in *The Blue Book*, 68, and in "Through All the Days to Be," in *The New Americanism*, 60. It is worth noting that hymnody, too, is characterized by a limited number of strict forms, Common Meter, Short Meter, and Long Meter. For a description of these forms, see: Reynolds, *Survey of Christian Hymnody*, xi–xiii.

111. William James, *Essays in Radical Empiricism and a Pluralistic Universe*, Ralph Barton Perry, ed., Dutton paperback edition (New York: E. P. Dutton, 1971), 146, passim.

112. Richard Bernstein, "Introduction," in James, *A Pluralistic Universe*, xxv.

113. James, *A Pluralistic Universe*, 143.

114. *The Blue Book*, 145.

115. Quoted in Bloom, "Emerson: The Glory and Sorrows of American Romanticism," 156.

116. Archibald MacLeish, *Poetry and Experience* (Cambridge, MA: Riverside Press, 1960), 118; see also: 113–20 for general remarks on the withdrawal of poetry from public life.

117. Abraham Heschel, *The Prophets*, Colophon edition, v. 1 (New York: Harper and Row), 106. The situational nature of true prophecy is stressed in almost all works on the subject. Martin Buber in fact makes this the distinguishing mark

of true prophecy. See: Martin Buber, *The Prophetic Faith,* Torchbook edition (New York: Harper and Row, 1960), 178f.

118. James L. Crenshaw, *Prophetic Conflict* (Berlin: Walter de Gruyter, 1971).

NOTES TO CHAPTER 9

1. Edmund White, "The Political Vocabulary of Homosexuality," in David Berman, ed., *The Burning Library* (New York: Knopf, 1994), 70.

2. In addition to White, see: Howard Brown, *Familiar Faces, Hidden Lives: The Story of Homosexual Men in America Today* (New York: Harcourt Brace Jovanovich, 1976), 201–2; Jonathan Katz, *Gay American History: Lesbians and Gay Men in the U.S.A.* (New York: Thomas Y. Crowell, 1976), 7; Martin P. Levine, "Introduction," in Martin P. Levine, ed., *Gay Men: The Sociology of Male Homosexuality,* Colophon edition (New York: Harper and Row, 1979), 238.

3. Kenneth Burke, like Malinowski, often focuses on the essential differences among magic, science, and religion, but the repeated grouping of the three suggests their essential kinship. Burke occasionally explicitly acknowledges this as when he writes: "Magic, religion, and science are alike in that they foster a body of thought concerning the nature of the universe and man's relation to it." Kenneth Burke, *Counter-Statement,* (Berkeley and Los Angeles: University of California Press, 1968), 163. See also: Bronislaw Malinowski, *Magic, Science and Religion,* Anchor edition (Garden City, NY: Doubleday Anchor, 1954).

4. Michael Riordon's "Capital Punishment: Notes of a Willing Victim," reprinted in Levine, *Gay Men,* 78–99, is particularly revealing. See also: Katz, *Gay American History,* 131.

5. Bruce Bawer, *A Place at the Table: The Gay Individual in American Society* (New York: Simon and Schuster, 1993), 125.

6. Richard D. Mohr, "Why Sodomy Laws Are Bad," in *Gays/Justice: A Study of Ethics, Society, and Law* (New York: Columbia University Press, 1988), 49–62; James K. Feibleman, "Sexual Behavior, Morality and the Law," in Ralph Slovenko, ed., *Sexual Behavior and the Law* (Springfield, IL: Charles C. Thomas, 1965), 176, 177; Walter Barnett, *Sexual Freedom and the Constitution: An Inquiry into the Constitutionality of Repressive Sex Laws* (Albuquerque, NM: University of New Mexico Press, 1973), 75, passim.; Edwin M. Schur, *Crimes without Victims: Deviant Behavior and Public Policy* (Englewood Cliffs, NJ: Prentice-Hall 1965), 78. A 1996 survey of sodomy laws, occasioned by the tenth anniversary of a Georgia Supreme Court decision upholding the constitutionality of that state's sodomy law, while noting that much has changed in this area since *Bowers v. Hardwick* in 1986, bears witness to the continuing validity of Schur's observation. Twenty-one states still have statutes which prohibit "crimes against nature," "sexual misconduct," "sodomy and buggery," "buggery," "deviate sexual conduct," or "unnatural intercourse." Lisa Neff, "The State of Sodomy Laws," *Windy City Times* (March 21, 1996), 9.

7. For a more detailed examination of the gay response to each member of the triumvirate, see: James Darsey, "Vessels of the Word: Studies of the Prophetic Voice in American Public Address," unpublished dissertation, University of Wisconsin, Madison, 1985, 422–33.

8. Patricia L. Schmidt, "The Role of Moral Idealism in Social Change: Lord Ashley and the Ten Hours Factory Act," *Quarterly Journal of Speech* 63 (1977), 15.

9. Irving Louis Horowitz, "The Pluralistic Bases of Modern American Liberalism," in *Ideology and Utopia in the United States, 1956–1976* (London: Oxford University Press, 1977), 377–97; see also: Murray Edelman, "The Political Language of the Helping Professions," in *Political Language: Words That Succeed and Policies That Fail* (New York: Academic Press, 1977), 20–21, 57–75.

10. Dennis Altman, *Homosexual: Oppression and Liberation,* Discus edition (New York: Avon, 1973), 185.

11. Weinberg and Williams, *Male Homosexuals: Their Problems and Adaptations* (New York: Oxford University Press, 1974), find a re-evaluation of sexual mores after the Second World War to be a major factor in the formation of the homophile liberation movement in America, and John D'Emilio, *Sexual Politics, Sexual Communities: The Making of a Homosexual Minority in the United States, 1940–1970* (Chicago: University of Chicago Press, 1983), traces the disruptive influences of the war and of new patterns of living following the war.

12. William Lee Miller, "The Rise of Neo-Orthodoxy," in Arthur M. Schlesinger, Jr. and Morton White, eds., *Paths of American Thought,* Sentry edition (Boston: Houghton Mifflin, 1970), 331.

13. For this analysis and use of the term "civil religion," see: John Murray Cuddihy, *No Offense: Civil Religion and Protestant Taste* (New York: Seabury Press, 1978).

14. Arthur M. Schlesinger, Jr., "The One against the Many," in Schlesinger and White, *Paths of American Thought,* 538.

15. Edwin M. Schur, "The Sociologist Comments," in Edwin M. Schur and Hugo Adam Bedau, *Victimless Crimes: Two Sides of a Controversy* (Englewood Cliffs, NJ: Prentice-Hall, 1974), 118. See also: Dwight Oberholtzer, "Introduction: Subduing the Cyclops," in W. Dwight Oberholtzer, ed., *Is Gay Good? Ethics, Theology, and Homosexuality* (Philadelphia: Westminster Press, 1971), 52.

16. Edward Sagarin, *Odd Man In: Societies of Deviants in America* (Chicago: Quadrangle Books, 1972), 82–84.

17. D'Emilio, *Sexual Politics, Sexual Communities,* 18.

18. Grant Gilmore, *The Ages of American Law* (New Haven, CT: Yale University Press), 110, passim.

19. Gilmore, *The Ages of American Law,* 95f.

20. For additional evidence on this argument, see: James Darsey, "From 'Commies' and 'Queers' to 'Gay is Good,' " in James W. Chesebro, ed., *Gayspeak: Gay Male and Lesbian Communication* (New York: Pilgrim Press, 1981); and James Darsey, "*Die Non:* Gay Liberation and the Rhetoric of Pure Tolerance," in R. Jeffrey

Ringer, ed., *Queer Words, Queer Images: Communication and the Construction of Homosexuality* (New York: New York University Press, 1994), 53–55.

21. Andrew Sullivan, *Virtually Normal: An Argument about Homosexuality* (New York: Alfred A. Knopf, 1995), 24.

22. Sullivan, *Virtually Normal*, 24.

23. "Justices Must Do the Right Thing," *Windy City Times* (October 19, 1995), 13.

24. James K. Mumaugh, "Supreme Court Must Consider the Rights of All in Colorado Case," *Windy City Times* (October 19, 1995), 12. Emphasis added.

25. Mumaugh, "Supreme Court Must Consider the Rights of All," 12.

26. Stuart A. Scheingold, *The Politics of Rights: Lawyers, Public Policy, and Political Change* (New Haven: Yale University Press, 1974), 17.

27. Ronald Dworkin, *Taking Rights Seriously* (Cambridge, MA: Harvard University Press, 1977), xii.

28. For an overview of gay rights rhetoric, 1948–90, see: Darsey, "From 'Commies' and 'Queers' to 'Gay is Good,' " in Chesebro, *Gayspeak;* and James Darsey, "From 'Gay is Good' to the Scourge of AIDS," *Communication Studies* 42 (1991), 43–66.

29. Both these campaigns are analyzed in Darsey, *"Die Non,"* in Ringer, *Queer Words, Queer Images*.

30. Richard Steele with Tony Fuller, "God's Crusader," *Newsweek* (June 6, 1977), 20.

31. Anita Bryant, *The Anita Bryant Story: The Survival of Our Nation's Families and the Threat of Militant Homosexuality* (Old Tappan, NJ: Fleming H. Revell Co., 1977), 37–38, quoted in Ronald Fischli, "Anita Bryant's Stand against 'Militant Homosexuality': Religious Fundamentalism and the Democratic Process," *Central States Speech Journal* 30 (1979), 267.

32. Steele, "God's Crusader"; Fischli, "Anita Bryant's Stand against 'Militant Homosexuality,' " esp. 270.

33. Fischli, "Anita Bryant's Stand against 'Militant Homosexuality,' " 270.

34. Featured in Deborah Fort and Ann Skinner-Jones, "The Great Divide," DNA/Crow Productions, 1993.

35. Gays and lesbians regularly do very poorly in opinion polls. Though recent results have improved over times when gays and lesbians ranked regularly among the greatest threats to civilization, 1992 data for the American National Election Study, run by the Survey Research Center of the University of Michigan, reveals gays and lesbians scoring only more favorably than people on welfare on a "feeling thermometer" where 100 was the "warmest" feeling, 50 neutral, and 0 the coldest. People on welfare had a mean score of 50.1; gays and lesbians, 39.2. Posted to Queer-net by Mark Hertzog.

36. Paul Varnell, "Theory of Gay Progress," *Windy City Times* (February 1, 1996), 15.

37. Judy Rohrer, "Is It Right to Focus on 'Rights'?" *Harvard Gay and Lesbian Review* 3 (1966), 56.

38. Will Perkins, founder of Colorado for Family Values, in "The Great Divide."

39. From the text of Oregon Proposition 9, presented in "Fighting for Our Lives," Feather and Fin Productions, 1992.

40. According to Jerry Bunge, one of the engineers of the Columbus ordinance, it was a strategic decision to maintain a very low profile until the period allowed for public opposition had expired. Personal conversation, July 6, 1992.

41. For some germane remarks on "liberty" as a "feminization of power," see: Michael Calvin McGee, "The Origins of 'Liberty': A Feminization of Power," *Communication Monographs* 47 (1980), 23–45.

42. Hocquenghem's analysis of the antipolitical nature of homosexuality as "desire" rather than "revolution," a desire which is, in fact, directionless, is relevant here. Guy Hocquenghem, *Homosexual Desire,* Daniella Dangoor, trans. (London: Allison and Busby, 1978), 120–25, 104.

43. Marshall Kirk and Hunter Madsen, *After the Ball: How America Will Conquer Its Fear and Hatred of Gays in the '90s* (New York: Doubleday, 1989), xxxvi, xxvi, 161, 207, 187, 276.

44. For a more complete analysis, see: Darsey, *"Die Non."*

45. David Jernigan, "Why Gay Leaders Don't Last: The First Ten Years after Stonewall," *Out/Look* (Summer 1988), 35.

46. Bawer, *A Place at the Table.* Many prominent members of this group are included in Bruce Bawer, ed., *Beyond Queer: Challenging Gay Left Orthodoxy* (New York: Free Press, 1996).

47. Urvashi Vaid, *Virtual Equality: The Mainstreaming of Gay and Lesbian Liberation* (New York: Anchor Books, 1995).

48. Turned by a well-meaning copy editor into "bright red clothes." Darsey, *"Die Non,"* 63.

49. Posted on the internet to Queerlaw, May 6, 1996.

50. John Reid, *The Best Little Boy in The World* (New York: G. P. Putnam, 1973).

51. Quoted in John Powers, "Toxic Shock Syndrome," *L.A. Weekly* (May 17, 1991), reprinted as program material for screening of *Poison,* Wexner Center for the Arts, Columbus, Ohio (June 1, 7, 8, 1991).

52. Candace Chellew, "The Naked Truth," *Advocate* (September 6, 1994), 5.

53. David Harvey, *The Condition of Postmodernity: An Inquiry into the Origins of Cultural Change* (Cambridge, MA: Blackwell, 1990), 102.

54. Harvey, *The Condition of Postmodernity,* 103.

55. Lee Goodman, "The Politics of Patience," *GPU News* (October 1977), 12–13.

56. Stephen Miller, "Ends and Means: Should the Gay Movement Mimic Its Enemies?" *New York Native* (January 22, 1996), 26.

57. Scott Tucker, *Fighting Words: An Open Letter to Queers and Radicals* (New York: Cassell, 1995), 40.

58. Thomas Paine, *The Rights of Man,* Introduction by Eric Foner (New York: Penguin, 1984), 85.

59. Herbert Marcuse, "Repressive Tolerance," in Robert Paul Wolff, Barrington Moore, Jr., and Herbert Marcuse, *A Critique of Pure Tolerance,* paperback edition (Boston: Beacon Press, 1969), 81. See also: Leo Strauss, *Natural Right and History* (Chicago: University of Chicago Press, 1953), 5f. In Thomas Mann's *The Magic Mountain,* Herr Settembrini cautions Hans Castorp: "Do not forget that tolerance becomes crime, if extended to evil." *The Magic Mountain,* H. T. Lowe-Porter, trans., Vintage Books edition (New York: Random House, 1969), 516.

60. Marcuse, "Repressive Tolerance," 83, 88, 98, passim.

61. Part One: Millennium Approaches (New York: Theatre Communications Group, 1992), 90.

62. John Gallagher, "Money Talks: Gay and AIDS Activists Are Increasingly Banking on Hired Professionals to Help Reach Republicans in Congress," *Advocate* (July 25, 1995), 42.

63. "Campaign Fund PAC Ranks among Top 50 PACs," *Momentum: The Newsletter for Members of the Human Rights Campaign Fund* (Fall 1993), 1.

64. Though she rightly contrasts the situation of lesbians and gay men, Danae Clark allows some important similarities as advertisers seek to colonize gay and lesbian styles and transform them into a salable commodity. "Commodity Lesbianism," reprinted in Henry Abelove, Michèle Aina Barale, and David Halperin, eds., *The Lesbian and Gay Studies Reader* (New York: Routledge, 1993), 186–201.

65. *POZ* (June/July 1995), 77.

66. Daniel Harris, "Out of the Closet, and into Never-Never Land: The New Gay Magazines Gloss Over Politics to Penetrate a Market," *Harper's* (December 1995), 52–53.

67. Letter to the editor from Sarah Pettit, Editor, *Out, Harper's* (February 1996), 6.

68. Letter to the editor from Sarah Pettit, 6.

69. Advertisement, *New York Native* (April 1, 1996), 128.

70. *New York Native* (April 8, 1996), 23.

71. "Soundbites," reporting on a story from the *Wall Street Journal* (March 22, 1996), *New York Native* (April 1, 1996), 4. For examples of the ads, see: *Windy City Times* (March 21, 1996), 2; *Windy City Times* (March 28, 1996), 2; *Outlines* (April, 1996), 2. In addition, Subaru is a "proud founding sponsor" of the Rainbow Card Foundation, a Visa card that supports lesbian and gay causes. See: advertisement, *Advocate* (February 20, 1996), 5.

72. *Advocate* (November 28, 1995), 3.

73. Advertisement in *New York Native* (May 27, 1996), 32.

74. R. Daniel Foster, "Shopping for Life," *Advocate* (November 28, 1995), 37.

75. Paul Varnell, "Enjoy Being a Market," *Windy City Times* (March 28, 1996), 15.

76. Varnell, "Enjoy Being a Market."

77. Bruce Bawer, "Up (with) the Establishment," *Advocate* (January 23, 1996), 112.

78. See: advertisement in *Advocate* (December 12, 1995), 41.

79. *Advocate* (December 12, 1995), 11.

80. Stephen H. Miller, "Ends and Means: Should the Gay Movement Mimic Its Enemies?" *New York Native* (January 22, 1996), 22–24.

81. *New York Native* (January 22, 1996), 23.

82. See: Jan Carl Park, "Referendum Campaigns vs. Gay Rights," in Chesebro, *Gayspeak,* 286–90; see especially: news of economic boycotts against Disney, for its movie *Priest,* for its domestic partners policy, and for allowing a convicted pedophile to direct the film *Powder.* John Gallagher, "A Fairy-Tale Ending," *Advocate* (November 28, 1995), 25.

83. Marcuse, "Repressive Tolerance," 94.

84. Bawer, *A Place at the Table,* 51.

85. Bawer, "Up (with) the Establishment," 112.

86. Advertisement, *New York Native* (February 12, 1996), 2.

87. I took the survey by phone, May 22, 1996.

88. Arlene Zarembka, "The Gay Marketeers," *Washington Blade* (December 1995), posted to Queerlaw by Ms. Zarembka.

89. Scalia, dissenting opinion, *Romer v. Evans,* posted on the Internet.

90. Posted on the Internet.

91. Bawer, *A Place at the Table,* 155.

92. Scalia, dissenting opinion, *Romer v. Evans.*

93. Camille Paglia, "That Old-Time Religion," *Advocate* (December 26, 1995), 72.

94. Paglia, "That Old-Time Religion," *Advocate* (December 26, 1995), 72.

95. For example, Stephen H. Miller, "Weighty Issues," *New York Native* (May 6, 1996), 21.

96. Jeff Getty, quoted in Rachel Gotbaum, "Jungle Fever," *Advocate* (September 5, 1995), 36.

97. Conte and Scarce, "Here's Your Wake-Up Call," *COQZ: Central Ohio Queer 'Zine* (May, 1994), 2.

98. Conte and Scarce, "Queers Read This. I Hate Straights: A leaflet distributed at the 1990 pride march in New York City published anonymously by Queers," *COQZ: Central Ohio Queer 'Zine* (May 1994), 3–4.

99. *Southern Voice* (March 15, 1990), 6.

100. Tucker, *Fighting Words,* 19.

101. Guy Debord, *Comments of the Society of the Spectacle,* Malcolm Imrie, trans. (New York: Verso, 1990), 2, 7.

102. Mickey Wheatley, "Beyond the Melting Pot," *Out/Look* (Summer, 1989), 57.

103. Rick Moody, *The Ring of Brightest Angels around Heaven: A Novella and Stories* (Boston: Little Brown, 1995), 155, 157, 167.

NOTES TO CHAPTER 10

1. Louis Hartz, *The Liberal Tradition in America* (New York: Harcourt, Brace and World, 1955), passim.

2. Edwin Black, "The 'Vision' of Martin Luther King," in *Literature as Revolt and Revolt as Literature: Three Studies in the Rhetoric of Non-Oratorical Forms,* The Proceedings of the Fourth Annual University of Minnesota Spring Symposium in Speech- Communication (May 3, 1969), Minneapolis, MN, 7.

3. Hartz, *The Liberal Tradition in America,* 63.

4. Hartz, *The Liberal Tradition in America,* 10, 42–43, 58; cf. 47.

5. Henry F. May, *Ideas, Faiths, and Feelings: Essays on American Intellectual and Religious History, 1952–1982* (New York: Oxford University Press, 1983), 172.

6. Northrop Frye, *The Critical Path: An Essay on the Social Context of Literary Criticism,* Midland edition (Bloomington: Indiana University Press, 1973), 57.

7. I intend my use of the word "culture" here and elsewhere to correspond to something like Michael Polanyi's idea that culture is a kind of knowledge based on tradition and an expression of a desire for excellence. Polanyi writes: "Thus we may regard, in the last analysis, the entire superior knowledge embodied in a modern highly articulate culture as the sum total of what its classics have uttered and its heroes and saints have done." Michael Polanyi, *Personal Knowledge: Towards a Post-Critical Philosophy,* Corrected edition (Chicago: University of Chicago Press, 1962), 376ff. Polanyi's notion shares much with Matthew Arnold's idea, developed in *Culture and Anarchy,* that culture is a striving toward perfection. It stands to reason, then, that the story of a culture at some level can be found in its fondest myths.

8. Matthew Arnold, in *Literature and Dogma,* James C. Livingston, ed. (New York: Frederick Ungar, 1970), 73.

9. Karlyn Kohrs Campbell and Kathleen Hall Jamieson, *Form and Genre: Shaping Rhetorical Action* (Falls Church, VA: Speech Communication Association, [1978]), 24f.

10. See: Polanyi's remarks on commitment in *Personal Knowledge,* 299–324.

11. See: chapter 1 regarding the literature referred to here.

Index

abolitionism, 27, 61–84; and American radical tradition, 114, 208; gay liberation compared to, 185
A-bomb, 131, 133
Acheson, Dean, 139, 143
ACT-UP, 190, 194, 195, 196
Adams, John, 36, 47, 76, 80
Adams, Samuel, 41, 76, 80
Advocate magazine, 189, 190, 191
AIDS, 190, 191
Algren, Nelson, on Debs, 107
allegory, 32
Altgeld, John Peter, Debs compared to, 107
Altman, Dennis, 177
Amerasia magazine, 134
American Law Institute, Model Penal Code, 180
American Revolution, 10, 22, 35–60, 89, 91, 133, 178; and American radical tradition, 122, 200, 201, 202, 203, 204, 208; and community, 112, 113; in Eugene Debs's rhetoric, 89, 90; epistemology of, 51–58; gay liberation compared to, 194; contrasted with Martin Luther King, Jr., 126; contrasted with Joe McCarthy, 139; in Wendell Phillips's rhetoric, 75–76, 80; Wendell Phillips compared to, 65; Robert Welch compared to, 161, 165, 167
Amos, 16, 18, 23, 95
Andrews, James, on Debs, 86
Angels in America, 188
anomie, 23
anonymity, prophetic, 32
apocalyptic: and chaos, 118; dualism and, 116–17; and fantasy, 119; and judgment, 117; as metaphorical, 118; Old Testament origins of, 114–19; as pessimistic, 117, 140–41; pseudonyms in, 118

apodeictic, 19, 22, 91
argumentum ad personam, 31, 56
Aristotle: on civility, 1, 4; on demonstration, 19, 52; on modes of proof, 15; on natural law, 123; on virtue, 30, 49
Army-McCarthy Hearings, 137; Clarence Thomas confirmation compared to, 129
Arnold, Matthew, ix, x, 7, 207; "Dover Beach," 208–9; "The Proof from Prophecy," 201
asceticism, 29
Auden, W. H., *The Age of Anxiety,* 131–32
Augustine, 15
authority: governmental, legitimate, 42–47, 62; prophetic, 30–31, 32, 85, 122

Bailey, F. G., 33
Bailyn, Bernard, on American Revolutionaries, 36, 45
Baptist faith, and poetic, 156
Barrett, George, on Robert Welch, 151–52
Bartlett, Irving, on Debs, 62, 71
Baskerville, Barnet, on Joe McCarthy, 136
Bataille, Georges, on dualism, 116
"Battle Hymn of the Republic," 158
Bawer, Bruce, 176, 191, 192
Becker, Carl, on Declaration of Independence, 59
Beecher, Lyman, 69; Wendell Phillips compared to, 61
Bell, Daniel, x, 133
Bellah, Robert, ix, 3, 9, 22, 49, 126
Bellamy, Edward, *Looking Backward,* 87
Bercovitch, Sacvan, on American jeremiad, 7, 69
Berger, Peter, x, 23; on secularization in society, 124, 126
Berlin, Sir Isaiah, 51
Bernstein, Richard, 172

Bible: in American culture and rhetoric, 6, 10, 16, 201–2; in American Revolution, 22, 47; in Debs's rhetoric, 90, 91; in William Lloyd Garrison's rhetoric, 73; in Phillips's rhetoric, 67–68, 71, 72; in slavery debate, 67

biography (prophetic), 34, 106–8

Bisson, T. A., 134

Bittner, Egon, on radicalism, 21, 39

Black, Edwin, xii; on exhortation v. argumentation, 77; on the genuinely revolutionary, 200

Blair, Hugh, 15

Blake, William: "The Marriage of Heaven and Hell," 199; and Romanticism, 159

Blank, Sheldon, 19, 20

Bloom, Harold, on Emerson, 160

Blumenfeld, Warren J., 185

Bollinger, Lee, 3

Bolton, Thomas, 36

Boyer, Paul, on the psychological impact of the atomic bomb, 132

Branagan, Thomas, 71

British Empiricism: in the American Revolution, 51; Romantic view of, 158

Brooks, Peter, on melodrama, 82–83

Brothers Karamozov, 125, 126

Brown, John: Debs compared to, 98; in Debs's rhetoric, 97, 98; Phillips on, 62, 70, 80

Browning, Elizabeth Barrett, as influence on Phillips, 156

Brueggemann, Walter: on prophetic community, 20; on subversive power of poetry, 120

Brutus, 49

Bryant, Anita, campaign against gay rights, 182, 183

Bryant, Donald C., on rhetoric and poetic, 122

Bryant, William Cullen, influence on Welch, 156

Budenz, Louis, 144

Burke, Edmund: on the value of freedom in the colonies, 46; on Parliament and higher law, 44

Burke, Kenneth, xi; on economics as usurper of religion, 9; on *ethos,* 85; as part of Graeco-Roman rhetorical tradition,

16; on martyrdom as exhibitionism, 32; on rhetoric as adaptation, 5

Bush, George, accused by Clinton campaign of McCarthyism, 129

Bynner, Witter, on Debs, 101

Byron, Lord (George Gordon Noel), and Romanticism, 159

Calhoun, John C., Phillips's grudging admiration of, 72

calling, prophetic, 28–29, 32, 156. *See also* rebirth, prophetic

Calvin, John, 44; in American thought, 201

Calvinism, 70, 159, 204; Phillips and, 69–70

Campbell, George, 15; and Eugene Debs, 105; and Wendell Phillips, 78

Camus, Albert, *The Plague,* 132

Carlyle, Thomas: on history, 162; on poetry, 158; in Welch's rhetoric, 156

Carmichael, Stokely, and economic bases of black power, 196

Carter, Jimmy, "national malaise," 113

Castorp, Hans, 79

Chadwick, Nora Kershaw, on prophecy and poetry, 121

Chalmers, James, 57

Channing, Edward T., 79

Chapman, Maria Weston, 71, 74

charisma, 31–32, 33, 94, 96, 121, 122; in Debs, 95, 104

Chellew, Candace, 186

Christ, 33, 34, 79; Debs compared to, 98, 99–102; in Debs's rhetoric, 91, 96, 97; as model for Debs, 108

Cicero, 1, 5, 15, 22; and virtue, 49

Cincinnati, gay rights struggle in, 182, 191

civility: in American Revolution, 35–37; Matthew Arnold's view of, 7; decay of in contemporary U.S., ix, 2–4; misplaced value of, 209. *See also* etiquette (manners)

Claessens, August, on Debs, 94

Clay, Henry, 72; Phillips compared to, 61

Clinton, Bill: accuses Bush campaign of McCarthyism, 129; gay and lesbian support of, 189; "New Covenant," 203

Cochran, Bert, on Debs, 86

Cole, Thomas, 4

Coleridge, Samuel Taylor: on pedantry, 173; and Romanticism, 158

Collins, John J., on apocalyptic, 118
Colorado, gay rights battle in, 182, 183;
    Amendment 2, 181, 191; Colorado for
    Family Values, 182
Columbus, OH, gay rights initiative in,
    184
come-outerism, 67
community: American, x, 1–3, 8, 12, 39,
    90, 112, 123–24; Debs and, 106; erosion
    of, 133; McCarthy and, 129; and proph-
    ecy, 81, 111–12, 174
Compromise of 1850, 72
compromise: nature of, 68; versus prophecy,
    22; versus reasonableness in Debs, 92
Comte, August, and postmodern epistemol-
    ogy, 132
conservatism, xi; in American radical tradi-
    tion, 203, 204; in American Revolution,
    36, 40, 199; in Debs, 87, 89; and the urge
    to order, 205; in poetic, 120, 170; reac-
    tion to radicalism, 37; in rhetoric of self-
    evidence, 20
conspiracy, argument from: in American
    Revolution, 36; American Revolution
    compared to abolitionism, 73; used
    against gay liberation, 193; McCarthy's
    use of, 138, 139, 142–43; slave power,
    72–73; in Welch's rhetoric, 154, 161–62
Constitution, U.S.: compared to Declaration
    of Independence, 65; gay liberation ap-
    peal to, 180–81; legalistic view in Martin
    Luther King, Jr., 126; Phillips on, 62; radi-
    cal abolitionist view of, 65
Constitutional Courant, 55
Conte[fag], Marc, 195
covenant: American, 48, 114, 129, 201; in
    American Revolution, 47, 59; versus
    apocalyptic, 114; and community, 20,
    114, 126; and Debs, 91; in eighteenth-
    century political theory, 41; Old Testa-
    ment, 11, 17, 18, 25, 115
Cowper, William, 155
Crenshaw, James, 31, 174
crisis: in antebellum United States, 69; in *fin
    de siècle* America, 86–87; McCarthy and,
    129, 133–34, 146, 148; nature of, 23, 60,
    63, 178; Wendell Phillips and, 68; of
    prophecy itself, 116; rhetorical role of,
    69; Welch and, 169–70

Crowley, Mort, "The Boys in the Band," 176
cummings, e. e., 170
Curry, Harriet, on Debs, 99
Curry, Mabel, on Debs, 99

Dahrendorf, Ralf, on the logic of econom-
    ics as basis of politics, 197
D'Amato, Alfonse, Whitewater committee
    compared to McCarthyism, 129
Daniel (biblical book of), 111, 128
Davis, David Brion, on slavery, 64, 71
deafness (as metaphor for moral ignorance),
    56; Wendell Phillips's use of, 65
Debord, Guy, on contemporary spectacle,
    196
Debs, Eugene, 10, 34, 85–108, 133, 178;
    and American community, 112, 113; and
    American radical tradition, 114, 200, 202,
    203, 204; Bible and, 90, 91, 95; and cha-
    risma, 93–95; versus compromise, 92;
    epistemology of, 90–92; gay liberation
    compared to, 181; martyrdom and, 96–
    102; contrasted to McCarthy, 139;
    Camille Paglia compared to, 194; poetry
    in, 156; rebirth, 93–95; on slavery, 89; on
    virtue and manhood, 88–90; Welch com-
    pared to, 11, 12, 161, 163–64, 165, 167,
    196
Debs, Katherine Metzel, on Debs, 94–95
Declaration of Independence, 43, 46, 48,
    49, 51, 206; as abolitionist ideal, 65; as ju-
    dicial rhetoric, 58
D' Emilio, John, 179
Democratic Party, 189
Denton, Jeremiah, compared to McCarthy,
    128
Descartes, René, 52; Cartesian method, 37
Deutero-Isaiah, 32, 141
Dewey, John: on the decay of community in
    America, 124, 182; *The Public and Its Prob-
    lems,* 106
Dickens, Charles, *Hard Times,* 87
Dickinson, John, 57; "Letters from a Farmer
    in Pennsylvania," 37
"DINK," 189
Dreiser, Theodore, Debs compared to, 107
drunkenness. *See* intoxication, as metaphor
DuBois, W. E. B., on economics as basis of
    power, 196

Duché, Jacob, 47–48
Dukakis, Michael, accuses Bush campaign of McCarthyism, 128
Dulany, Daniel, 43
Durkheim, Emile, on the power of the sacred, 21
duty: in American Revolution, 48–49; in American tradition, 200, 203; in Debs, 102–4; in Phillips, 80–81; prophetic, 80; in Welch, 166–68
Dworkin, Ronald, 181
Dyer, Mary, celebrated by Phillips as martyr, 80

economics (v. politics), 9, 125–27, 187–89
Economist magazine, 187
Edelman, Murray, xi; on crisis, 69
Einstein, Albert, and postmodern epistemology, 132
Eisenhower, Dwight, 141, 142, 152, 161, 162
Eisenstadt, S. N., 63; on centrifugal movement of modern world, 123, 124
Eliade, Mircea, on religious symbolism, 104
Elijah, 28
Elshtain, Jean Bethke, on reasonable public discourse, 4, 8
Emerson, Ralph Waldo, 70; "American Scholar," 160; Debs compared to, 106; criticized by William James, 172; "The Poet," 157; as prophet, 160; "The Reformer," 169; and Romanticism, 159; on speaking the truth, 160–61; as model for Welch, 122, 156, 166, 168–69, 173, 204
epideictic rhetoric, 39; and community, 111
Epstein, Benjamin, 151
ethos: in American Revolution, 38–39; Aristotle on, 15; Debs's, 96, 106; and *logos* in prophecy, 85; McCarthy's, 145–46; and melodrama, 83–84; and *pathos* in prophecy, 26, 79–80, 96; prophetic, 10, 26, 27–34, 85–86, 93
etiquette (manners), 2; in persuasion, 4–5; as pseudo-principle, 178
Eugene V. Debs Foundation, 107
Everett, Edward, 69; Phillips compared to, 61

Exile, Babylonian, 116, 174
Existentialism, 132
Exodus, American, 201
Ezekiel, 16, 17, 85, 111, 116, 151, 199

fantastic: versus community, 136; nature of, 135–36; noncontradiction in, 147–48; as secular apocalyptic, 119, 136
Faulkner, William, Nobel Prize acceptance speech, 131
Field, Frederick Vanderbilt, 134
fire (as radical metaphor), 26–27; in American Revolution, 37; "fire and strength," ix, x, 7, 8, 208, 209
First Continental Congress, 40
Fischli, Ronald, on Anita Bryant, 182
Fliegleman, Jay, on late-eighteenth-century rhetoric, 37, 38, 39
Forster, Arnold, on John Birch Society, 151
Fortas, Abe, on radical discourse of 1960s, 3, 8
Foster, Hal: on postmodern pluralism, 113; on lack of tradition in postmodern art, 122
Foster, Stephen S., and come-outerism, 67
Fox, Michael, on ancient Hebrew rhetorical tradition, 7
Franklin, Benjamin, 90
Freedman, David, on prophecy and poetry, 121
freedom: and duty in American tradition, 49, 87, 161, 200–201, 203; and duty in prophecy, 30, 78; economics and, 92, 126–27, 187–94; as inalienable, 42; as liberal value, 205; martyrdom as, 81; versus slavery in American Revolution, 42, 45–47; versus slavery in antebellum America, 63–64; versus slavery in Debs, 89; freedom of speech in Phillips, 73–74; contemporary trivialization of, 9, 206
Freud, Sigmund, and postmodern epistemology, 132
Frye, Northrop, 26, 27, 103, 207; on Romantic poets, 158, 159, 166
Fugitive Slave Act, 72

Gallagher, John, 189
Galloway, Joseph, 37, 43
Gamson, William, rational exchange theory of social change, 9

Garrison, William Lloyd, 62, 65, 67, 69, 71, 72, 73, 74, 77, 80; in Debs's rhetoric, 92, 93

Gay Agenda, 193

Gay and Lesbian Victory Fund, 189

gay liberation, 12, 127, 175–98; and American radical tradition, 200, 206; assimilationist tendencies in, 184–88; use of boycott, 191–19; argument based on economics, 188–97; versus the law, 12, 175–76; as narrowly legalistic, 179–82; versus religion, 12, 175–77; 182–84; versus science, 12, 175–76

Gay Men's Health Crisis, 189

Gay Rights, Special Rights, 193

genre, 6, 11; and prophecy, 111. *See also* epideictic rhetoric; fantastic, nature of; judicial rhetoric; melodrama; *and other specific genres*

Getty, Jeff, 195

Gilmore, Grant, on the evolution of American law, 179–80

Ginger, Ray, on Debs, 96

Gitlin, Todd, on the decay of contemporary community, 2, 4, 8, 11

Giuliani, Rudolph, and Gay and Lesbian Business Expo, 190

Glendon, Mary Ann, on the decay of public discourse, 3, 4, 8

Goddard, 56

Godkin, E. L., on Wendell Phillips, 62

Goodman, Lee, 187

GPU News, 187

Graeco-Roman tradition (in rhetoric), 4, 5, 6, 15; contrasted to Hebraic tradition, 7, 16, 111

Graham, Billy, on decay of American society, 1, 2, 3, 4, 11

Gregg, Richard, on ego-functions of rhetoric, 105

Gusfield, Joseph, on Temperance and slavery, 64

Gutman, Herbert, on industrialization in America, 87

Habermas, Jürgen: on crisis, 23; on tendencies toward rationalization of the world, 124, 126, 182

Haiman, Franklyn, "Farewell to Rational Discourse," 3, 8

Hamilton, Charles, economic program for black power, 196

Hancock, John, 76

Hanson, Paul, on apocalyptic, 117, 141

Hariman, Robert, on civility in public discourse, 4

Harper's magazine, 190

Harris, Daniel, on consumer orientation of gay magazines, 189

Hartz, Louis, on conflicts in the American tradition, 200, 201

Harvey, David, on the postmodern, 112, 113, 187

Hawthorne, Nathaniel, *The Blithedale Romance,* 84

Haynes, Todd, on assimilationist gay cinema, 186

Hays, Samuel, on industrialization in America, 102

Hazelton, R., on vision as metaphor for knowing, 54

Hebraism, Matthew Arnold's conception of, 6–7, 201, 208

Hegel, G. W. F.: absolute idealism criticized by William James, 172; and Romanticism, 158

Hellenism, Matthew Arnold's conception of, 6–7, 201, 209

Henry, Patrick: in Debs's rhetoric, 92, 93; in Phillips's rhetoric, 76

Heschel, Abraham: on absolutism in prophecy, 22; on covenantal obligation, 18; on prophecy as demonstration, 19; on *pathos* in prophecy, 25, 26, 77; on the prophetic calling, 28; on the prophet as messenger, 17; on prophetic timeliness, 173; on prophetic vision, 56

Himmelfarb, Gertrude, on the decay of contemporary society, 2, 8

Hiss, Alger, McCarthy's indictment of, 143

history: absence of, in McCarthy's rhetoric, 149; absence of, in postmodernism, 122, 205–6; in apocalyptic, 118; Carlyle's theory of, 158; cyclical versus progressive, x; as didactic narrative, 158–59, 162–63; sacred, 71, 115; Spengler's theory of, 162

Hobbes, Thomas, 180; on the senses, 54; on the social contract, 41, 46

Hoffman, Abbie, *Revolution for the Hell of It,* 3

Hofstadter, Richard: on industrialization in America, 87, 88; on Phillips, 68

Holloway, John, on the prophetic in nineteenth-century poetry, 159

Holmes, Oliver Wendell, as poetic inspiration for Welch, 155, 156

Hoover, J. Edgar, 137, 171

Hopkins, Stephen, 46; "An Essay on the Trade of the Northern Colonies," 35

Horowitz, Irving, on pluralism, 123

Hosea, 23, 32

Howe, Irving, on Debs, 101, 105

Hudson, W. D., on self-sufficiency of prophetic *ethos*, 19

Hugo, Victor, *Les Miserables*, 156

Human Rights Campaign Fund, 186, 197; PAC, 189

Hume, David: on passion and reason, 78; on sensory data, 52

Hurt, Walter, on Debs, 100, 102, 106

Hutchinson, Ann, celebrated by Phillips as martyr, 80

hymnody, 156. *See also* poetic

IKEA, marketing to gay community, 189, 190

industrialization in U.S., 86–87

Ingersoll, Robert Green, as model for Debs, 105

Inglis, Charles, 53

intoxication, as metaphor, 18; in abolitionist rhetoric, 65; in American Revolution, 57; McCarthy's use of, 133; Wendell Phillips's use of, 64–65, 68

Isaiah, 18, 20, 29, 32, 35, 57, 61, 62, 108, 199

Isbell, Mike, 189

Isherwood, Christopher, 188

Jackson, Rosemary, on the fantastic, 135, 137, 138, 147, 149

James, Henry, on melodrama, 83

James, William: on martyrdom, 33–34; on Nietzsche, 30; pluralist philosophy, 171–72; and postmodern epistemology, 132; on rebirth, 29; on self-consciousness as first premise, 52; "the will to believe," 57, 204

Jamieson, Kathleen, on argumentative function of natural law, 123

Jefferson, Thomas, x, 36, 45, 51; epistemology of "Summary View," 52; as heroic figure for Debs, 90; as heroic figure for Phillips, 76

Jensen, Merrill, on basis of colonial rights, 40

jeremiad, 69, 114

Jeremiah, 16, 19, 20, 23, 27, 28, 30, 31, 32, 34, 45, 72, 73, 85, 151

Jernigan, David, 185

Joan of Arc, 34; in Debs's rhetoric, 97; in rhetoric about Debs, 98; George Bernard Shaw's, 8, 31

Joel, 35

John Birch Society, 150, 151–74

Johnson, Lyndon Baines, "Great Society" theme, 203

Johnson, Samuel, *Dictionary*, 37

Jonah, 28, 29

judgment, 25, 27; in American radical tradition, 133; in American Revolution, 58–60, 71; Debs's of workers, 88–89; failure of, in apocalyptic, 117; as prophetic speech form, 24; rhetorical function, 75; as separation in rhetoric of Wendell Phillips, 74–75

judicial rhetoric, 21; in American Revolution, 58–60; in prophecy, 111

Kameny, Frank, 192

Kansas-Nebraska Act, 72

Kant, Immanuel, 57, 133

Kelly, Walt, *Pogo*, 129, 131

Kemp, Harry, 155; "God the Architect," 154

Kennedy, John F., "New Frontier," 203; versus Nixon on Cold War, 171

Kierkegaard, Soren, and postmodern epistemology, 132

King, Martin Luther, Jr., 171; "I Have a Dream," 126

Kinsey, Alfred, *Sexual Behavior in the Human Male*, 178

Kirk, Marshall, 184–85

Kopelin, Louis, on Debs, 94, 100

Korean War, 130, 134, 141, 171

Kraditor, Aileen: on Debs, 90, 104; on martyrdom in abolitionism, 80

Kramer, Aaron, on prophecy in nineteenth-century poetry, 160–67

Kushner, Tony, 188

Lasky, Melvin, on metaphor and radicalism, 120

Lattimore, Owen, 134, 135; Budenz's testimony against, 144

Laurens, Henry, 59

law v. gay liberation, 175–76; changing nature of, 179; v. religion, 180–81

Lee, Ronald, on Debs, 86

legend, 34; Debs's, 93–102, 106

Lens, Sidney, on Debs, 86

Leonard, Daniel, 55, 56

LePrade, Ruth, on Debs, 98

Levenberg, Steve, 190

Lewis, Sinclair, on Debs, 99

Lincoln, Abraham: allusions to, by Welch, 154; Debs compared to, 34, 107

Lippman, Walter, on McCarthy's power, 145

Lipset, Seymour Martin, on John Birch Society, 151

Locke, John: in American Revolutionary thought, 10, 45, 46, 47, 52, 58; and liberalism in American thought, 200, 201; influence on Phillips, 75; on reason, 53; on the senses, 54

logos: in abolitionism, 71; in American Revolution, 10, 35–60; Aristotle on, 15; related to *ethos*, 85; related to *pathos*, 25, 71, 86; prophetic, 10, 16–22, 85

Lomas, Charles, on Debs, 86

Long, Burke, 30

Longfellow, Henry Wadsworth, influence on Welch, 156

Longtime Companion, 186

Lovejoy, Elijah: in Debs's rhetoric, 97; Wendell Phillips on, 64, 76, 80

Lowell, James Russell, 155

Lucas, Stephen, xi; on American Revolution, 39, 40

Luther, Martin, 104

Machiavelli, x

MacLeish, Archibald, on poetry's retreat from politics, 173

Madison, Charles, on Debs, 86

Madsen, Hunter, 184–85

Making Love, 186

Malachi, 27

Malcolm X, 196; and argument from principle, 126

manners. *See* etiquette

Marcuse, Herbert, on tolerance and referenda, 192

Marshall, George, 135, 143, 144

martyrdom, 31, 32, 33; in abolitionist thought, 79–81; in Debs's rhetoric, 96–102; in Welch's rhetoric, 154, 166–168. See also *pathos*; Brown, John; Christ; Joan of Arc

Marxism: in Debs's rhetoric, 90, 91; as science versus religion, 91

Massachusettensis, 53, 55

Mattachine Society, 185, 186

May, Henry, on decay of consensus in America, 204

McCarran-Walter Act, 128

McCarthy, Joseph, 11, 128–50; and American radical tradition, 200, 204–5; and apocalyptic, 119; on U.S. China policy, 135, 144–45; use of darkness metaphor, 139–40; and the *ethos* of the Senate, 145–46; and the media, 145–46; objectivity, 136–37; Robert Welch compared to, 151, 161–62, 169, 171

McCauley, Thomas Babington, 157

McCormick, Richard L., on Debs, 86

McIlwain, Charles, on constitutional basis of American Revolution, 41

melodrama, 82–83; in Debs, 106; and *ethos*, 84

Meredith, Owen, "Last Words of a Sensitive Second-Rate Poet," 169

messenger (prophet as), 21, 26, 28

messenger formula, 17, 24; and poetry, 156

Miami (Dade Co.), gay rights struggle in, 182, 183

Micah, 23, 24, 25

Mill, John Stuart, 10

Miller, Arthur, on McCarran-Walter Act, 128

Miller, Perry, 63

Miller, Stephen, 187

Miller, William Lee, 178

Milton, John, 156; in Philips's rhetoric, 75

Miss Manners (Judith Martin), 2

Moody, Rick, *The Ring of Brightest Angels around Heaven*, 197–98

Moses, 66

Mulryan, Dave, 191

nabi, 28. *See also* calling, prophetic
Nahum, 23
Nathan, 81
Nation, The, magazine, on Phillips, 62
National Gay and Lesbian Business and Consumer Expo, 190
National Gay and Lesbian Task Force, 191, 197
natural law: in American Revolution, 37, 39–41; argument from, 123; relation to charter, 41; decay of in American thought, 179; versus gay liberation, 176, 178; relation to human law in American Revolution, 40–45; in Phillips's rhetoric, 76. *See also* sacred principle
negotiation, secular argument as, 125
Newfield, Jack, on radical rhetoric of 1960s, 3, 8
New Israel, United States as, 16, 39
Niebuhr, Reinhold, *Children of Light, Children of Darkness,* 140
Niebuhr, Richard, on the anxieties of the 1950s, 132
Nietzsche, Friedrich: admiration for Old Testament mythology, 207; on martyrdom, 30; and postmodern epistemology, 132
1950s, 130–33, 171
1960s, ix, 3, 5, 8, 151, 171, 186, 204, 206
1980s, 5, 8
1990s, 3, 5, 8
Nixon, Richard: contrasted to Kennedy on Cold War, 171; on radical rhetoric of 1960s, 3, 8
Norris, Frank, 15
Novanglus, 46, 47, 53
Noyes, Alfred, 155; in Welch's rhetoric, 156; "To Alfred Noyes," 171

Oakley, Ronald J., on the anxieties of the 1950s, 132
O'Hare, Kate Richards, on Debs, 94, 99
Ohmann, Richard, 26
Olbrechts-Tyteca, L., 1
O'Leary, Stephen, 114
Oregon, gay rights struggle in, 182, 183
Osborn, Michael, on darkness metaphor, 139
Oshinsky, David, on McCarthy, 145, 147
Otis, James, 40, 41, 44, 45, 48, 53, 56; and

American radical tradition, 204; *Out* magazine, 189; in Phillips's rhetoric, 76, 80
Overholt, Thomas, 32

Paglia, Camille, 194
Paine, Thomas, 44, 50, 55, 56, 57; and American radical tradition, 204; "Common Sense," epistemology of, 53; in Debs's rhetoric, 90; on reason, 37; on tolerance, 188
pan-determinism in fantasy, 142
pan-signification in fantasy, 142–43
Parks, Rosa, 5
Parrington, Vernon, on "the mind of New England" in American thought, 159
pathos: abolitionist, 71; in American Revolution, 37–39; Aristotle on, 15; in Debs's rhetoric, 96–100, 104–5; related to *ethos,* 26, 79–81; related to *logos,* 25, 71, 79; McCarthy's, 135; and passion, 76; Wendell Phillips's, 10, 76–78; prophetic, 10, 23–27, 61–84, 203; and reason in nineteenth century, 78–79; in rhetoric about Debs, 101–2; as suffering, 33
Paul, the Apostle, 34
Pearson, Drew, 139
Peeperkorn, Mynheer, 79
Perelman, Chaim, 1, 16; on self-evidence, 19
perfectionism, 114, 164; in Welch, 165, 203
Persian dualism, 116, 141, 143
Phillips, Wendell, 10, 27, 61–84, 89, 133, 178; and American community, 112, 113; and American radical tradition, 200, 203, 204; American Revolution as model, 73, 75–76; and John Brown, 62, 70; on the Church, 67; on U.S. Constitution, 62, 65–66; influence on Debs, 89, 92, 105; "In Defense of Lovejoy," 76; free speech v. slavery in, 73–74; gay liberation compared to, 181; "The Lost Arts," 62; on madness, 82; on martyrdom, 80–81; contrasted to McCarthy, 139; Camille Paglia compared to, 194; *pathos* in, 76–77; poetry in, 156; on politics and politicians, 66; Welch compared to, 161, 163, 164, 165, 167
Pierce, Charles, and postmodern epistemology, 132
Plato, x, 15; on poetry and madness, 121;

and Romanticism, 158; and transcendental law, 179

pluralism: versus covenant, 126; and postmodernism, 113, 122, 123; and Welch, 172–73

poetic, 114, 119–22; in Baptism, 156; as form, 119, 122, 170–71; and history, Romantic view, 158; Old Testament as, 119, 121; and prophecy in nineteenth-century America, 160; and rhetoric, 121–22; as ritual, 119, 171; routinization of charisma, 122; as sign of charisma, 121; in Unitarianism, 156; in Welch, 155–57, 161. *See also particular poets*

Poison, 186

pollution (as economic right), 196

Pope, Alexander, as influence on Phillips, 156

popular sovereignty, 42

Port Huron Statement, 186

postmodernism, 11, 111–27, 175; and apocalyptic, 114; and decay of community, 112–13; absence of history in, 122; and religious decay, 178, 179

POZ magazine, 189, 190

prophecy, 15–34, 114–15, 202–3; and community, 113; and monotheism, 115, 140; optimism of, 27, 114, 140, 163

Psalms, 111

psychopathology: Debs and, 102; and gay liberation, 175, 177; martyrdom and, 33, 102; McCarthy and, 149; Phillips on, 82; Plato on, 121; poetry and, 120–21; and prophecy, 31; radicalism conceived as, 79, 81, 111, 126; and rebirth, 29; Welch and, 152

Pullman strike, 99

purity: and American Revolution, 59; and the metaphor of fire, 26; and prophecy, 27; and radical abolitionism, 74

Queer Nation, 195

Quintilian, 15

Raab, Earl, on Robert Welch, 151

Rabkin, Eric, on fantasy, 135, 136, 137, 138

radicalism, ix, x, 63; American, 8, 9, 39, 199–200; versus compromise, 57; and conservatism, 21, 204; versus economics, 9, 197; versus the personal, 9, 172; and

prophecy, 57; versus reasonableness, 21; as witness bearing, 57

Reagan, Ronald, revival of McCarran-Walter Act, 128

reason: as civility, 36, 209; as economics, 9, 122–27; eighteenth-century conception of, 37; liberal view of, 8, 209; and natural law in American Revolution, 53; as negotiation, 58, 92, 126; related to passion, 78; versus religion, 180

rebirth: Debs's, 93–95; Wendell Phillips's, 69–70; prophetic, 29, 93

Reid, John, 186

Reid, Thomas, 52, 54

religious right, 2, 182–83

Republican Party, 142, 183, 189

Reynolds, Stephen Marion, on Debs, 95, 98, 105

rîb pattern in prophetic speech, 21, 111

Richards, I. A., on sincerity, 85

Ricouer, Paul, 118

Riley, James Whitcomb, 156

ritual, conservatism of, 171

Roman Catholic Church, 97, 194, 196; versus Calvinism, 70; mass, pre–Vatican II, 122

Romanticism, 158–59

Romer v. Evans, 180; Antonin Scalia's dissent, 193, 194

Roosevelt, Franklin Delano, the "New Deal," 203

Roosevelt, Theodore, 102

Rovere, Richard, on McCarthy, 147, 149

sacred: diminution of, 205; nature of, 25. *See also* science, versus religion

sacred principle, x, 177; argument from, in American Revolution, 39–40, 47–48; argument from, in Debs, 92; argument from, in Phillips, 65–68; postmodern erosion of, 133

Sagarin, Edward, 178

Salvatore, Nick, on Debs, 90, 95, 96, 99

Scarce [Homoscarce], Mike, 195

Scheingold, Stuart, on "the myth of rights," 181

Schlesinger, Arthur, Jr.: on Debs, 106; on the 1950s, 132; on tolerance, 178

Schmidt, Patricia, on moral principle and argument, 177

Schrecker, Ellen, on McCarthy, 149
Schur, Edwin, on morality and the law, 178
science: and homosexuality, 175, 176; Marxism as, 91; versus religion, 91, 124–25, 170, 178–79, 180
Scott, Donald M., on abolitionist commitment, 64, 69
Scott, R. B. Y.: on prophecy and crisis, 23; on prophecy and poetry, 121; on the prophetic calling, 28
Scottish Common Sense philosophy: in American Revolution, 51; erosion of, 133; in nineteenth-century U.S., 76. *See also* Reid, Thomas
Second Continental Congress, 36, 50; epistemology of, 53
Second Great Awakening, 63, 69, 76, 82
self-control, in nineteenth-century thought, 63–64. *See also* virtue
self-evidence, 35, 53; in argument, 19; conservatism of, 20; elitism and, 56, 90; McCarthy versus, 144; radicalism of, 20, 57
self-righteousness: and Debs, 92; and Phillips, 71
servitude (in prophecy), 27–33, 85–86. *See also ethos,* prophetic; messenger formula; *pathos*
Sexual Behavior in the Human Male, 178–79
Shannon, David A., on Debs, 107
Sharp, Granville, 71
Shaw, George Bernard, *Saint Joan,* 8, 31
Shelley, Percy Bysshe, 155, 159
Sidney, Algernon, 75
Sinclair, Upton, on Debs, 94, 99, 101
slavery, and U.S. Constitution: in Debs's rhetoric, 88, 89, 98; nineteenth-century conception, 63–64; radical abolitionist view, 65; Whig conception, 43, 46–47, 48, 49
sleep (as metaphor for moral failure): in the American radical tradition, 203; in American Revolution, 57; in Debs's rhetoric, 91; as used by McCarthy, 139–40, 143; in Old Testament, 18, 56, 68, 175; as used by Phillips, 77; as used by Welch, 161
Sloan, John, on Emerson, 161
Smart, Barry, on postmodernism, 112
Smith, Adam, theory of sympathy, 105
Smith, John, on crisis, 23
Smith, Timothy, on nineteenth-century social reform, 63

social contract, in eighteenth-century thought, 41
social disintegration, 1–5
Socrates, Debs compared to, 98
Soviet Union, 131
Spargo, John, on Debs, 98
Spengler, Oswald, cyclical theory of history, 162
Spoerri, Theophil, on conservatism in poetry, 120
Spooner, Lysander, 65
Sputnik, 154
Stackhouse, Max, on Calvinism, 70
Stanton, Elizabeth Cady, on radicalism, 57
Stevenson, Adlai, accused by McCarthy, 141
Stewart, James, on Phillips, 61, 76, 78
Stonewall Rebellion, 177
Strauss, Leo, x, 26
style, rhetorical: Henry Peacham's *Garden of Eloquence,* 157; Welch's, 153–57
Subaru, ad campaign to gays and lesbians, 190
Sullivan, Andrew, 180

Tebedo, Kevin, 182
Temperance movement, 64. *See also* self control, in nineteenth-century thought; virtue
Tennyson, Alfred Lord: influence on Welch, 155; quoted by Welch, 170
Thacher, Peter (Boston Massacre Oration), 38
This Side of Paradise, 106
Thomas, Clarence, compares confirmation process to McCarthyism, 129
Thomas, John L., on perfectionism, 165
Thomas, Norman, on Debs, 107
Thoreau, Henry David, 206
Time magazine, 184
Todorov, Tzvetan, on the fantastic, 135, 142
tolerance, 178; and economics, 126; nature of, 125, 188
tradition, American radical, 5–6, 10–11, 16, 89, 90, 122, 165, 199–210
Truman, Harry, 131, 139, 143, 162
Tucker, Scott, 188, 196
Tydings, Millard, 145
Tydings Committee, 134

Uncle Tom's Cabin, 67; as melodrama, 83
Uncommon Clout Card, 191

Unitarianism, 158, 169; versus Calvinism in American thought, 159–60; and poetic, 156
United Steelworkers, Eugene V. Debs Local, 107
Untermeyer, Louis, on Debs, 107
U.S. Constitution: abolitionist view, 65; Phillips's view, 62

Vaid, Urvashi, 185
Varnell, Paul, on gays as market, 191
Vawter, Bruce: on *pathos* of Yahweh, 25; on poetry in Old Testament, 119; on the prophetic calling, 32; on rationality of prophecy, 21
Vietnam War, 171
virtue: in American Revolution, 49–50; in antebellum thought, 64; Debs on, 88–89; and manliness, 88; Welch and, 165
vision, as metaphor for moral (in)capacity, 18, 19, 56, 68, 91, 140, 203; Debs's use of, 92, 94, 95; and eighteenth-century epistemology, 54–55; Emerson's "transparent eyeball," 160; McCarthy's use of, 139; in nineteenth-century poetry, 160; Phillips's use of, 65, 69; Welch's use of, 164. *See also* sleep (as metaphor for moral failure), in American Revolution
vocation: for Debs, 103; for Phillips, 70. *See also* calling, prophetic
von Rad, Gerhard, 30, 34, 115

Wagner, Richard, x
Waldheim, Kurt, accuses accusers of McCarthyism, 128
Walters, Ronald, 70
Warren, Joseph (Boston Massacre Oration), 51
Warren, Robert Penn, 15
Washington, George, 1, 34, 90
Watts, Isaac, as influence on Phillips, 156
Wayland, J. H., on Debs, 99
Weaver, Richard, x, 19; *Ideas Have Consequences*, 118, 130
Weber, Max: on charisma, 31, 32; on secularization in society, 122, 123–24, 126, 182
Webster, Daniel, Phillips compared to, 61
Welch, Joseph, 137
Welch, Robert, 11, 12, 122, 155–74; and the American covenant, 166; and American radical tradition, 204, 205; cyclical view of history, 155, 162; compared to Debs, 11, 12; didacticism, 163–64; and duty, 166–68; Emerson as model, 122, 156, 162, 168–69; gay liberation compared to, 181; as imitator, 122, 173; "A Letter to Krushchev," 154; compared to Joe McCarthy, 11, 151; "More Stately Mansions," 155; idealization of nineteenth century, 157–58; optimism, 163; rhetorical style, 153–55
West, Samuel, 42, 45
Westermann, Claus, 21, 24
Whately, Richard, 15
Wheatley, Mickey, 197
White, Edmund, 175, 177
White, James Boyd, 5, 111
White, Morton, on American Revolution, 48, 56, 57
Whitman, Walt: influence on Debs, 156; and Romanticism, 159
Whittier, John Greenleaf, 155; influence on Debs, 156; *Proem,* 152
Wichelns, Herbert, on Emerson, 160–61, 167
Wiebe, Robert, on *fin de siècle* America, 86
Wisconsin, gay rights struggle in, 182, 183
Wolf, Hazel Catherine, on martyrdom in abolitionism, 79, 80
Wolff, Robert Paul, on tolerance and negotiation, 125
Wolpe, Stefan, 171
Wood, Gordon, on radicalism of American Revolution, 36
Wordsworth, William, and Romanticism, 158
World War I, 107, 133, 178; as catalyst for social change, 113; Debs's dissent, 99
World War II, 128, 133, 146, 178; contrasted with World War I, 130; as marker of postmodernism, 113, 114, 118–19, 122, 130, 171, 175, 179, 204
Wrage, Ernest, 40

Yale Law School Storrs Lectures, 179

Zarembka, Arlene, 193
Zephaniah, 23, 116, 128
Zulick, Margaret, 16, 17, 30, 34